Say I Love You.

6

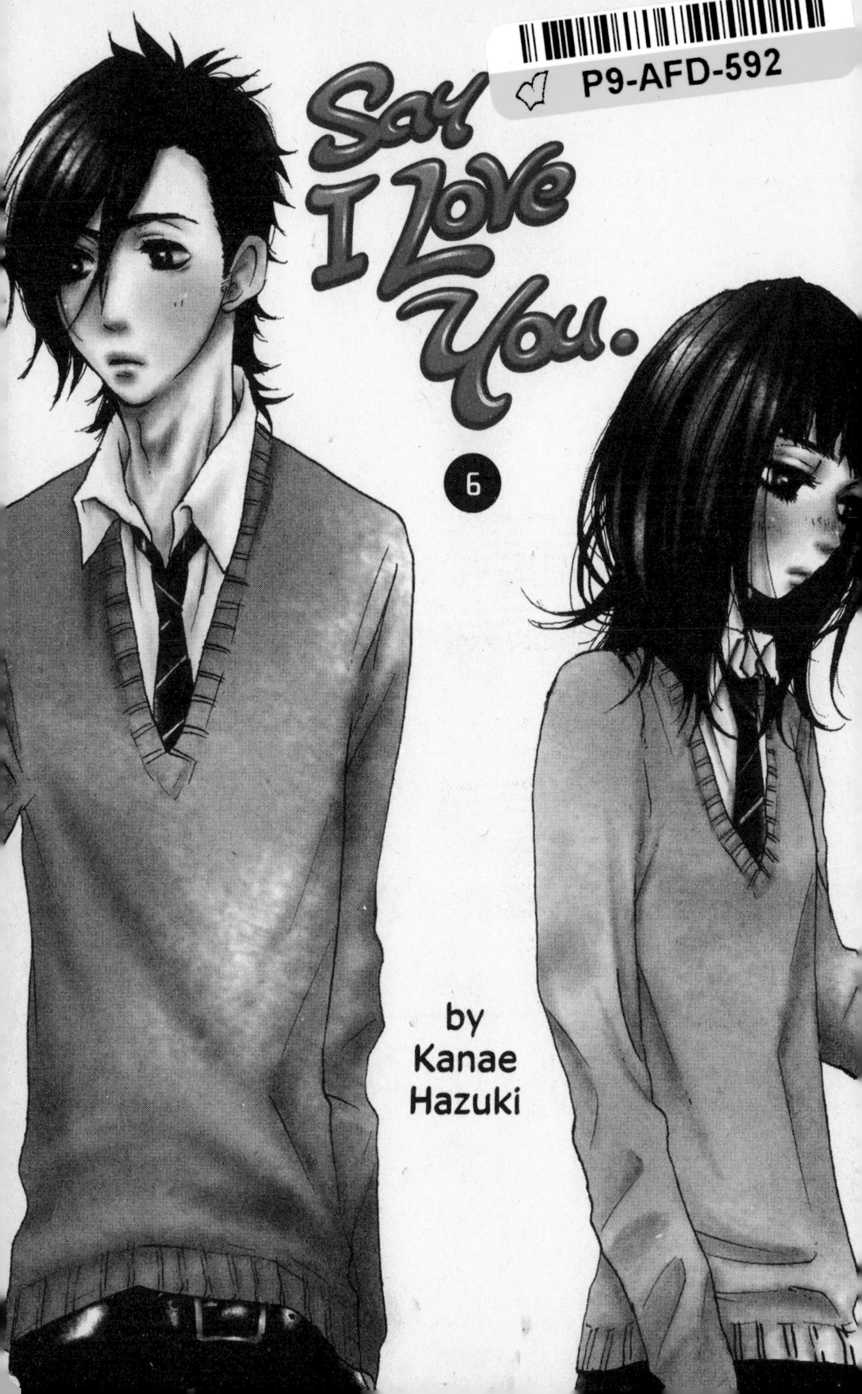

by
Kanae
Hazuki

Kanae Hazuki
presents

Chapter 21

Chapter 22

Chapter 23

Chapter 24

CHARACTERS

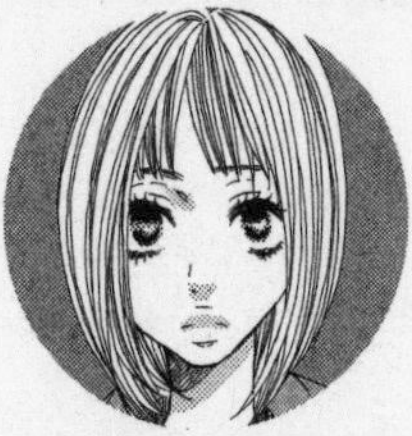

Mei Tachibana

A girl who hasn't had a single friend, let alone a boyfriend, in sixteen years, and has lived her life trusting no one. She finds herself attracted to Yamato, who, for some reason, just won't leave her alone, and they start dating.

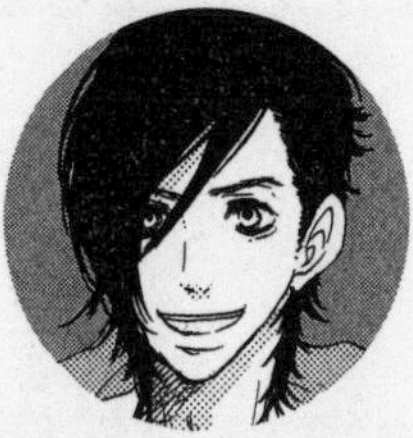

Yamato Kurosawa

The most popular boy at Mei's school. He has the love of many girls, yet for some reason, he is obsessed with Mei, the brooding weirdo girl from another class.

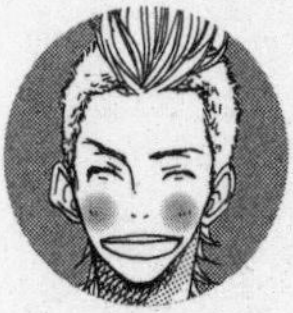

Kai

Yamato's classmate from middle school who had been the victim of bullying. For his own reasons, he started high school a year late. He is a regular customer at Mei's work, and a Land lover.

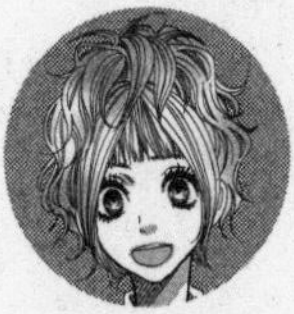

Megumi

An amateur model who has her sights set on Yamato. She transferred to his school and got him a modeling job. The two gradually got closer, and she is currently plotting to pull Mei and Yamato apart.

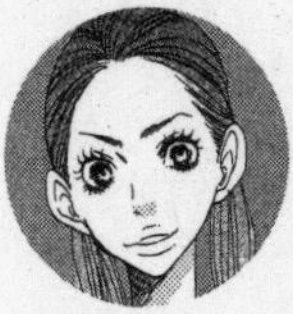

Aiko

She likes Yamato and was jealous of Mei, but now that she has seen Mei trying so hard to confront her own insecurities, she has decided to cheer her on. They were put in the same class in their second year of high school.

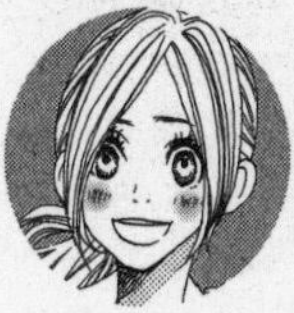

Asami

A girl who treats Mei as a real friend. She had a thing for Yamato, but now she is dating his friend Nakanishi. She and Mei were put in different classes in their second year of high school.

STORY

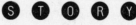

Mei Tachibana spent sixteen years without a single friend or boyfriend. One day she accidentally injured Yamato Kurosawa, the most popular boy in her school. Ironically, that made him like her, and he unilaterally decided that they were friends. He even kissed her like he meant it. Mei was gradually drawn in by Yamato's kindness and sincerity, and started to realize that she was in love. However, the amateur model Megumi has her sights on Yamato; she transfers to their school and implements various schemes to get closer to him. Furthermore, Yamato's friend from middle school Kai has a secret crush on Mei, and he's starting to act on it?!

Say
"I love you".
Kanae Hazuki

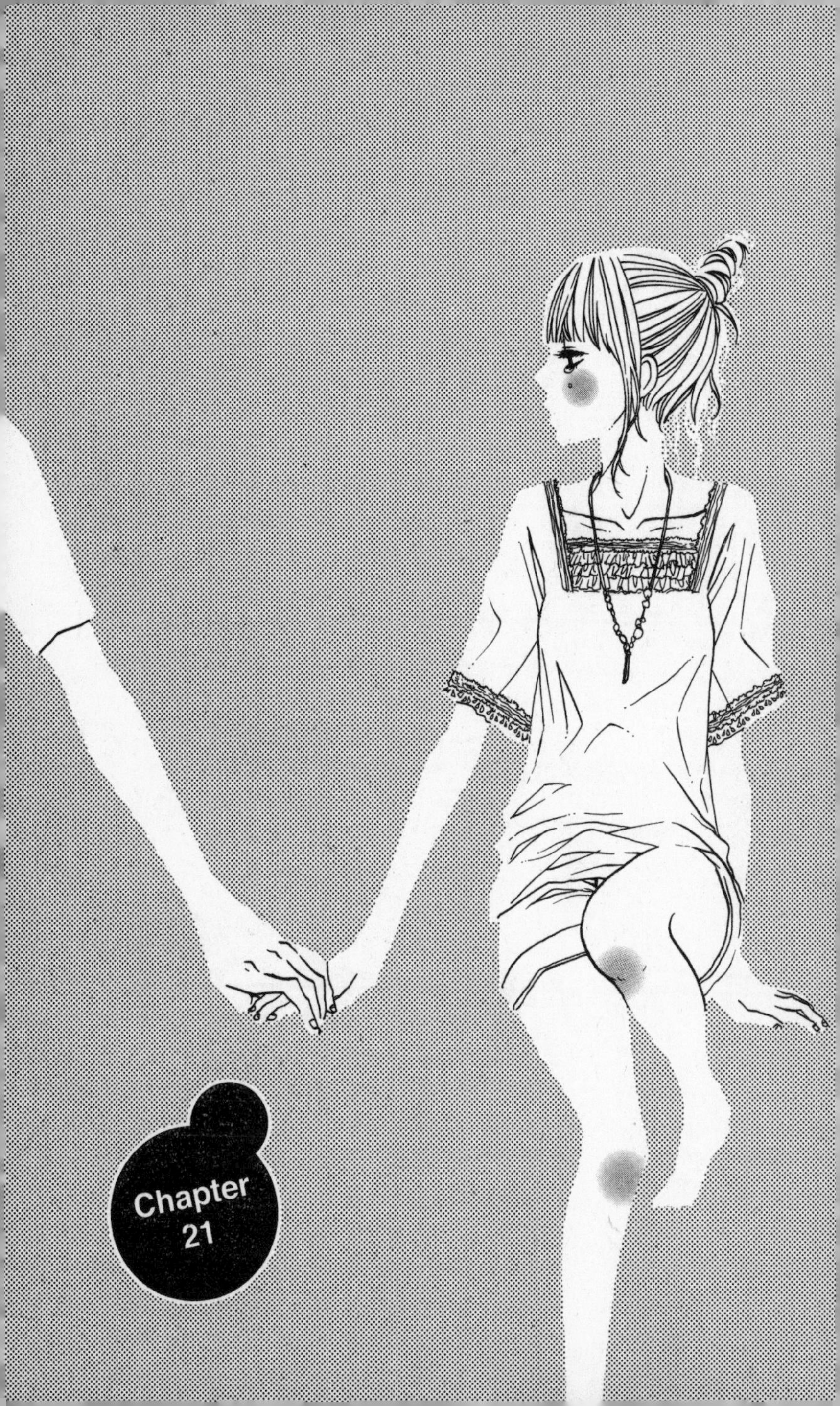
Chapter 21

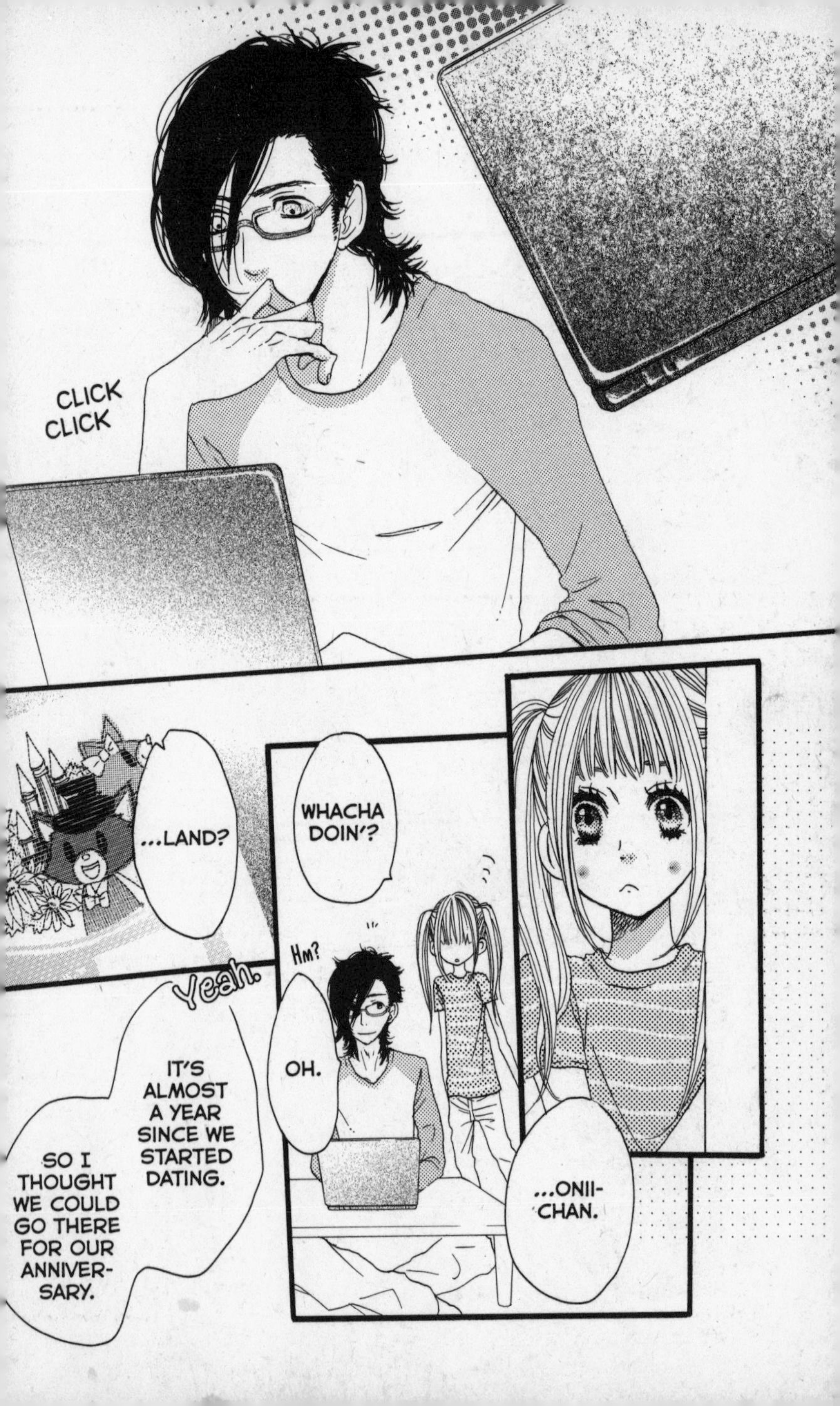
CLICK
CLICK
...ONII-CHAN.
WHATCHA DOIN'?
Hm?
OH.
...LAND?
Yeah.
IT'S ALMOST A YEAR SINCE WE STARTED DATING.
SO I THOUGHT WE COULD GO THERE FOR OUR ANNIVERSARY.

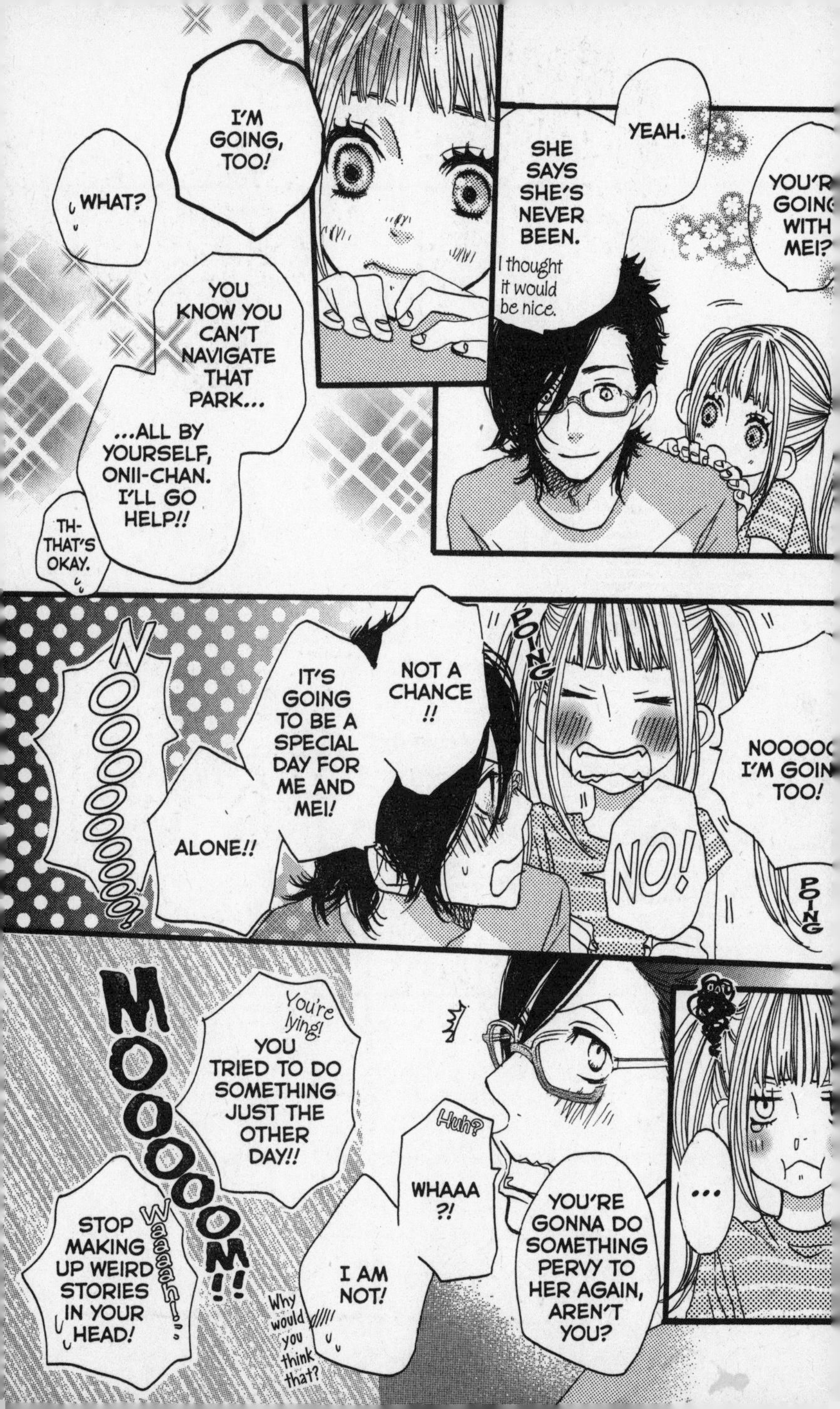
YOU'R GOIN WITH MEI?
YEAH.
SHE SAYS SHE'S NEVER BEEN.
I thought it would be nice.
I'M GOING, TOO!
WHAT?
YOU KNOW YOU CAN'T NAVIGATE THAT PARK...
...ALL BY YOURSELF, ONII-CHAN. I'LL GO HELP!!
TH-THAT'S OKAY.
NOOOO I'M GOIN TOO!
POING
NO!
POING
NOT A CHANCE!!
IT'S GOING TO BE A SPECIAL DAY FOR ME AND MEI!
ALONE!!
NOOOOOOOOOOO!
...
YOU'RE GONNA DO SOMETHING PERVY TO HER AGAIN, AREN'T YOU?
Huh?
WHAAA?!
I AM NOT!
Why would you think that?
You're lying!
YOU TRIED TO DO SOMETHING JUST THE OTHER DAY!!
MOOOOOOM!!
Waaaah!
STOP MAKING UP WEIRD STORIES IN YOUR HEAD!

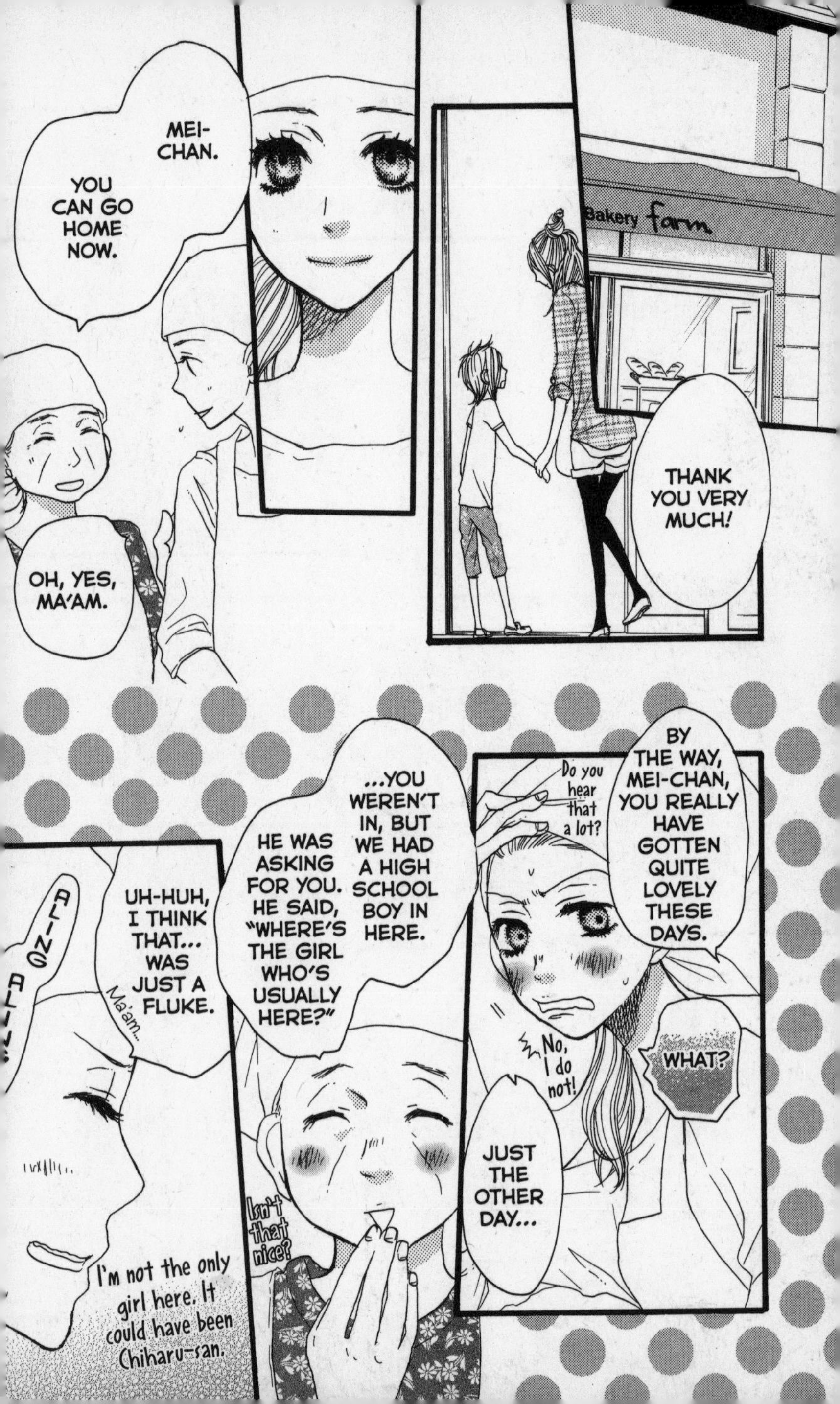

Bakery farm
THANK YOU VERY MUCH!
MEI-CHAN.
YOU CAN GO HOME NOW.
OH, YES, MA'AM.
BY THE WAY, MEI-CHAN, YOU REALLY HAVE GOTTEN QUITE LOVELY THESE DAYS.
Do you hear that a lot?
WHAT?
No, I do not!
JUST THE OTHER DAY...
...YOU WEREN'T IN, BUT WE HAD A HIGH SCHOOL BOY IN HERE.
HE WAS ASKING FOR YOU. HE SAID, "WHERE'S THE GIRL WHO'S USUALLY HERE?"
Isn't that nice?
UH-HUH, I THINK THAT... WAS JUST A FLUKE.
Ma'am...
ALING
I'm not the only girl here. It could have been Chiharu-san.

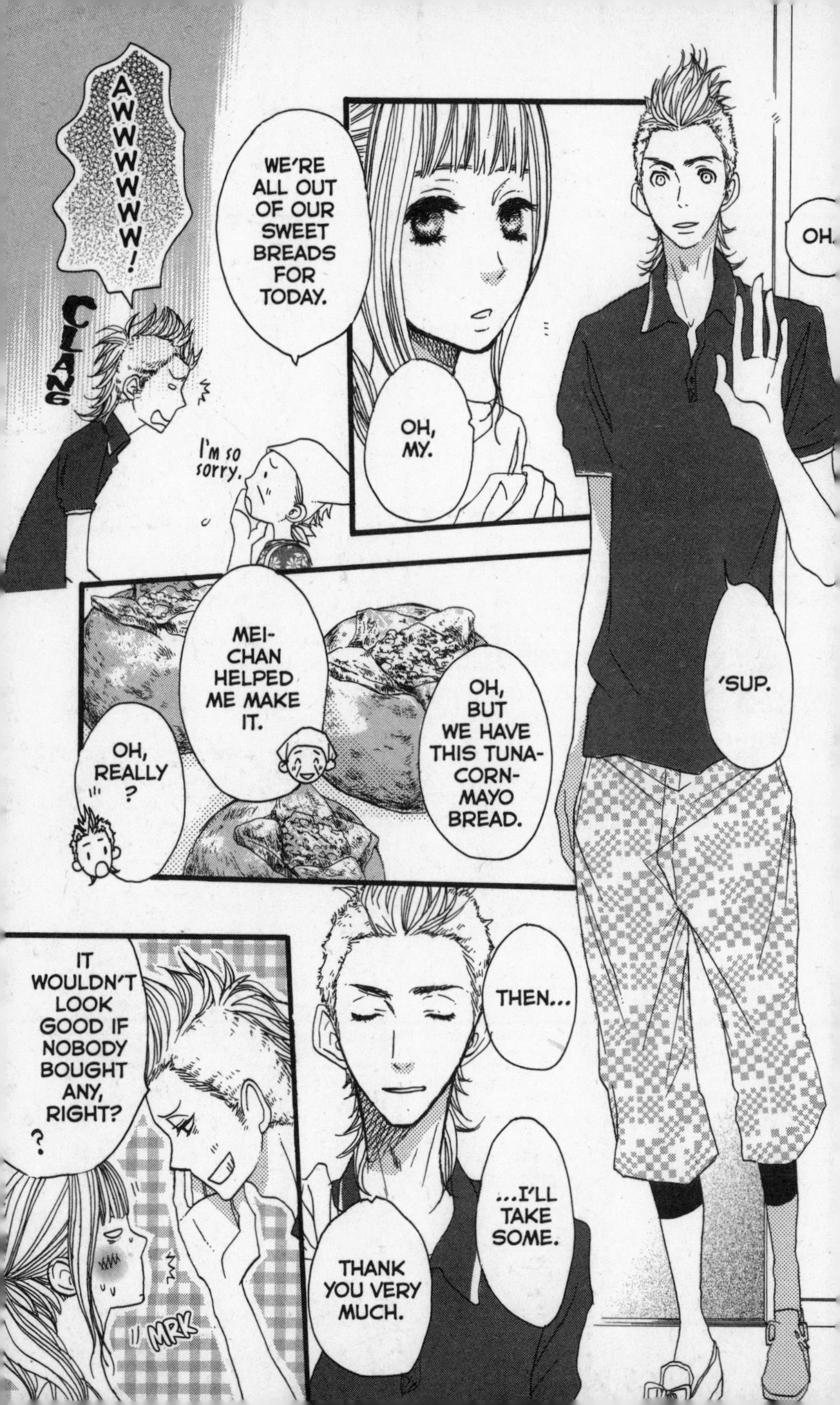
OH.
'SUP.
OH, MY.
WE'RE ALL OUT OF OUR SWEET BREADS FOR TODAY.
AWWWWWW!
CLANG
I'm so sorry.
OH, BUT WE HAVE THIS TUNA-CORN-MAYO BREAD.
MEI-CHAN HELPED ME MAKE IT.
OH, REALLY?
THEN...
...I'LL TAKE SOME.
THANK YOU VERY MUCH.
IT WOULDN'T LOOK GOOD IF NOBODY BOUGHT ANY, RIGHT?
MRK

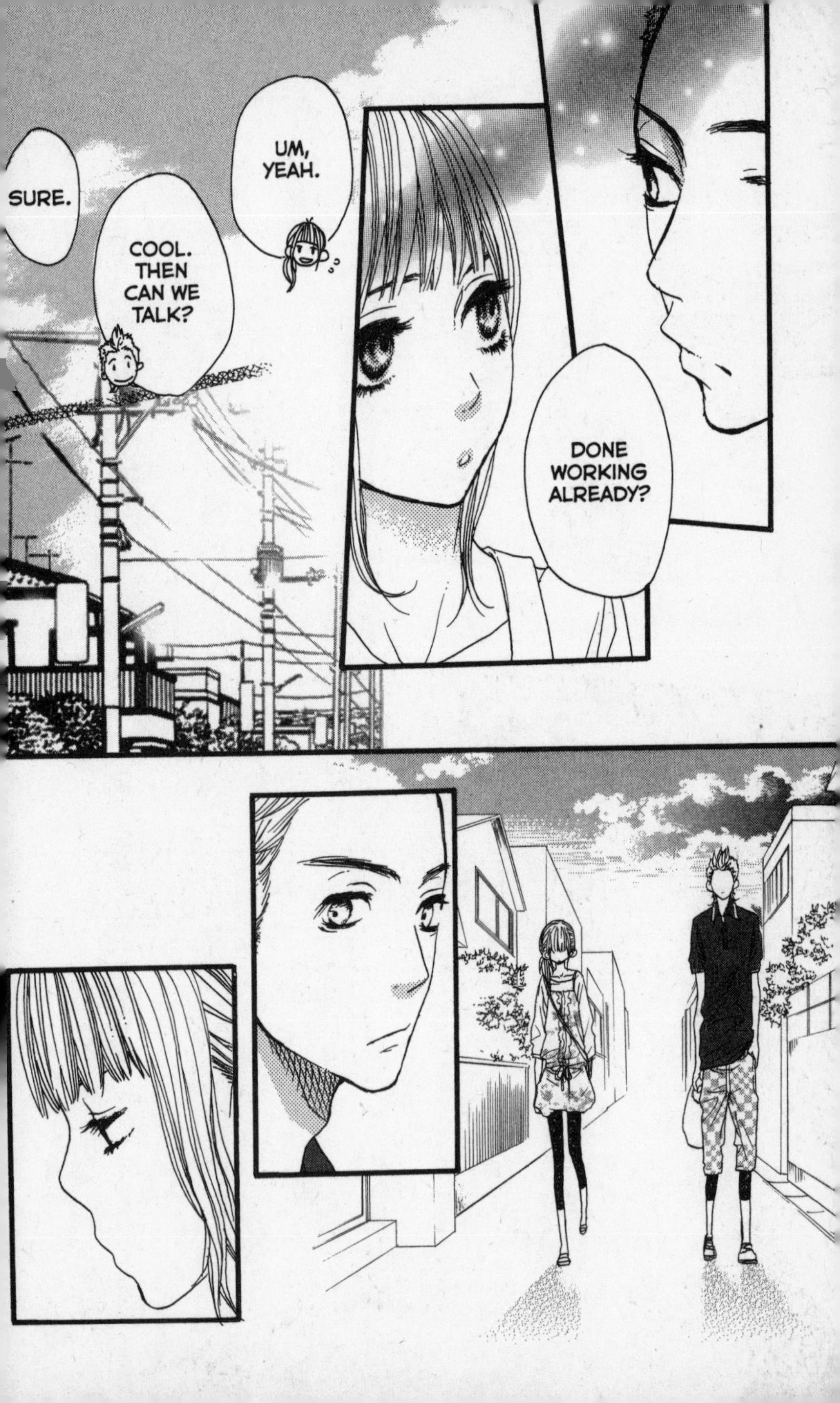
DONE WORKING ALREADY?
UM, YEAH.
COOL. THEN CAN WE TALK?
SURE.

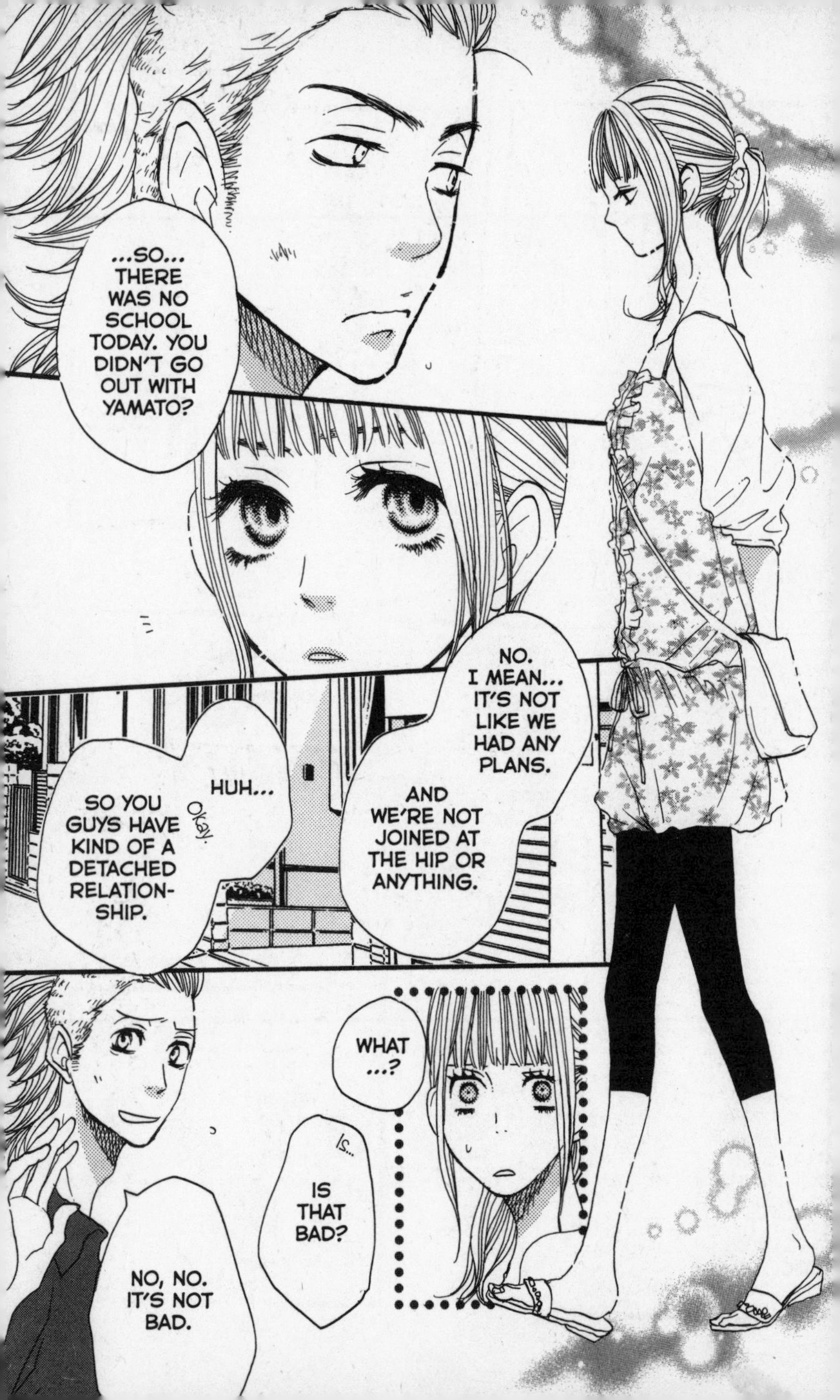
...SO... THERE WAS NO SCHOOL TODAY. YOU DIDN'T GO OUT WITH YAMATO?
NO. I MEAN... IT'S NOT LIKE WE HAD ANY PLANS.
AND WE'RE NOT JOINED AT THE HIP OR ANYTHING.
HUH...
Okay.
SO YOU GUYS HAVE KIND OF A DETACHED RELATION-SHIP.
WHAT ...?
IS...
IS THAT BAD?
NO, NO. IT'S NOT BAD.

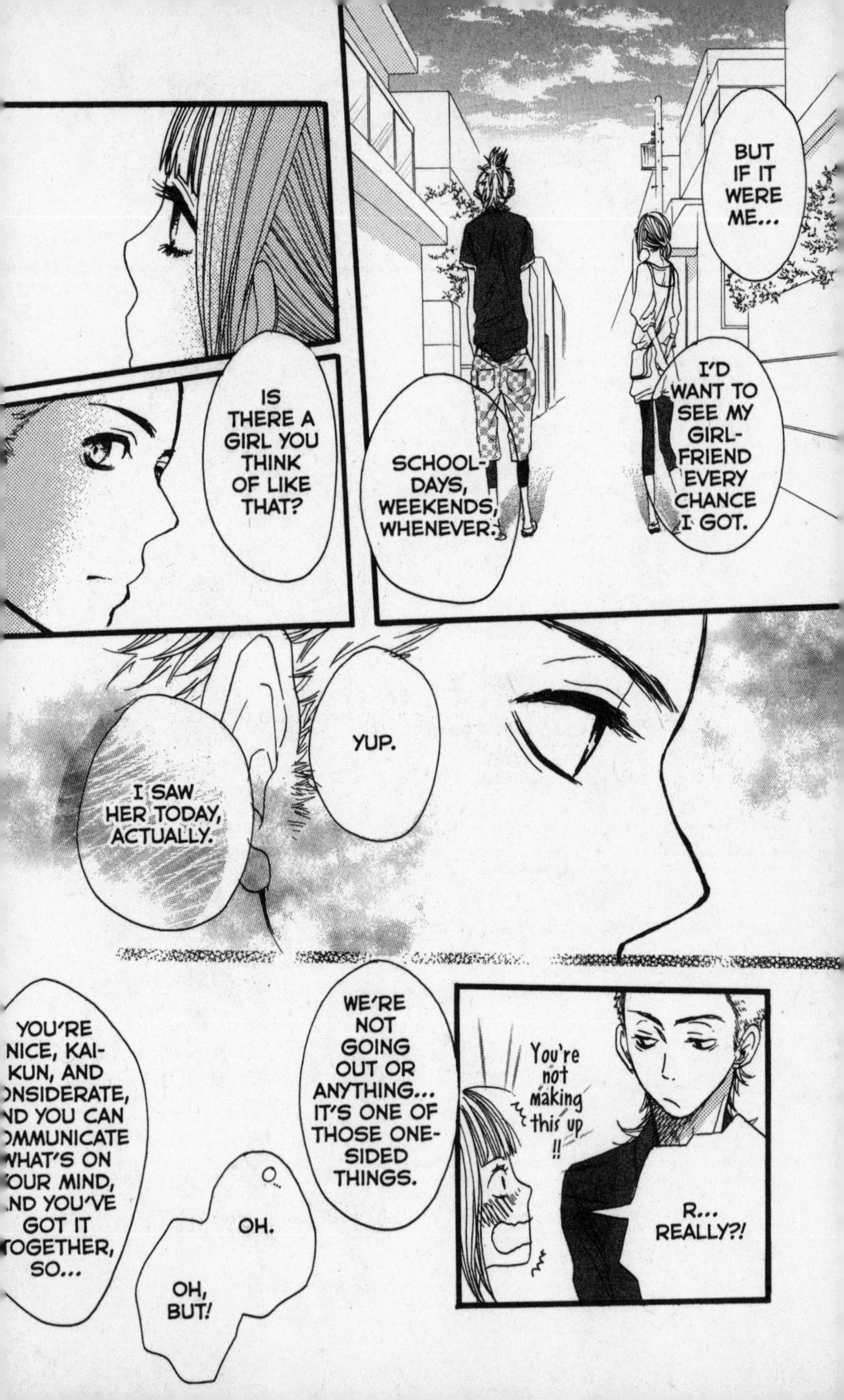
BUT IF IT WERE ME...
I'D WANT TO SEE MY GIRL-FRIEND EVERY CHANCE I GOT.
SCHOOL-DAYS, WEEKENDS, WHENEVER.
IS THERE A GIRL YOU THINK OF LIKE THAT?
YUP.
I SAW HER TODAY, ACTUALLY.
R... REALLY?!
You're not making this up!!
WE'RE NOT GOING OUT OR ANYTHING... IT'S ONE OF THOSE ONE-SIDED THINGS.
O...
OH.
OH, BUT!
YOU'RE NICE, KAI-KUN, AND ONSIDERATE, ND YOU CAN OMMUNICATE HAT'S ON OUR MIND, ND YOU'VE GOT IT OGETHER, SO...

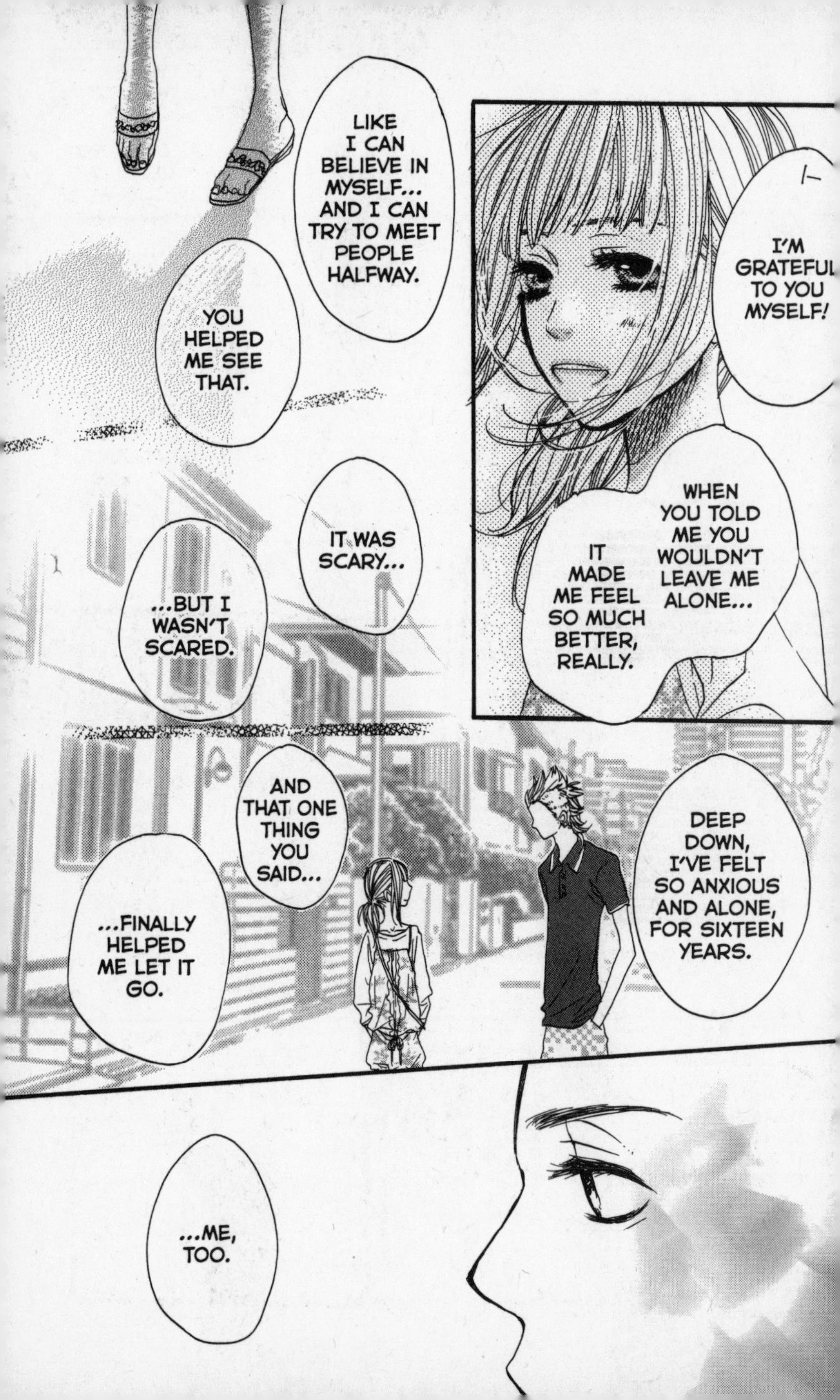
I–
I'M GRATEFUL TO YOU MYSELF!
WHEN YOU TOLD ME YOU WOULDN'T LEAVE ME ALONE...
IT MADE ME FEEL SO MUCH BETTER, REALLY.
LIKE I CAN BELIEVE IN MYSELF... AND I CAN TRY TO MEET PEOPLE HALFWAY.
YOU HELPED ME SEE THAT.
IT WAS SCARY...
...BUT I WASN'T SCARED.
DEEP DOWN, I'VE FELT SO ANXIOUS AND ALONE, FOR SIXTEEN YEARS.
AND THAT ONE THING YOU SAID...
...FINALLY HELPED ME LET IT GO.
...ME, TOO.

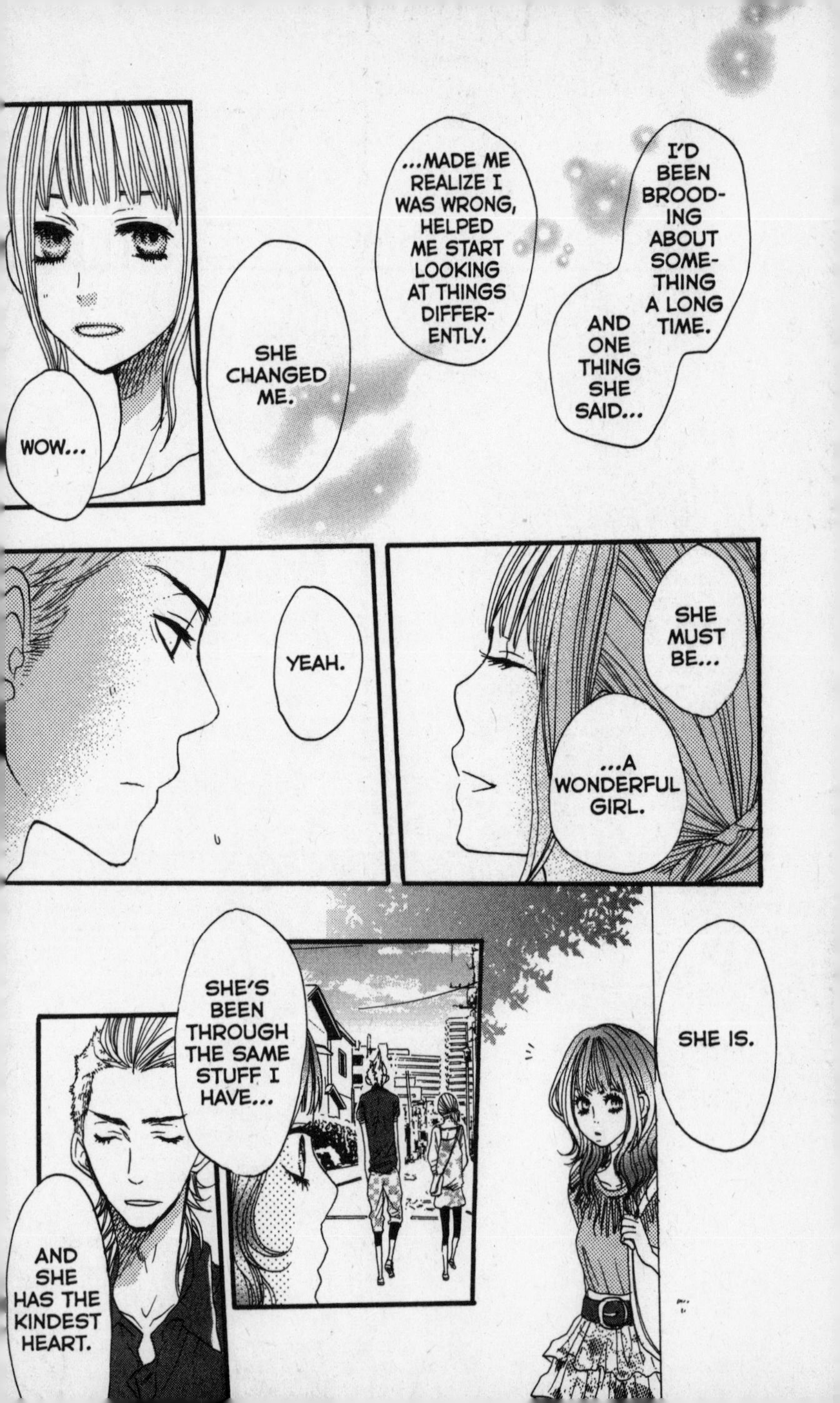
I'D BEEN BROODING ABOUT SOMETHING A LONG TIME. AND ONE THING SHE SAID...
...MADE ME REALIZE I WAS WRONG, HELPED ME START LOOKING AT THINGS DIFFERENTLY.
SHE CHANGED ME.
WOW...
SHE MUST BE...
...A WONDERFUL GIRL.
YEAH.
SHE IS.
SHE'S BEEN THROUGH THE SAME STUFF I HAVE...
AND SHE HAS THE KINDEST HEART.

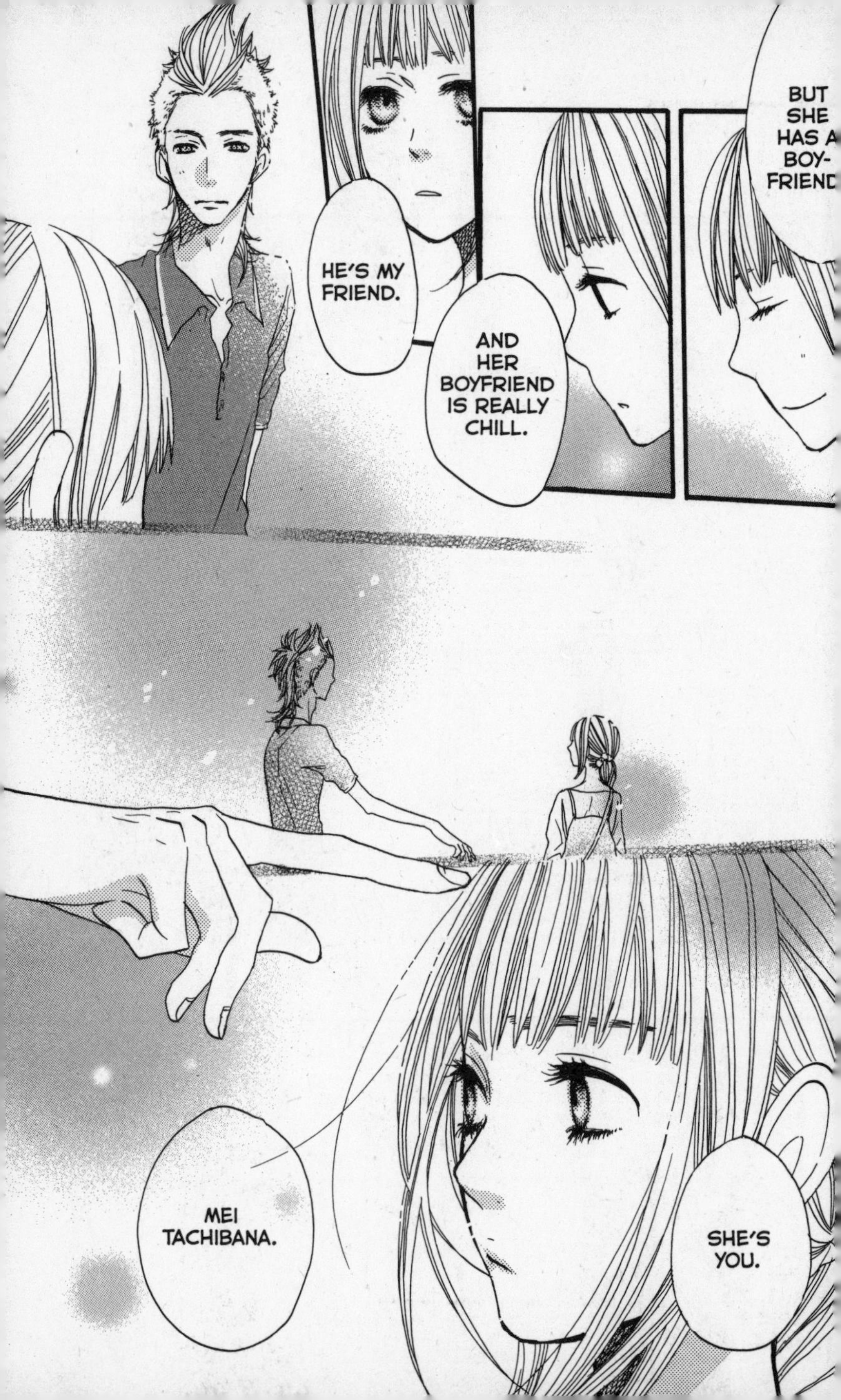
BUT SHE HAS A BOY-FRIEND
AND HER BOYFRIEND IS REALLY CHILL.
HE'S MY FRIEND.
SHE'S YOU.
MEI TACHIBANA.

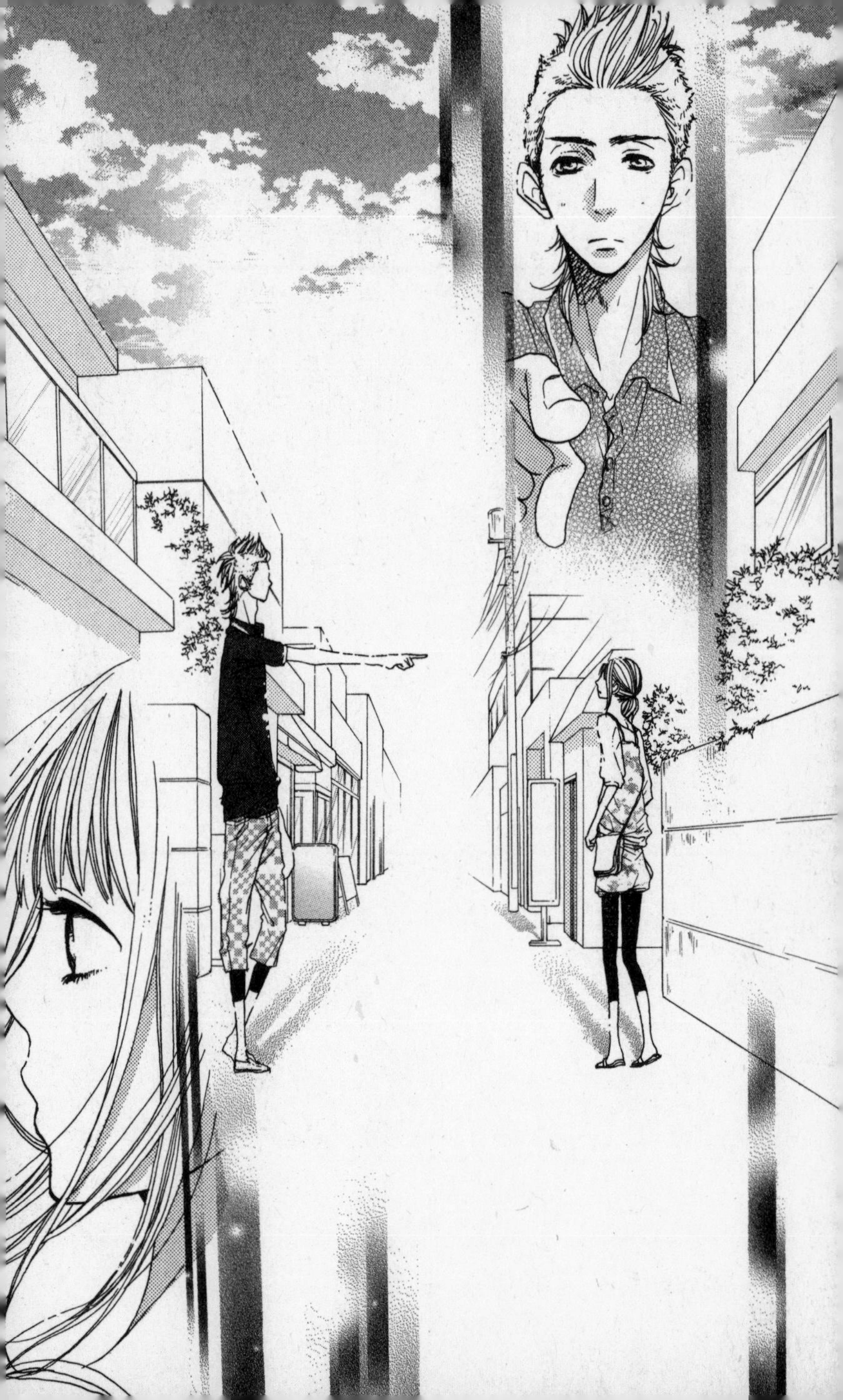

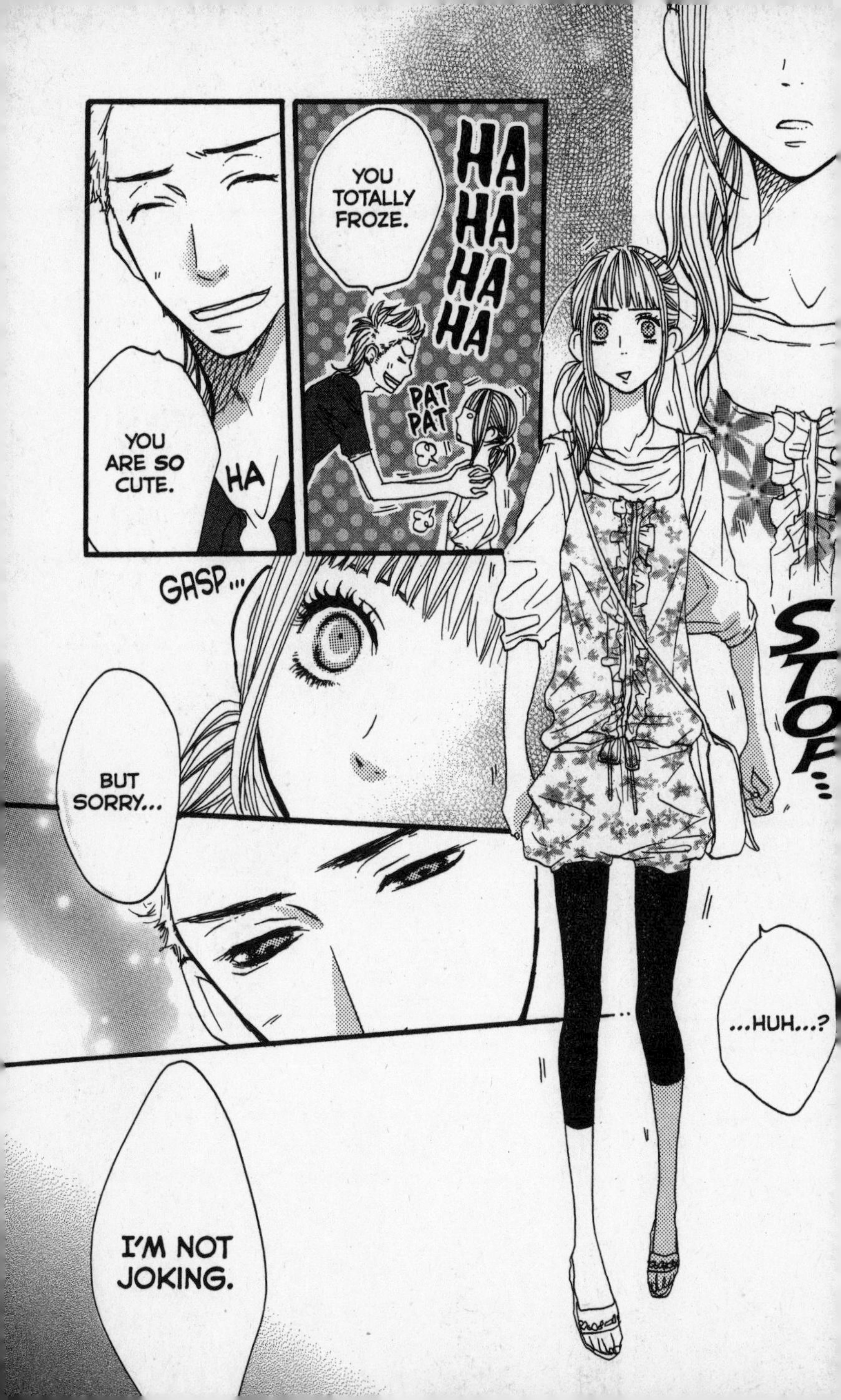

STOP...
...HUH...?
YOU TOTALLY FROZE.
HA HA HA HA HA HA HA HA
PAT PAT
YOU ARE SO CUTE.
HA
GASP...
BUT SORRY...
I'M NOT JOKING.

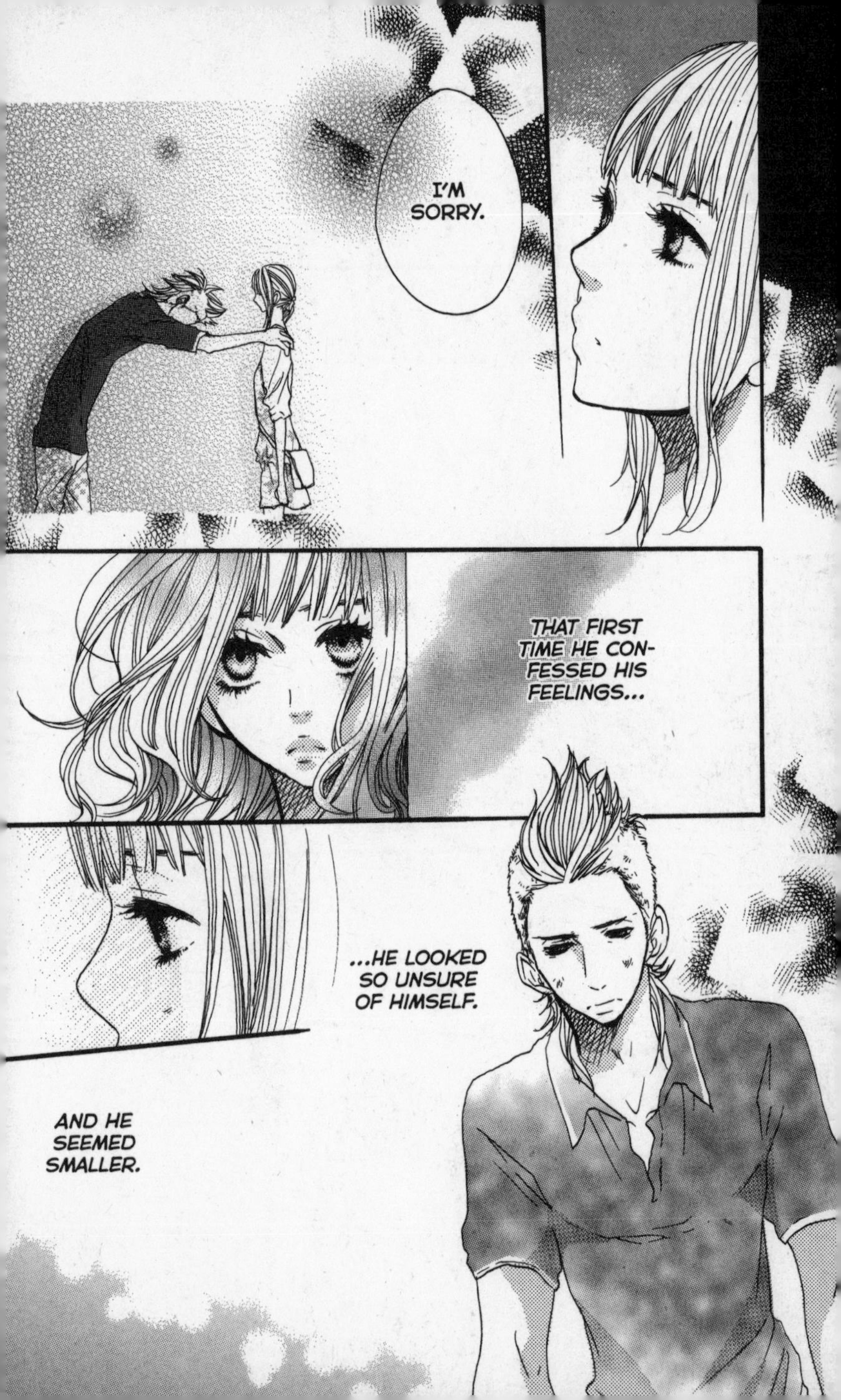
I'M SORRY.
THAT FIRST TIME HE CON-FESSED HIS FEELINGS...
...HE LOOKED SO UNSURE OF HIMSELF.
AND HE SEEMED SMALLER.

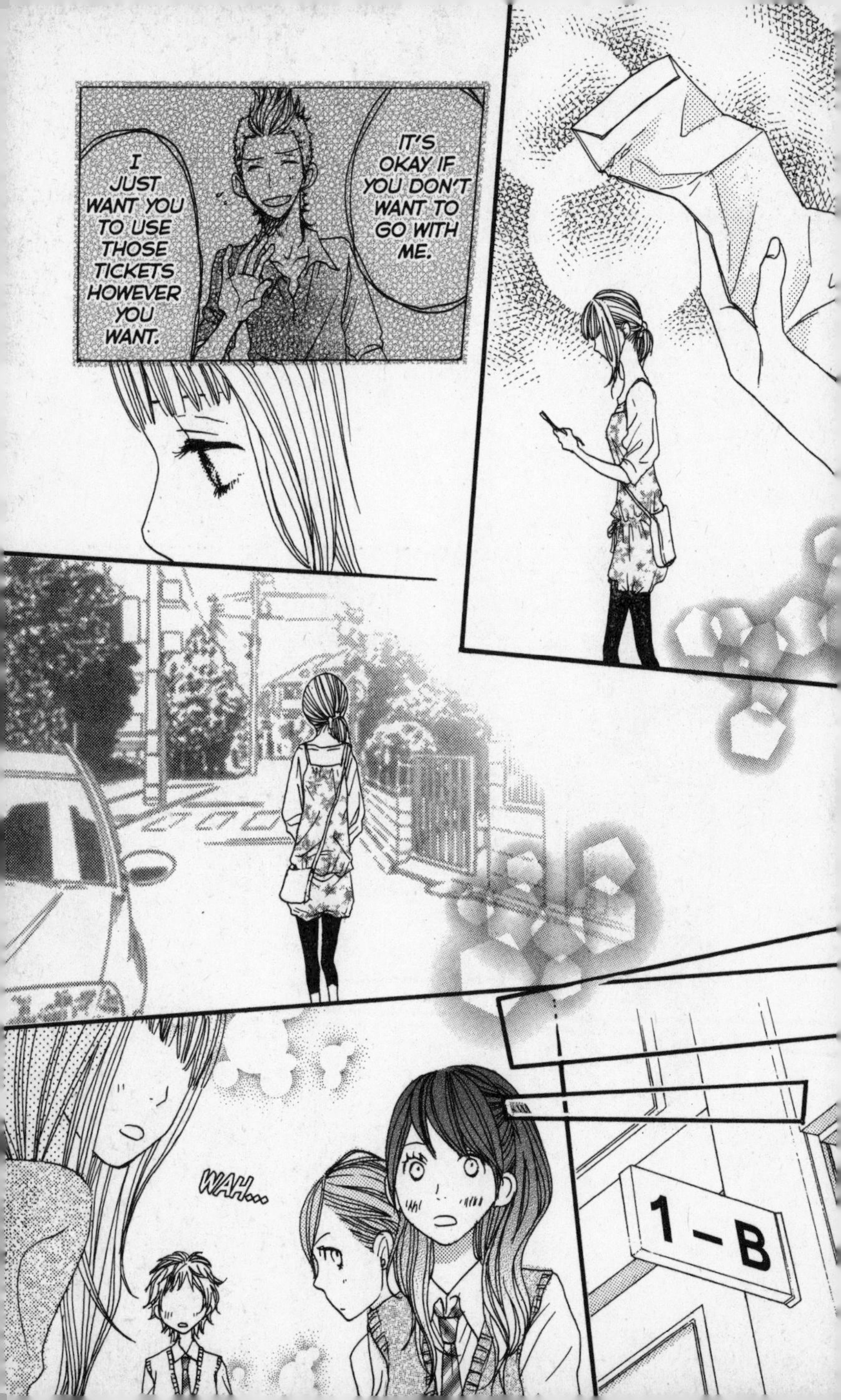
IT'S OKAY IF YOU DON'T WANT TO GO WITH ME.
I JUST WANT YOU TO USE THOSE TICKETS HOWEVER YOU WANT.
1-B
WAH...

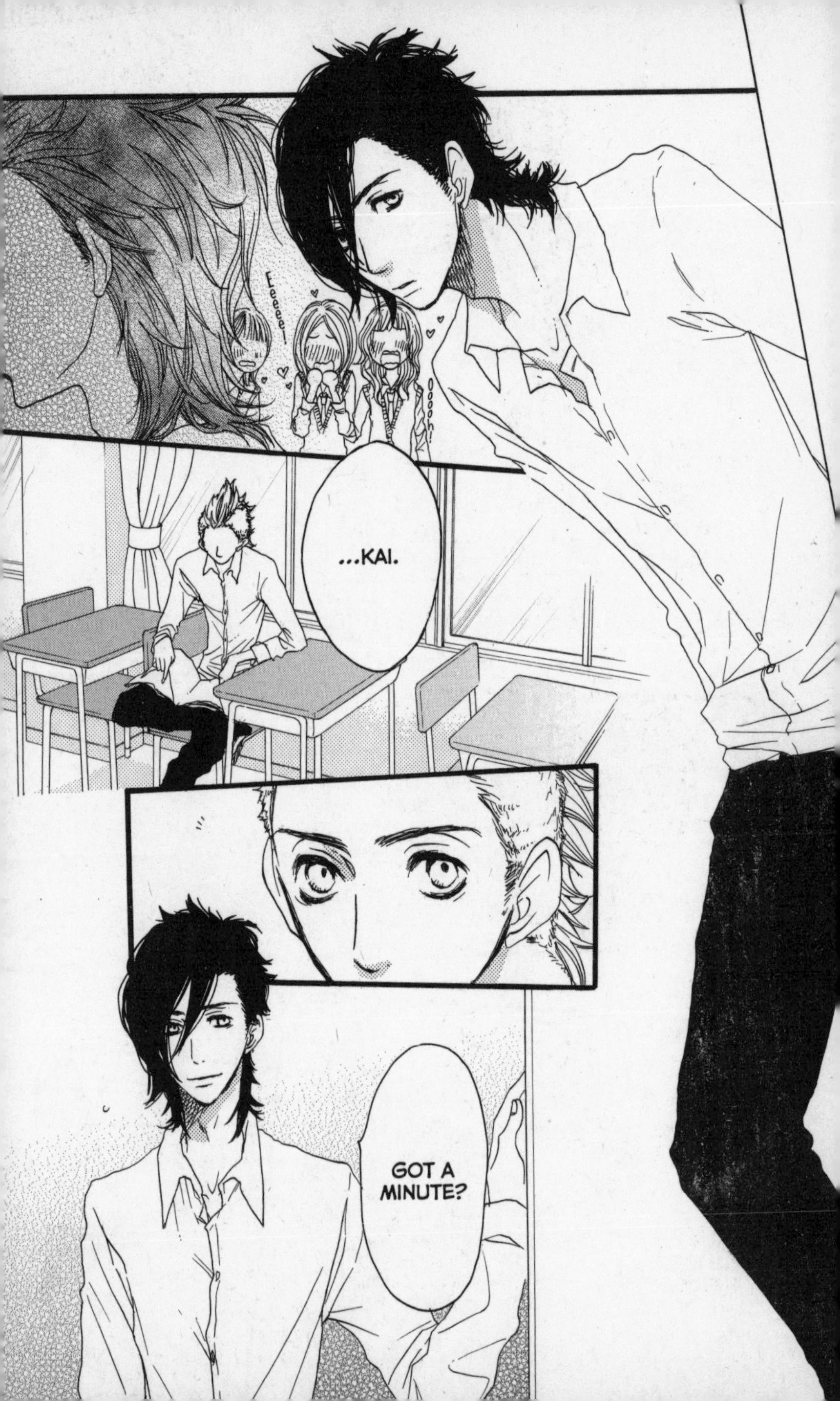
Ooooh!
Eeeee!
...KAI.
GOT A MINUTE?

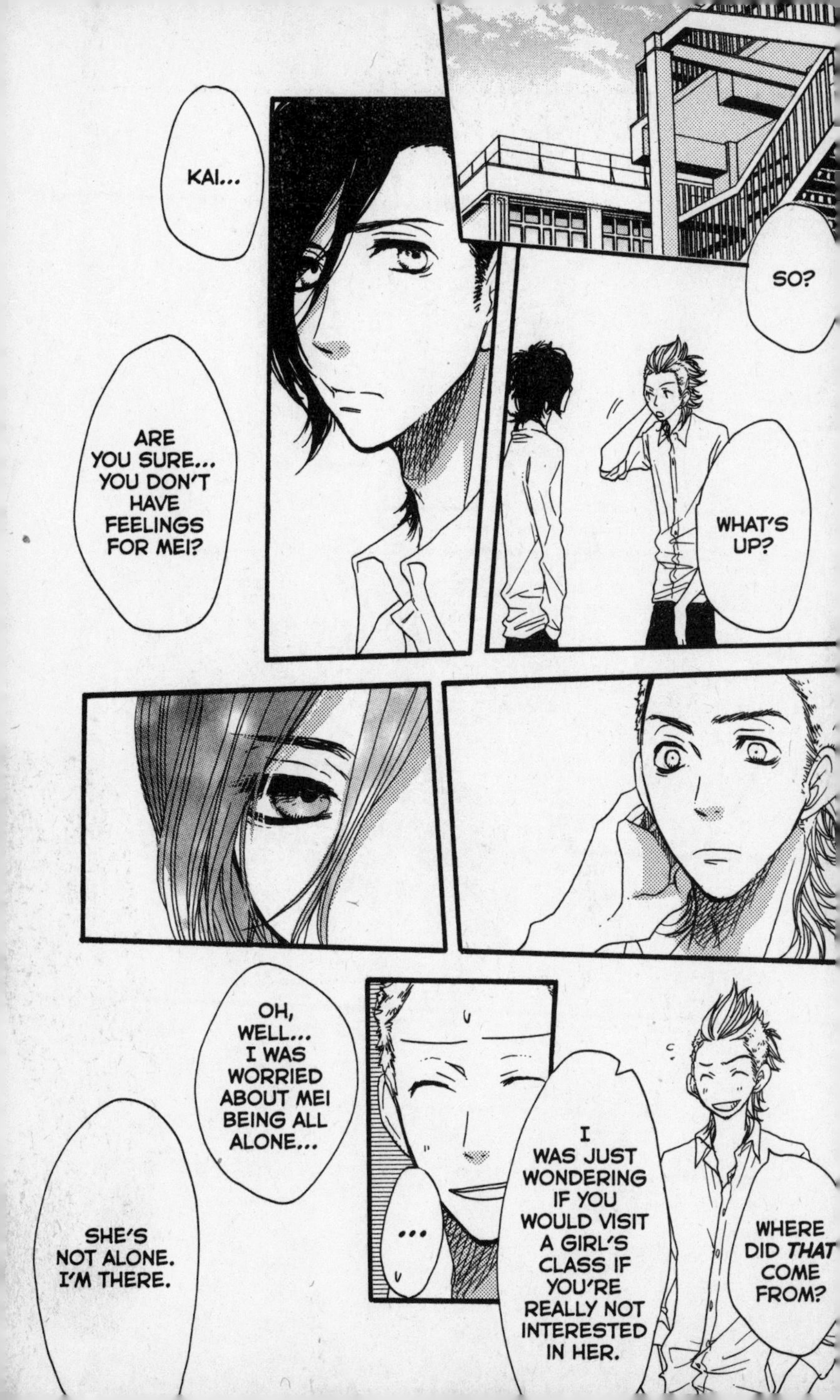
SO?
WHAT'S UP?
KAI...
ARE YOU SURE... YOU DON'T HAVE FEELINGS FOR MEI?
WHERE DID *THAT* COME FROM?
I WAS JUST WONDERING IF YOU WOULD VISIT A GIRL'S CLASS IF YOU'RE REALLY NOT INTERESTED IN HER.
...
OH, WELL... I WAS WORRIED ABOUT MEI BEING ALL ALONE...
SHE'S NOT ALONE. I'M THERE.

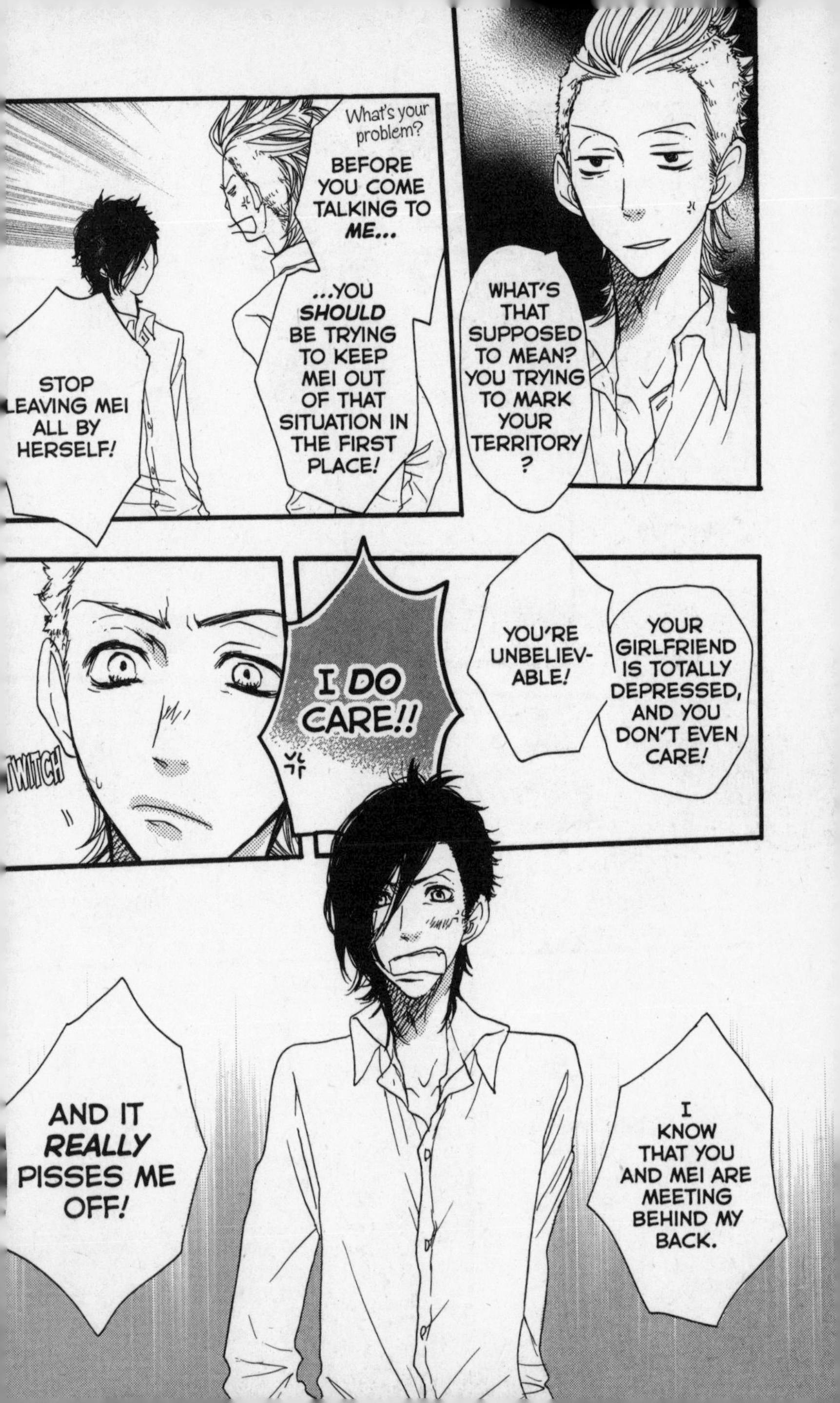
WHAT'S THAT SUPPOSED TO MEAN? YOU TRYING TO MARK YOUR TERRITORY?
What's your problem?
BEFORE YOU COME TALKING TO *ME*...
...YOU *SHOULD* BE TRYING TO KEEP MEI OUT OF THAT SITUATION IN THE FIRST PLACE!
STOP LEAVING MEI ALL BY HERSELF!
YOUR GIRLFRIEND IS TOTALLY DEPRESSED, AND YOU DON'T EVEN CARE!
YOU'RE UNBELIEV-ABLE!
I *DO* CARE!!
TWITCH
I KNOW THAT YOU AND MEI ARE MEETING BEHIND MY BACK.
AND IT *REALLY* PISSES ME OFF!

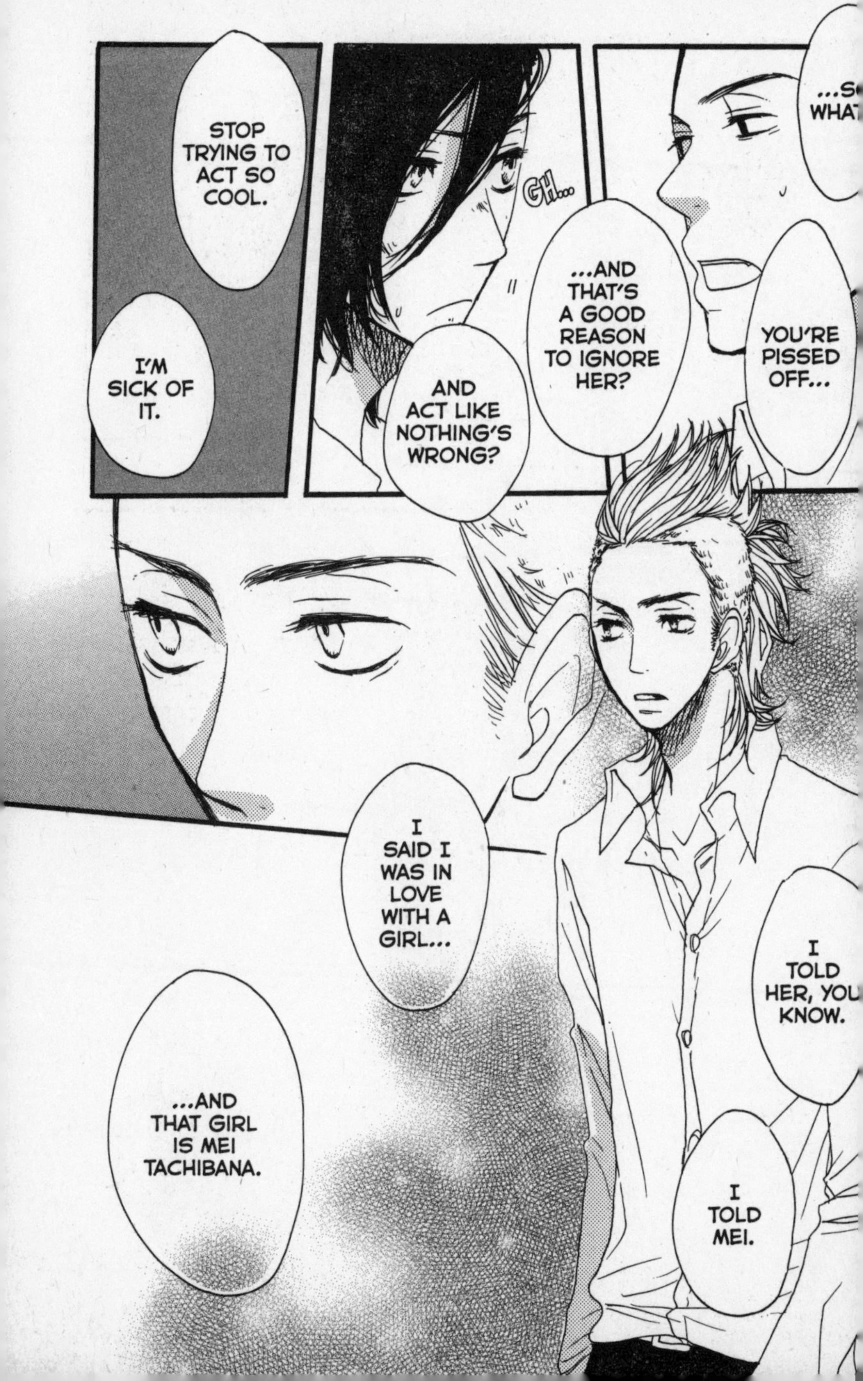
...S WHAT
YOU'RE PISSED OFF...
...AND THAT'S A GOOD REASON TO IGNORE HER?
GH...
AND ACT LIKE NOTHING'S WRONG?
STOP TRYING TO ACT SO COOL.
I'M SICK OF IT.
I TOLD HER, YOU KNOW.
I TOLD MEI.
I SAID I WAS IN LOVE WITH A GIRL...
...AND THAT GIRL IS MEI TACHIBANA.

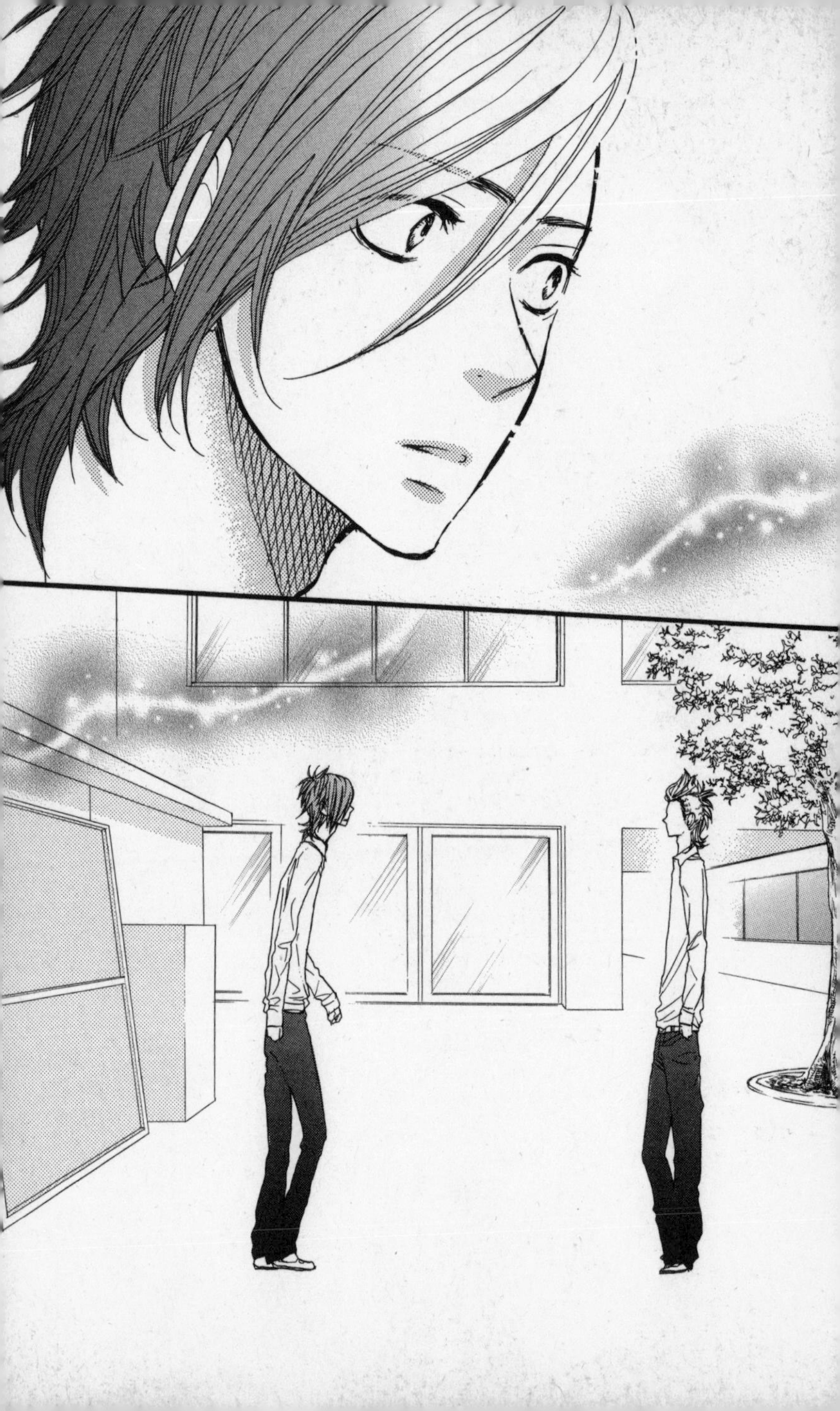

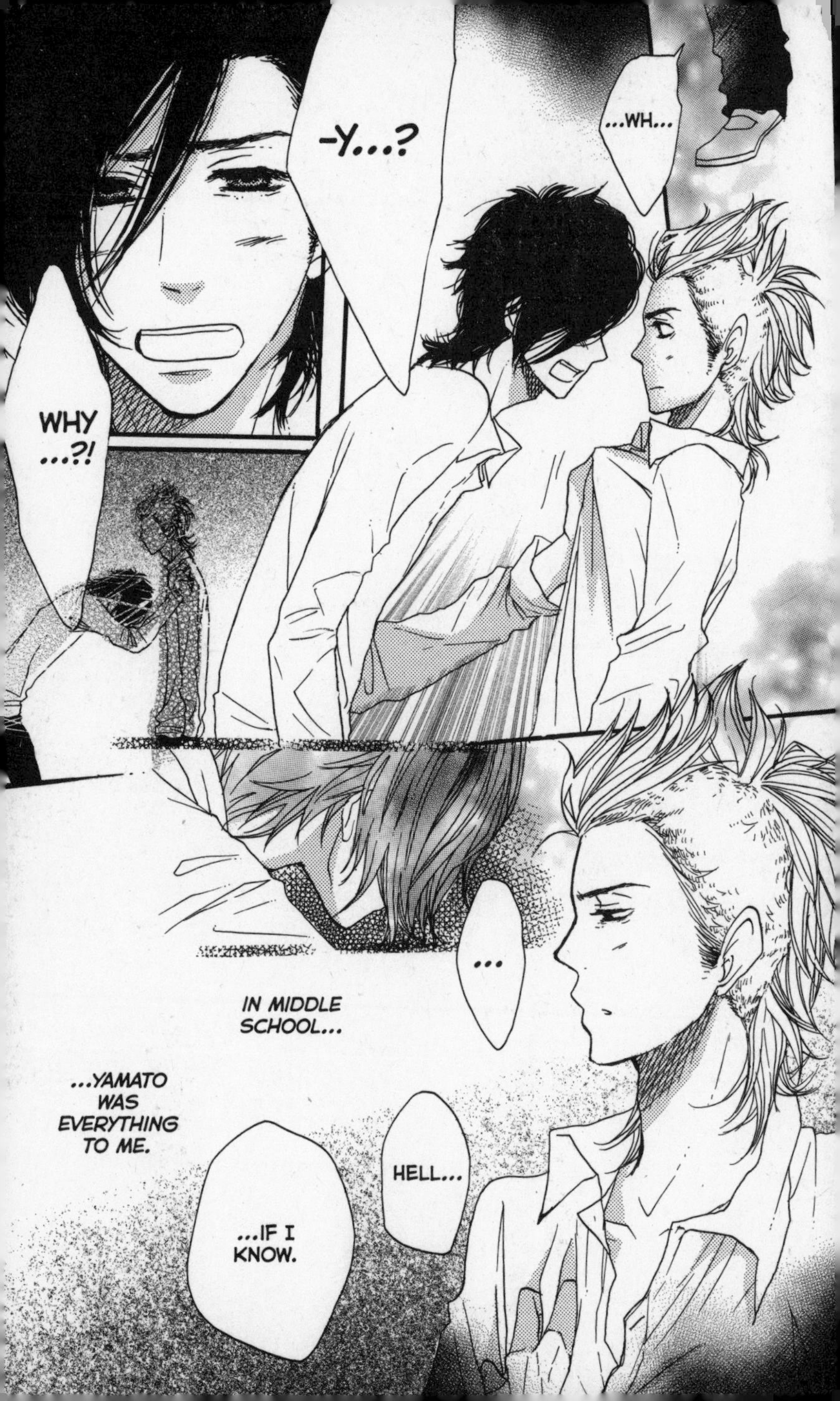
...WH...
-Y...?
WHY ...?!
...
IN MIDDLE SCHOOL...
...YAMATO WAS EVERYTHING TO ME.
HELL...
...IF I KNOW.

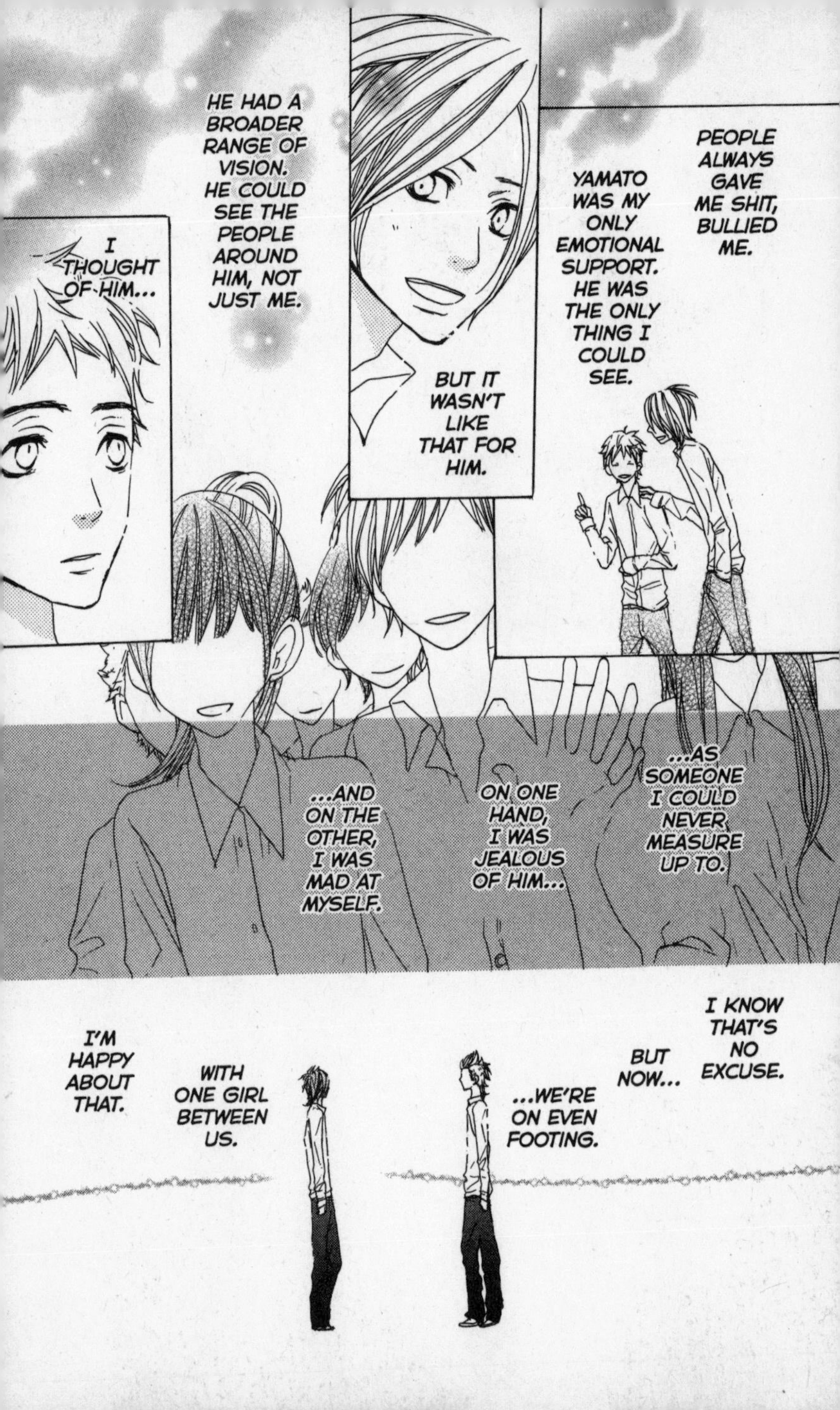

PEOPLE ALWAYS GAVE ME SHIT, BULLIED ME.
YAMATO WAS MY ONLY EMOTIONAL SUPPORT. HE WAS THE ONLY THING I COULD SEE.
BUT IT WASN'T LIKE THAT FOR HIM.
HE HAD A BROADER RANGE OF VISION. HE COULD SEE THE PEOPLE AROUND HIM, NOT JUST ME.
I THOUGHT OF HIM...
...AS SOMEONE I COULD NEVER MEASURE UP TO.
ON ONE HAND, I WAS JEALOUS OF HIM...
...AND ON THE OTHER, I WAS MAD AT MYSELF.
I KNOW THAT'S NO EXCUSE.
BUT NOW...
...WE'RE ON EVEN FOOTING.
WITH ONE GIRL BETWEEN US.
I'M HAPPY ABOUT THAT.

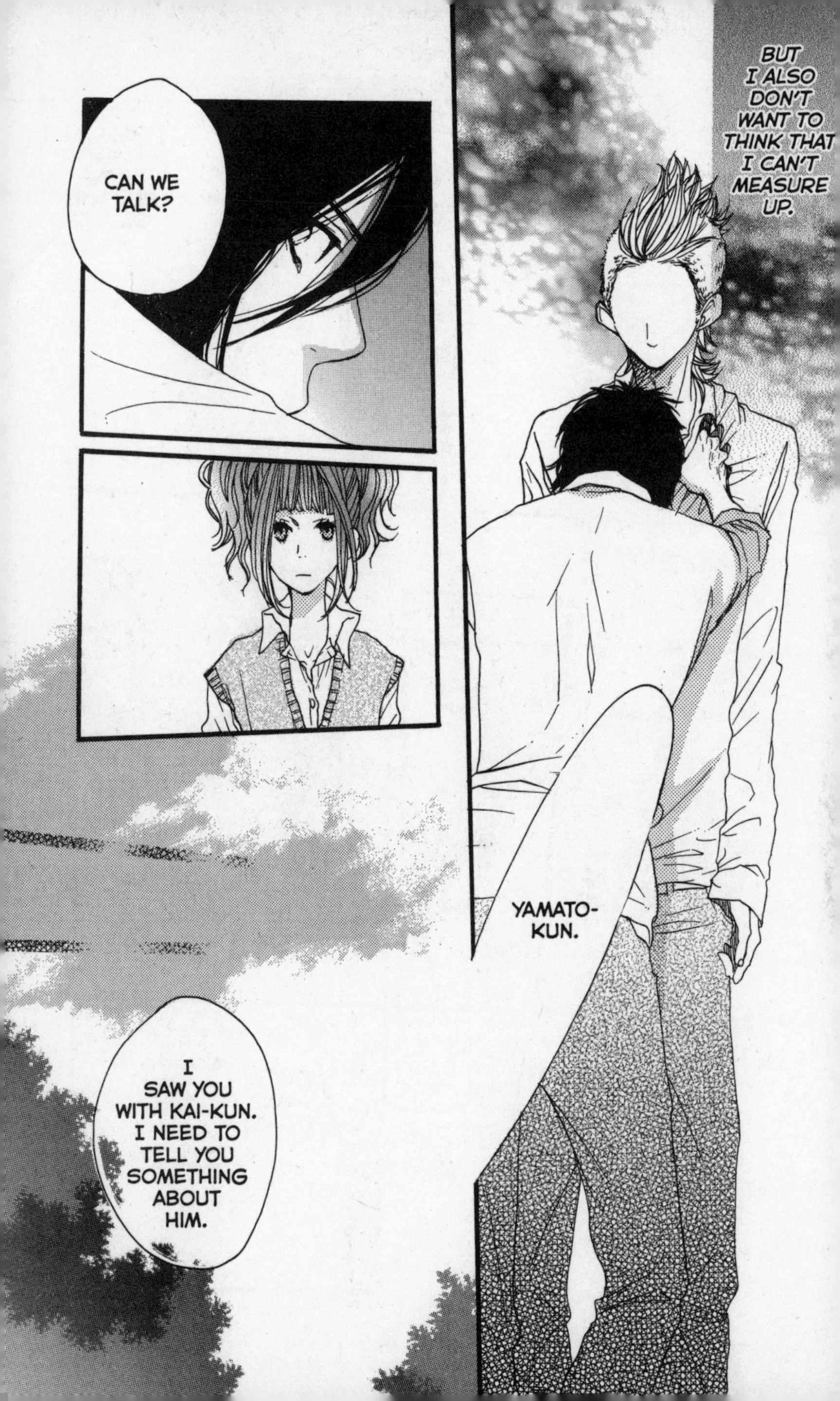
BUT I ALSO DON'T WANT TO THINK THAT I CAN'T MEASURE UP.
YAMATO-KUN.
CAN WE TALK?
I SAW YOU WITH KAI-KUN. I NEED TO TELL YOU SOMETHING ABOUT HIM.

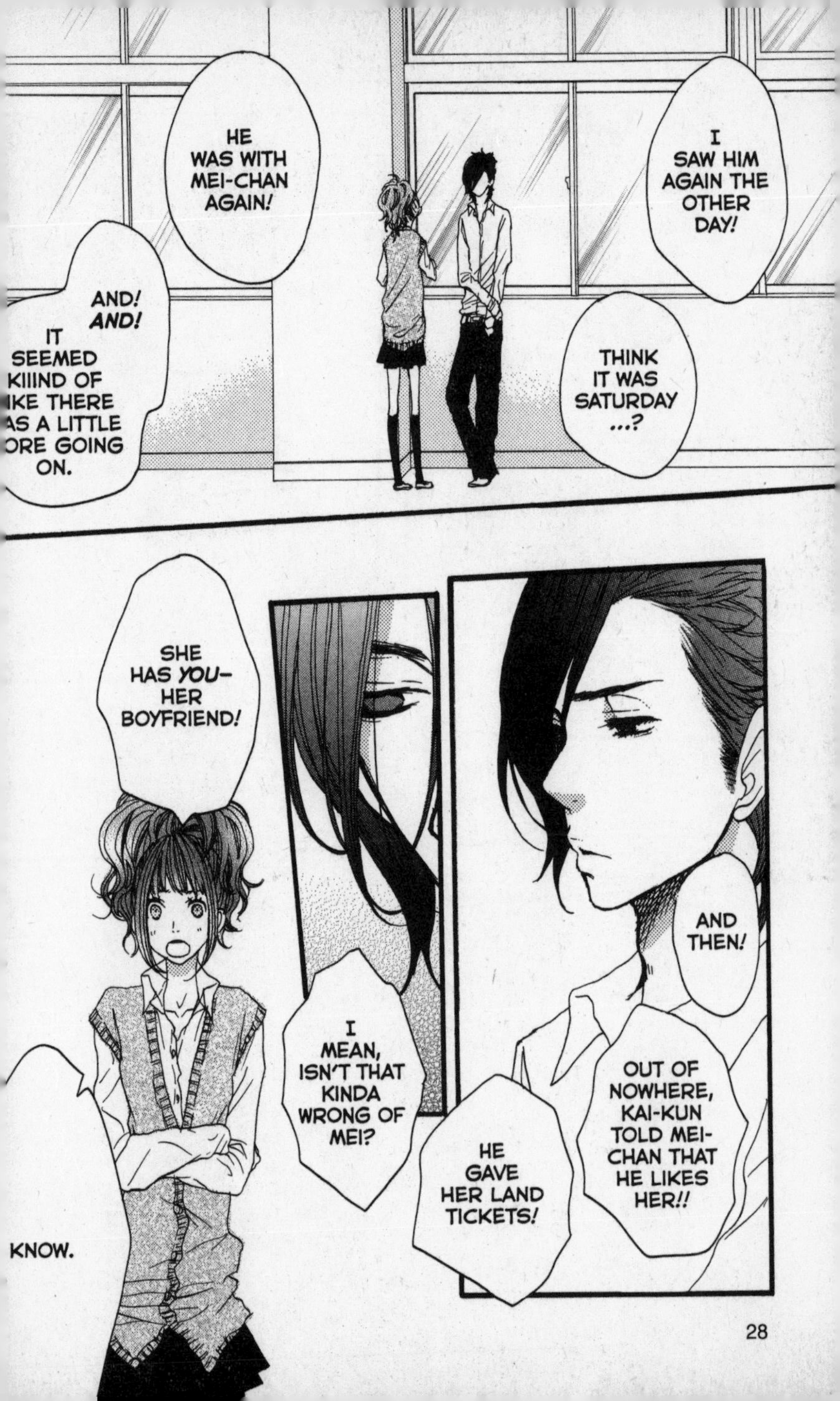
I SAW HIM AGAIN THE OTHER DAY!
THINK IT WAS SATURDAY ...?
HE WAS WITH MEI-CHAN AGAIN!
AND! *AND!* IT SEEMED KIIIND OF IKE THERE AS A LITTLE ORE GOING ON.
AND THEN!
OUT OF NOWHERE, KAI-KUN TOLD MEI-CHAN THAT HE LIKES HER!!
HE GAVE HER LAND TICKETS!
I MEAN, ISN'T THAT KINDA WRONG OF MEI?
SHE HAS *YOU*—HER BOYFRIEND!
KNOW.

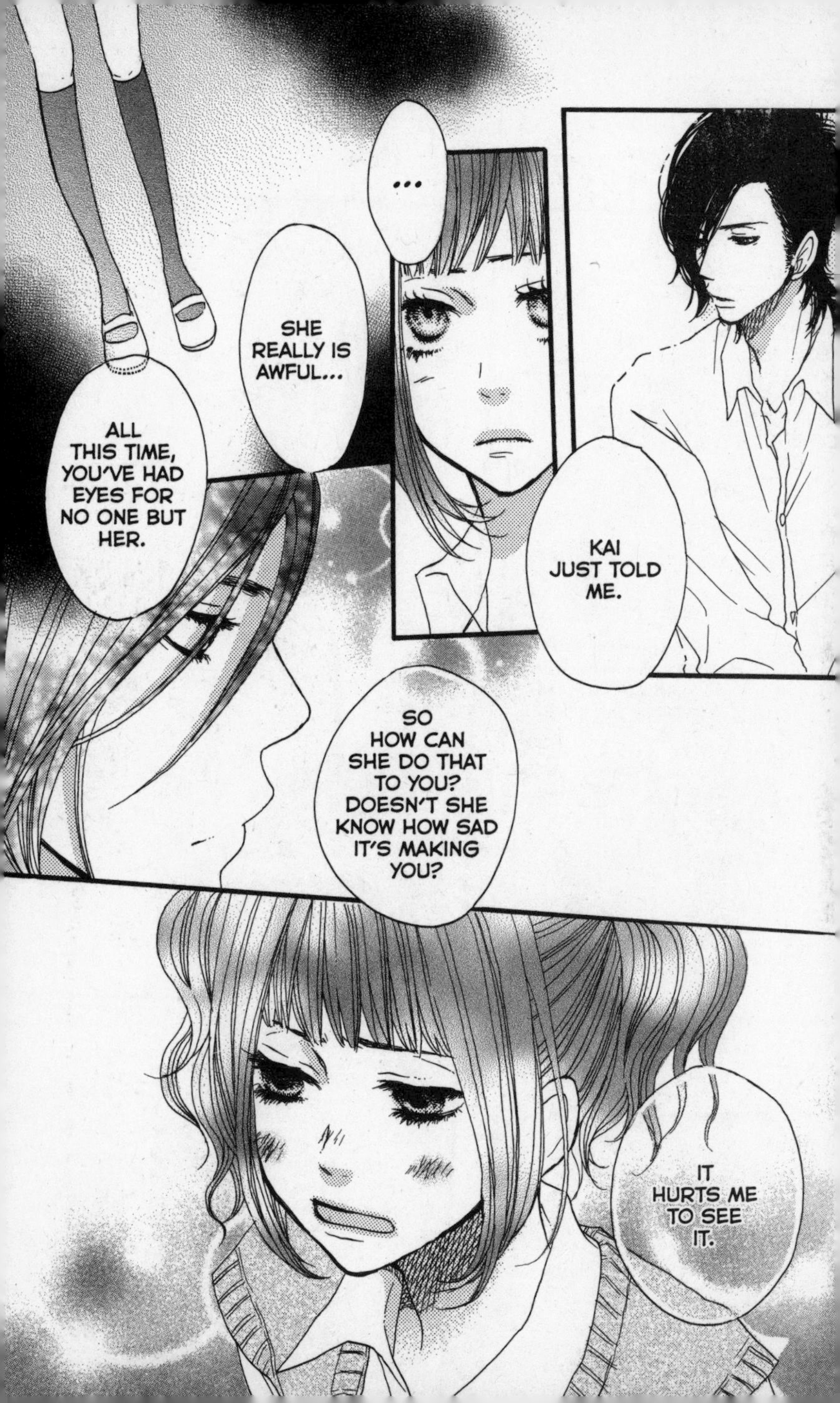
KAI JUST TOLD ME.
...
SHE REALLY IS AWFUL...
ALL THIS TIME, YOU'VE HAD EYES FOR NO ONE BUT HER.
SO HOW CAN SHE DO THAT TO YOU? DOESN'T SHE KNOW HOW SAD IT'S MAKING YOU?
IT HURTS ME TO SEE IT.

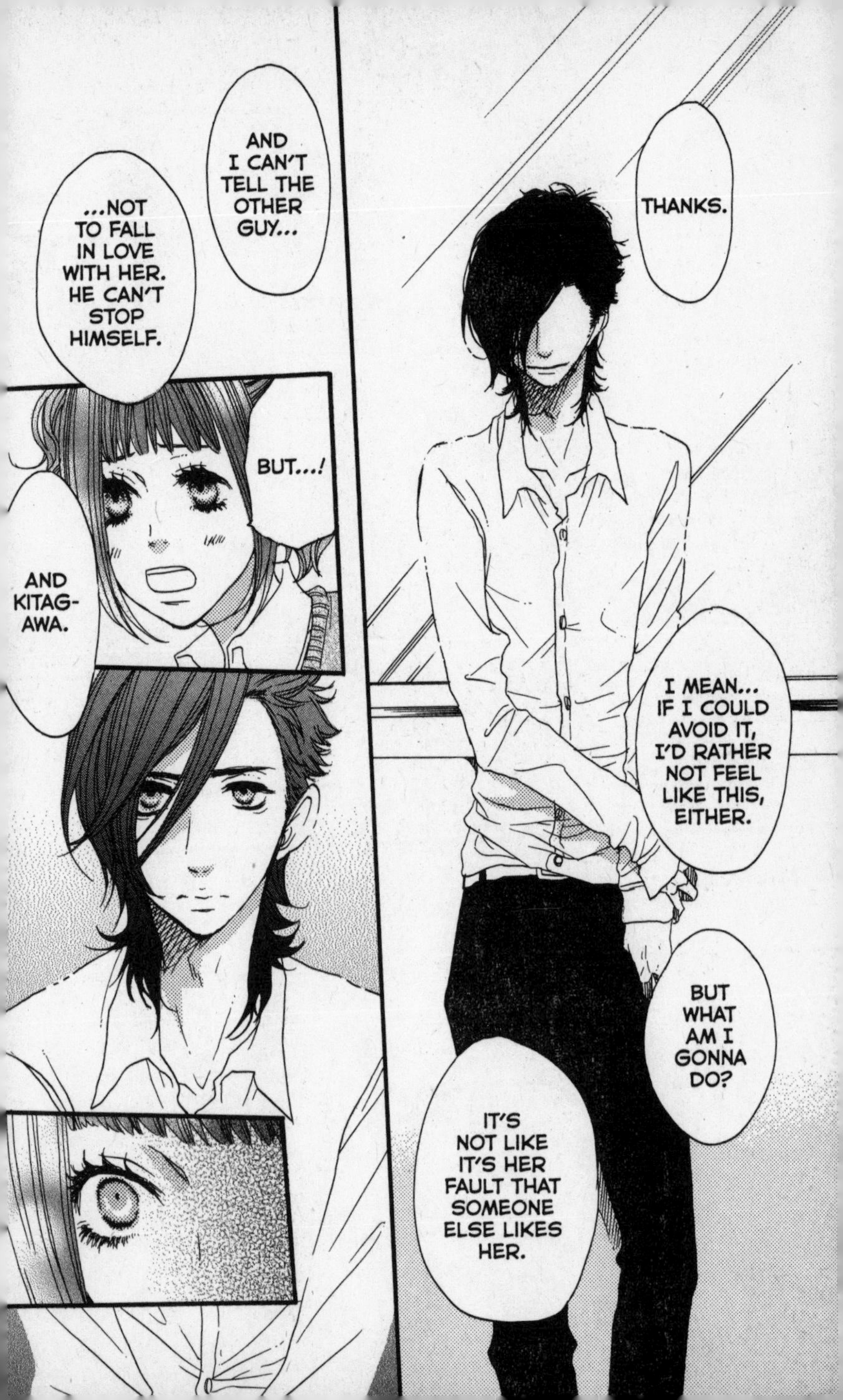
THANKS.
I MEAN... IF I COULD AVOID IT, I'D RATHER NOT FEEL LIKE THIS, EITHER.
BUT WHAT AM I GONNA DO?
IT'S NOT LIKE IT'S HER FAULT THAT SOMEONE ELSE LIKES HER.
AND I CAN'T TELL THE OTHER GUY...
...NOT TO FALL IN LOVE WITH HER. HE CAN'T STOP HIMSELF.
BUT...!
AND KITAGAWA.

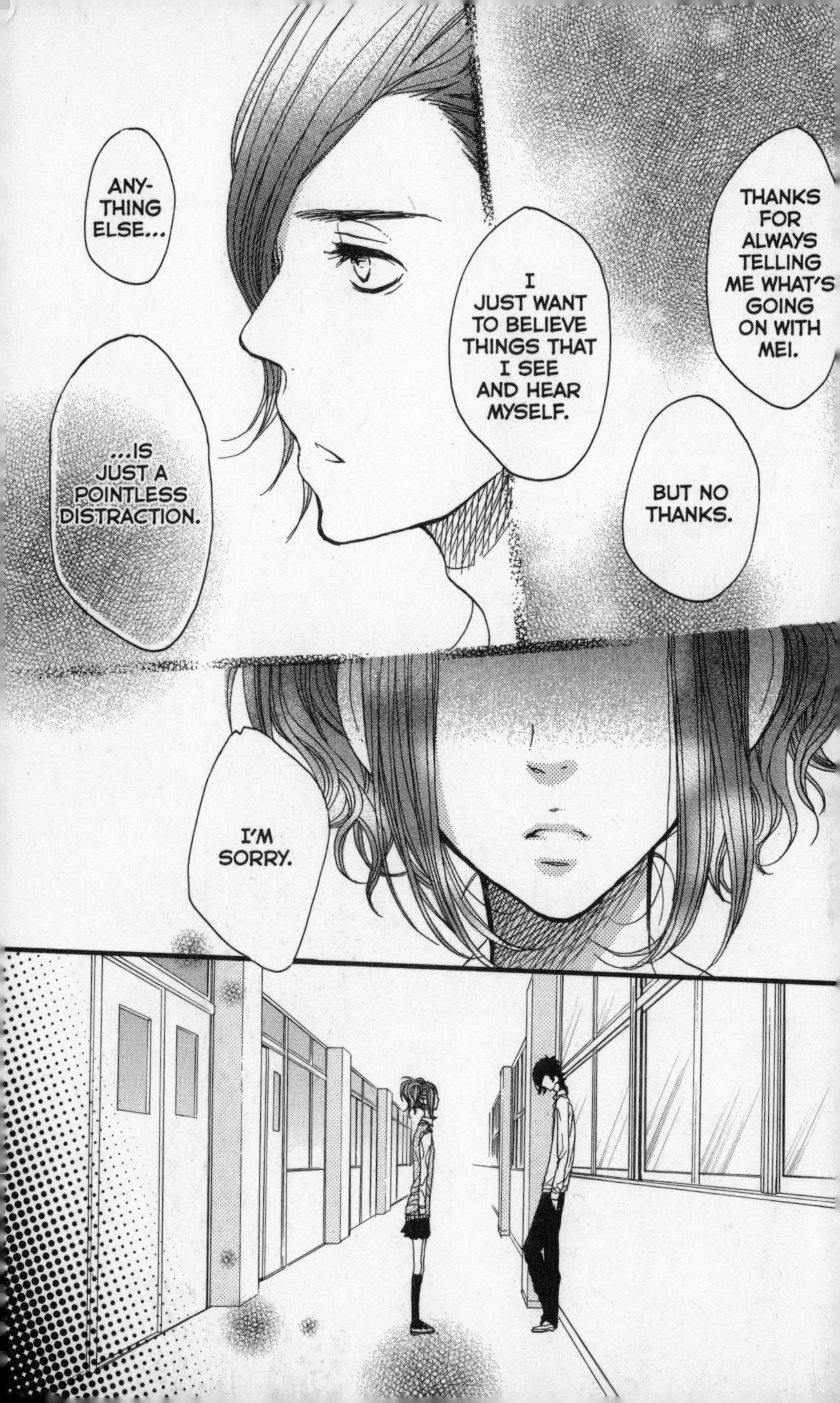
THANKS FOR ALWAYS TELLING ME WHAT'S GOING ON WITH MEI.
BUT NO THANKS.
I JUST WANT TO BELIEVE THINGS THAT I SEE AND HEAR MYSELF.
ANY-THING ELSE...
...IS JUST A POINTLESS DISTRACTION.
I'M SORRY.

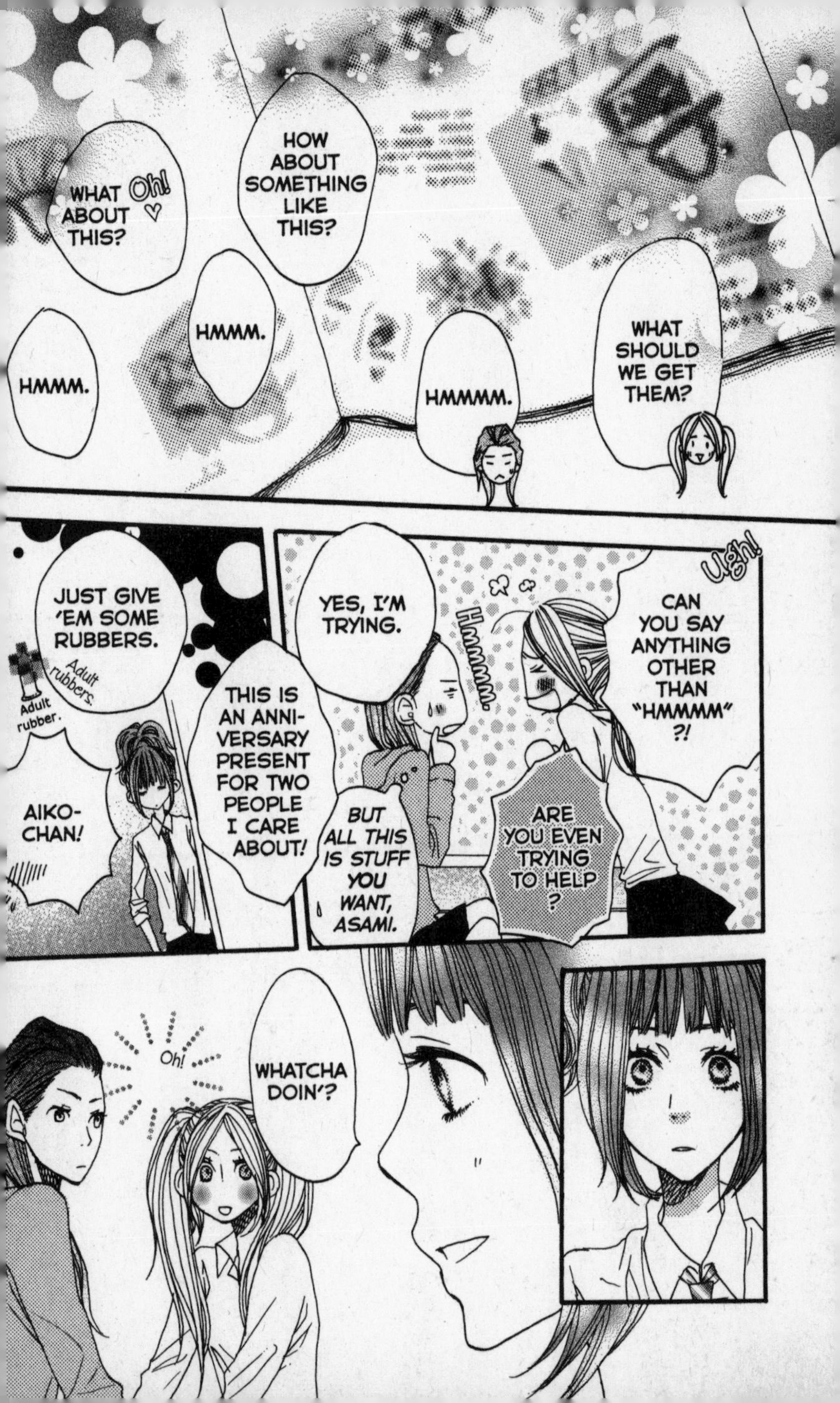

WHAT SHOULD WE GET THEM?
HMMMM.
HOW ABOUT SOMETHING LIKE THIS?
HMMM.
Oh! ♡
WHAT ABOUT THIS?
HMMM.
Ugh!
CAN YOU SAY ANYTHING OTHER THAN "HMMMM"?!
Hmmmm.
YES, I'M TRYING.
ARE YOU EVEN TRYING TO HELP?
BUT ALL THIS IS STUFF YOU WANT, ASAMI.
THIS IS AN ANNIVERSARY PRESENT FOR TWO PEOPLE I CARE ABOUT!
JUST GIVE 'EM SOME RUBBERS.
Adult rubbers.
Adult rubber.
AIKO-CHAN!
WHATCHA DOIN'?
Oh!

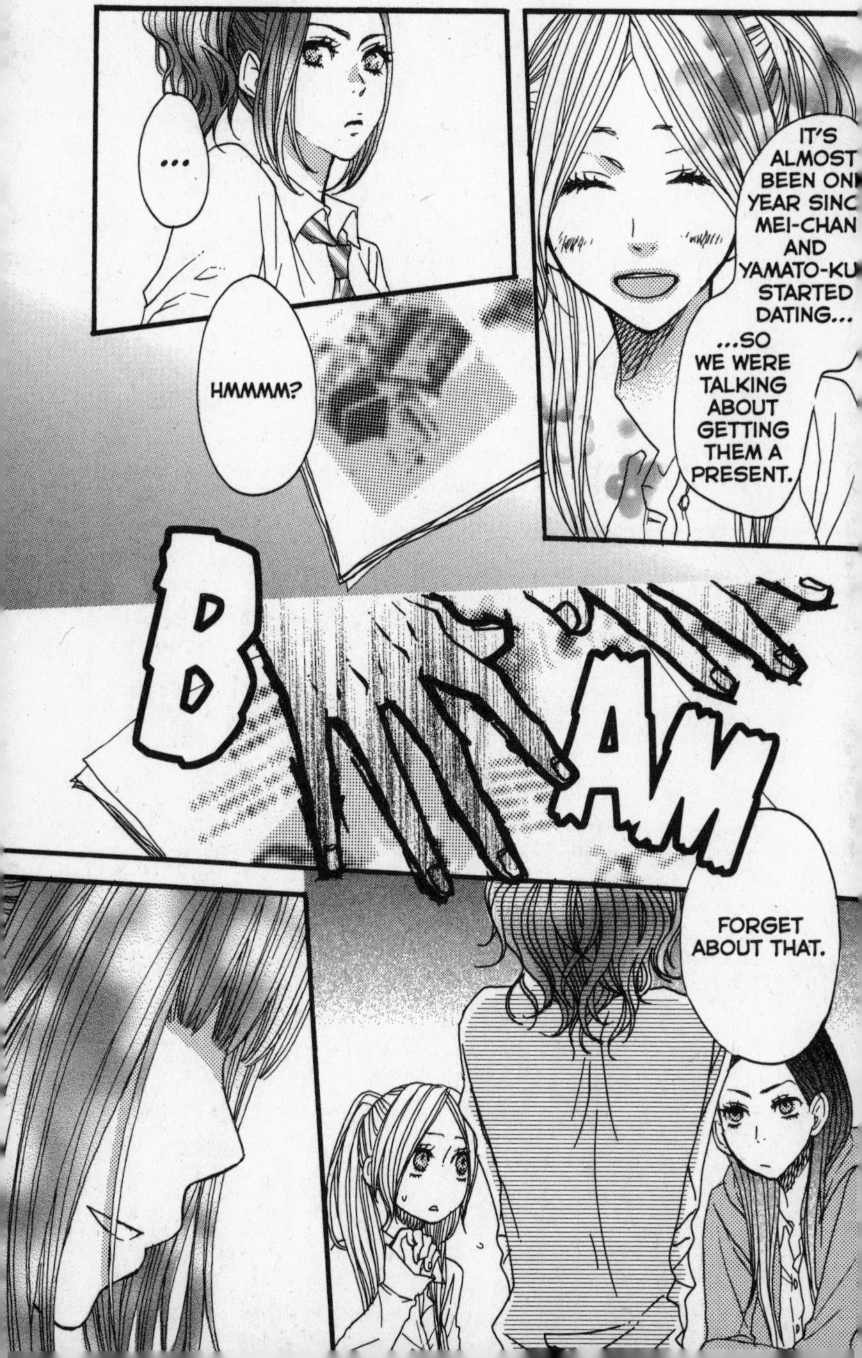
IT'S ALMOST BEEN ON YEAR SINC MEI-CHAN AND YAMATO-KU STARTED DATING...
...SO WE WERE TALKING ABOUT GETTING THEM A PRESENT.
...
HMMMM?
BAM
FORGET ABOUT THAT.

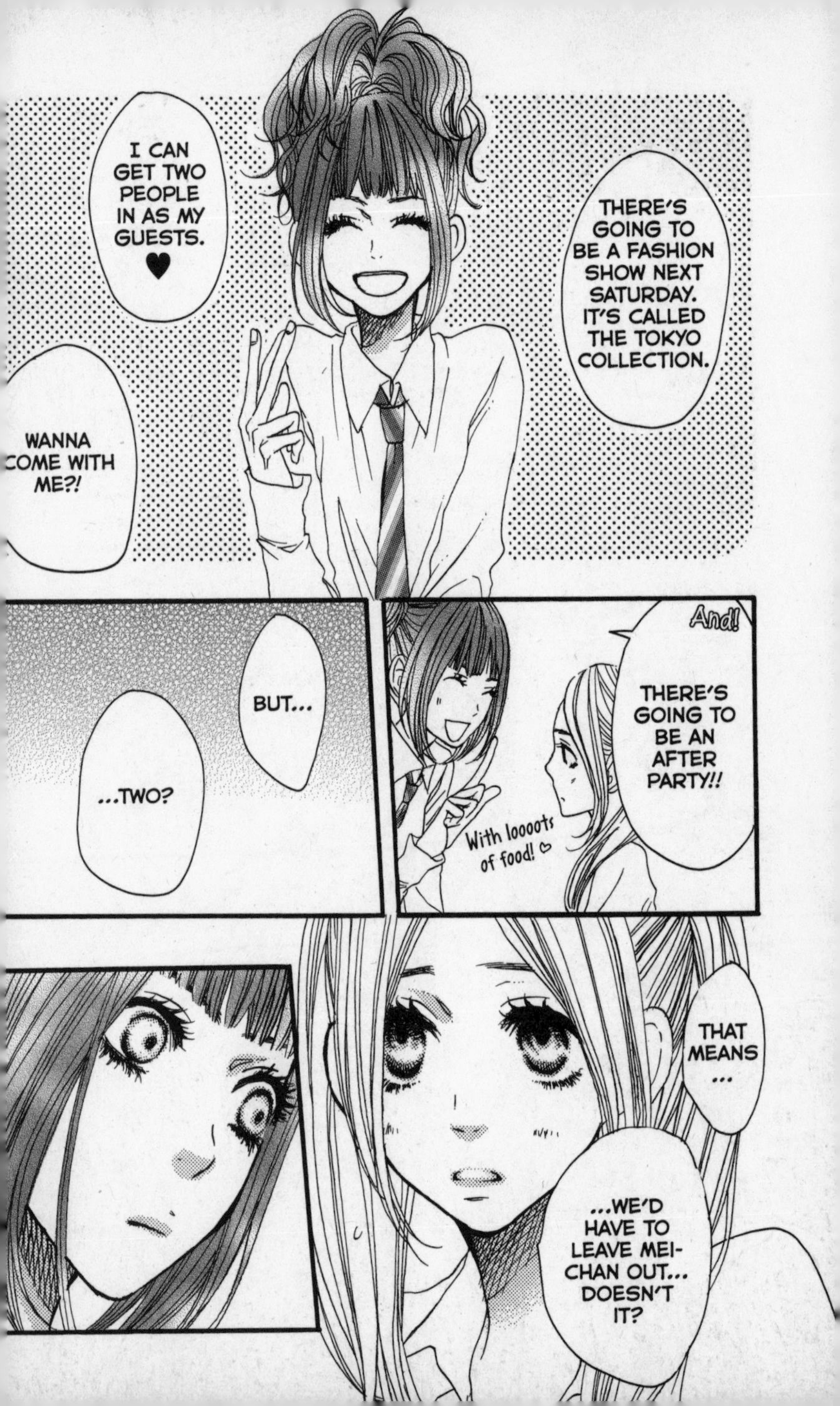
THERE'S GOING TO BE A FASHION SHOW NEXT SATURDAY. IT'S CALLED THE TOKYO COLLECTION.
I CAN GET TWO PEOPLE IN AS MY GUESTS. ♥
WANNA COME WITH ME?!
And!
THERE'S GOING TO BE AN AFTER PARTY!!
With loooots of food! ♡
BUT...
...TWO?
THAT MEANS ...
...WE'D HAVE TO LEAVE MEI-CHAN OUT... DOESN'T IT?

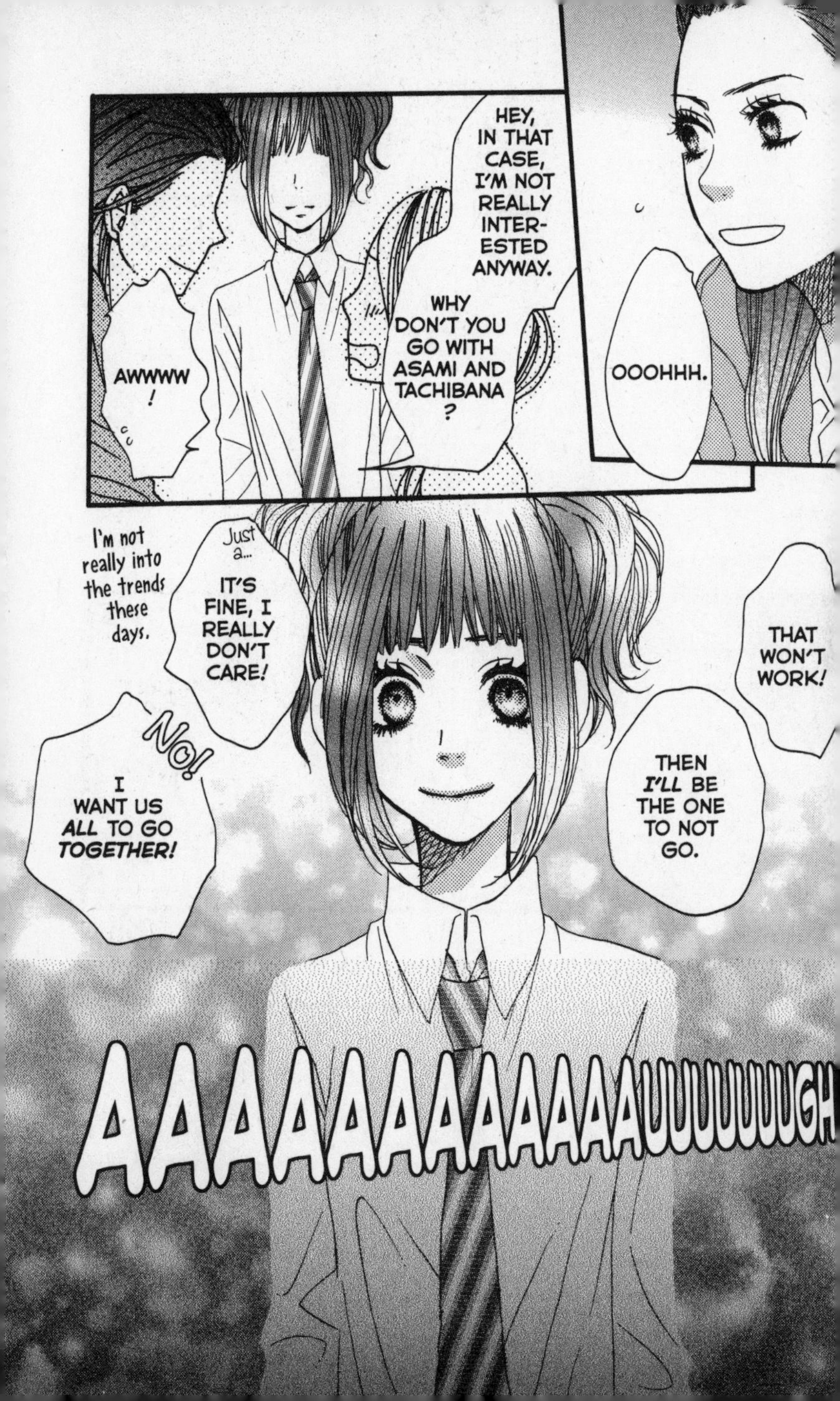
OOOHHH.
HEY, IN THAT CASE, I'M NOT REALLY INTER-ESTED ANYWAY.
WHY DON'T YOU GO WITH ASAMI AND TACHIBANA?
AWWWW!
THAT WON'T WORK!
THEN I'LL BE THE ONE TO NOT GO.
Just a...
IT'S FINE, I REALLY DON'T CARE!
I'm not really into the trends these days.
No!
I WANT US ALL TO GO TOGETHER!
AAAAAAAAAAAUUUUUUUGH

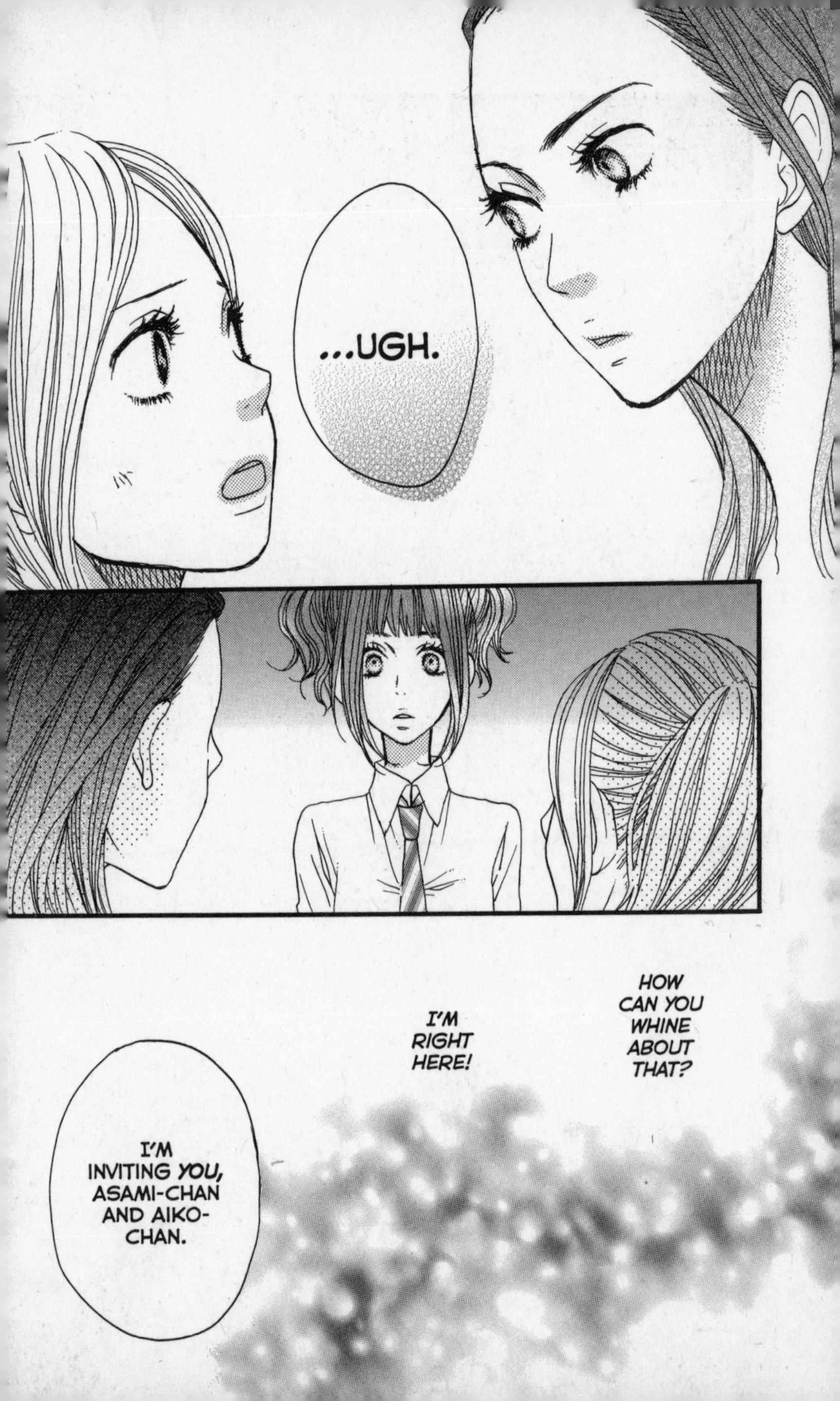
...UGH.
HOW CAN YOU WHINE ABOUT THAT?
I'M RIGHT HERE!
I'M INVITING *YOU*, ASAMI-CHAN AND AIKO-CHAN.

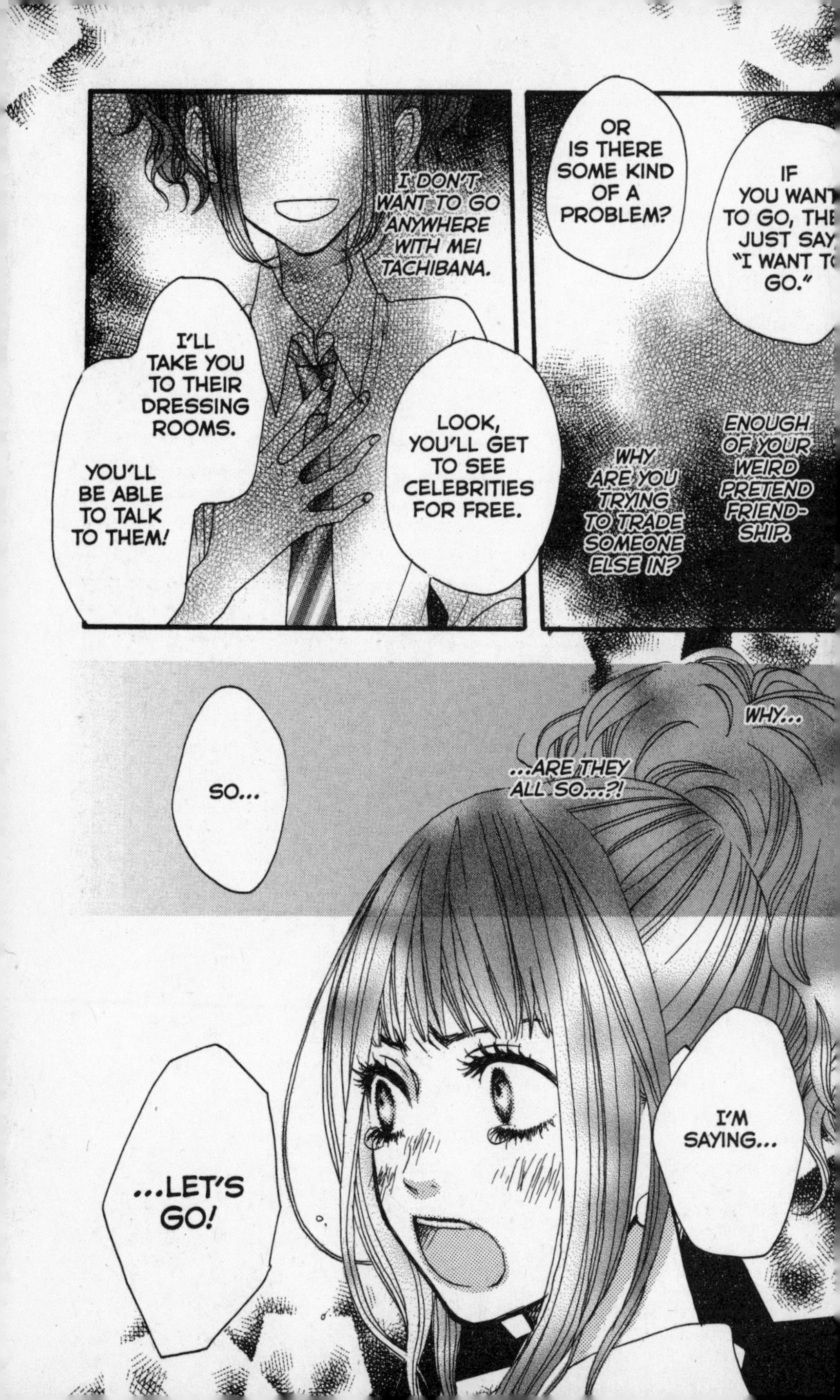
IF YOU WAN TO GO, THE JUST SAY "I WANT T GO."
OR IS THERE SOME KIND OF A PROBLEM?
ENOUGH OF YOUR WEIRD PRETEND FRIENDSHIP.
WHY ARE YOU TRYING TO TRADE SOMEONE ELSE IN?
I DON'T WANT TO GO ANYWHERE WITH MEI TACHIBANA.
LOOK, YOU'LL GET TO SEE CELEBRITIES FOR FREE.
I'LL TAKE YOU TO THEIR DRESSING ROOMS.
YOU'LL BE ABLE TO TALK TO THEM!
WHY...
...ARE THEY ALL SO...?!
SO...
I'M SAYING...
...LET'S GO!

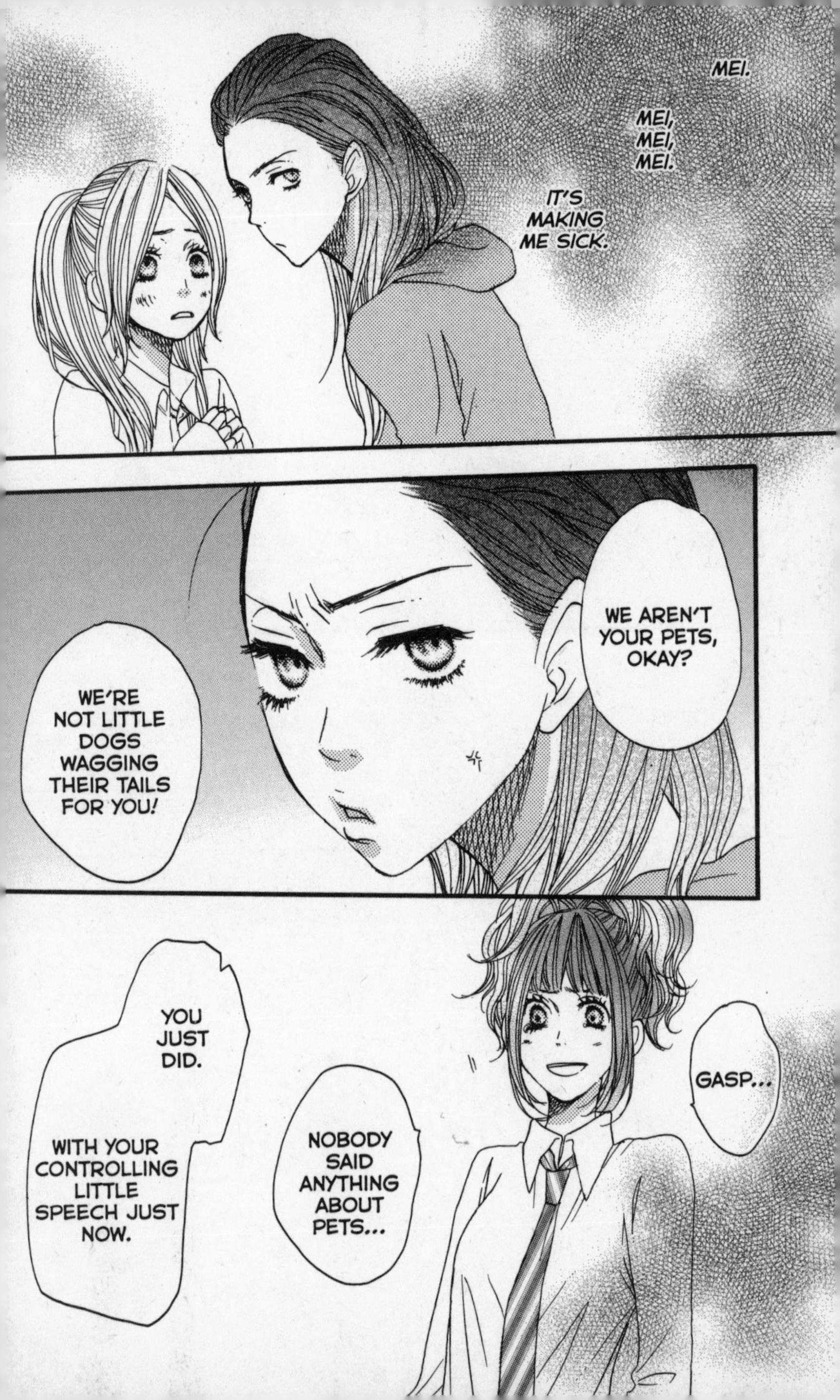
MEI.
MEI, MEI, MEI.
IT'S MAKING ME SICK.
WE AREN'T YOUR PETS, OKAY?
WE'RE NOT LITTLE DOGS WAGGING THEIR TAILS FOR YOU!
GASP...
NOBODY SAID ANYTHING ABOUT PETS...
YOU JUST DID.
WITH YOUR CONTROLLING LITTLE SPEECH JUST NOW.

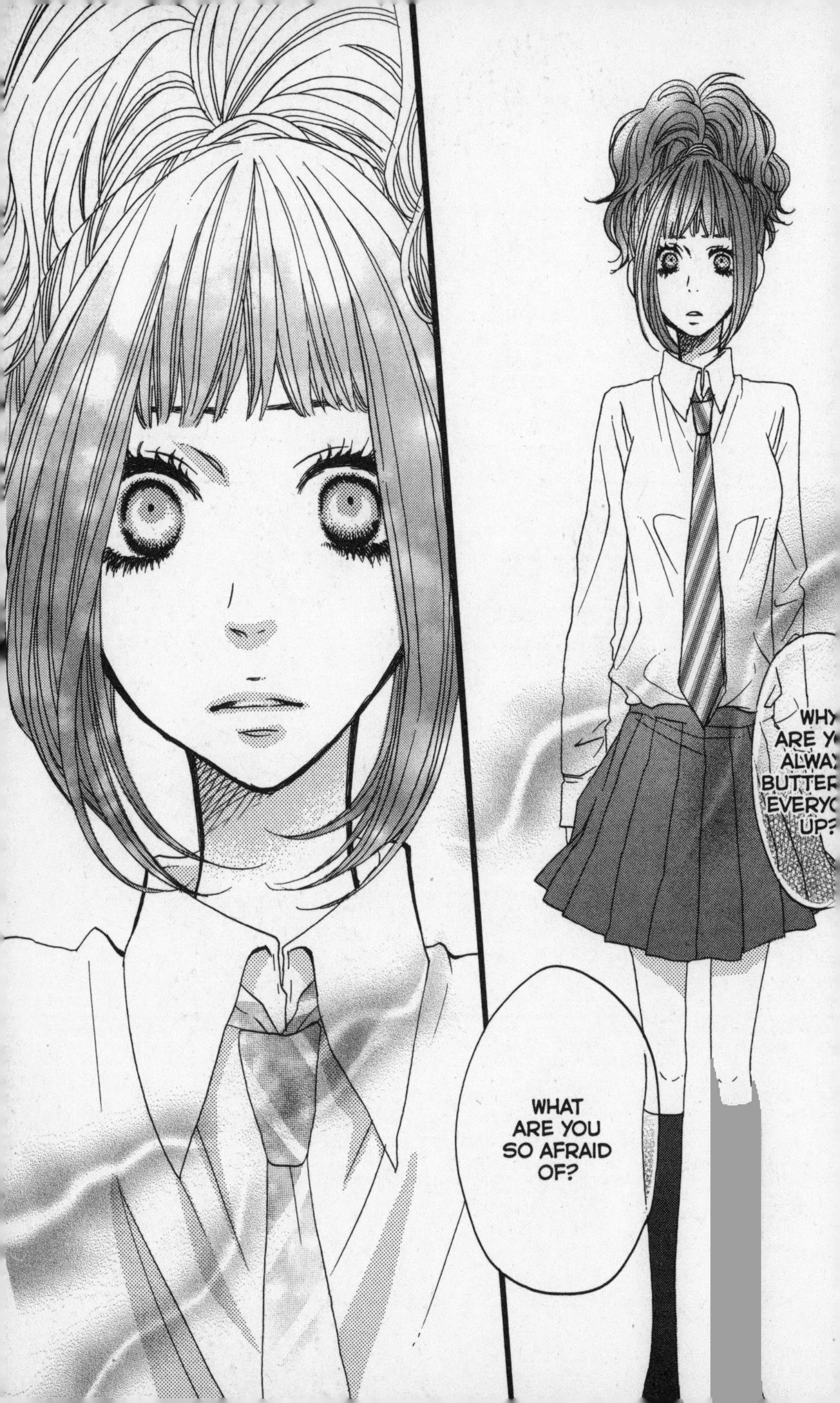
WHY ARE Y ALWAY BUTTER EVERYO UP?
WHAT ARE YOU SO AFRAID OF?

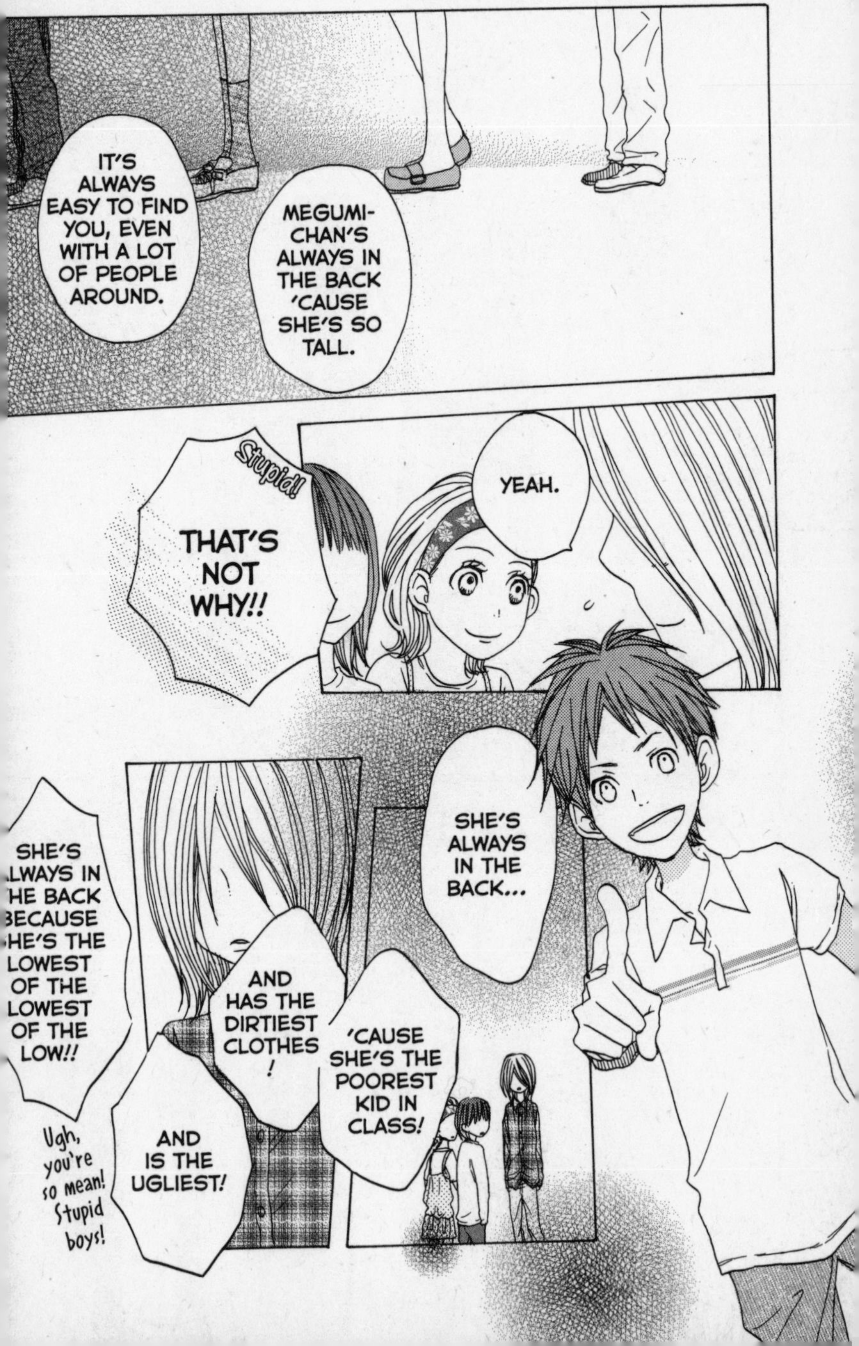
IT'S ALWAYS EASY TO FIND YOU, EVEN WITH A LOT OF PEOPLE AROUND.
MEGUMI-CHAN'S ALWAYS IN THE BACK 'CAUSE SHE'S SO TALL.
YEAH.
Stupid!!
THAT'S NOT WHY!!
SHE'S ALWAYS IN THE BACK...
'CAUSE SHE'S THE POOREST KID IN CLASS!
AND HAS THE DIRTIEST CLOTHES!
AND IS THE UGLIEST!
SHE'S LWAYS IN HE BACK ECAUSE HE'S THE LOWEST OF THE LOWEST OF THE LOW!!
Ugh, you're so mean! Stupid boys!

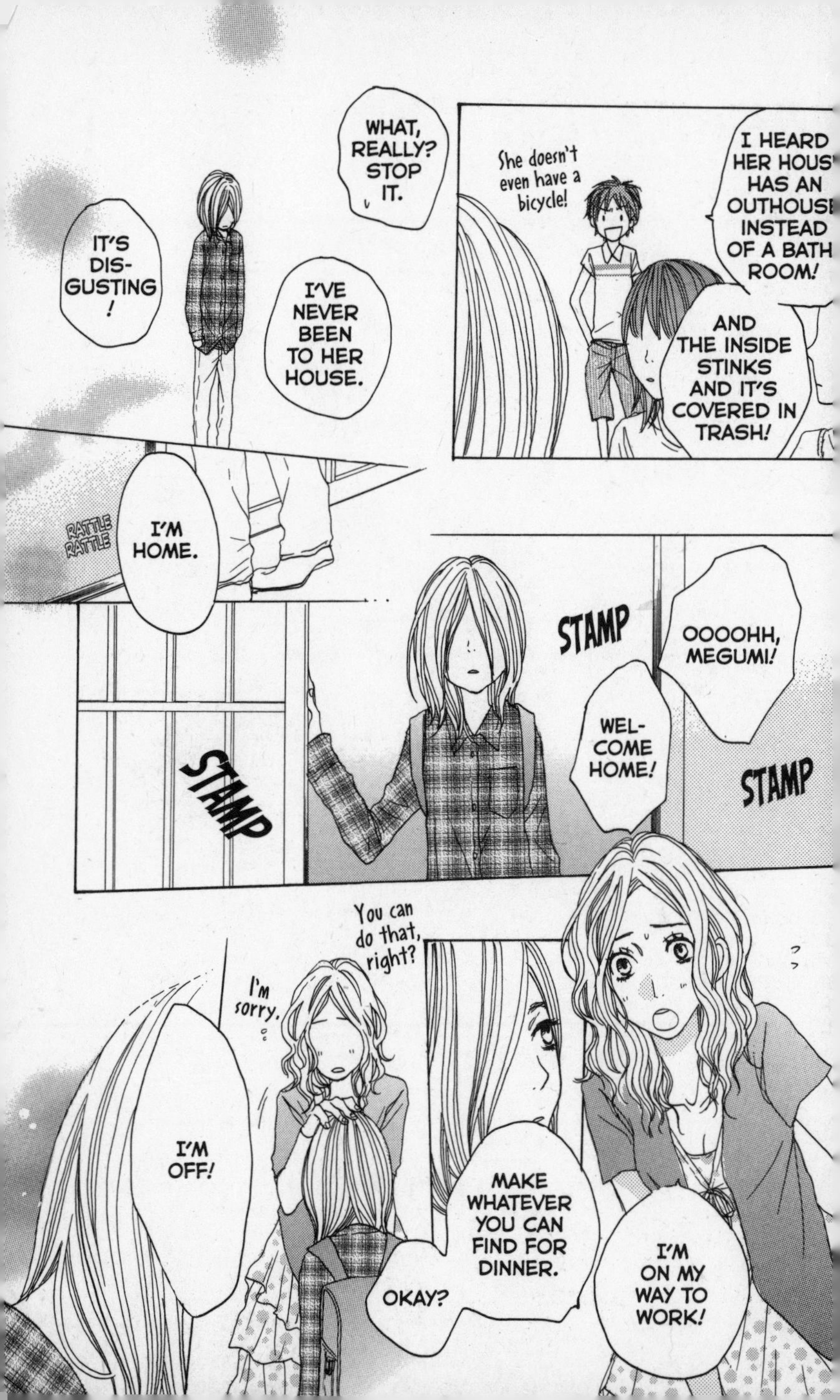
I HEARD HER HOUS HAS AN OUTHOUS INSTEAD OF A BATH ROOM!
She doesn't even have a bicycle!
AND THE INSIDE STINKS AND IT'S COVERED IN TRASH!
WHAT, REALLY? STOP IT.
I'VE NEVER BEEN TO HER HOUSE.
IT'S DIS-GUSTING!
I'M HOME.
RATTLE RATTLE
OOOOHH, MEGUMI!
STAMP
WEL-COME HOME!
STAMP
STAMP
I'M ON MY WAY TO WORK!
MAKE WHATEVER YOU CAN FIND FOR DINNER.
OKAY?
You can do that, right?
I'm sorry.
I'M OFF!

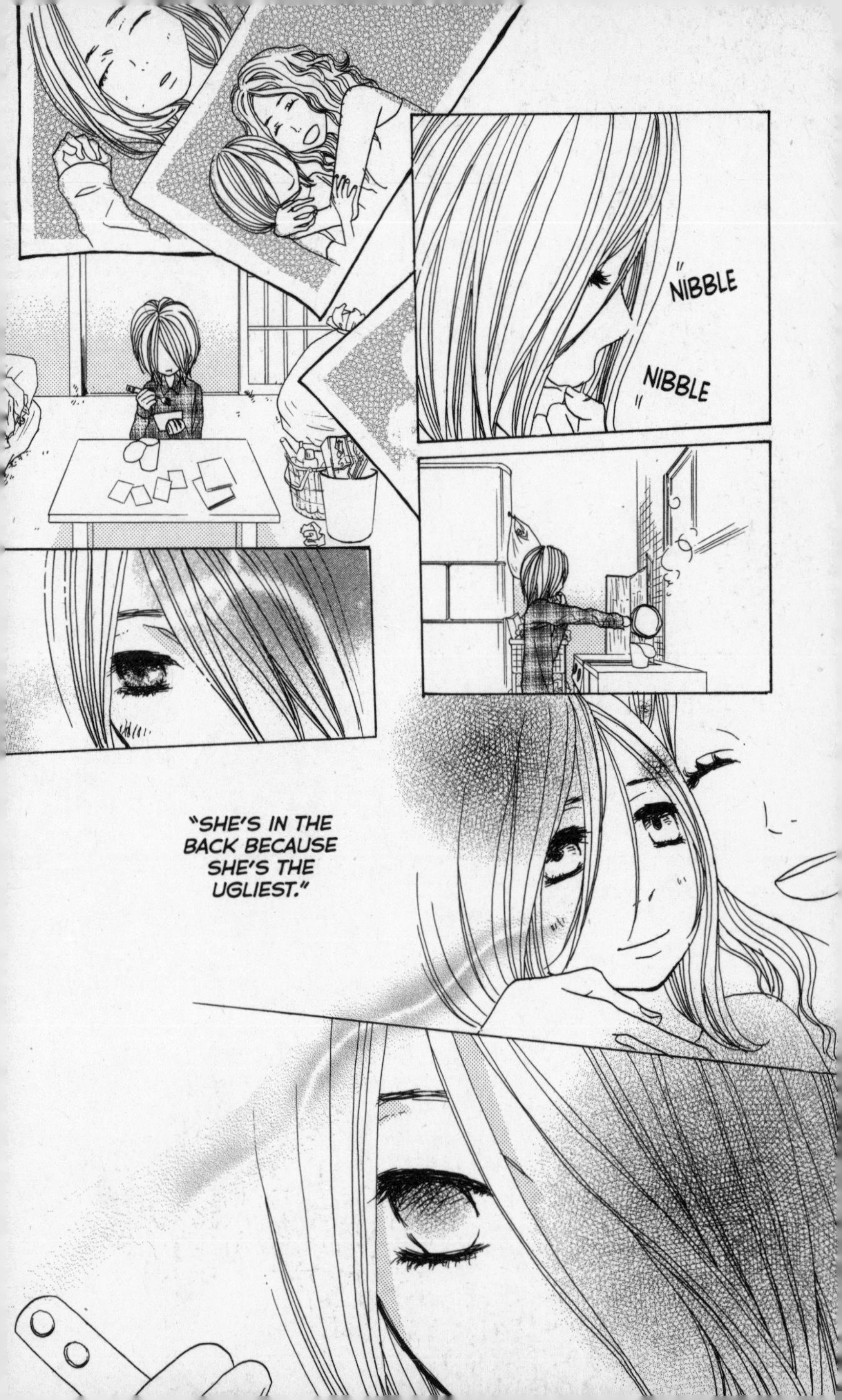
NIBBLE
NIBBLE
"SHE'S IN THE BACK BECAUSE SHE'S THE UGLIEST."

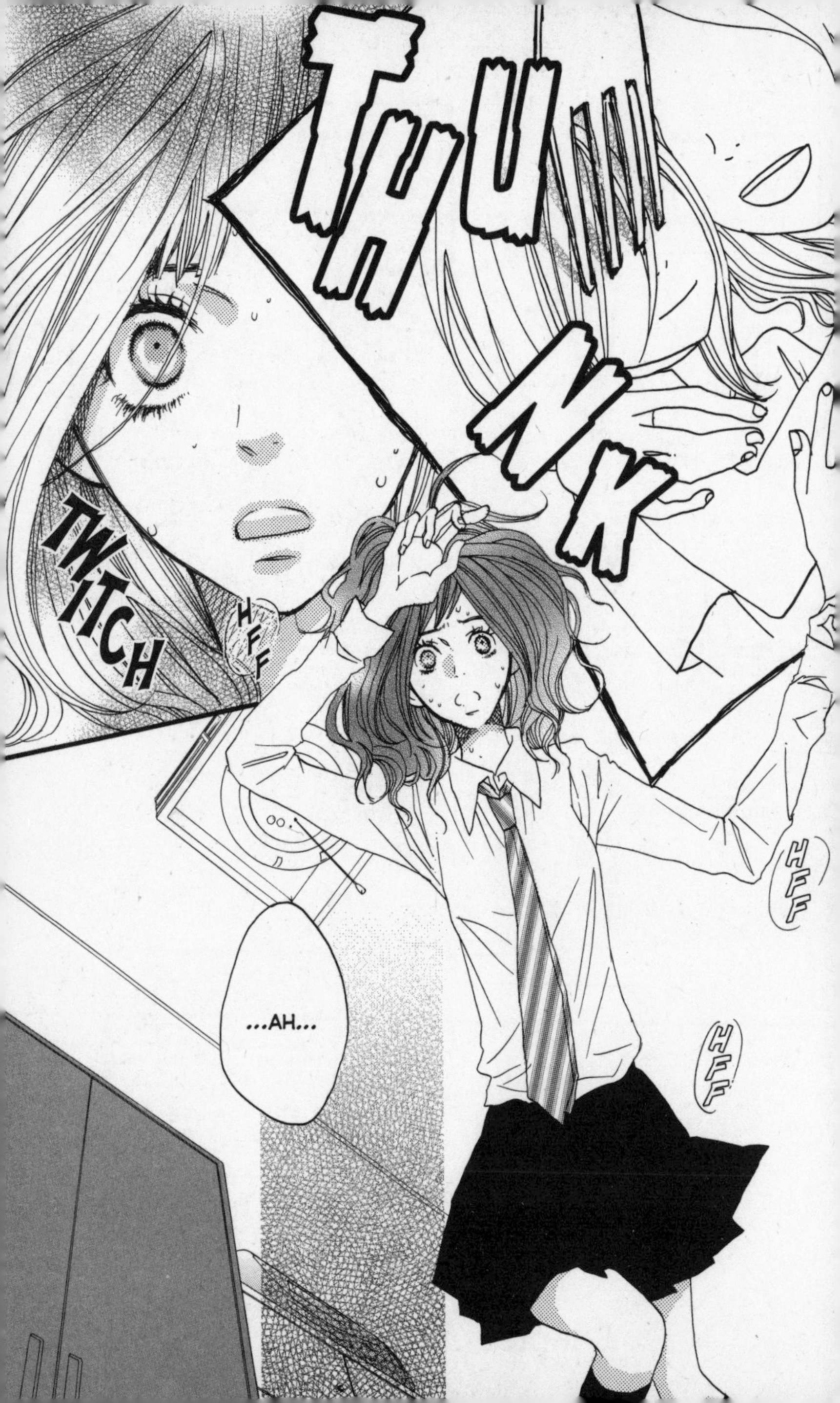
THUNK
TWITCH
HFF
HFF
HFF
...AH...

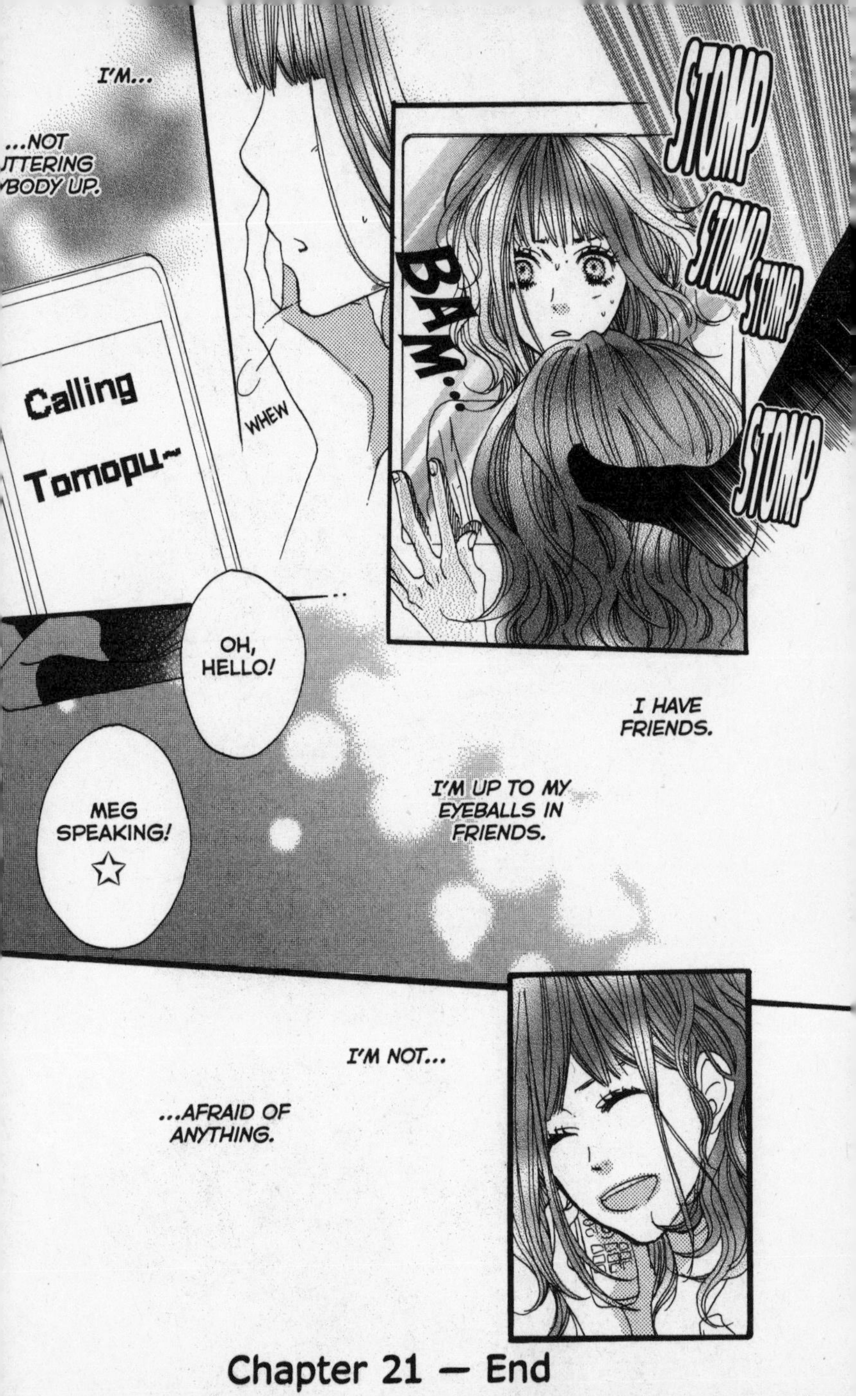
STOMP
STOMP STOMP STOMP
STOMP
BAM...
I'M...
...NOT
TTERING
BODY UP.
WHEW
Calling Tomopu~
I HAVE FRIENDS.
I'M UP TO MY EYEBALLS IN FRIENDS.
OH, HELLO!
MEG SPEAKING! ☆
I'M NOT...
...AFRAID OF ANYTHING.

Chapter 21 — End

Say
"I love you".

Kanae Hazuki

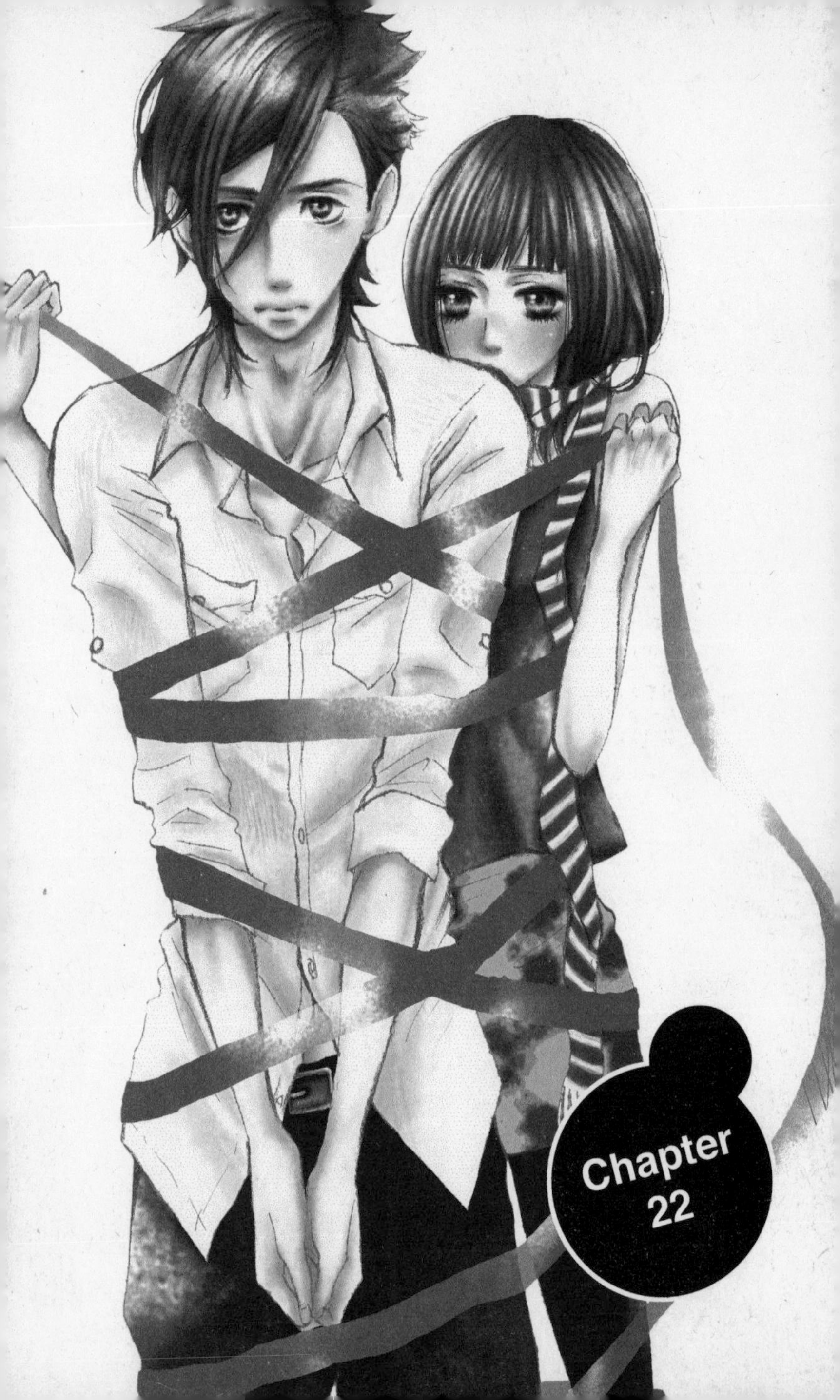
Chapter
22

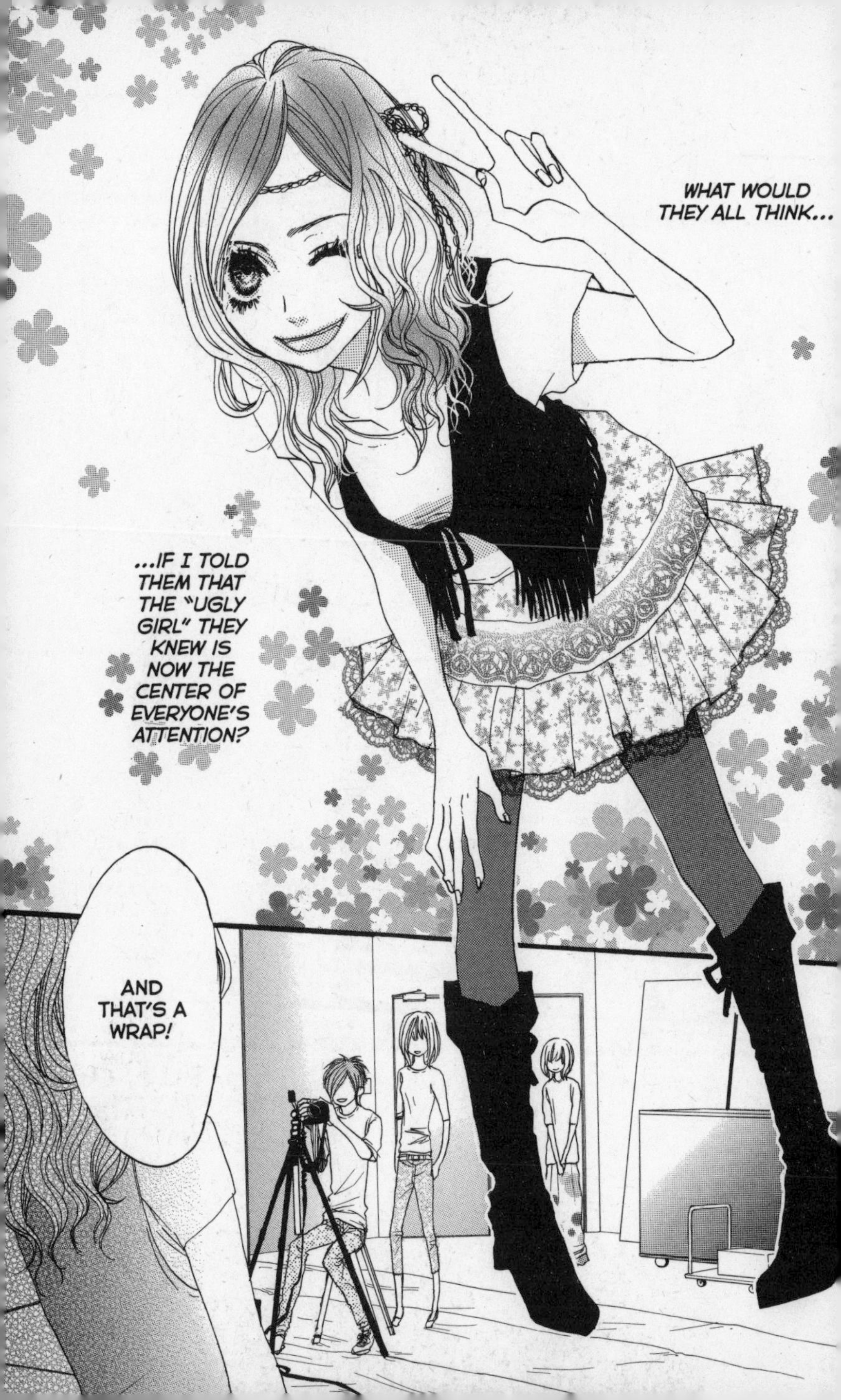
WHAT WOULD THEY ALL THINK...
...IF I TOLD THEM THAT THE "UGLY GIRL" THEY KNEW IS NOW THE CENTER OF EVERYONE'S ATTENTION?
AND THAT'S A WRAP!

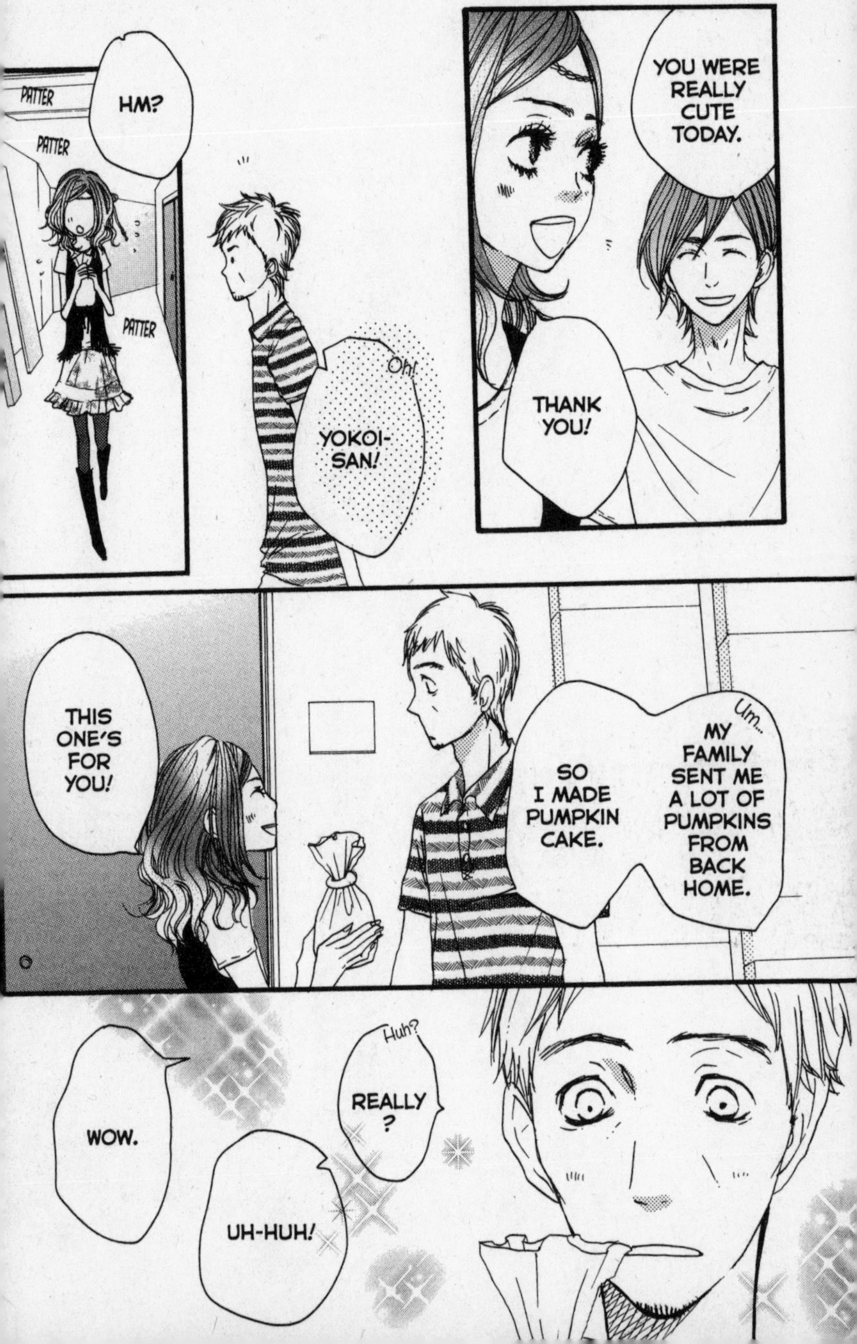
YOU WERE REALLY CUTE TODAY.
THANK YOU!
HM?
PATTER
PATTER
PATTER
Oh!
YOKOI-SAN!
Um...
MY FAMILY SENT ME A LOT OF PUMPKINS FROM BACK HOME.
SO I MADE PUMPKIN CAKE.
THIS ONE'S FOR YOU!
Huh?
REALLY?
UH-HUH!
WOW.

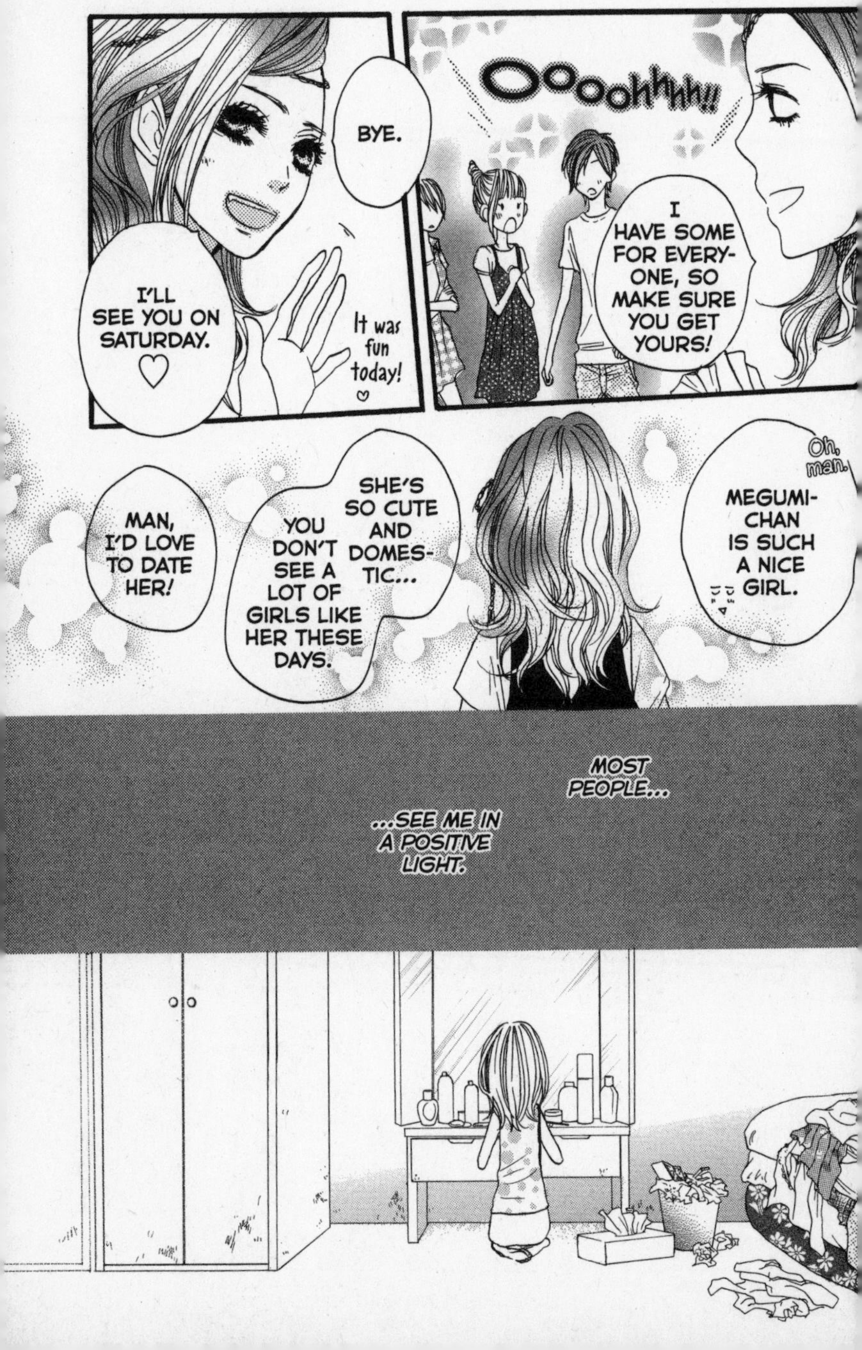
Oooohhhh!!
I HAVE SOME FOR EVERY-ONE, SO MAKE SURE YOU GET YOURS!
BYE.
I'LL SEE YOU ON SATURDAY. ♡
It was fun today! ♡
Oh, man.
MEGUMI-CHAN IS SUCH A NICE GIRL.
SHE'S SO CUTE AND DOMES-TIC...
YOU DON'T SEE A LOT OF GIRLS LIKE HER THESE DAYS.
MAN, I'D LOVE TO DATE HER!
MOST PEOPLE...
...SEE ME IN A POSITIVE LIGHT.

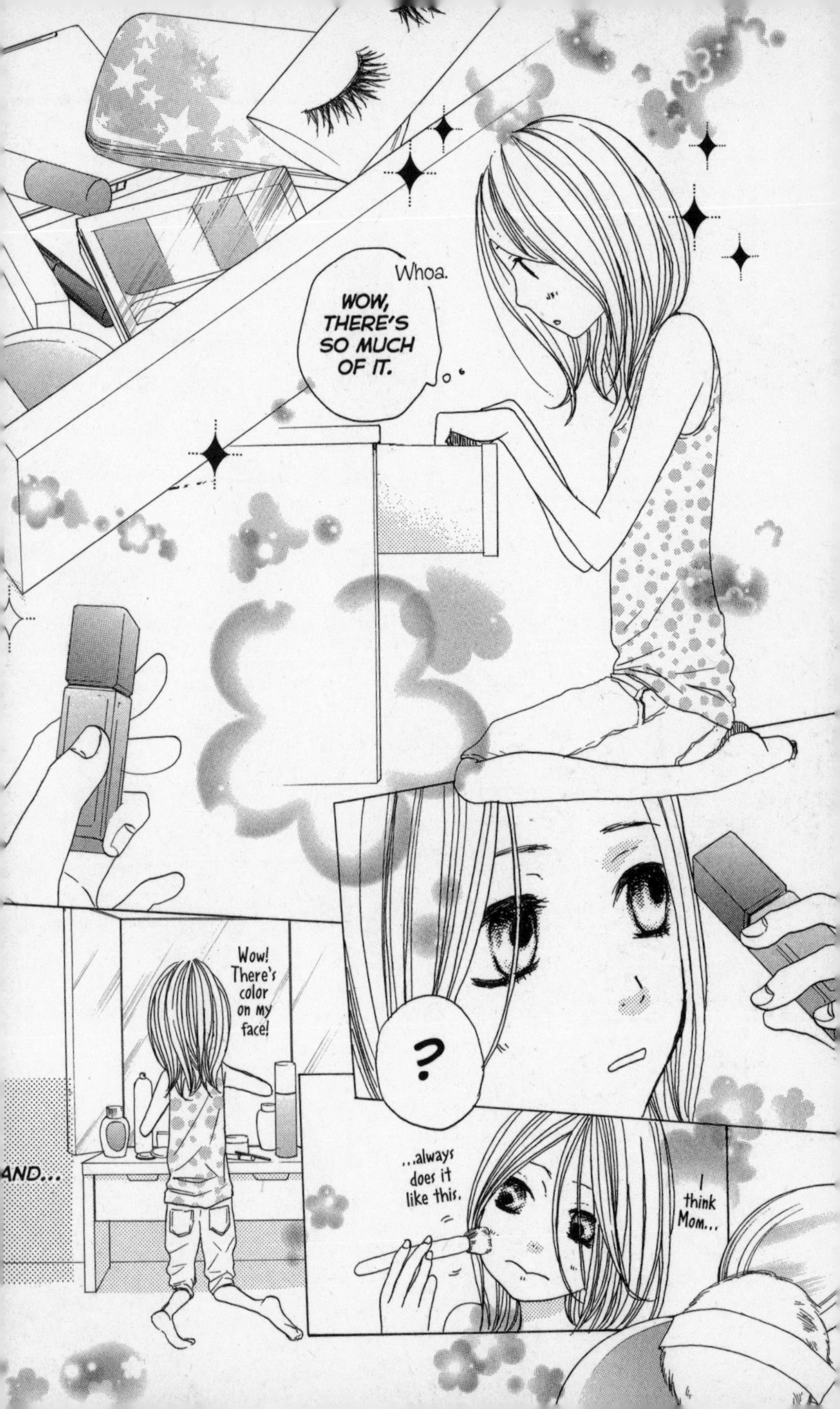

Whoa.
WOW, THERE'S SO MUCH OF IT.
?
I think Mom...
...always does it like this.
Wow! There's color on my face!
AND...

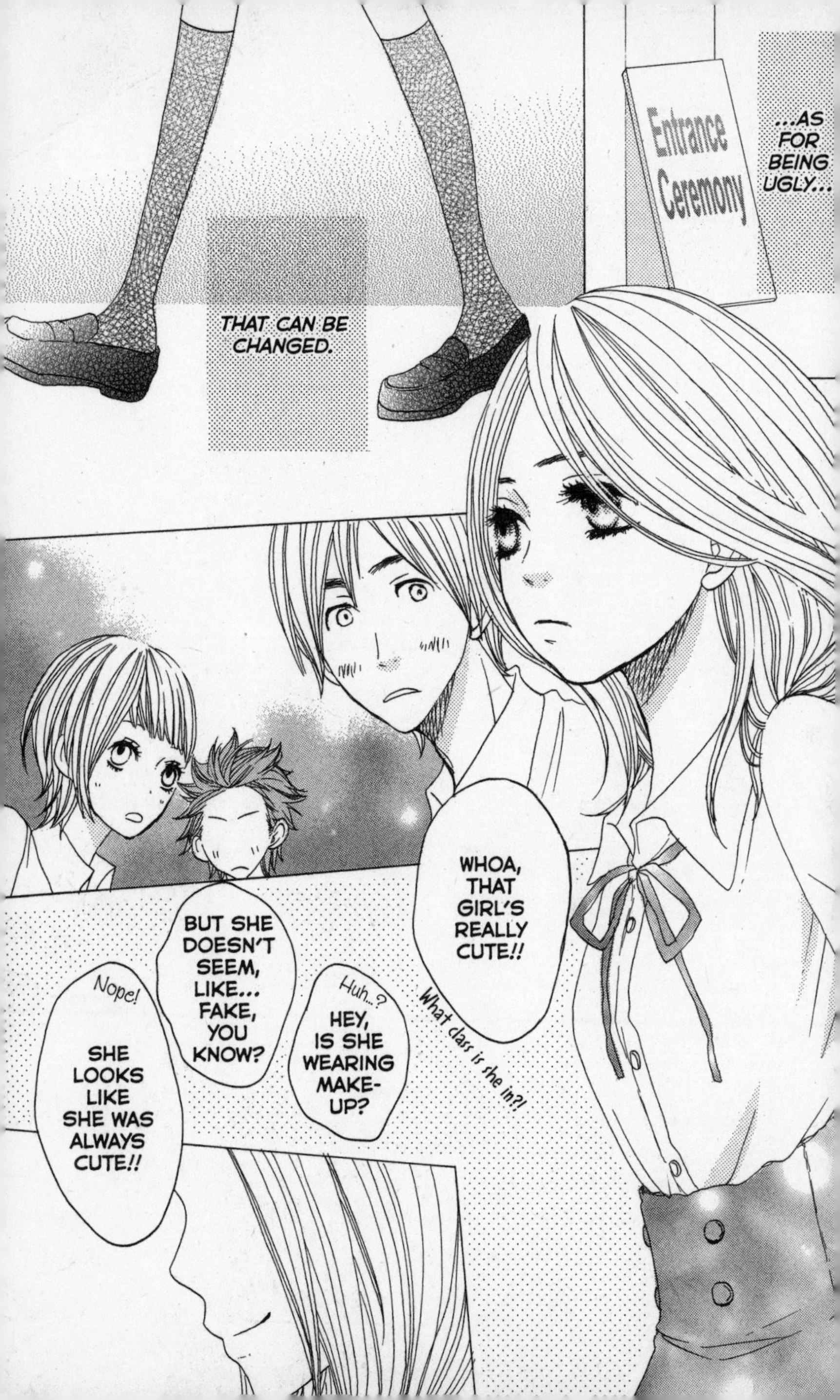
Entrance Ceremony
...AS FOR BEING UGLY...
THAT CAN BE CHANGED.
WHOA, THAT GIRL'S REALLY CUTE!!
What class is she in?!
Huh...?
HEY, IS SHE WEARING MAKE-UP?
BUT SHE DOESN'T SEEM, LIKE... FAKE, YOU KNOW?
Nope!
SHE LOOKS LIKE SHE WAS ALWAYS CUTE!!

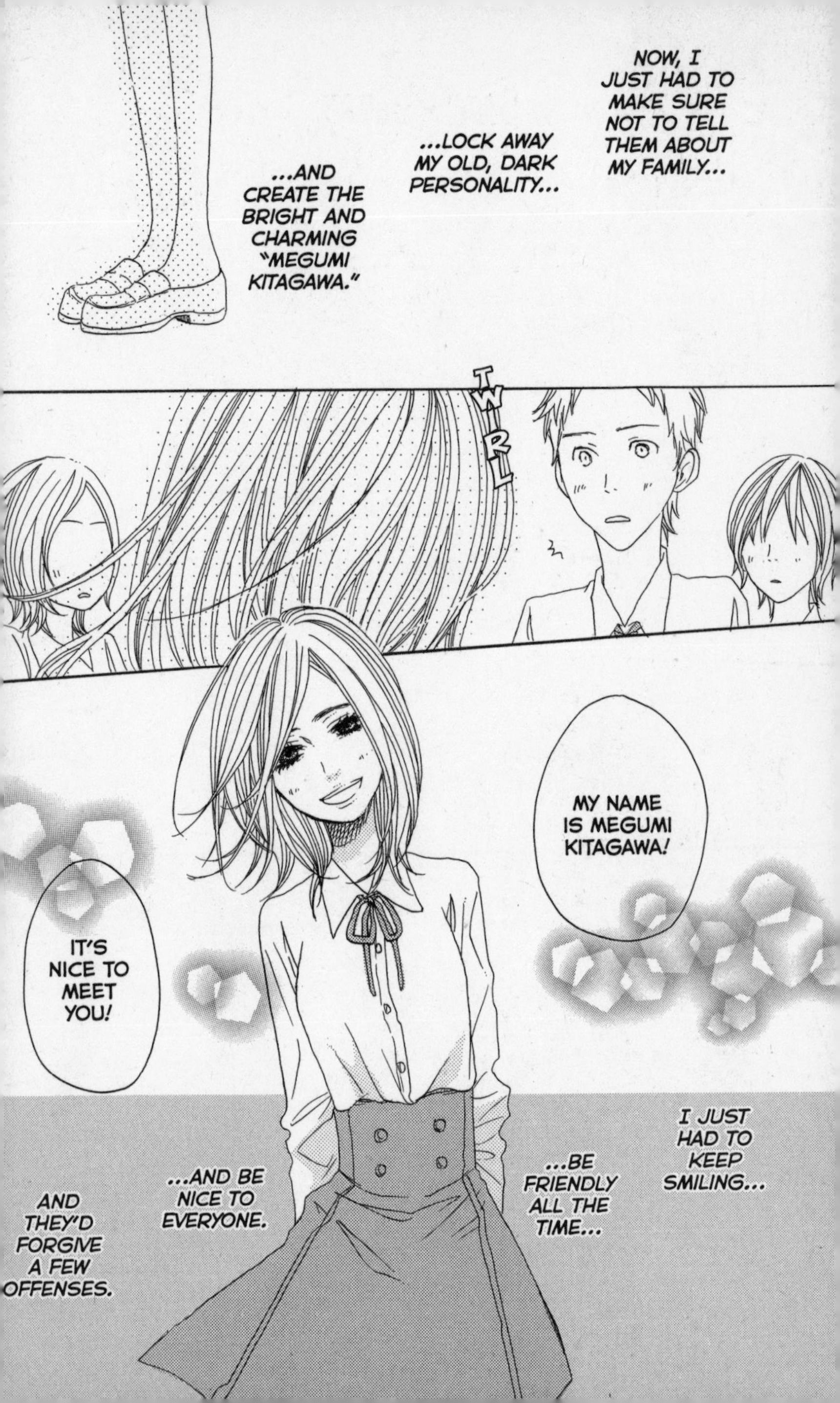
NOW, I JUST HAD TO MAKE SURE NOT TO TELL THEM ABOUT MY FAMILY...
...LOCK AWAY MY OLD, DARK PERSONALITY...
...AND CREATE THE BRIGHT AND CHARMING "MEGUMI KITAGAWA."
TWIRL
MY NAME IS MEGUMI KITAGAWA!
IT'S NICE TO MEET YOU!
I JUST HAD TO KEEP SMILING...
...BE FRIENDLY ALL THE TIME...
...AND BE NICE TO EVERYONE.
AND THEY'D FORGIVE A FEW OFFENSES.

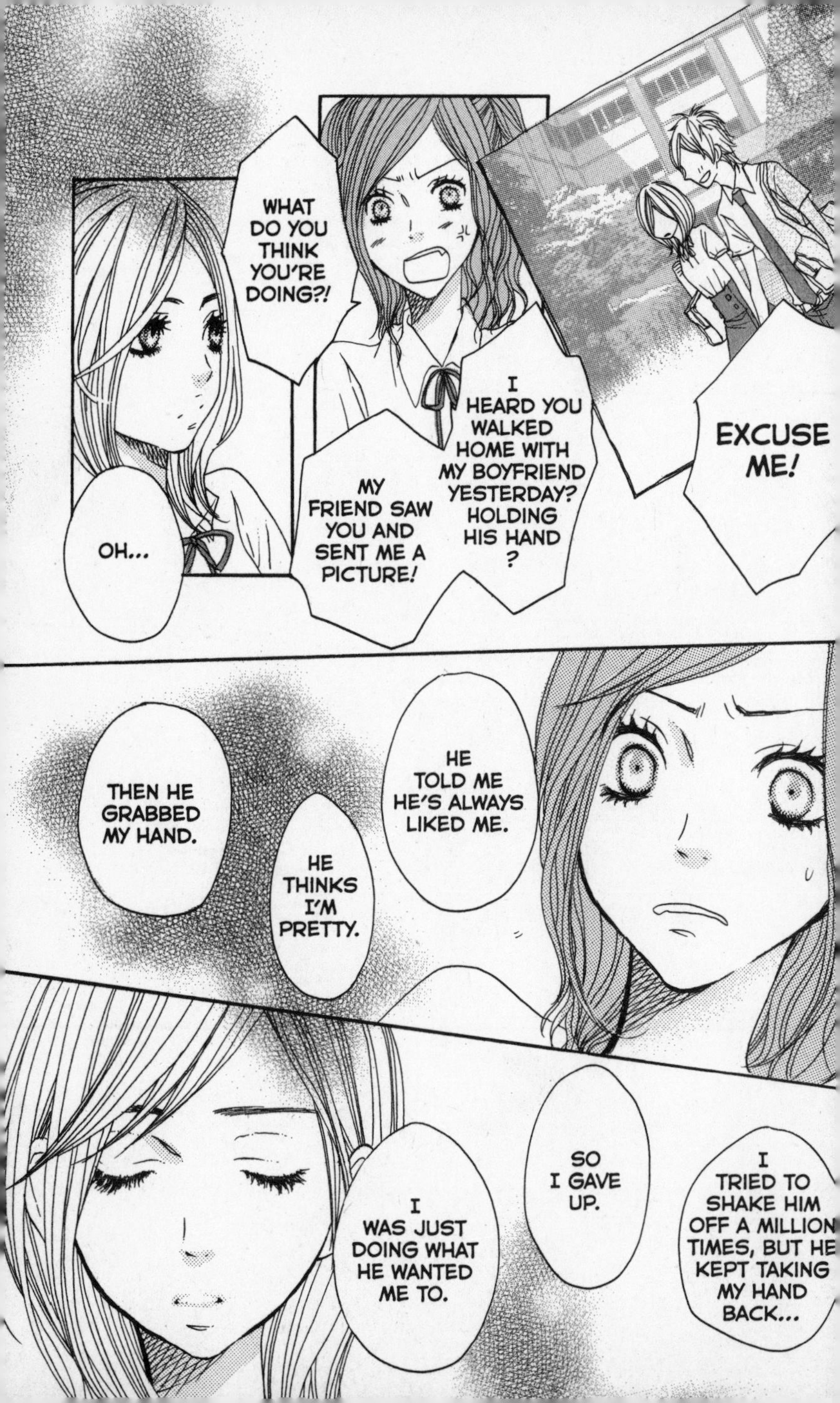
EXCUSE ME!
WHAT DO YOU THINK YOU'RE DOING?!
I HEARD YOU WALKED HOME WITH MY BOYFRIEND YESTERDAY? HOLDING HIS HAND?
MY FRIEND SAW YOU AND SENT ME A PICTURE!
OH...
HE TOLD ME HE'S ALWAYS LIKED ME.
HE THINKS I'M PRETTY.
THEN HE GRABBED MY HAND.
I TRIED TO SHAKE HIM OFF A MILLION TIMES, BUT HE KEPT TAKING MY HAND BACK...
SO I GAVE UP.
I WAS JUST DOING WHAT HE WANTED ME TO.

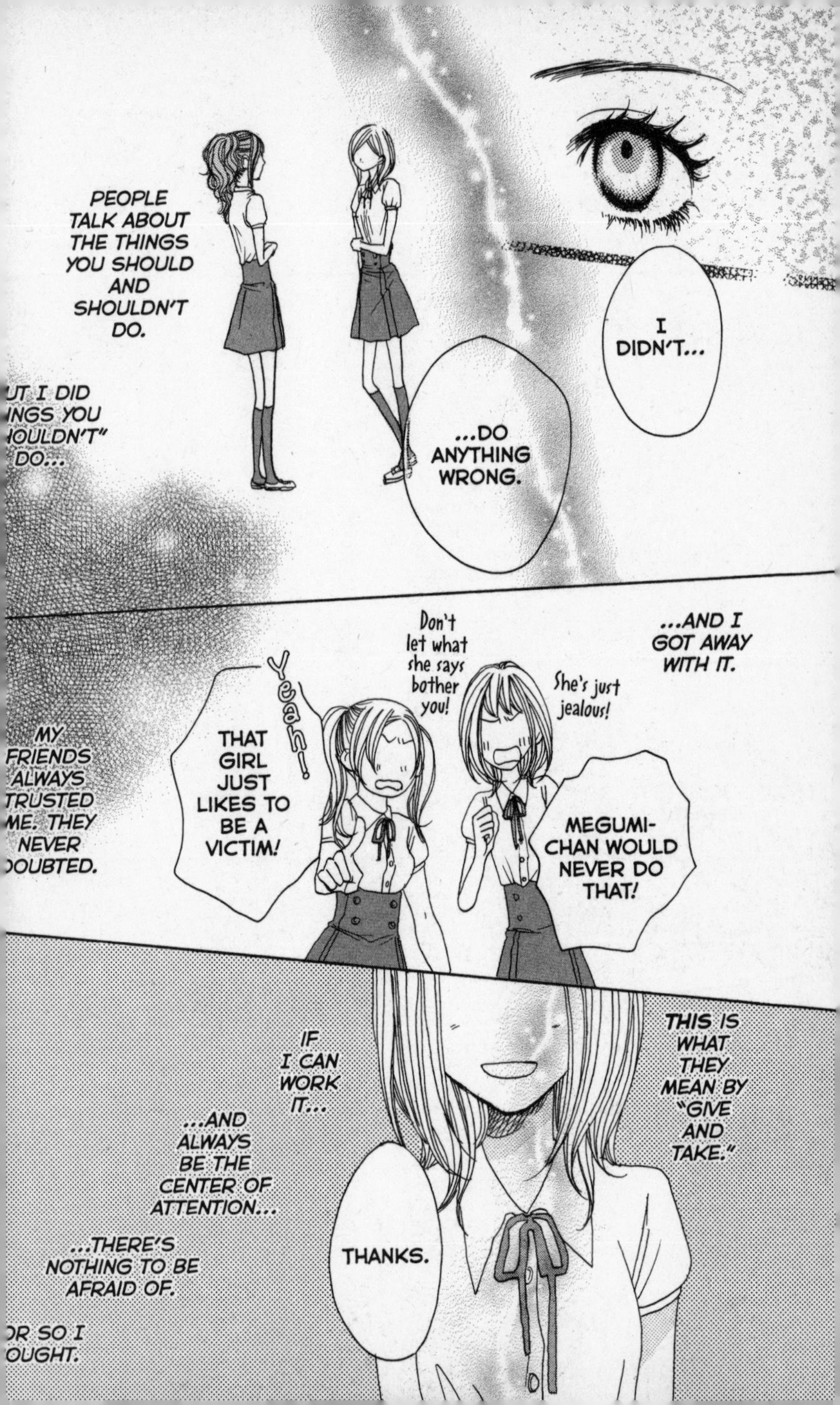
I DIDN'T...
...DO ANYTHING WRONG.
PEOPLE TALK ABOUT THE THINGS YOU SHOULD AND SHOULDN'T DO.
UT I DID INGS YOU OULDN'T" DO...
...AND I GOT AWAY WITH IT.
She's just jealous!
MEGUMI-CHAN WOULD NEVER DO THAT!
Don't let what she says bother you!
Yeah!
THAT GIRL JUST LIKES TO BE A VICTIM!
MY FRIENDS ALWAYS TRUSTED ME. THEY NEVER OUBTED.
THIS IS WHAT THEY MEAN BY "GIVE AND TAKE."
IF I CAN WORK IT...
...AND ALWAYS BE THE CENTER OF ATTENTION...
THANKS.
...THERE'S NOTHING TO BE AFRAID OF.
OR SO I OUGHT.

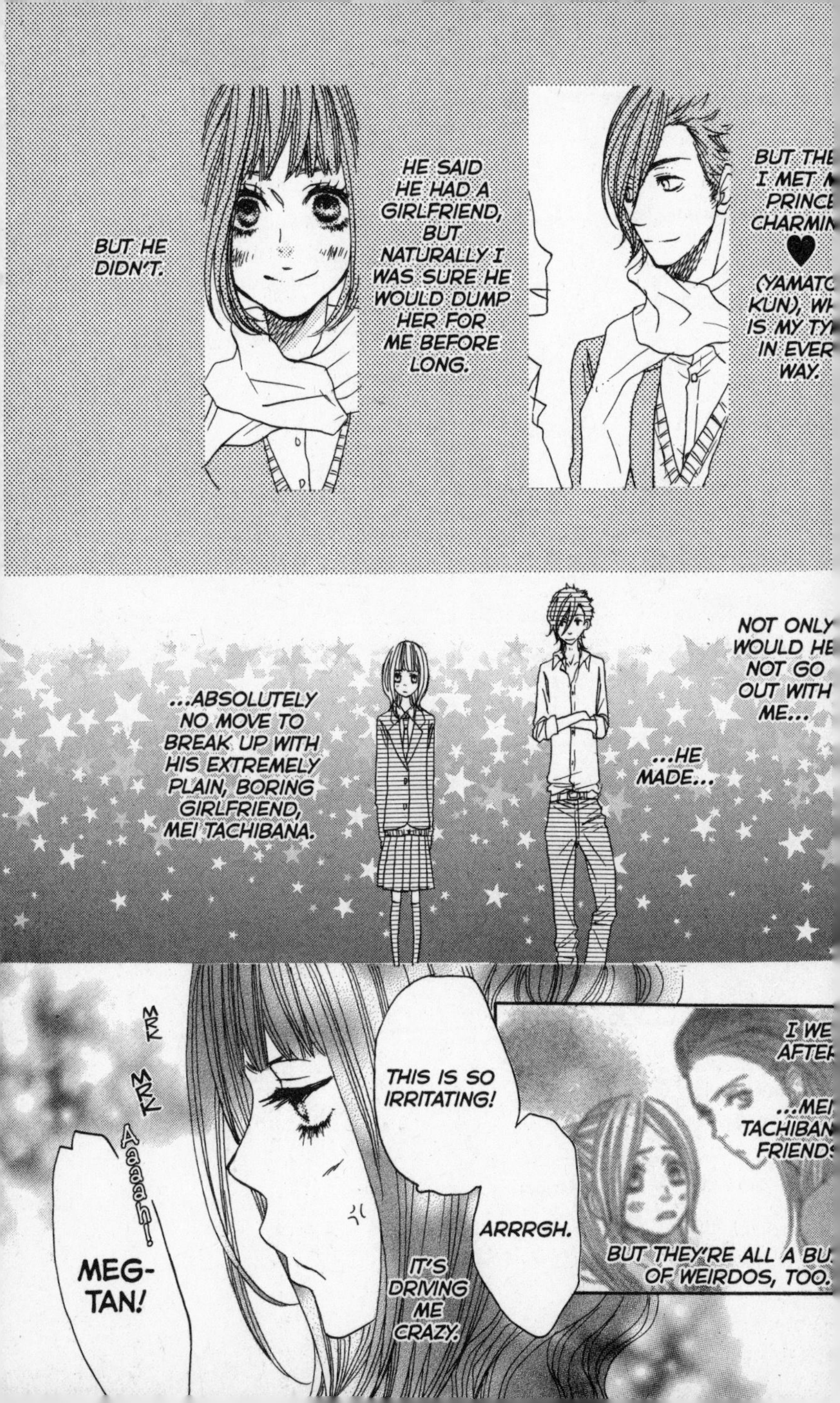

BUT THE I MET M PRINCE CHARMIN ♥ (YAMATO KUN), WH IS MY TY IN EVER WAY.
HE SAID HE HAD A GIRLFRIEND, BUT NATURALLY I WAS SURE HE WOULD DUMP HER FOR ME BEFORE LONG.
BUT HE DIDN'T.
NOT ONLY WOULD HE NOT GO OUT WITH ME...
...HE MADE...
...ABSOLUTELY NO MOVE TO BREAK UP WITH HIS EXTREMELY PLAIN, BORING GIRLFRIEND, MEI TACHIBANA.
I WE AFTER
...MEI TACHIBAN FRIENDS
BUT THEY'RE ALL A BU OF WEIRDOS, TOO.
THIS IS SO IRRITATING!
ARRRGH.
IT'S DRIVING ME CRAZY.
MRK
MRK
Aaaaah!
MEG-TAN!

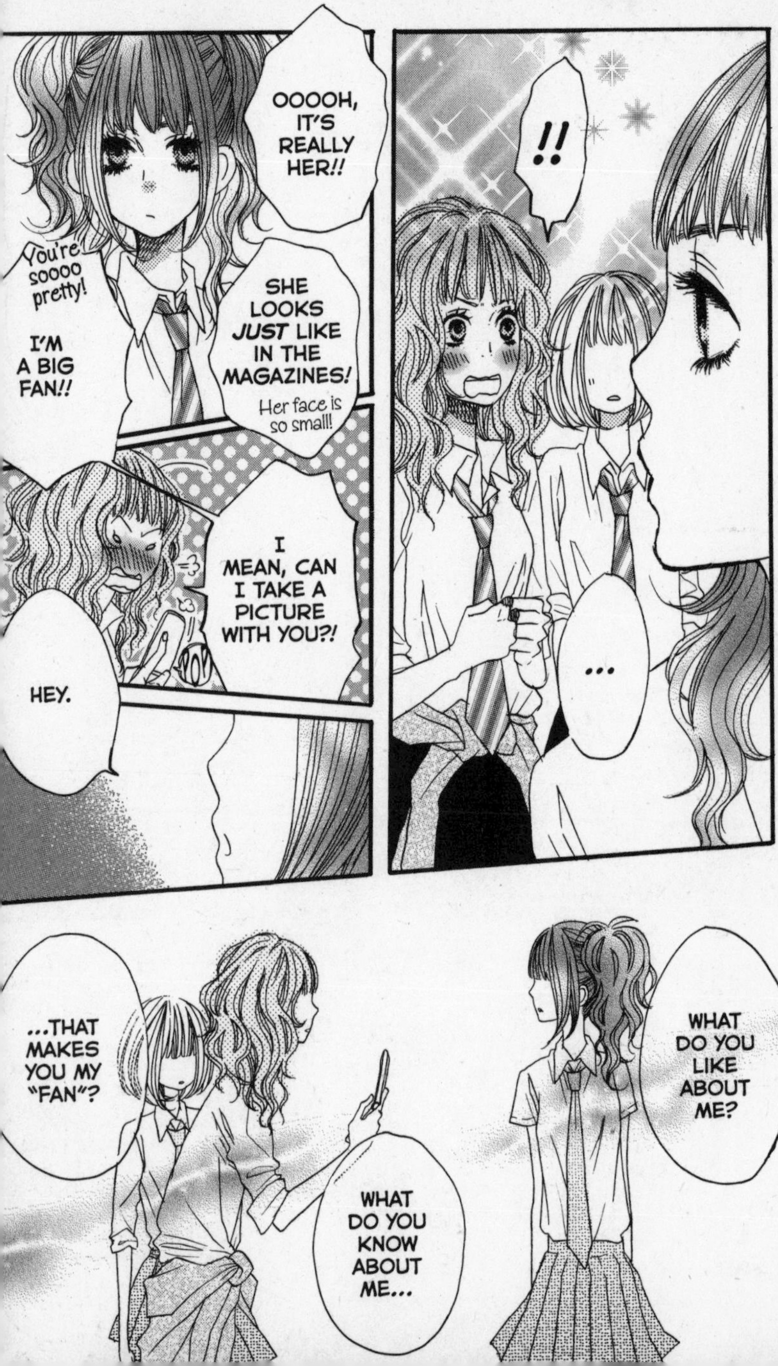
!!
...
OOOOH, IT'S REALLY HER!!
SHE LOOKS JUST LIKE IN THE MAGAZINES!
Her face is so small!
You're soooo pretty!
I'M A BIG FAN!!
I MEAN, CAN I TAKE A PICTURE WITH YOU?!
HEY.
WHAT DO YOU LIKE ABOUT ME?
WHAT DO YOU KNOW ABOUT ME...
...THAT MAKES YOU MY "FAN"?

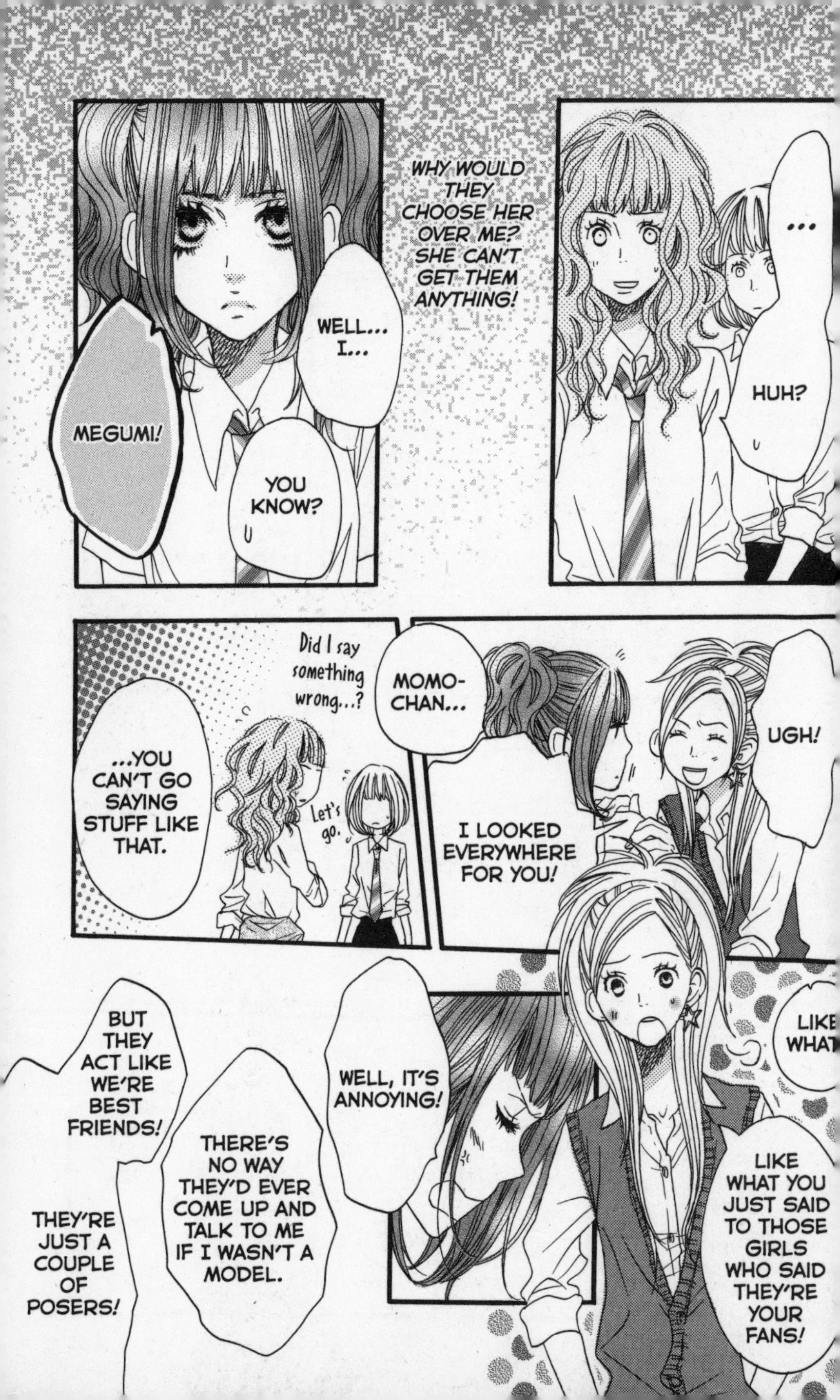
...
HUH?
WHY WOULD THEY CHOOSE HER OVER ME? SHE CAN'T GET THEM ANYTHING!
WELL... I...
YOU KNOW?
MEGUMI!
UGH!
MOMO-CHAN...
I LOOKED EVERYWHERE FOR YOU!
Did I say something wrong...?
...YOU CAN'T GO SAYING STUFF LIKE THAT.
Let's go.
LIKE WHAT
LIKE WHAT YOU JUST SAID TO THOSE GIRLS WHO SAID THEY'RE YOUR FANS!
WELL, IT'S ANNOYING!
BUT THEY ACT LIKE WE'RE BEST FRIENDS!
THERE'S NO WAY THEY'D EVER COME UP AND TALK TO ME IF I WASN'T A MODEL.
THEY'RE JUST A COUPLE OF POSERS!

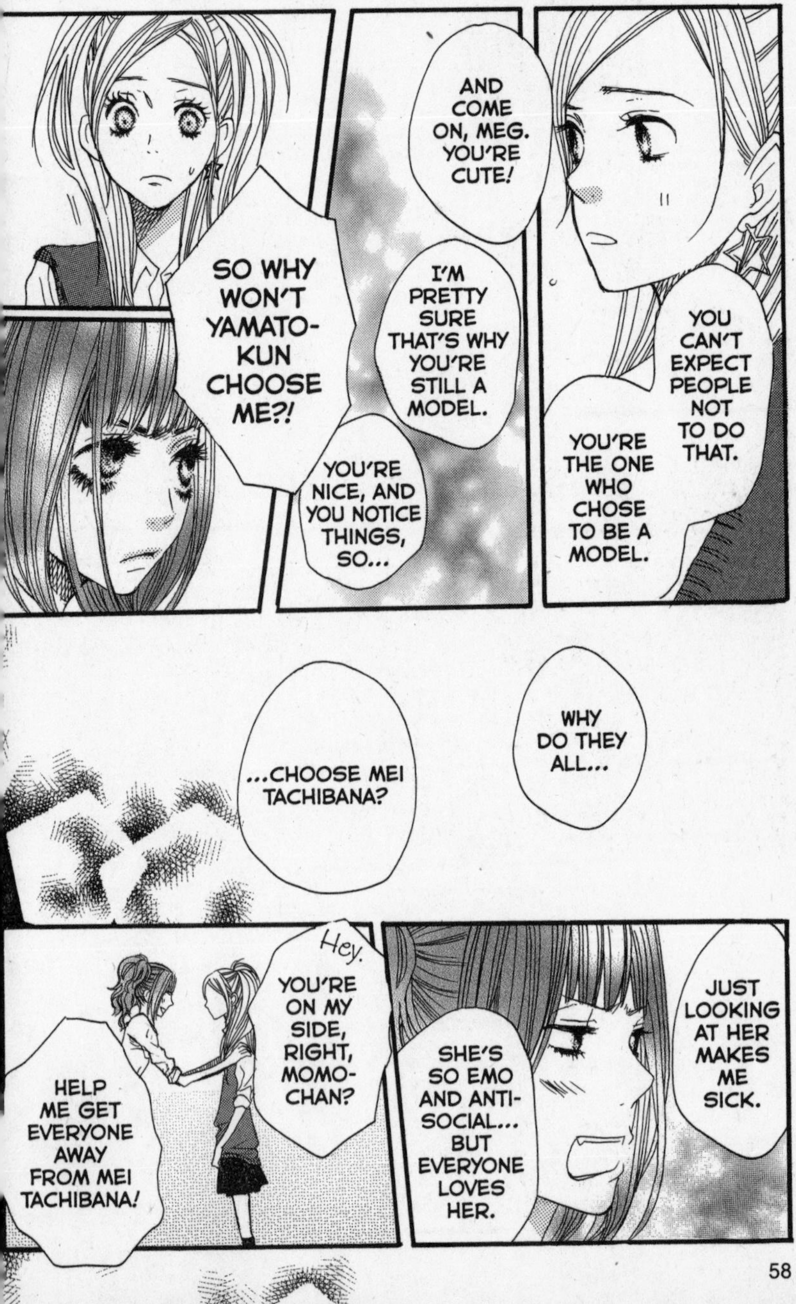

YOU CAN'T EXPECT PEOPLE NOT TO DO THAT.
YOU'RE THE ONE WHO CHOSE TO BE A MODEL.
AND COME ON, MEG. YOU'RE CUTE!
I'M PRETTY SURE THAT'S WHY YOU'RE STILL A MODEL.
YOU'RE NICE, AND YOU NOTICE THINGS, SO...
SO WHY WON'T YAMATO-KUN CHOOSE ME?!
WHY DO THEY ALL...
...CHOOSE MEI TACHIBANA?
JUST LOOKING AT HER MAKES ME SICK.
SHE'S SO EMO AND ANTI-SOCIAL... BUT EVERYONE LOVES HER.
Hey.
YOU'RE ON MY SIDE, RIGHT, MOMO-CHAN?
HELP ME GET EVERYONE AWAY FROM MEI TACHIBANA!

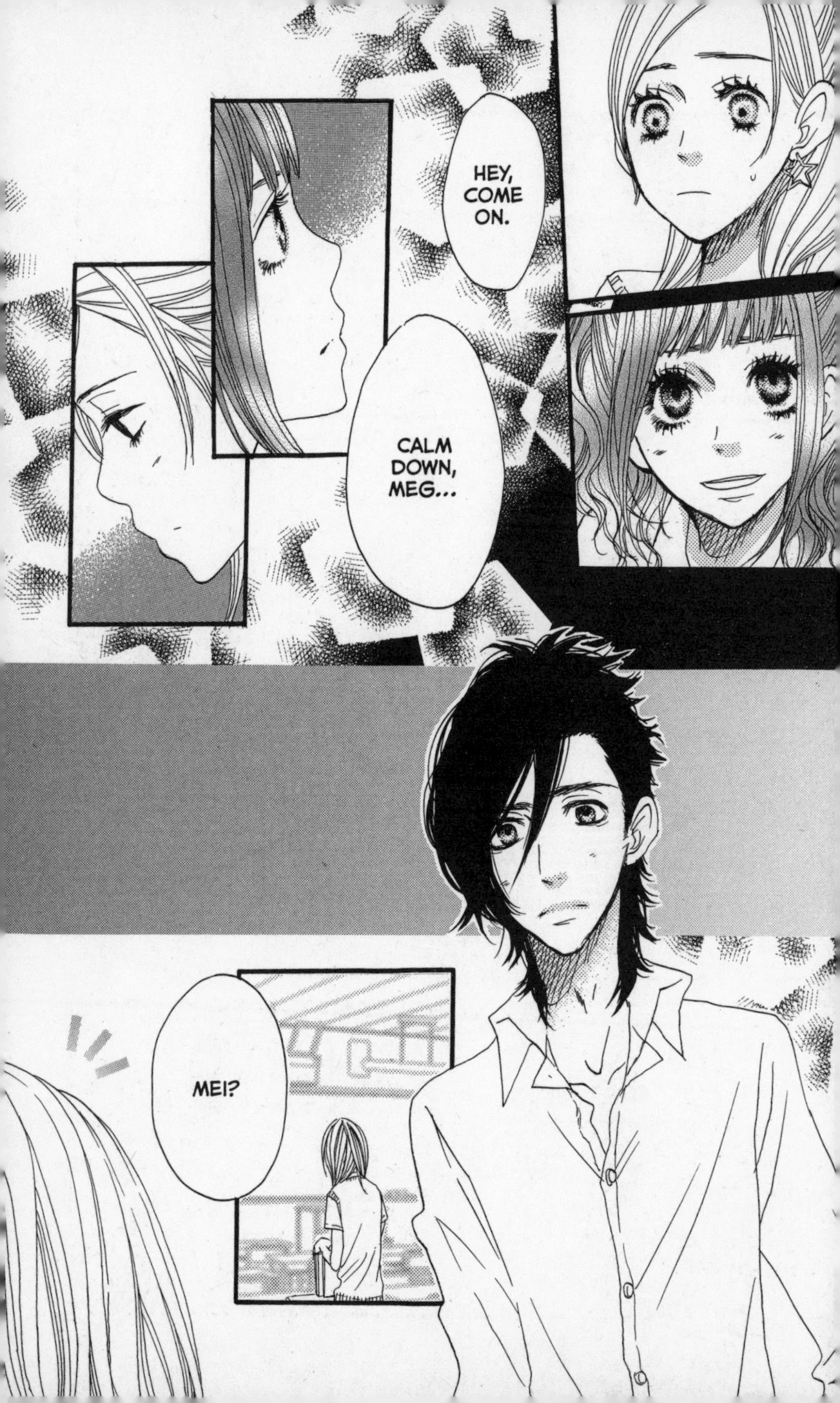
HEY, COME ON.
CALM DOWN, MEG...
MEI?

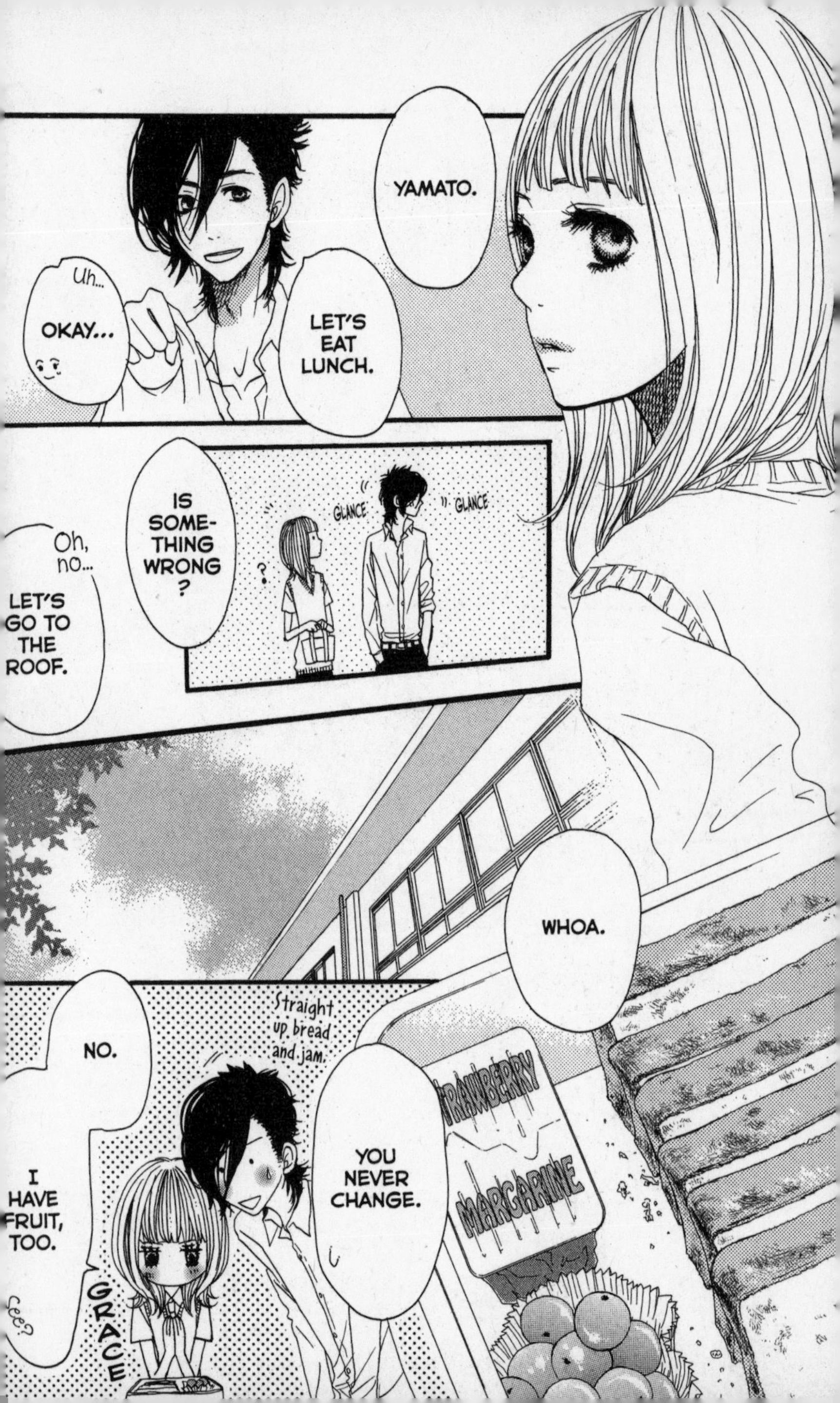
YAMATO.
LET'S EAT LUNCH.
Uh... OKAY...
IS SOME-THING WRONG?
GLANCE
GLANCE
Oh, no...
LET'S GO TO THE ROOF.
WHOA.
Straight up bread and jam.
YOU NEVER CHANGE.
TRAWBERRY
MARGARINE
NO.
I HAVE FRUIT, TOO.
GRACE

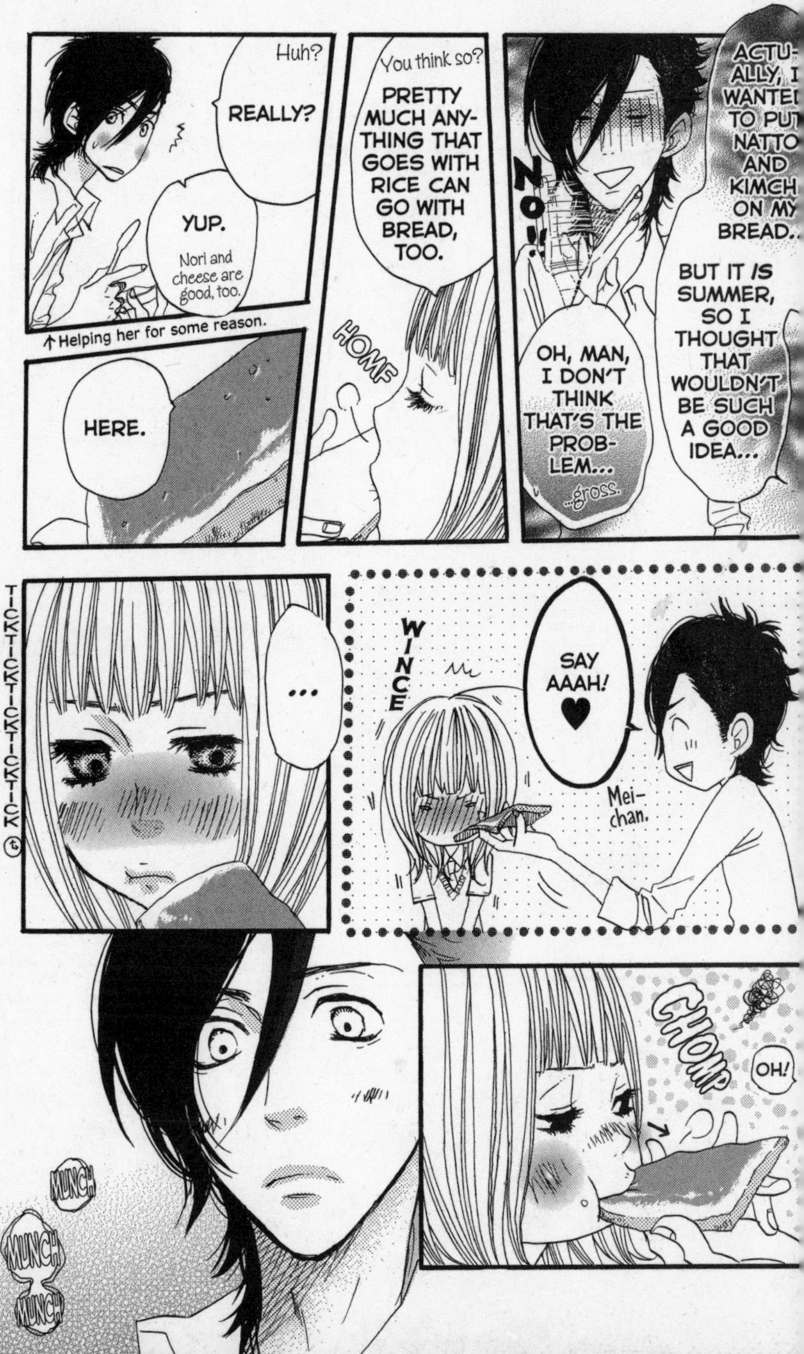
ACTU-ALLY, I WANTE TO PU NATTO AND KIMCH ON MY BREAD..
BUT IT IS SUMMER, SO I THOUGHT THAT WOULDN'T BE SUCH A GOOD IDEA...
NO!!
OH, MAN, I DON'T THINK THAT'S THE PROB-LEM...
...gross.
You think so?
PRETTY MUCH ANY-THING THAT GOES WITH RICE CAN GO WITH BREAD, TOO.
HOMF
Huh?
REALLY?
YUP.
Nori and cheese are good, too.
↑Helping her for some reason.
HERE.
SAY AAAH! ♥
Mei-chan.
WINCE
...
TICKTICKTICKTICKTICK
CHOMP
OH!
MUNCH
MUNCH
MUNCH

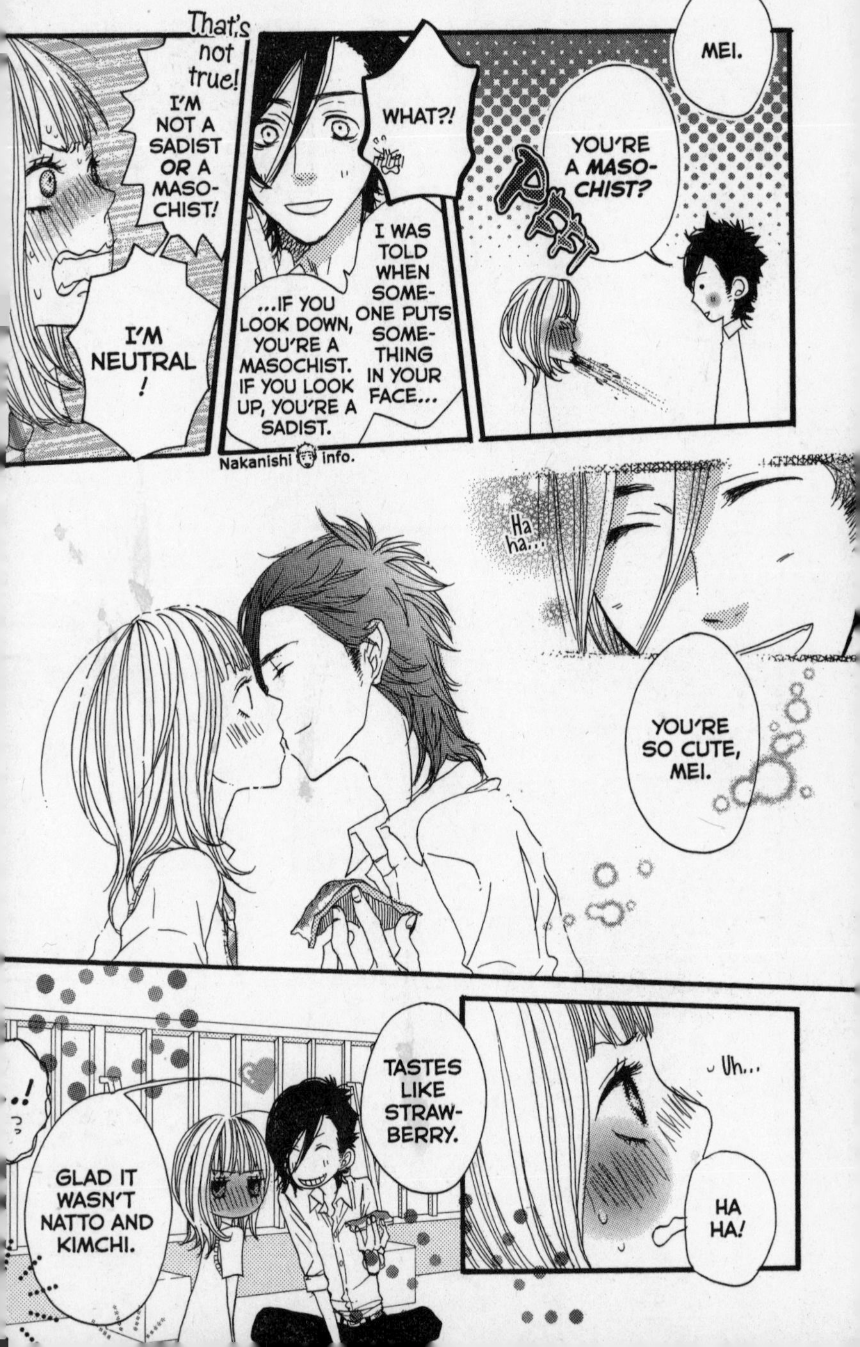
MEI.
YOU'RE A MASOCHIST?
PFFT
WHAT?!
I WAS TOLD WHEN SOMEONE PUTS SOMETHING IN YOUR FACE...
...IF YOU LOOK DOWN, YOU'RE A MASOCHIST. IF YOU LOOK UP, YOU'RE A SADIST.
Nakanishi info.
That's not true!
I'M NOT A SADIST OR A MASOCHIST!
I'M NEUTRAL!
Ha ha...
YOU'RE SO CUTE, MEI.
Uh...
HA HA!
TASTES LIKE STRAWBERRY.
GLAD IT WASN'T NATTO AND KIMCHI.

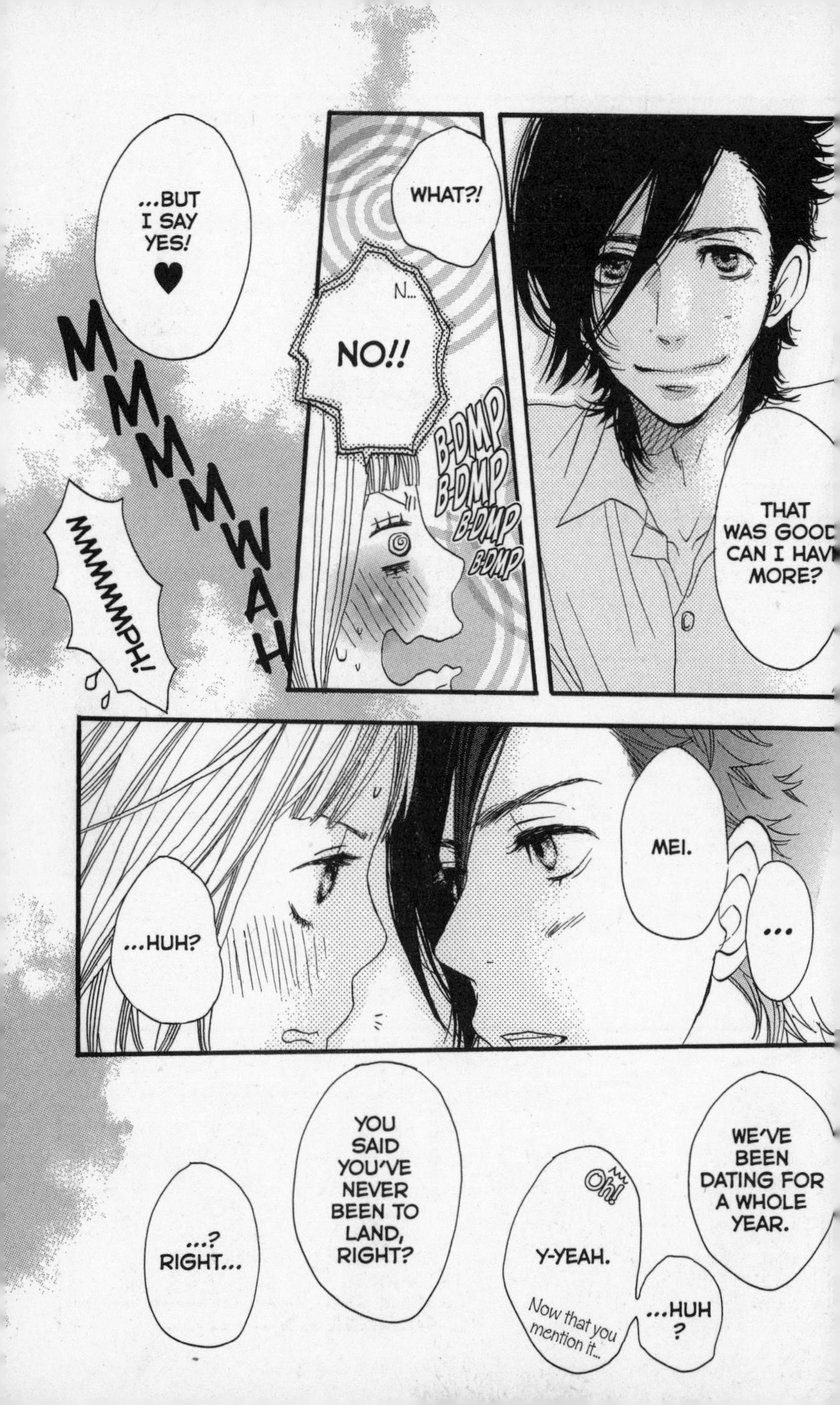

THAT WAS GOOD CAN I HAV MORE?
WHAT?!
N...
NO!!
B-DMP B-DMP B-DMP B-DMP
...BUT I SAY YES! ♥
MMMMWAH
MMMMMMPH!
MEI.
...
...HUH?
WE'VE BEEN DATING FOR A WHOLE YEAR.
...HUH ?
Oh!
Y-YEAH.
Now that you mention it...
YOU SAID YOU'VE NEVER BEEN TO LAND, RIGHT?
...? RIGHT...

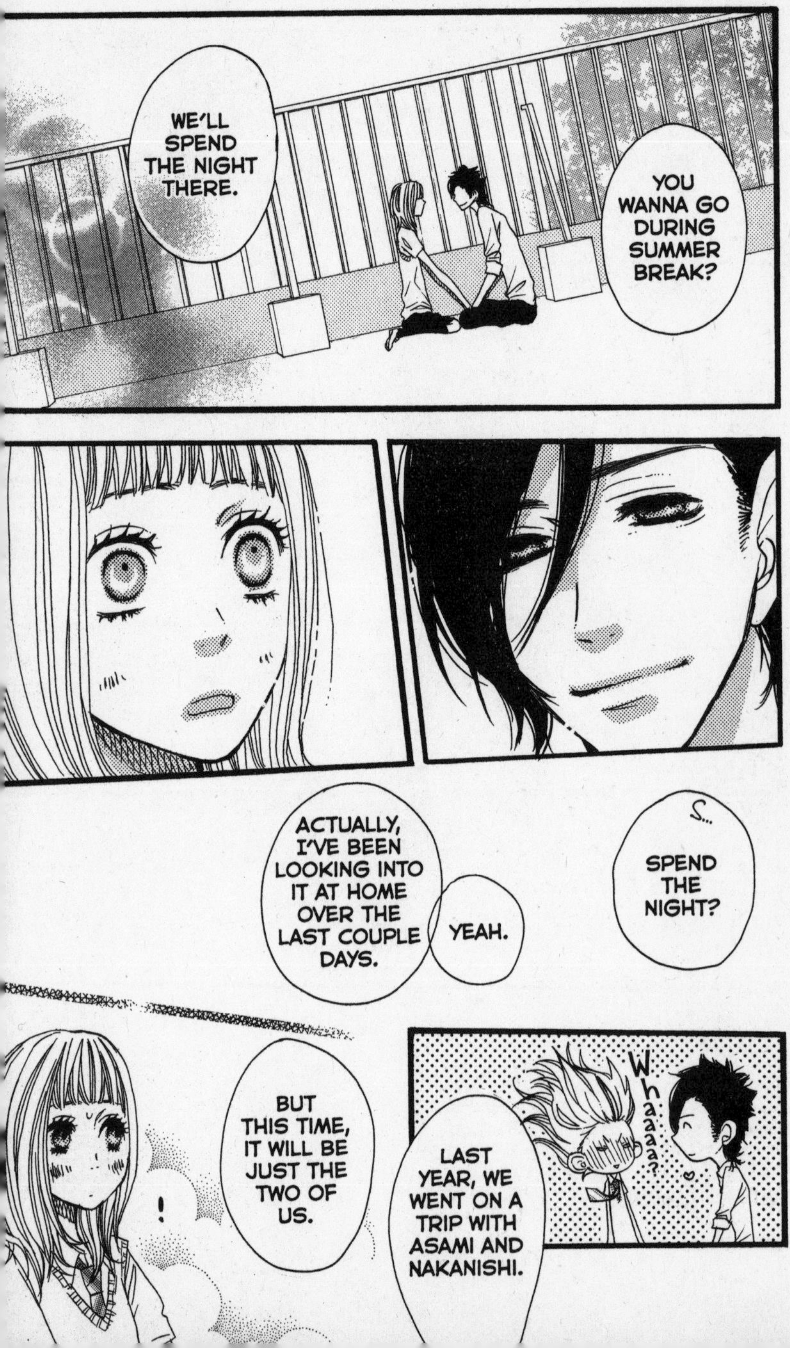
YOU WANNA GO DURING SUMMER BREAK?
WE'LL SPEND THE NIGHT THERE.
S... SPEND THE NIGHT?
YEAH.
ACTUALLY, I'VE BEEN LOOKING INTO IT AT HOME OVER THE LAST COUPLE DAYS.
Whaaaa?
LAST YEAR, WE WENT ON A TRIP WITH ASAMI AND NAKANISHI.
BUT THIS TIME, IT WILL BE JUST THE TWO OF US.
!

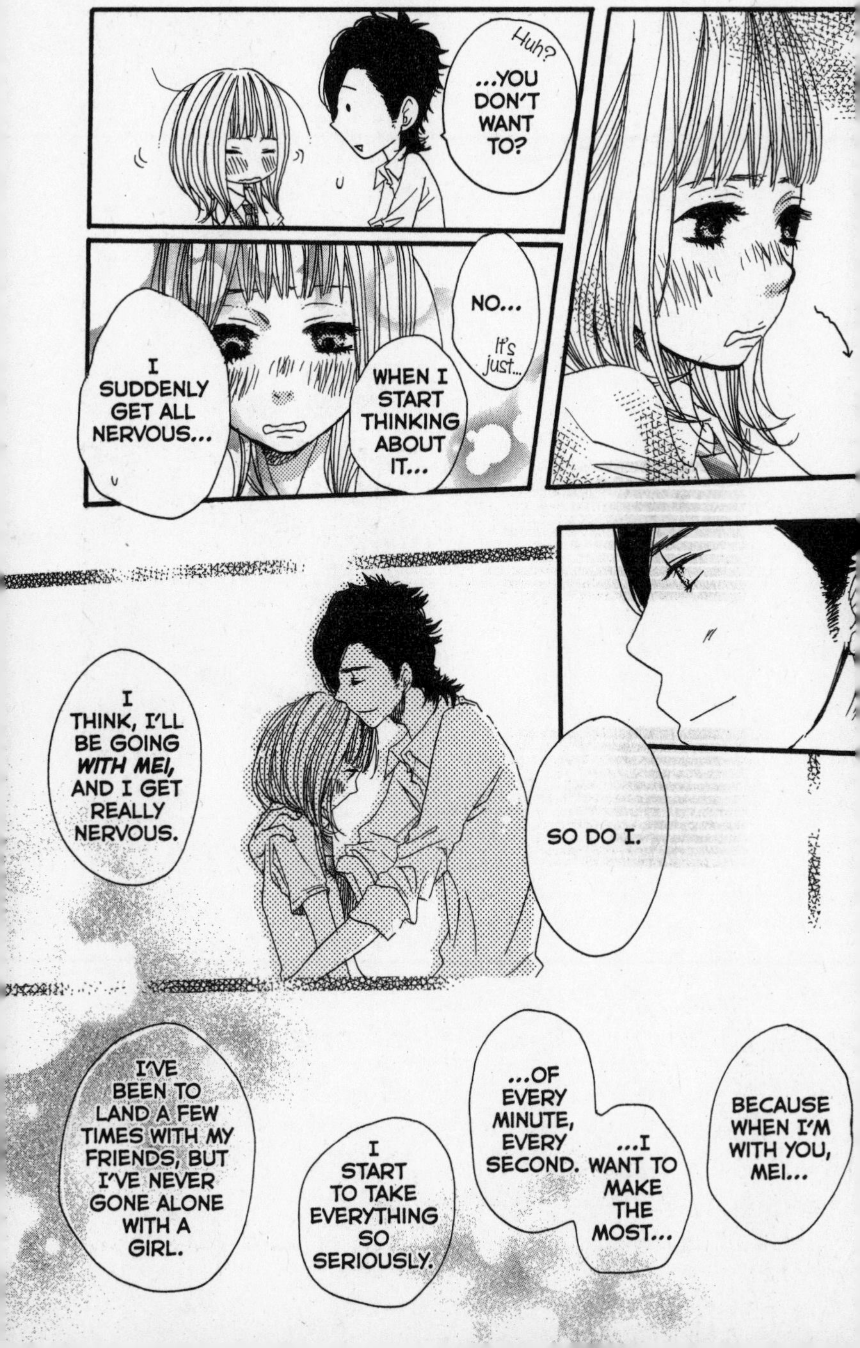
Huh?
...YOU DON'T WANT TO?
NO...
It's just...
WHEN I START THINKING ABOUT IT...
I SUDDENLY GET ALL NERVOUS...
SO DO I.
I THINK, I'LL BE GOING *WITH MEI,* AND I GET REALLY NERVOUS.
BECAUSE WHEN I'M WITH YOU, MEI...
...I WANT TO MAKE THE MOST...
...OF EVERY MINUTE, EVERY SECOND.
I START TO TAKE EVERYTHING SO SERIOUSLY.
I'VE BEEN TO LAND A FEW TIMES WITH MY FRIENDS, BUT I'VE NEVER GONE ALONE WITH A GIRL.

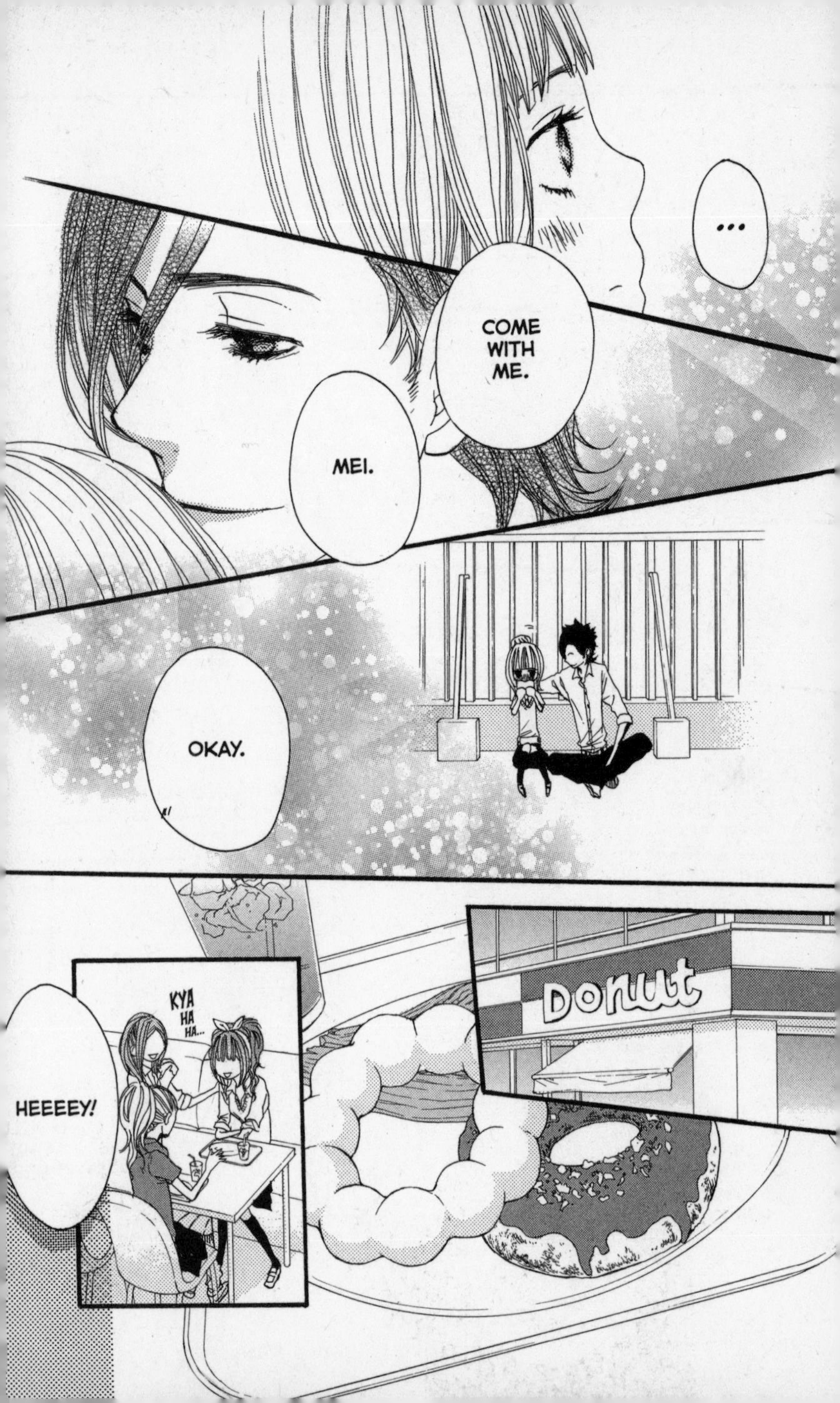

...
COME WITH ME.
MEI.
OKAY.
Donut
KYA HA HA...
HEEEEY!

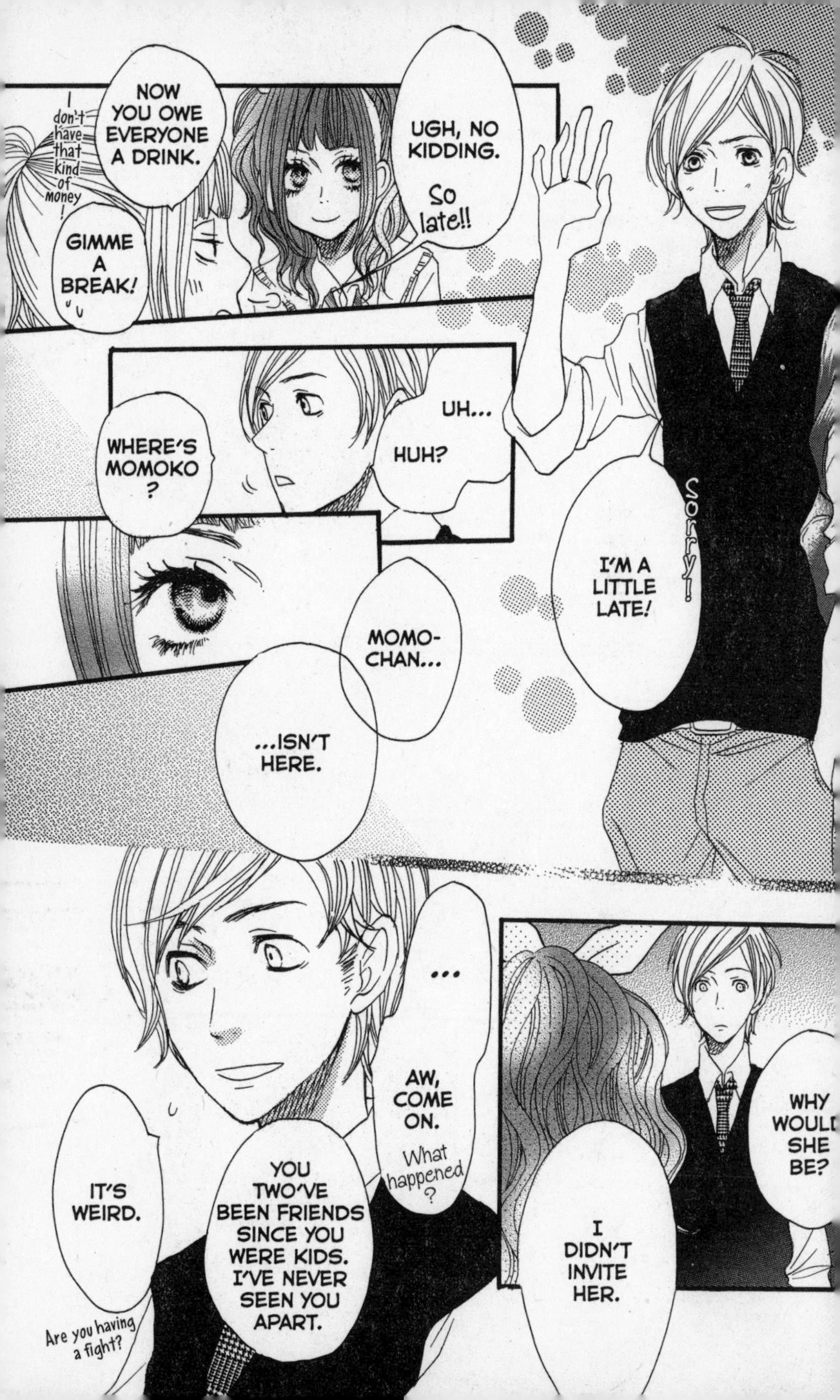
Sorry!
I'M A LITTLE LATE!
UGH, NO KIDDING.
So late!!
NOW YOU OWE EVERYONE A DRINK.
GIMME A BREAK!
I don't have that kind of money!
UH...
HUH?
WHERE'S MOMOKO?
MOMO-CHAN...
...ISN'T HERE.
WHY WOUL SHE BE?
I DIDN'T INVITE HER.
...
AW, COME ON.
What happened?
YOU TWO'VE BEEN FRIENDS SINCE YOU WERE KIDS. I'VE NEVER SEEN YOU APART.
IT'S WEIRD.
Are you having a fight?

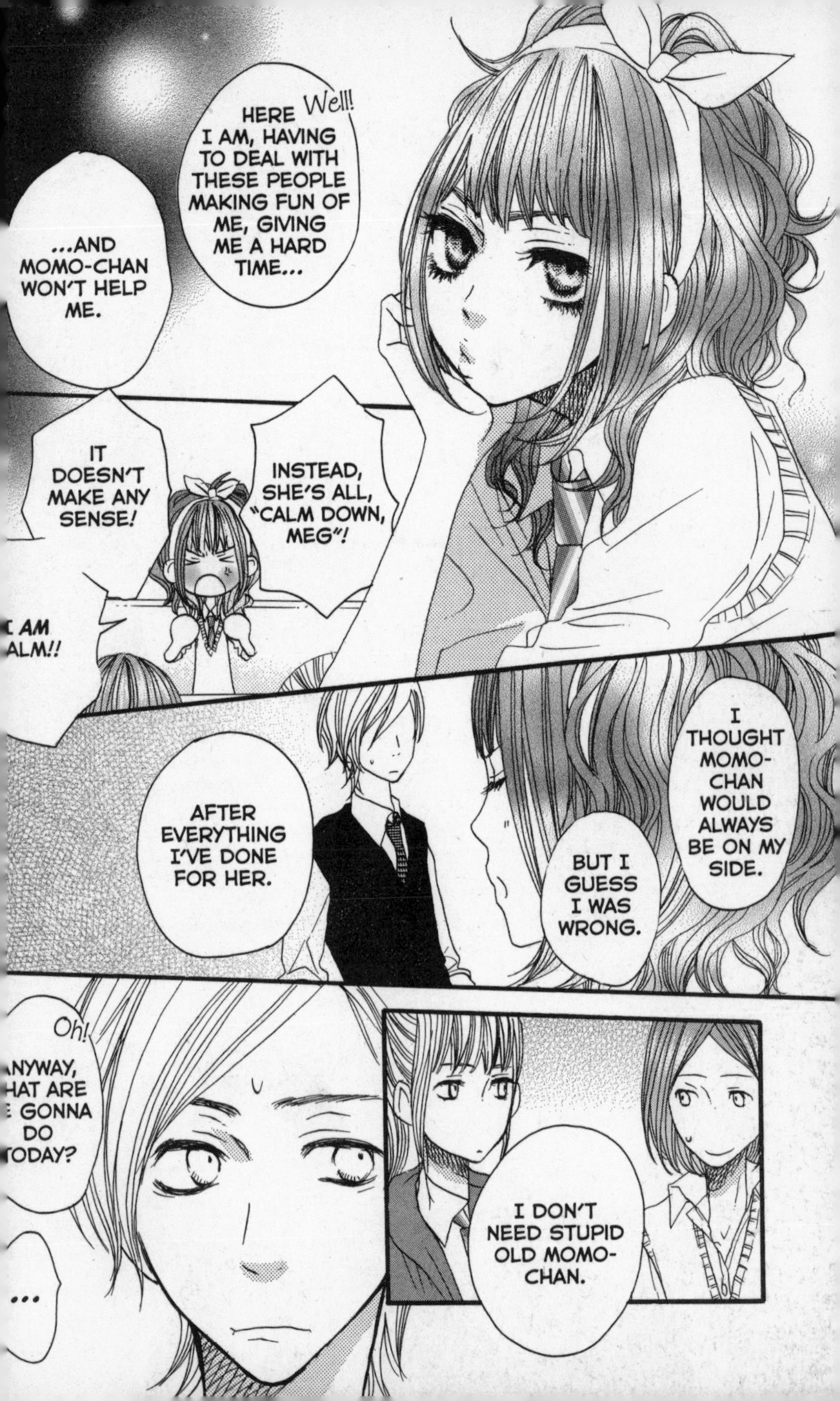

Well!
HERE I AM, HAVING TO DEAL WITH THESE PEOPLE MAKING FUN OF ME, GIVING ME A HARD TIME...
...AND MOMO-CHAN WON'T HELP ME.
INSTEAD, SHE'S ALL, "CALM DOWN, MEG"!
IT DOESN'T MAKE ANY SENSE!
AM ALM!!
I THOUGHT MOMO-CHAN WOULD ALWAYS BE ON MY SIDE.
BUT I GUESS I WAS WRONG.
AFTER EVERYTHING I'VE DONE FOR HER.
I DON'T NEED STUPID OLD MOMO-CHAN.
Oh!
NYWAY, HAT ARE GONNA DO ODAY?
...

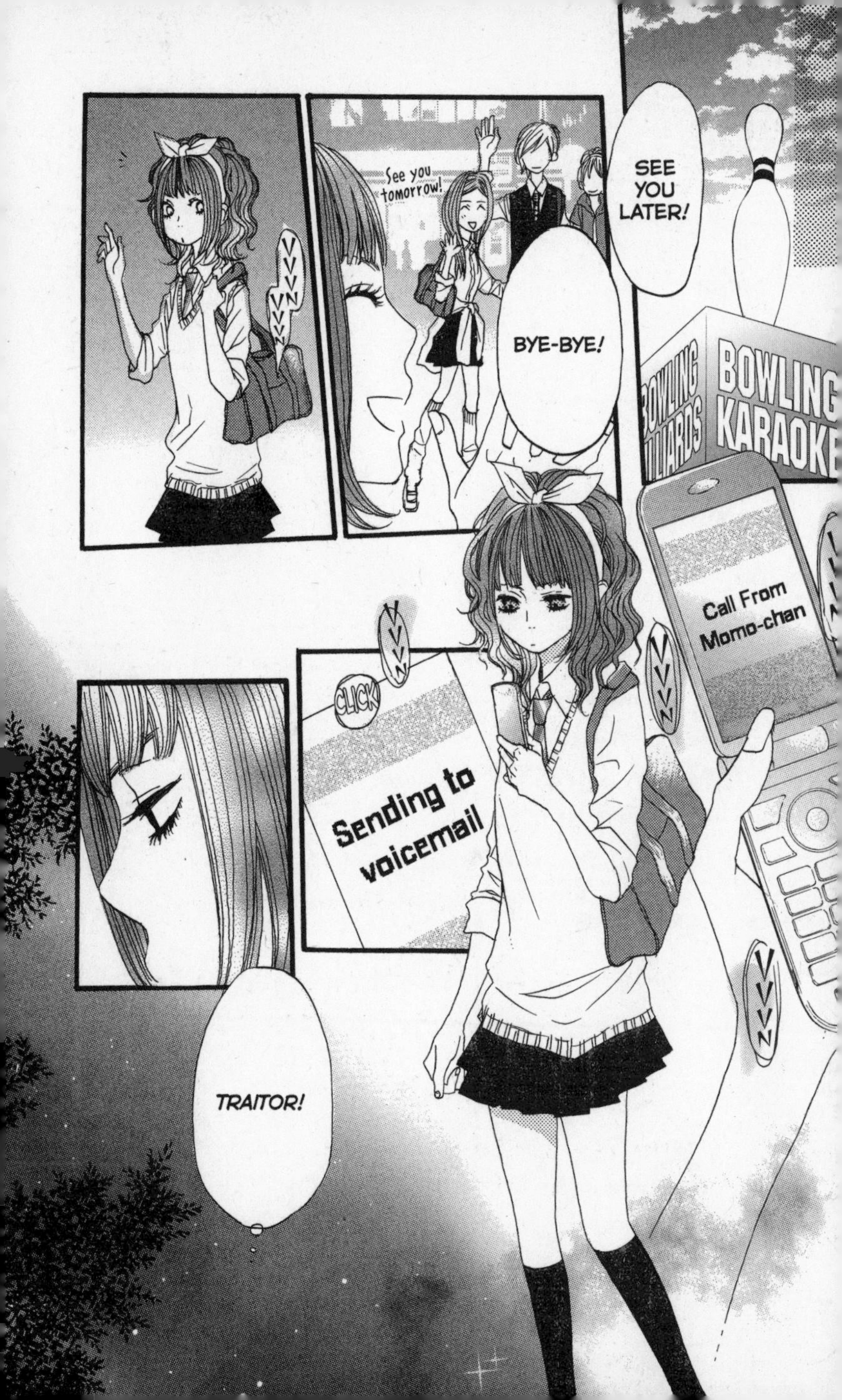
SEE YOU LATER!
BYE-BYE!
BOWLING KARAOKE
See you tomorrow!
VVVN
VVVN
Call From Momo-chan
VVVN
VVVN
CLICK
Sending to voicemail
VVVN
TRAITOR!

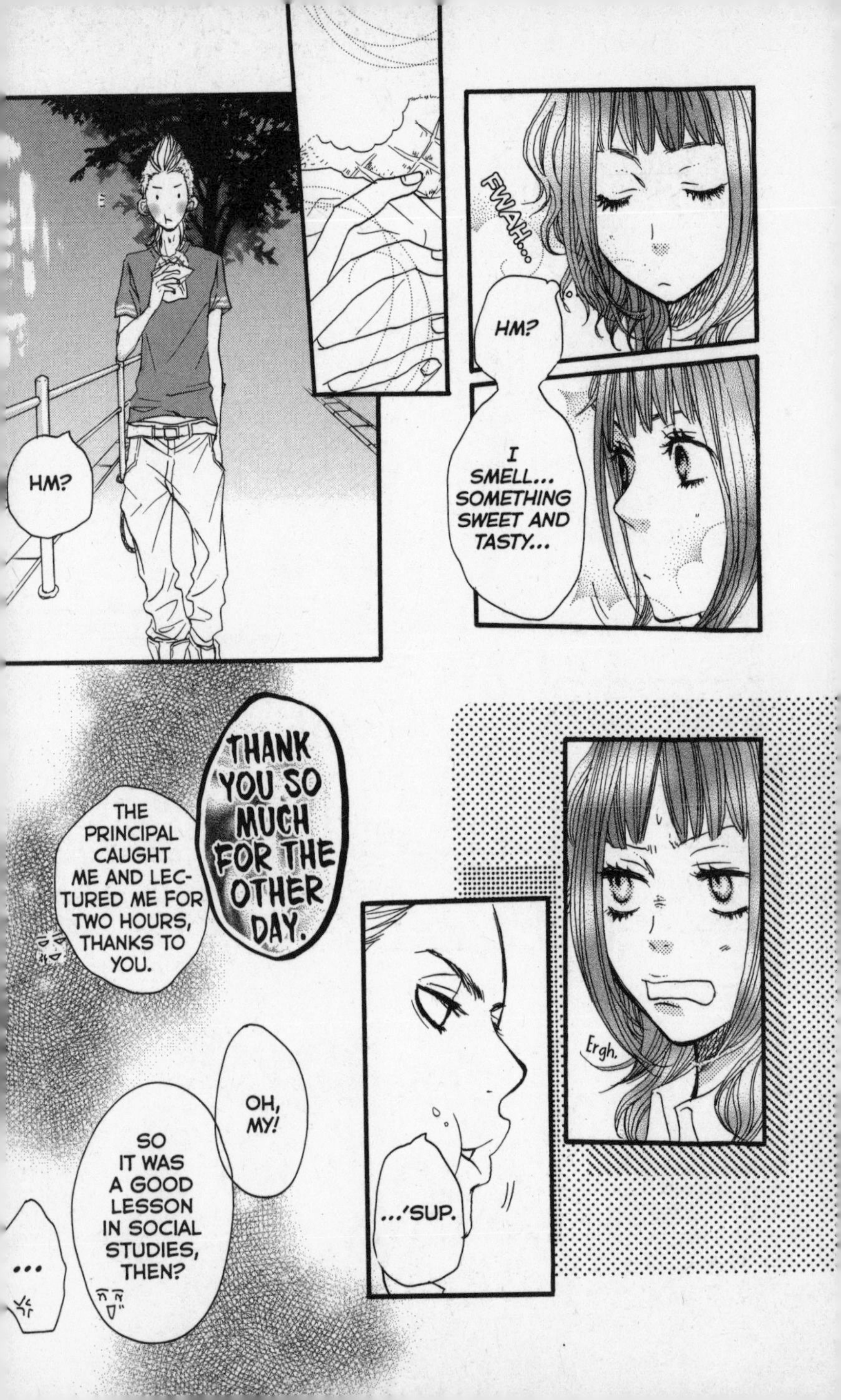
FWAH...
HM?
I SMELL... SOMETHING SWEET AND TASTY...
HM?
Ergh.
...'SUP.
THANK YOU SO MUCH FOR THE OTHER DAY.
THE PRINCIPAL CAUGHT ME AND LEC-TURED ME FOR TWO HOURS, THANKS TO YOU.
OH, MY!
SO IT WAS A GOOD LESSON IN SOCIAL STUDIES, THEN?
...

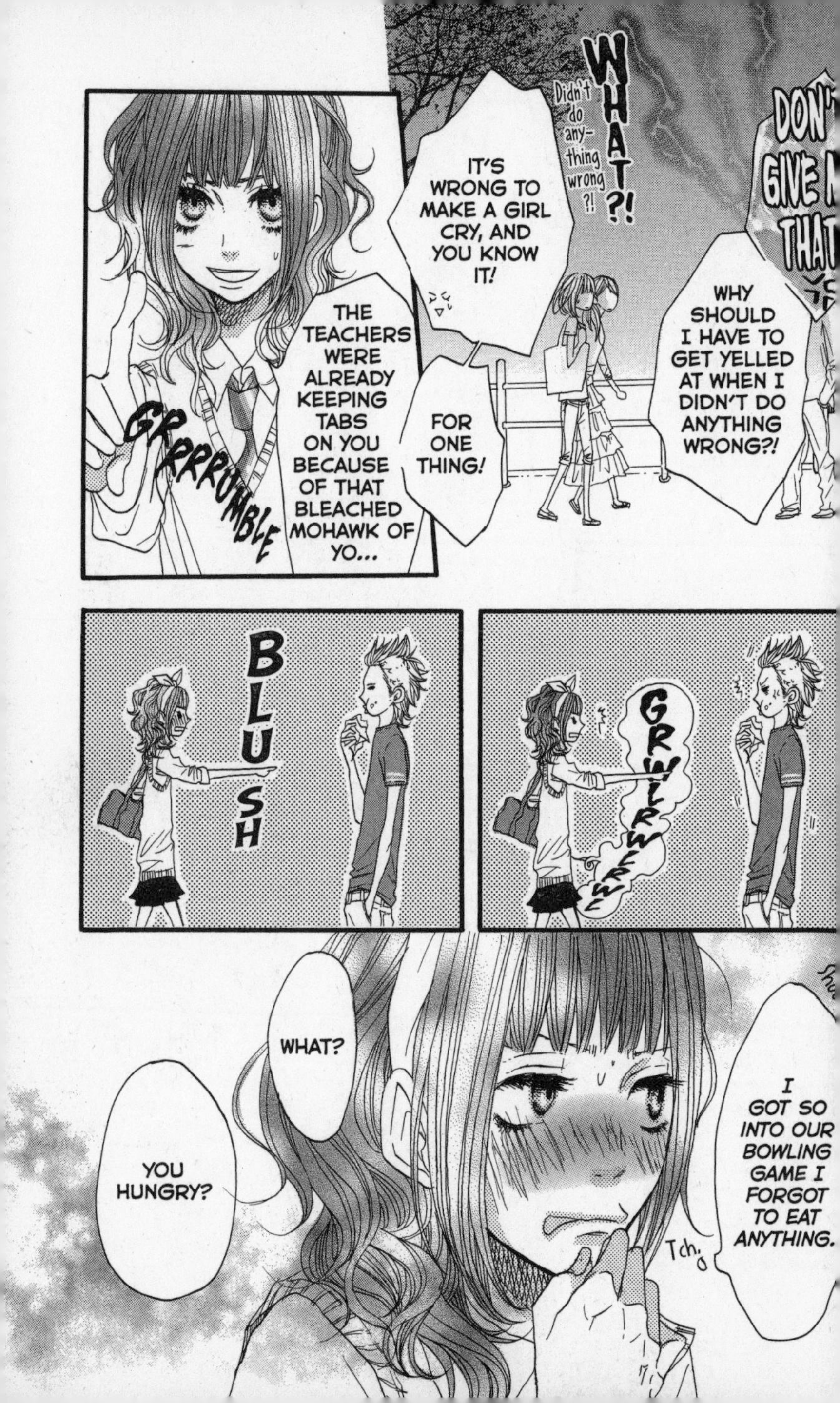
DON'T
GIVE
THAT
WHAT?!
Didn't do anything wrong?!
WHY SHOULD I HAVE TO GET YELLED AT WHEN I DIDN'T DO ANYTHING WRONG?!
IT'S WRONG TO MAKE A GIRL CRY, AND YOU KNOW IT!
FOR ONE THING!
THE TEACHERS WERE ALREADY KEEPING TABS ON YOU BECAUSE OF THAT BLEACHED MOHAWK OF YO...
GRRRRUMBLE
GRWLRWLRWL
BLUSH
I GOT SO INTO OUR BOWLING GAME I FORGOT TO EAT ANYTHING.
Tch.
WHAT?
YOU HUNGRY?

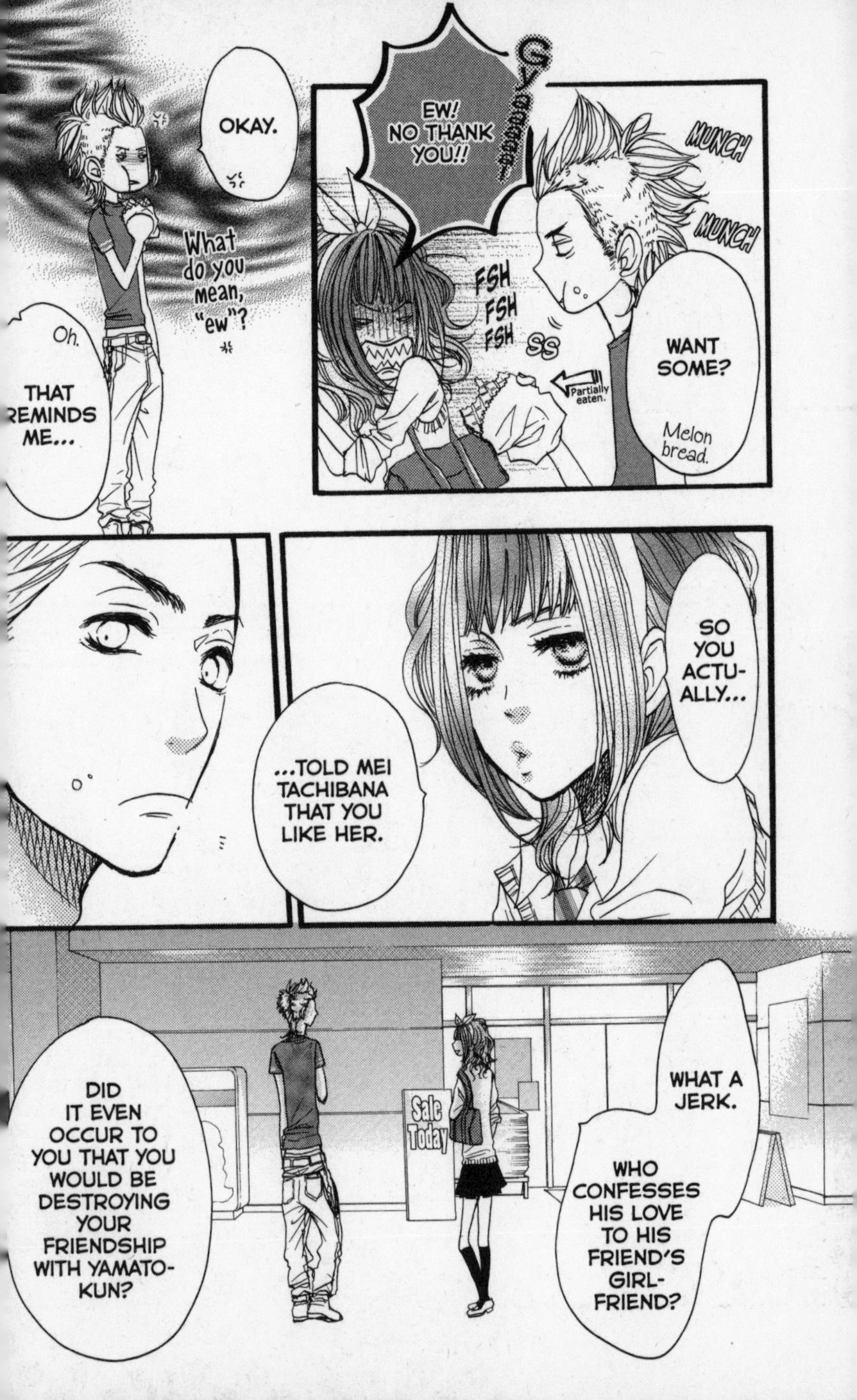
MUNCH
MUNCH
WANT SOME?
Melon bread.
Partially eaten.
SS
FSH FSH FSH
EW! NO THANK YOU!!
OKAY.
What do you mean, "ew"?
Oh.
THAT REMINDS ME...
SO YOU ACTU-ALLY...
...TOLD MEI TACHIBANA THAT YOU LIKE HER.
WHAT A JERK.
WHO CONFESSES HIS LOVE TO HIS FRIEND'S GIRL-FRIEND?
Sale Today
DID IT EVEN OCCUR TO YOU THAT YOU WOULD BE DESTROYING YOUR FRIENDSHIP WITH YAMATO-KUN?

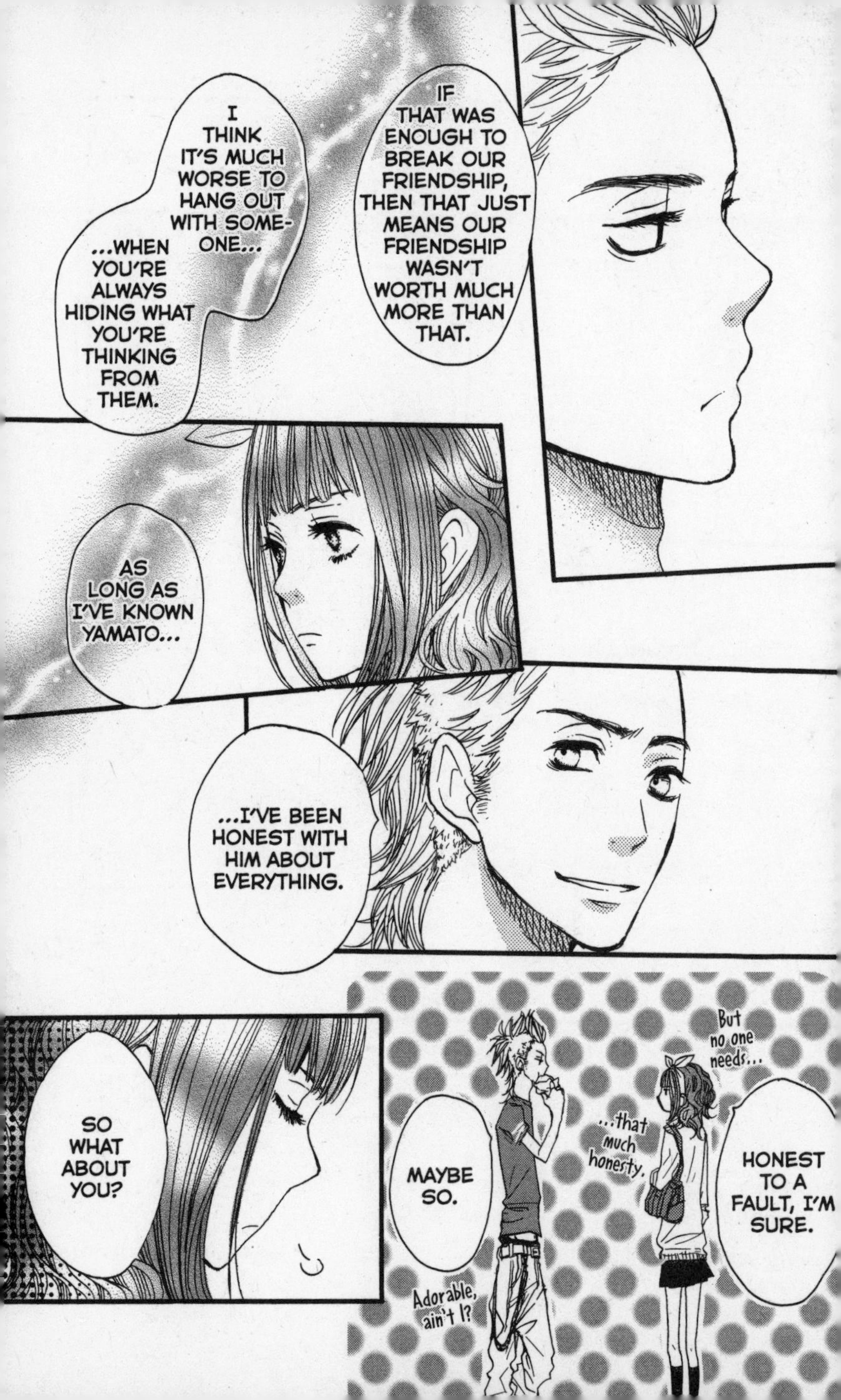
IF THAT WAS ENOUGH TO BREAK OUR FRIENDSHIP, THEN THAT JUST MEANS OUR FRIENDSHIP WASN'T WORTH MUCH MORE THAN THAT.
I THINK IT'S MUCH WORSE TO HANG OUT WITH SOME-ONE...
...WHEN YOU'RE ALWAYS HIDING WHAT YOU'RE THINKING FROM THEM.
AS LONG AS I'VE KNOWN YAMATO...
...I'VE BEEN HONEST WITH HIM ABOUT EVERYTHING.
HONEST TO A FAULT, I'M SURE.
But no one needs...
...that much honesty.
MAYBE SO.
Adorable, ain't I?
SO WHAT ABOUT YOU?

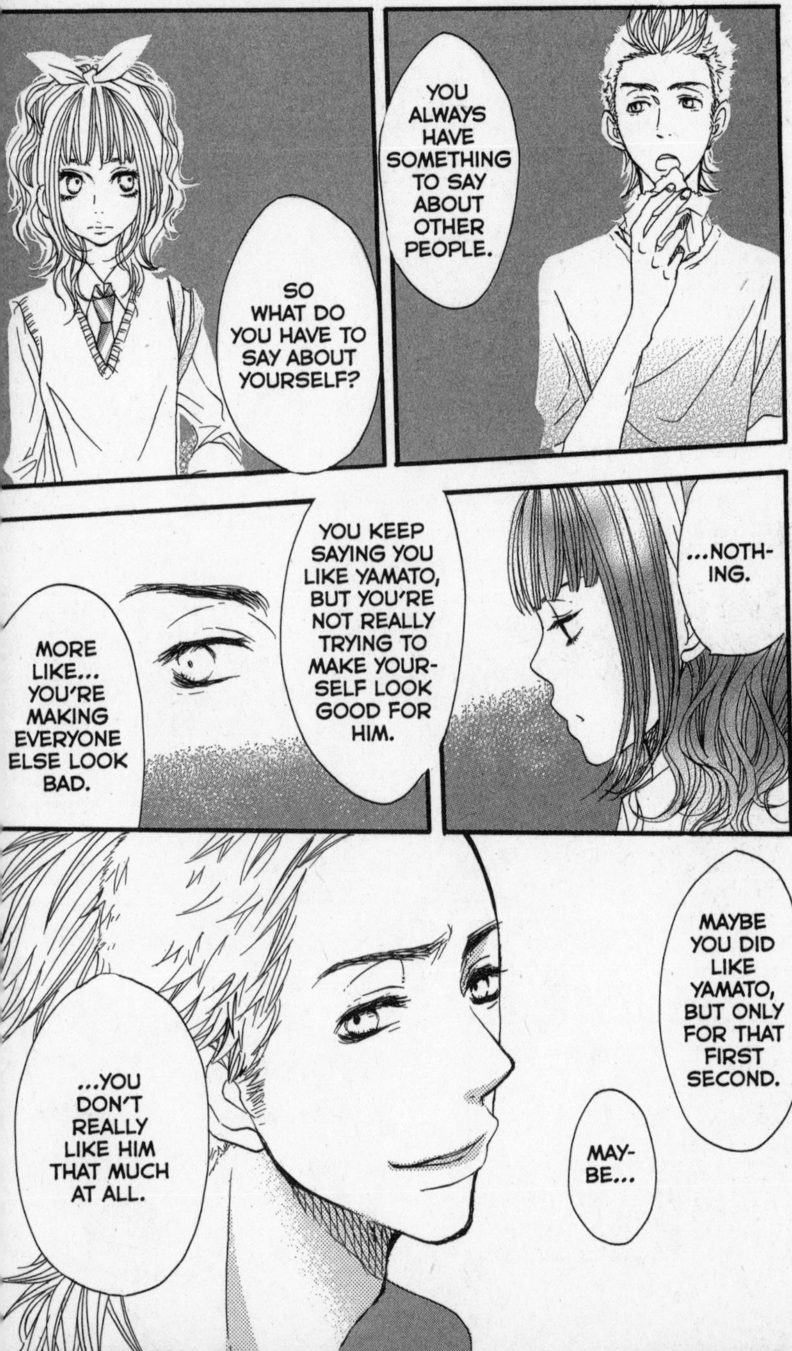
YOU ALWAYS HAVE SOMETHING TO SAY ABOUT OTHER PEOPLE.
SO WHAT DO YOU HAVE TO SAY ABOUT YOURSELF?
...NOTH-ING.
YOU KEEP SAYING YOU LIKE YAMATO, BUT YOU'RE NOT REALLY TRYING TO MAKE YOUR-SELF LOOK GOOD FOR HIM.
MORE LIKE... YOU'RE MAKING EVERYONE ELSE LOOK BAD.
MAYBE YOU DID LIKE YAMATO, BUT ONLY FOR THAT FIRST SECOND.
MAY-BE...
...YOU DON'T REALLY LIKE HIM THAT MUCH AT ALL.

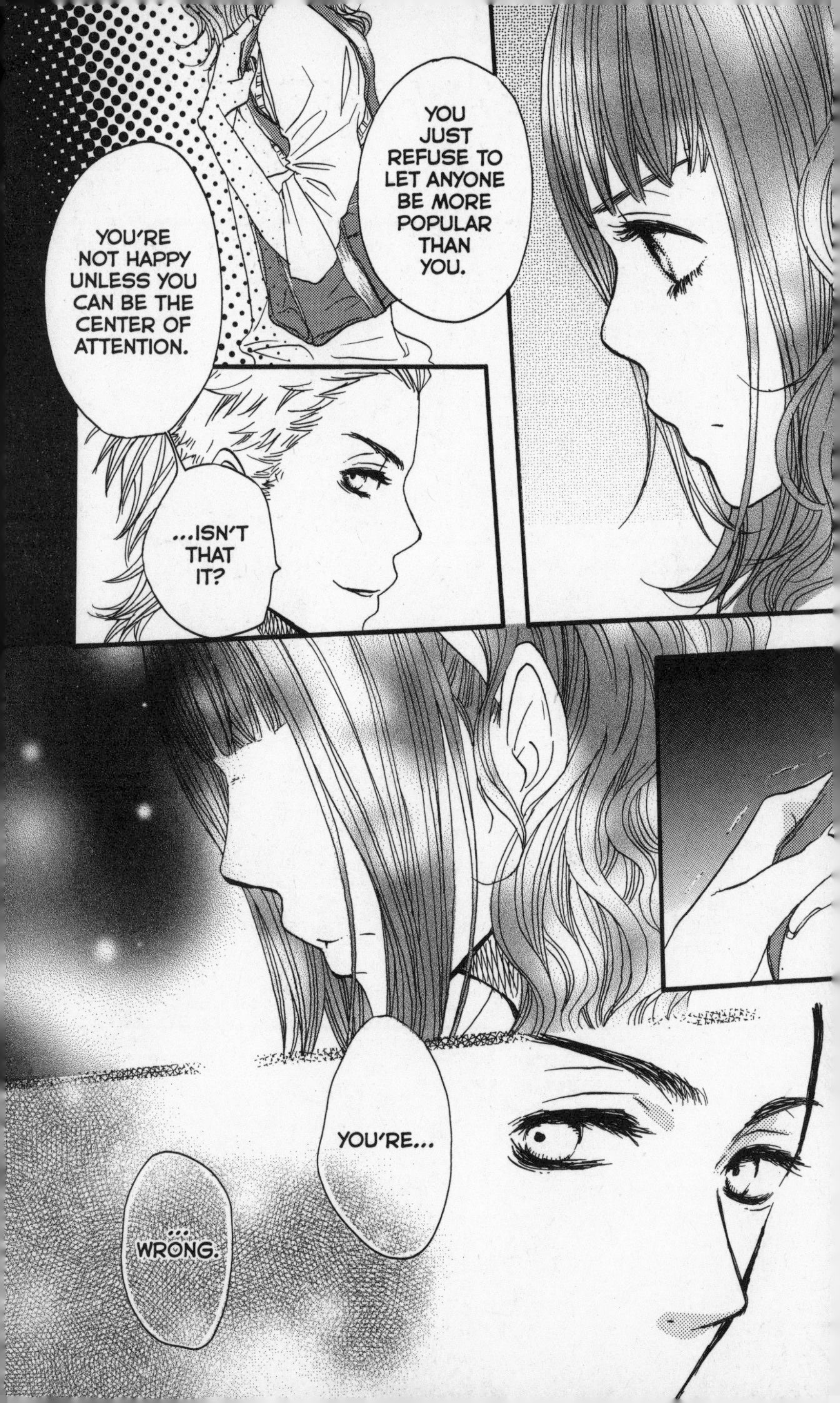
YOU JUST REFUSE TO LET ANYONE BE MORE POPULAR THAN YOU.
YOU'RE NOT HAPPY UNLESS YOU CAN BE THE CENTER OF ATTENTION.
...ISN'T THAT IT?
YOU'RE...
...WRONG.

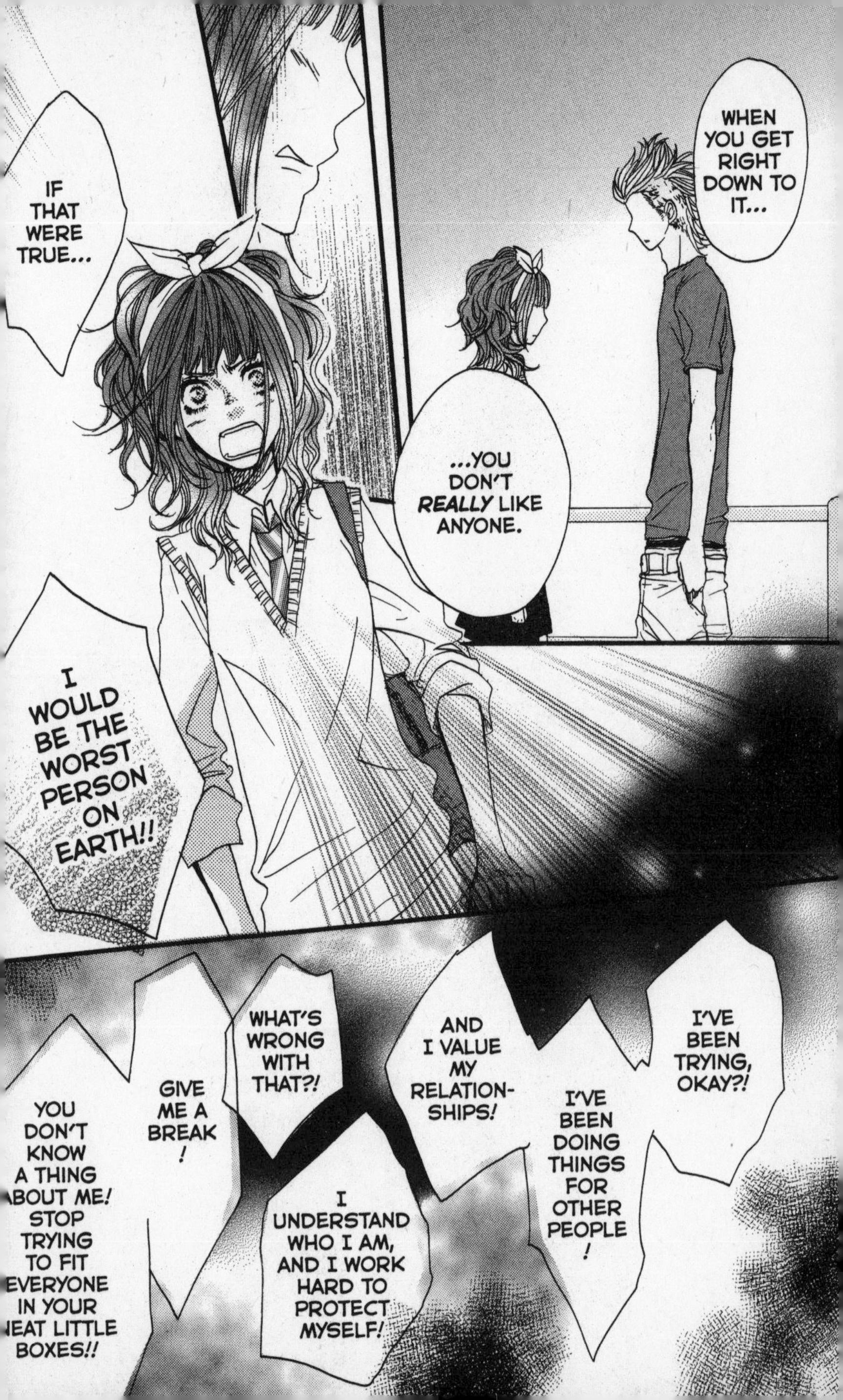
WHEN YOU GET RIGHT DOWN TO IT...
...YOU DON'T *REALLY* LIKE ANYONE.
IF THAT WERE TRUE...
I WOULD BE THE WORST PERSON ON EARTH!!
I'VE BEEN TRYING, OKAY?!
I'VE BEEN DOING THINGS FOR OTHER PEOPLE!
AND I VALUE *MY* RELATIONSHIPS!
WHAT'S WRONG WITH THAT?!
I UNDERSTAND WHO I AM, AND I WORK HARD TO PROTECT MYSELF!
GIVE ME A BREAK!
YOU DON'T KNOW A THING ABOUT ME! STOP TRYING TO FIT EVERYONE IN YOUR NEAT LITTLE BOXES!!

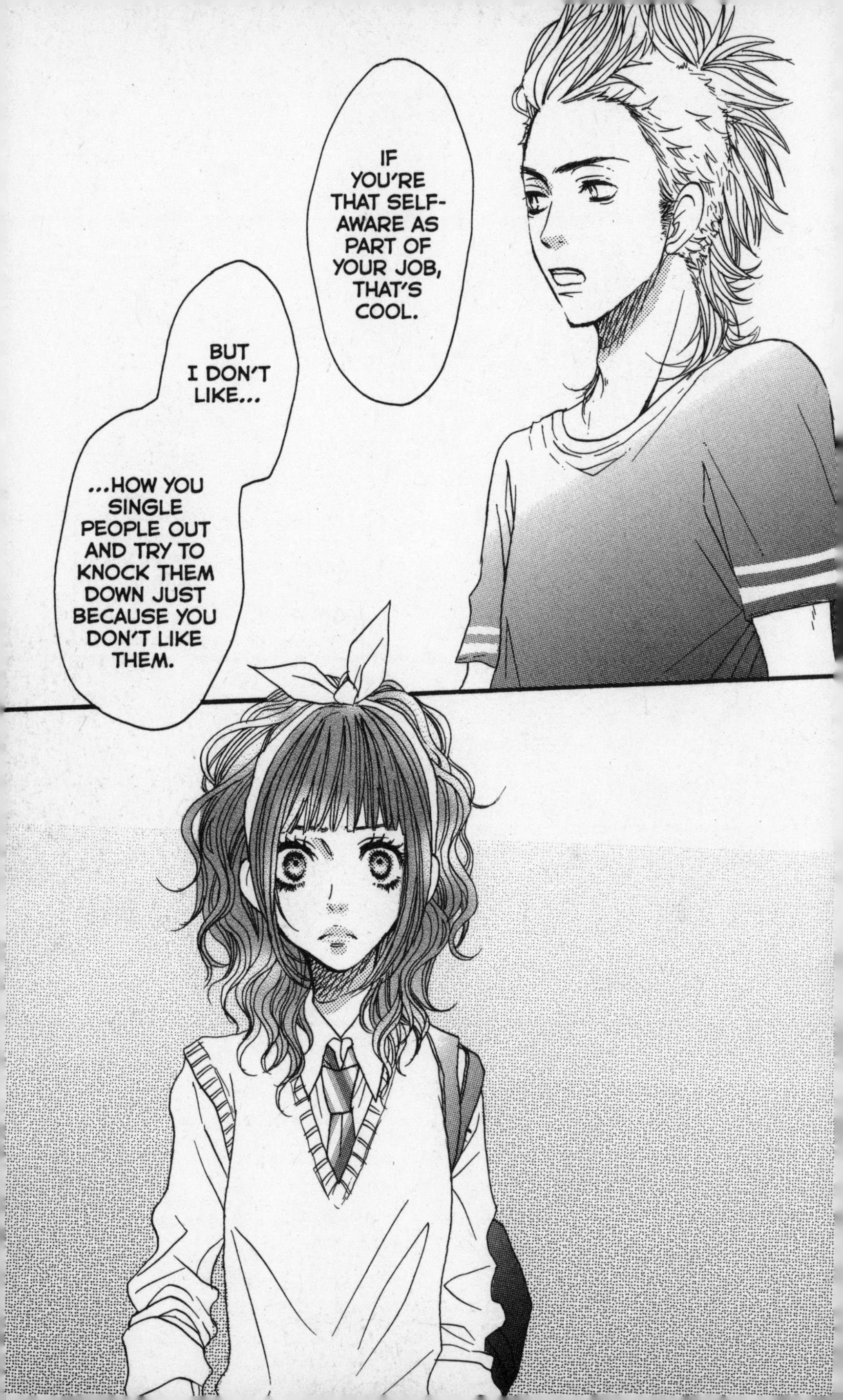
IF YOU'RE THAT SELF-AWARE AS PART OF YOUR JOB, THAT'S COOL.
BUT I DON'T LIKE...
...HOW YOU SINGLE PEOPLE OUT AND TRY TO KNOCK THEM DOWN JUST BECAUSE YOU DON'T LIKE THEM.

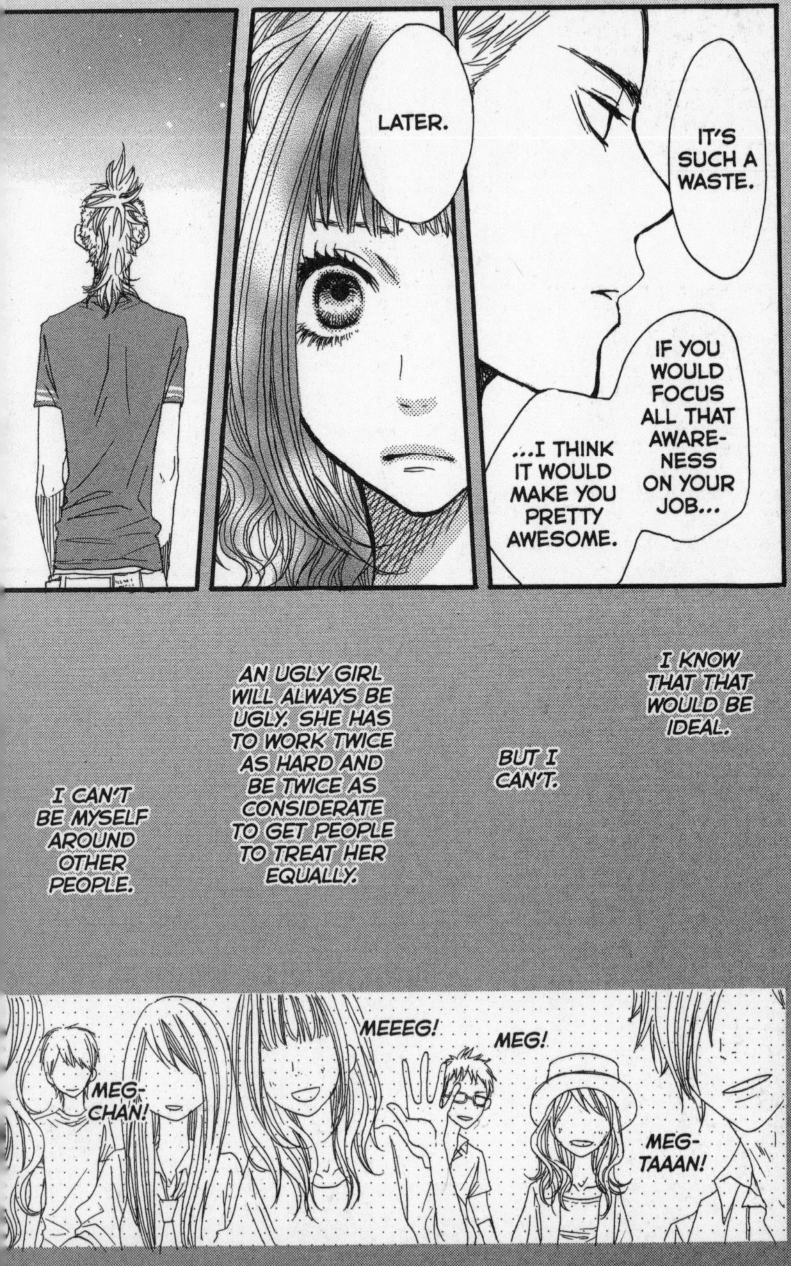
IT'S SUCH A WASTE.
IF YOU WOULD FOCUS ALL THAT AWARE-NESS ON YOUR JOB...
...I THINK IT WOULD MAKE YOU PRETTY AWESOME.
LATER.
I KNOW THAT THAT WOULD BE IDEAL.
BUT I CAN'T.
AN UGLY GIRL WILL ALWAYS BE UGLY. SHE HAS TO WORK TWICE AS HARD AND BE TWICE AS CONSIDERATE TO GET PEOPLE TO TREAT HER EQUALLY.
I CAN'T BE MYSELF AROUND OTHER PEOPLE.
MEG-TAAAN!
MEG!
MEEEG!
MEG-CHAN!

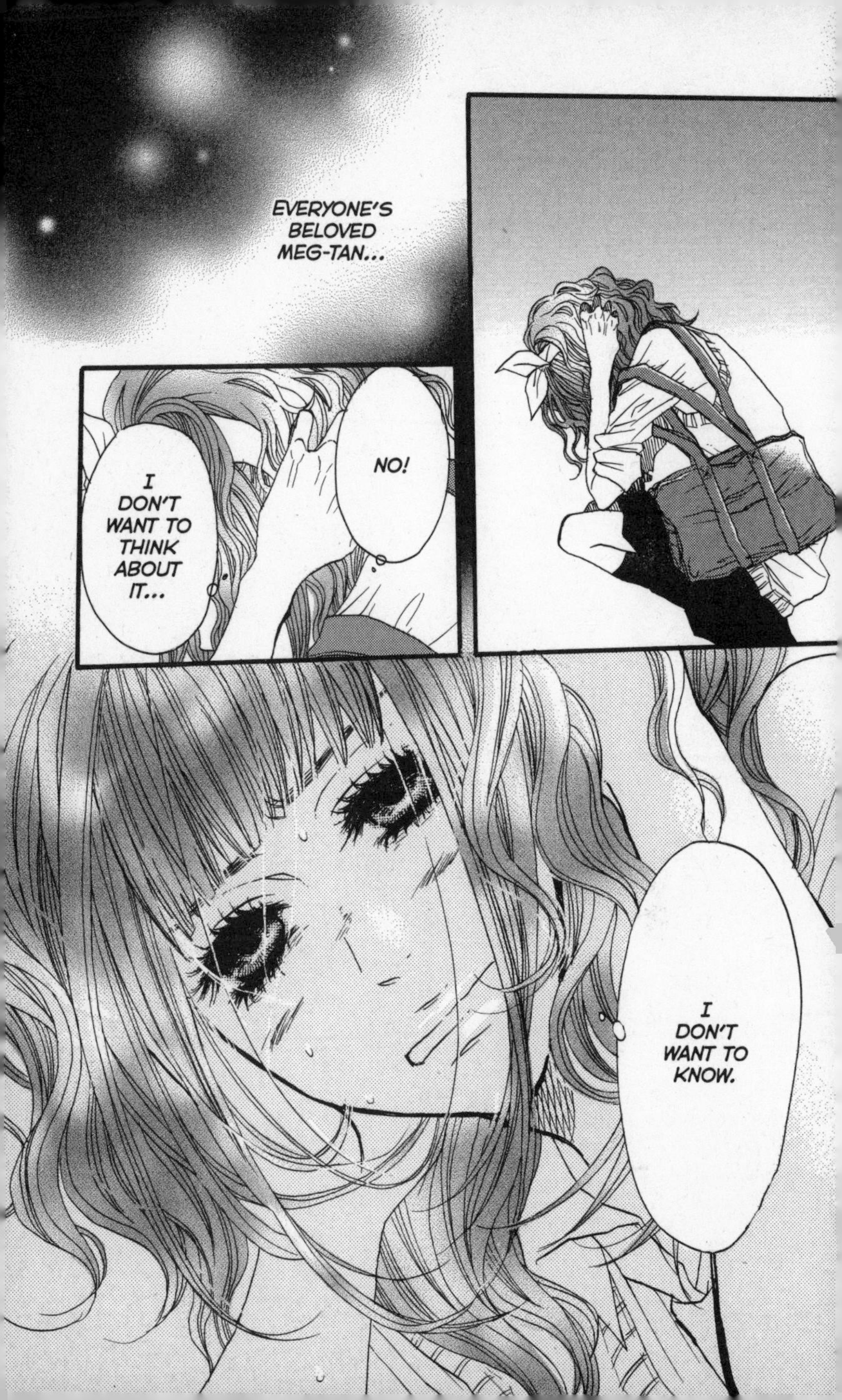
EVERYONE'S BELOVED MEG-TAN...
NO!
I DON'T WANT TO THINK ABOUT IT...
I DON'T WANT TO KNOW.

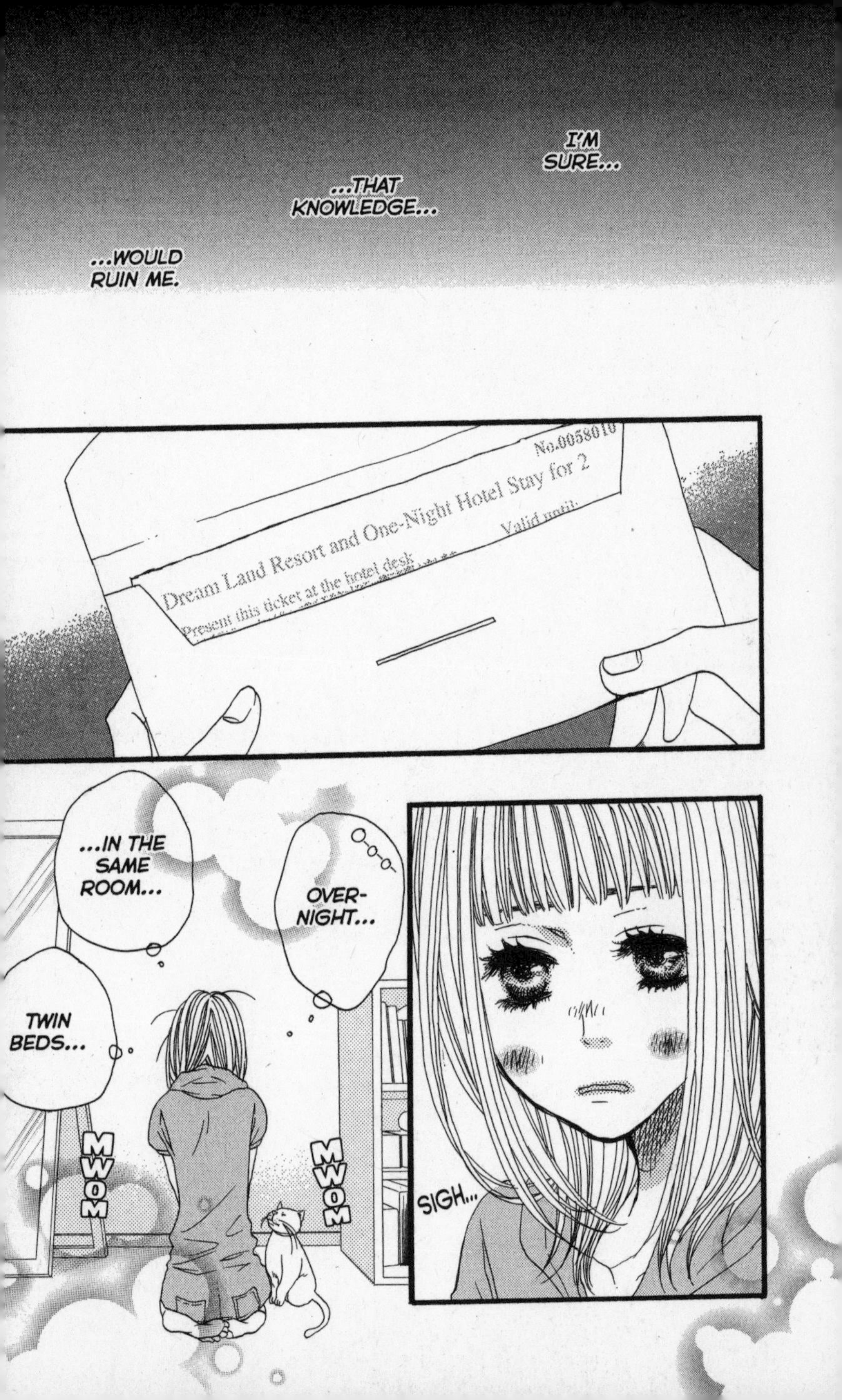

I'M SURE...
...THAT KNOWLEDGE...
...WOULD RUIN ME.
No.0058010
Dream Land Resort and One-Night Hotel Stay for 2
Present this ticket at the hotel desk
SIGH...
OVER-NIGHT...
...IN THE SAME ROOM...
TWIN BEDS...
MWOM
MWOM

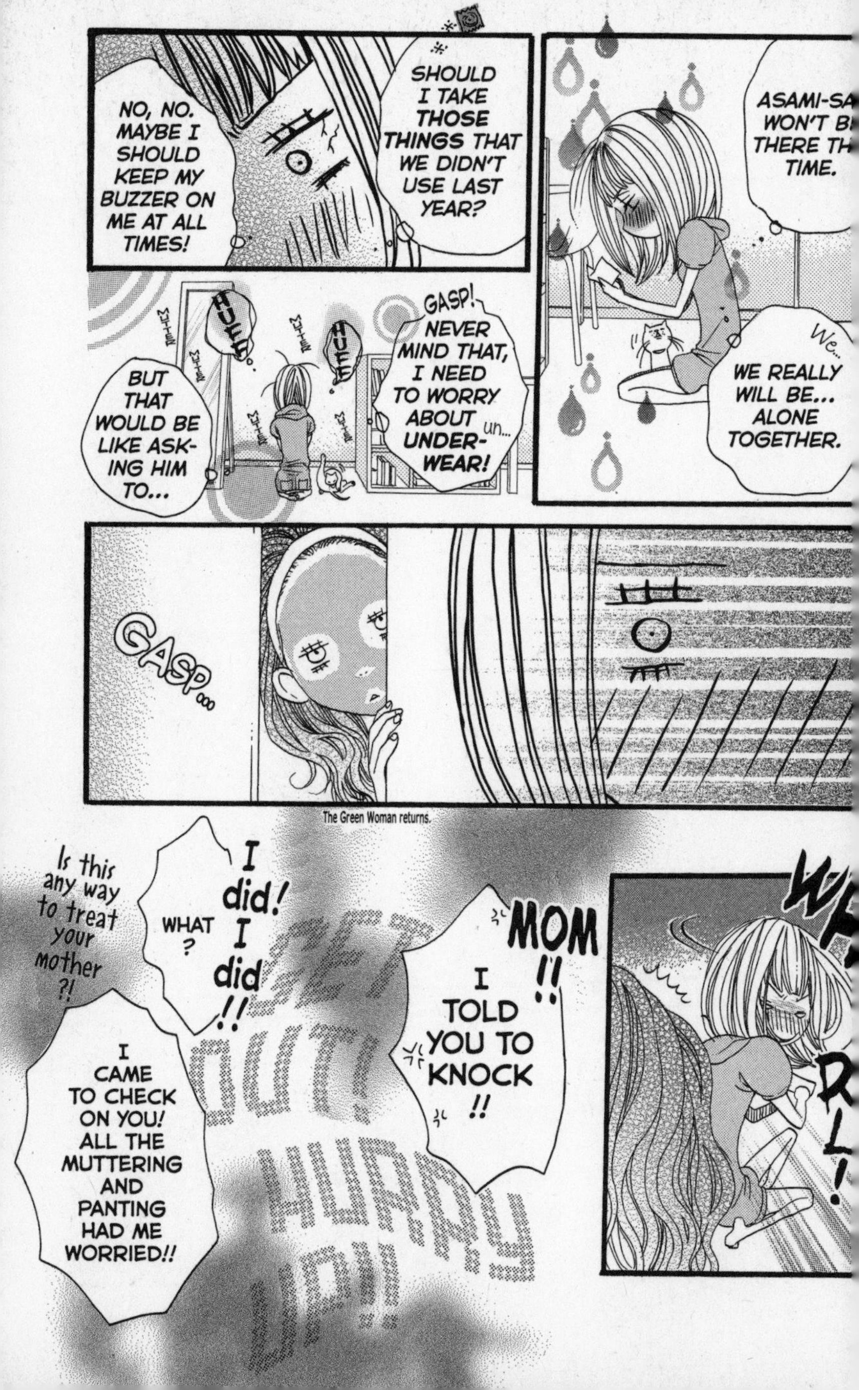
ASAMI-SA
WON'T B
THERE TH
TIME.
We...
WE REALLY WILL BE... ALONE TOGETHER.
SHOULD I TAKE THOSE THINGS THAT WE DIDN'T USE LAST YEAR?
NO, NO. MAYBE I SHOULD KEEP MY BUZZER ON ME AT ALL TIMES!
GASP! NEVER MIND THAT, I NEED TO WORRY ABOUT UNDER- WEAR!
un...
HUFF
HUFF
MUTTER
MUTTER
MUTTER
MUTTER
MUTTER
BUT THAT WOULD BE LIKE ASKING HIM TO...
GASP...
The Green Woman returns.
MOM!!
I TOLD YOU TO KNOCK!!
GET OUT!
HURRY UP!!
WHAT?
I did! I did!!
Is this any way to treat your mother?!
I CAME TO CHECK ON YOU! ALL THE MUTTERING AND PANTING HAD ME WORRIED!!

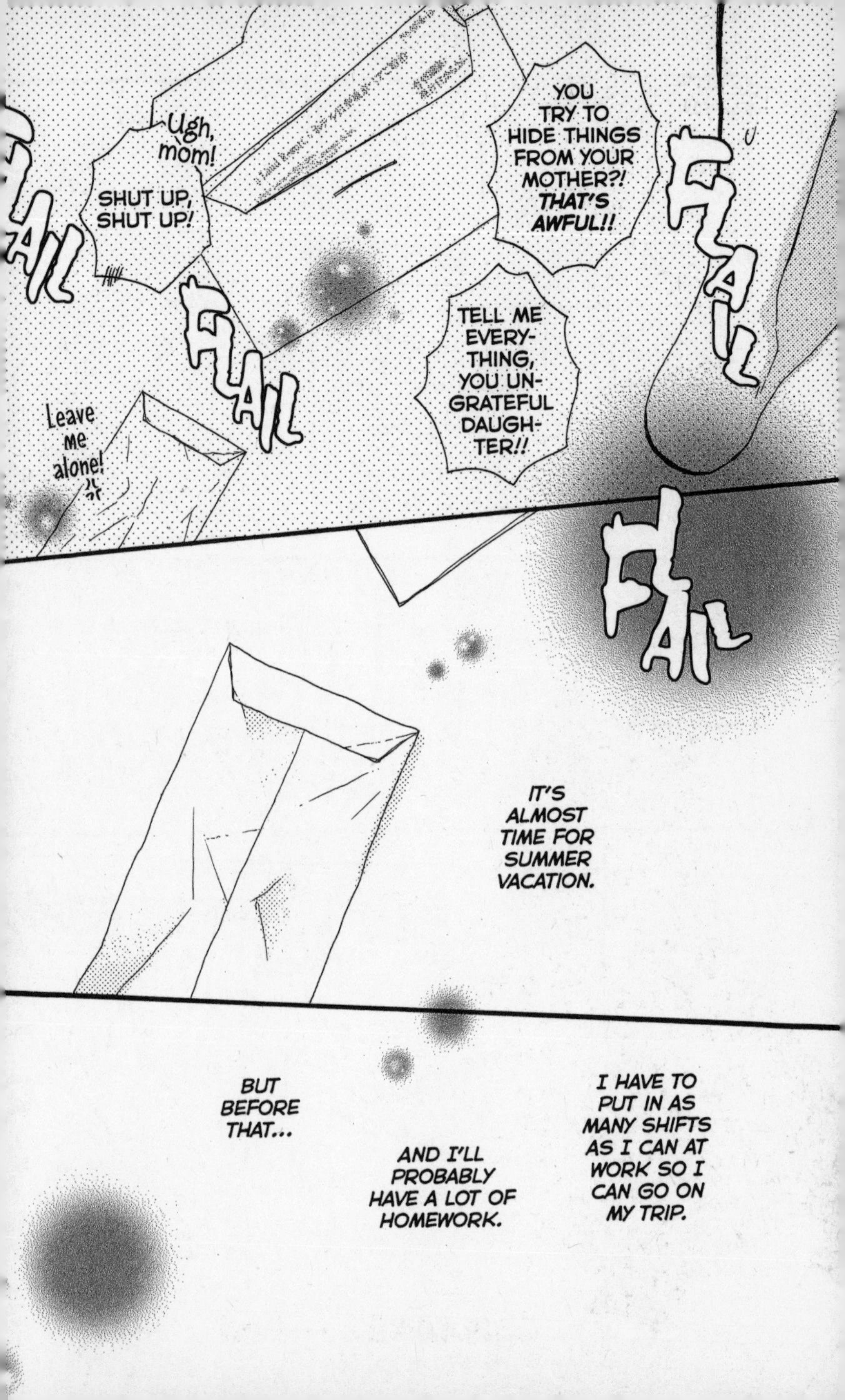
FLAIL
YOU TRY TO HIDE THINGS FROM YOUR MOTHER?! THAT'S AWFUL!!
TELL ME EVERYTHING, YOU UNGRATEFUL DAUGHTER!!
FLAIL
Ugh, mom!
SHUT UP, SHUT UP!
FLAIL
Leave me alone!
FLAIL
IT'S ALMOST TIME FOR SUMMER VACATION.
I HAVE TO PUT IN AS MANY SHIFTS AS I CAN AT WORK SO I CAN GO ON MY TRIP.
AND I'LL PROBABLY HAVE A LOT OF HOMEWORK.
BUT BEFORE THAT...

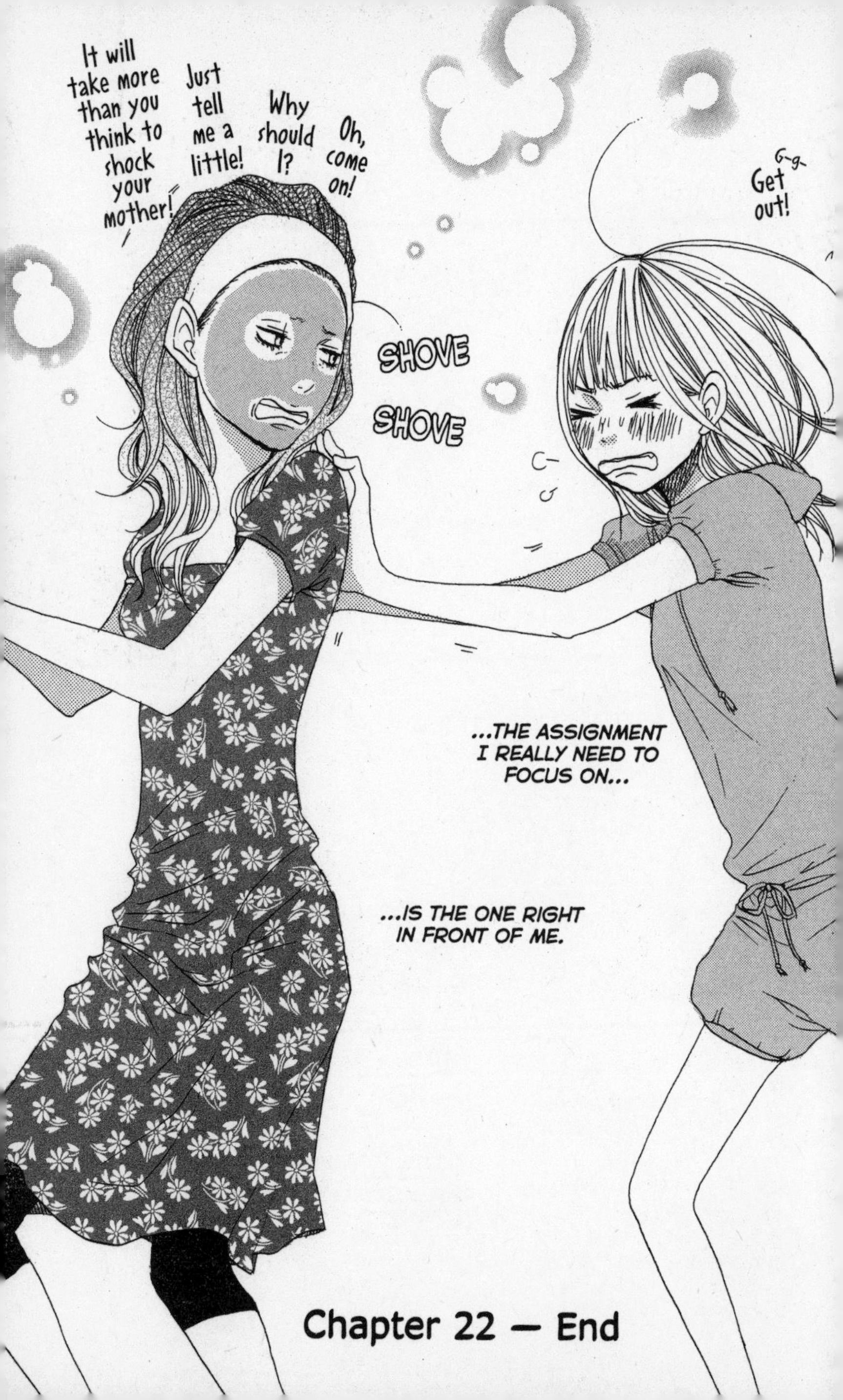
G-g- Get out!
Oh, come on!
Why should I?
Just tell me a little!
It will take more than you think to shock your mother!
SHOVE
SHOVE
...THE ASSIGNMENT I REALLY NEED TO FOCUS ON...
...IS THE ONE RIGHT IN FRONT OF ME.
Chapter 22 — End

Say "I love you".

Kanae Hazuki

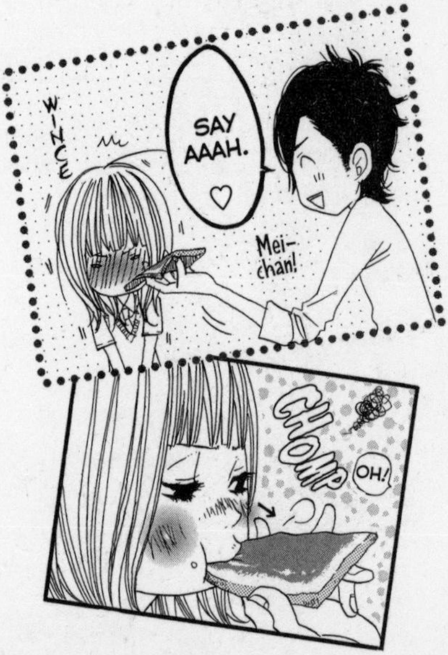
SAY AAAH. ♡
Mei-chan!
WINCE
CHOMP
OH!

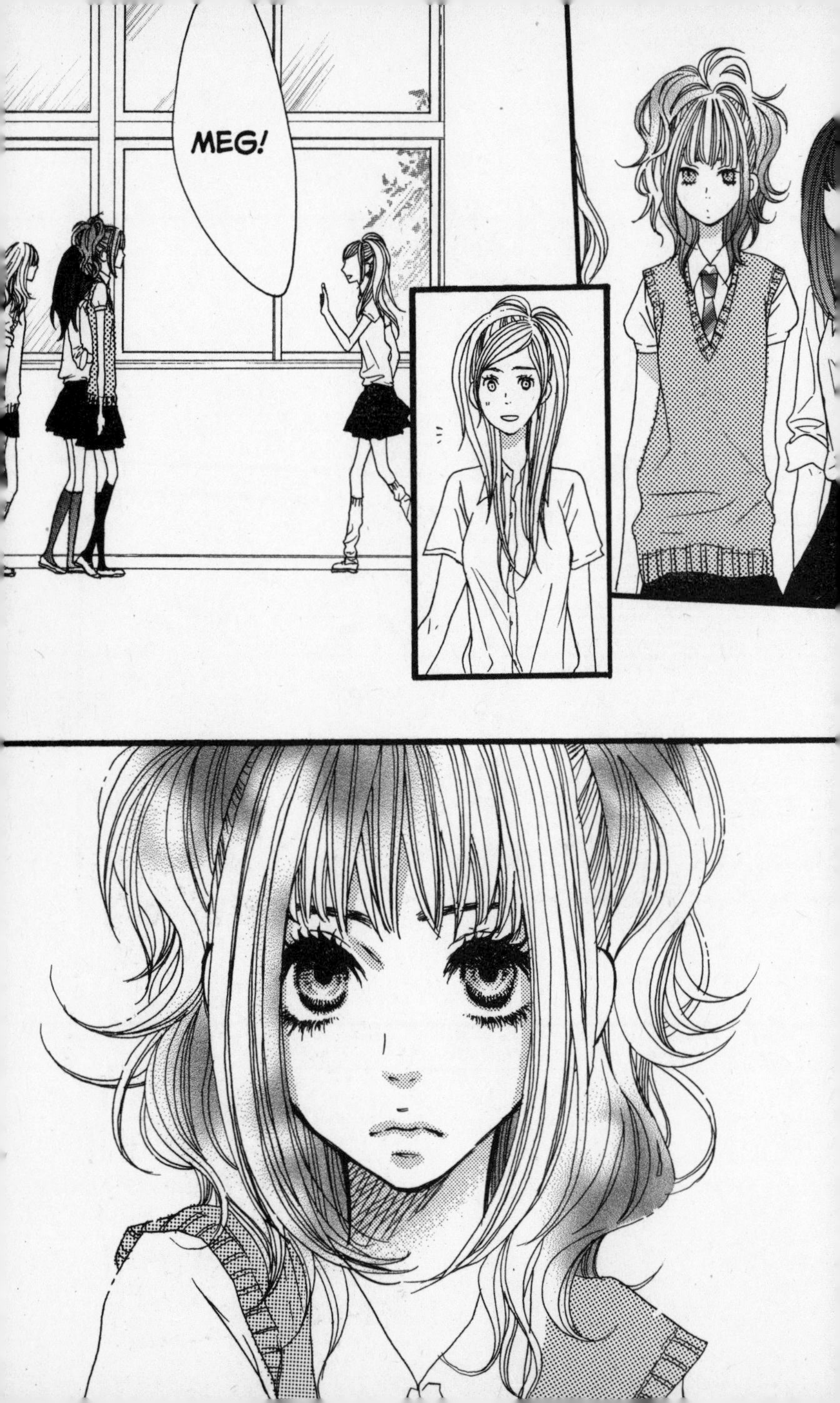
MEG!

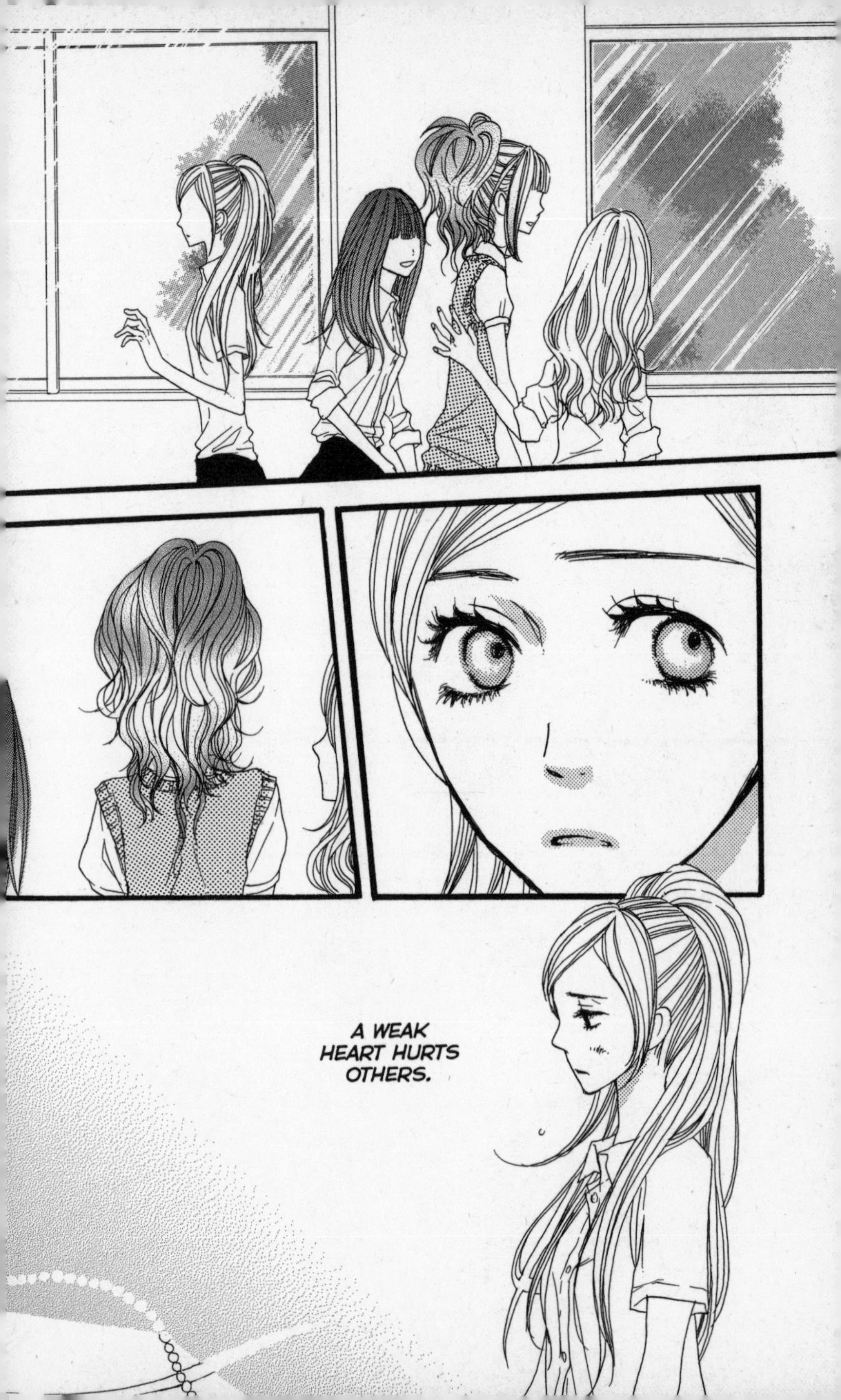
A WEAK HEART HURTS OTHERS.

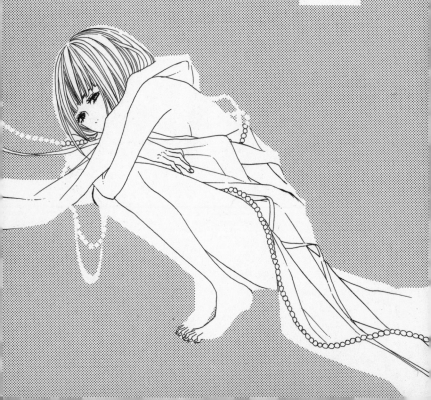

Chapter 23

EVERY-ONE IS STRUG-GLING.

EVERYONE IS TRYING TO GET STRONGER.

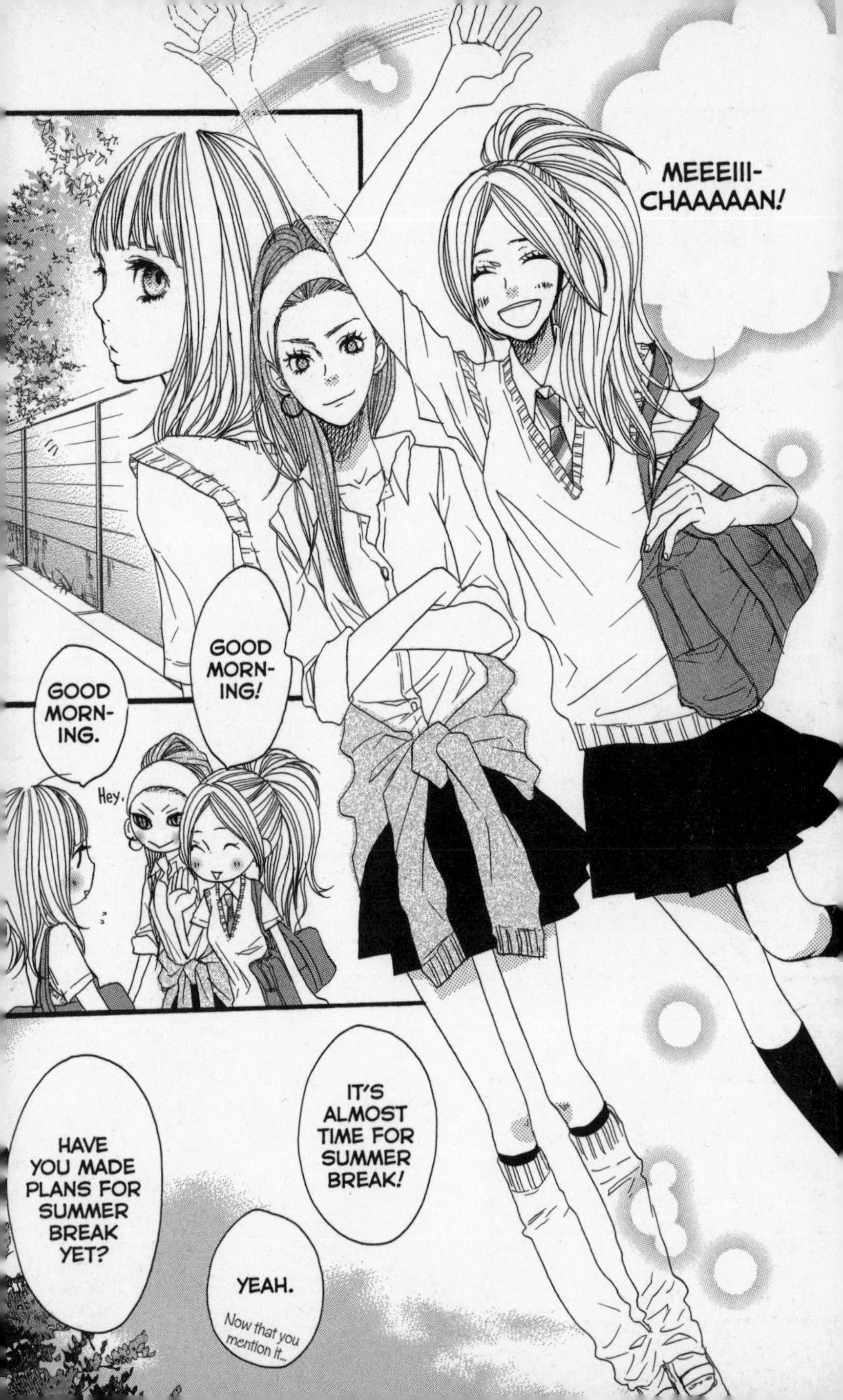
MEEEIII-
CHAAAAAN!
GOOD MORN-ING!
GOOD MORN-ING.
Hey.
IT'S ALMOST TIME FOR SUMMER BREAK!
HAVE YOU MADE PLANS FOR SUMMER BREAK YET?
YEAH.
Now that you mention it...

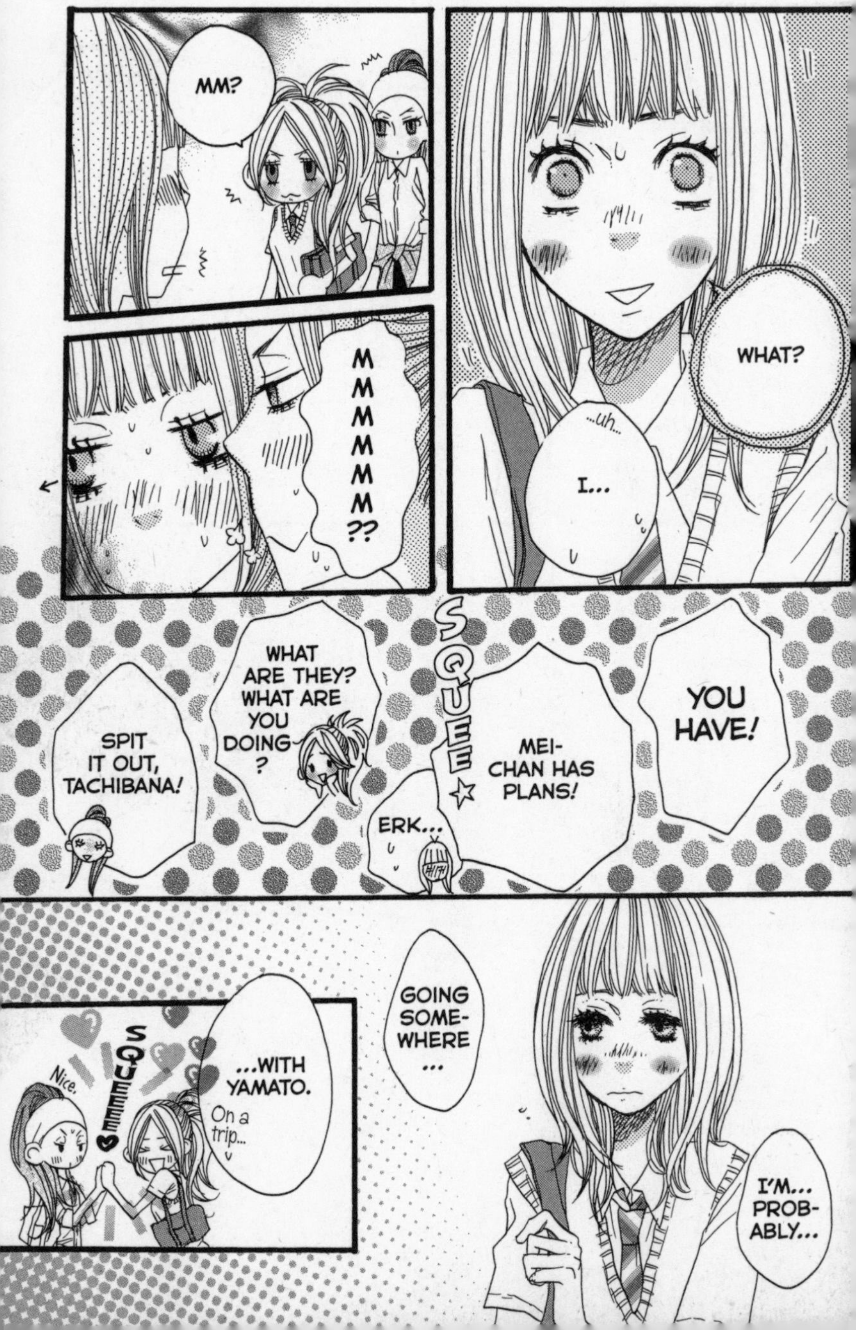
WHAT?
...uh...
I...
MM?
MMMMMMM??
YOU HAVE!
MEI-CHAN HAS PLANS!
SQUEE☆
ERK...
WHAT ARE THEY? WHAT ARE YOU DOING~?
SPIT IT OUT, TACHIBANA!
I'M... PROBABLY...
GOING SOMEWHERE...
...WITH YAMATO.
On a trip...
SQUEEEE♥
Nice.

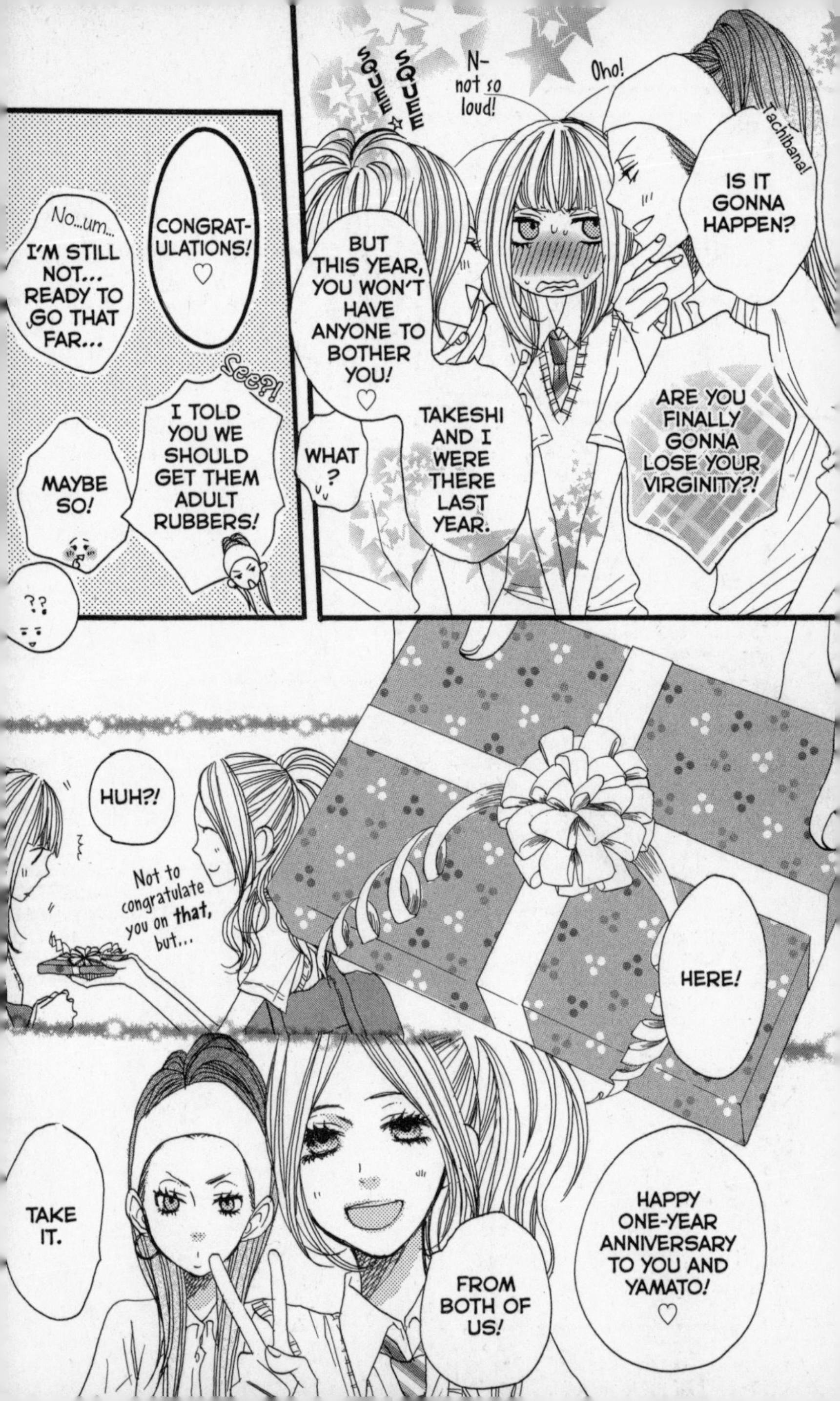
Oho!
Tachibana!
IS IT GONNA HAPPEN?
N- not so loud!
SQUEE ☆ SQUEE
ARE YOU FINALLY GONNA LOSE YOUR VIRGINITY?!
BUT THIS YEAR, YOU WON'T HAVE ANYONE TO BOTHER YOU! ♡
TAKESHI AND I WERE THERE LAST YEAR.
WHAT?
CONGRAT-ULATIONS! ♡
No...um... I'M STILL NOT... READY TO GO THAT FAR...
See?!
I TOLD YOU WE SHOULD GET THEM ADULT RUBBERS!
MAYBE SO!
??
Not to congratulate you on that, but...
HUH?!
HERE!
HAPPY ONE-YEAR ANNIVERSARY TO YOU AND YAMATO! ♡
FROM BOTH OF US!
TAKE IT.

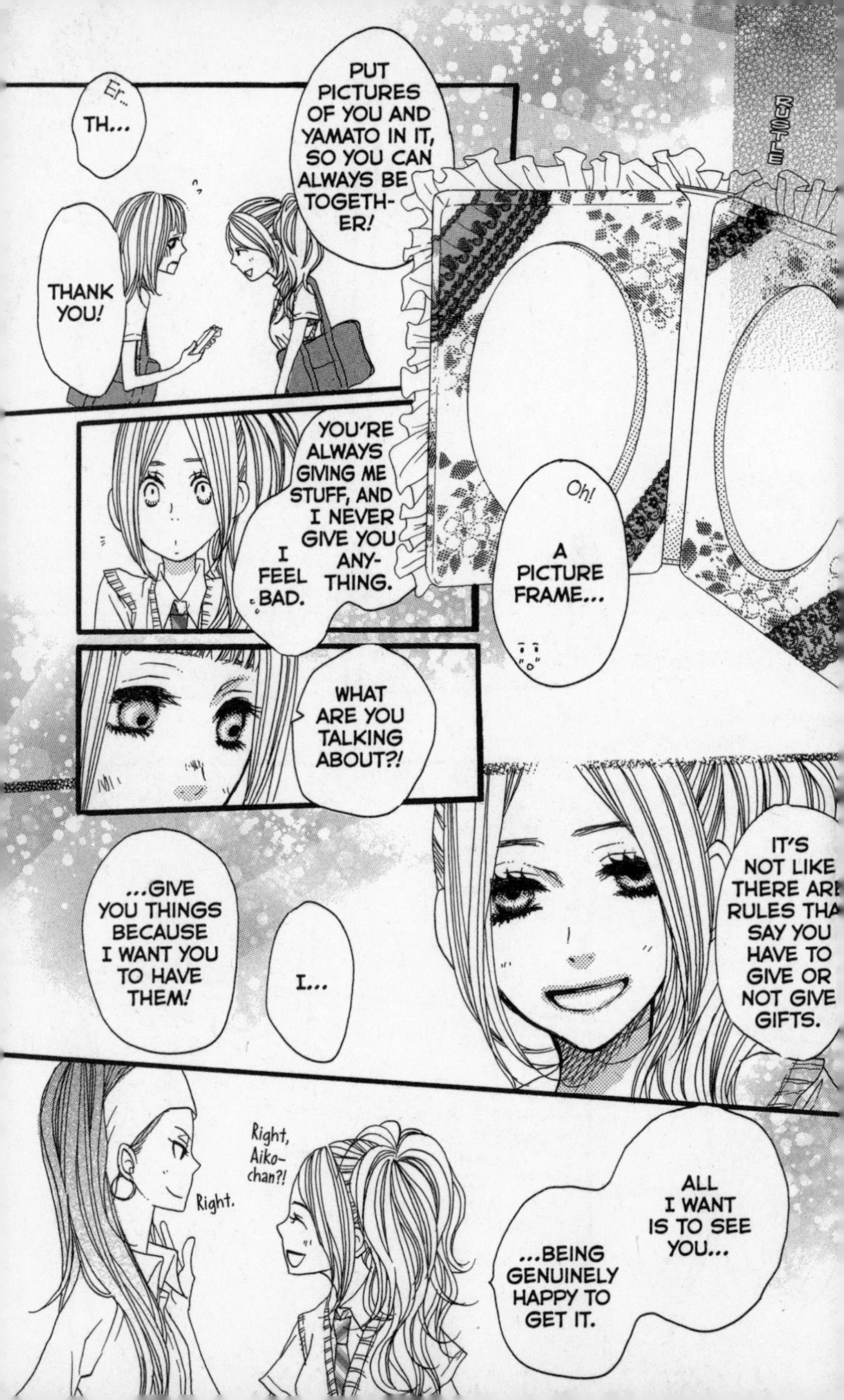
RUSTLE
Oh!
A PICTURE FRAME...
PUT PICTURES OF YOU AND YAMATO IN IT, SO YOU CAN ALWAYS BE TOGETH-ER!
Er... TH...
THANK YOU!
YOU'RE ALWAYS GIVING ME STUFF, AND I NEVER GIVE YOU ANY-THING.
I FEEL BAD.
WHAT ARE YOU TALKING ABOUT?!
IT'S NOT LIKE THERE ARE RULES THA SAY YOU HAVE TO GIVE OR NOT GIVE GIFTS.
I...
...GIVE YOU THINGS BECAUSE I WANT YOU TO HAVE THEM!
ALL I WANT IS TO SEE YOU...
...BEING GENUINELY HAPPY TO GET IT.
Right, Aiko-chan?!
Right.

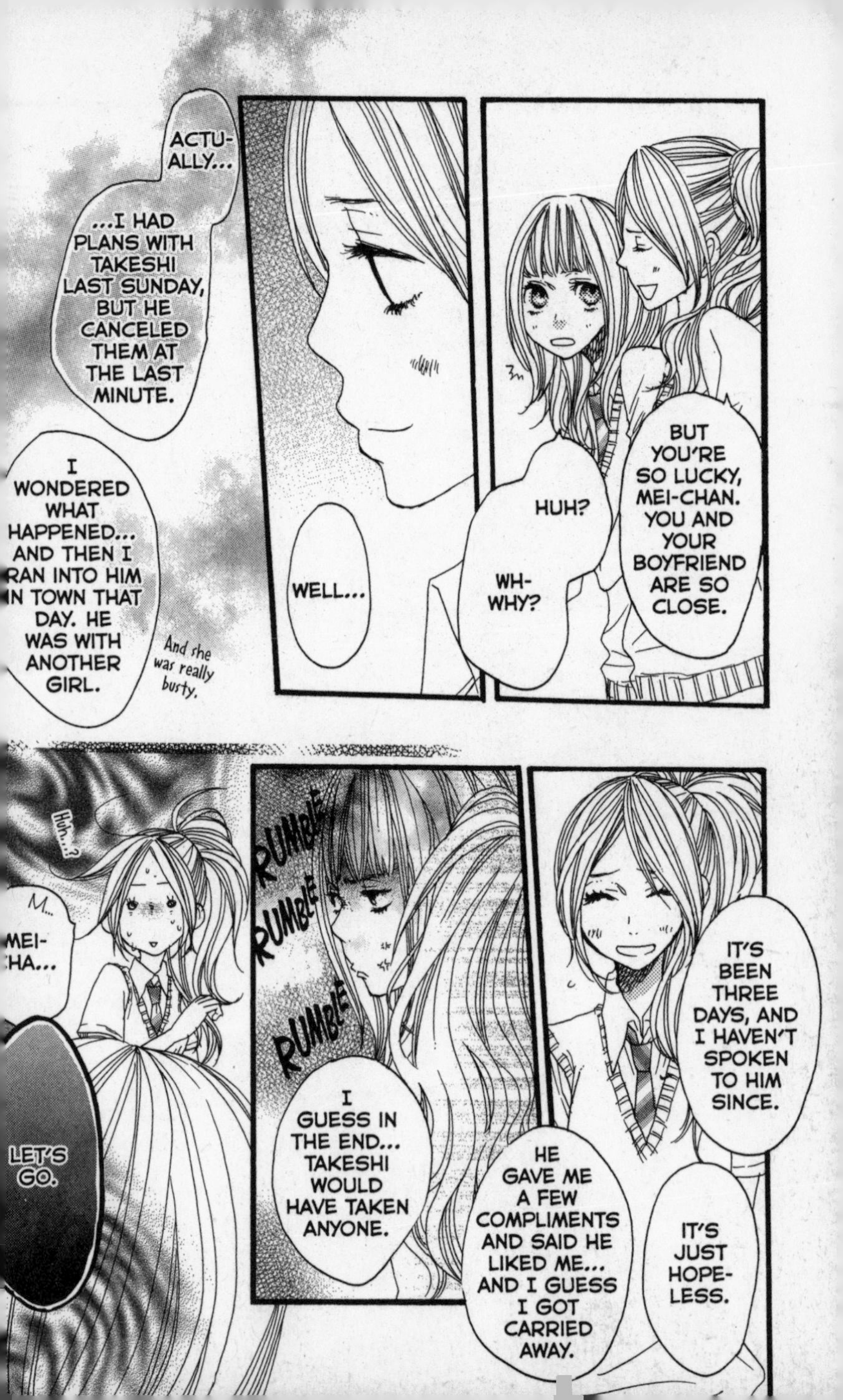
BUT YOU'RE SO LUCKY, MEI-CHAN. YOU AND YOUR BOYFRIEND ARE SO CLOSE.
HUH?
WH-WHY?
WELL...
ACTU-ALLY...
...I HAD PLANS WITH TAKESHI LAST SUNDAY, BUT HE CANCELED THEM AT THE LAST MINUTE.
I WONDERED WHAT HAPPENED... AND THEN I RAN INTO HIM IN TOWN THAT DAY. HE WAS WITH ANOTHER GIRL.
And she was really busty.
IT'S BEEN THREE DAYS, AND I HAVEN'T SPOKEN TO HIM SINCE.
IT'S JUST HOPELESS.
HE GAVE ME A FEW COMPLIMENTS AND SAID HE LIKED ME... AND I GUESS I GOT CARRIED AWAY.
RUMBLE
RUMBLE
RUMBLE
I GUESS IN THE END... TAKESHI WOULD HAVE TAKEN ANYONE.
Huh...?
M...
MEI-
HA...
LET'S GO.

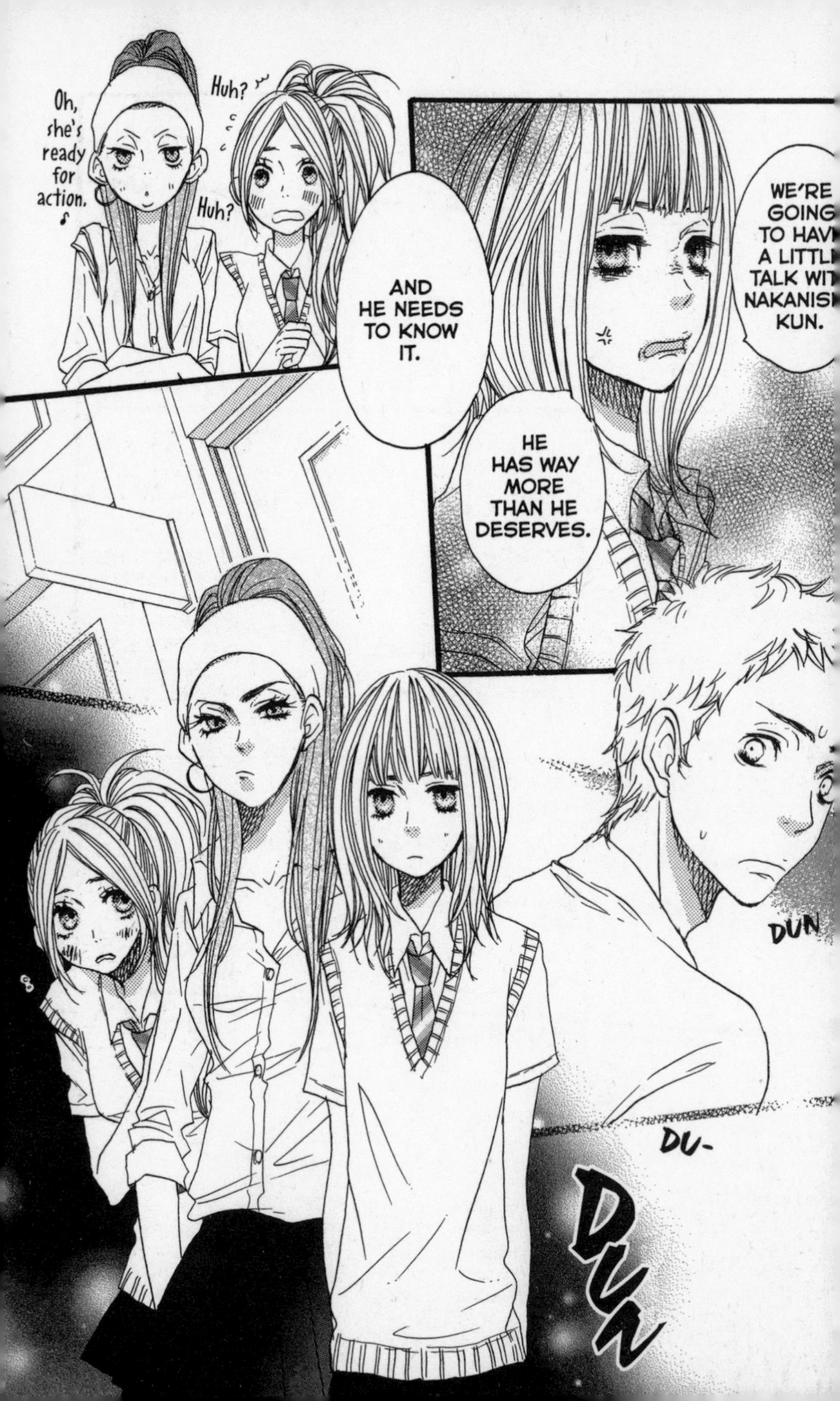
WE'RE GOING TO HAV A LITTL TALK WIT NAKANIS KUN.
HE HAS WAY MORE THAN HE DESERVES.
AND HE NEEDS TO KNOW IT.
Oh, she's ready for action.
Huh?
Huh?
DUN
DU-
DUN

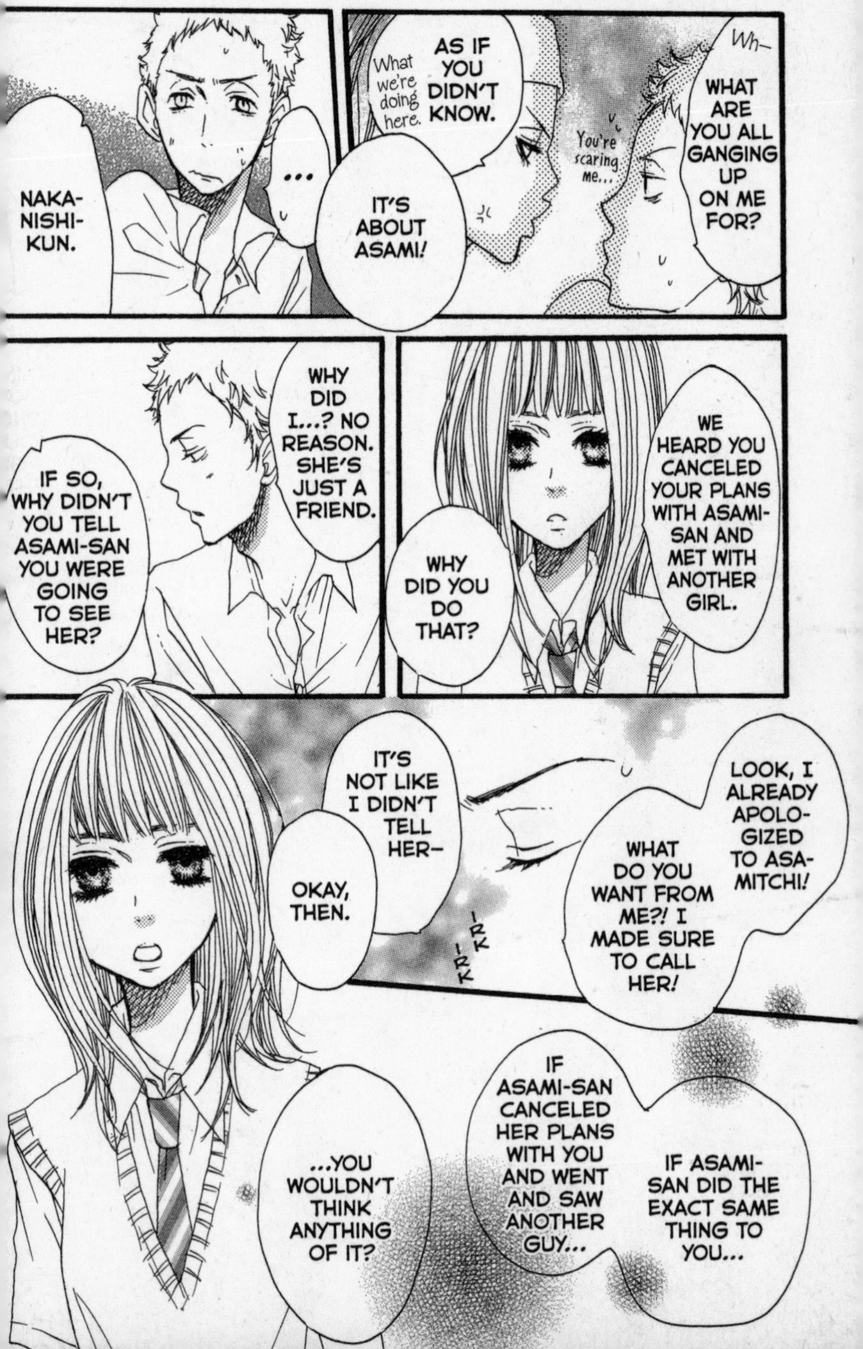
Wh–
WHAT ARE YOU ALL GANGING UP ON ME FOR?
You're scaring me...
AS IF YOU DIDN'T KNOW.
What we're doing here.
IT'S ABOUT ASAMI!
...
NAKA-NISHI-KUN.
WE HEARD YOU CANCELED YOUR PLANS WITH ASAMI-SAN AND MET WITH ANOTHER GIRL.
WHY DID YOU DO THAT?
WHY DID I...? NO REASON. SHE'S JUST A FRIEND.
IF SO, WHY DIDN'T YOU TELL ASAMI-SAN YOU WERE GOING TO SEE HER?
LOOK, I ALREADY APOLO-GIZED TO ASA-MITCHI!
WHAT DO YOU WANT FROM ME?! I MADE SURE TO CALL HER!
IT'S NOT LIKE I DIDN'T TELL HER–
IRK IRK
OKAY, THEN.
IF ASAMI-SAN DID THE EXACT SAME THING TO YOU...
IF ASAMI-SAN CANCELED HER PLANS WITH YOU AND WENT AND SAW ANOTHER GUY...
...YOU WOULDN'T THINK ANYTHING OF IT?

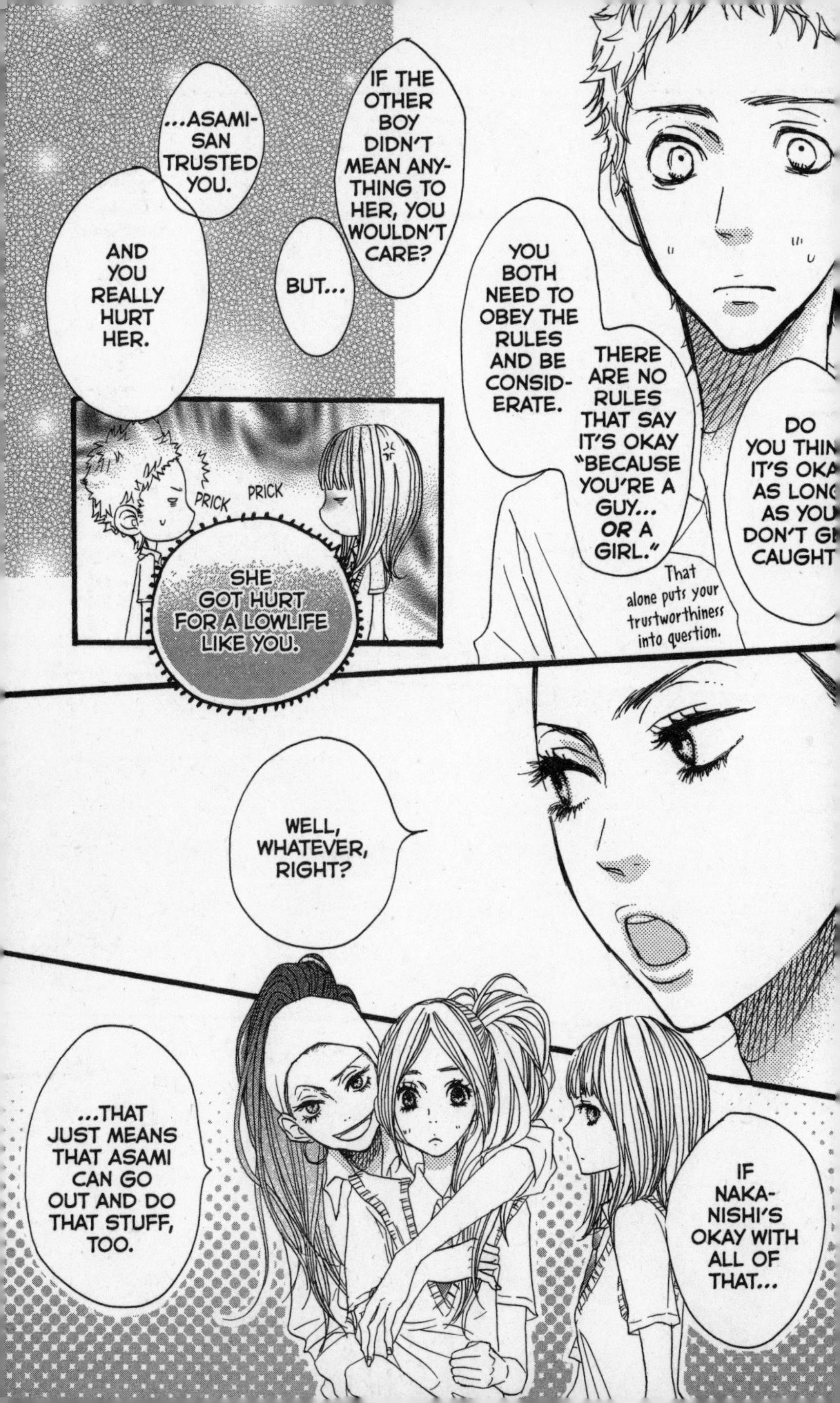

DO YOU THIN IT'S OKA AS LONG AS YOU DON'T G CAUGHT
THERE ARE NO RULES THAT SAY IT'S OKAY "BECAUSE YOU'RE A GUY... OR A GIRL."
That alone puts your trustworthiness into question.
YOU BOTH NEED TO OBEY THE RULES AND BE CONSIDERATE.
IF THE OTHER BOY DIDN'T MEAN ANYTHING TO HER, YOU WOULDN'T CARE?
BUT...
...ASAMI-SAN TRUSTED YOU.
AND YOU REALLY HURT HER.
PRICK
PRICK
SHE GOT HURT FOR A LOWLIFE LIKE YOU.
WELL, WHATEVER, RIGHT?
IF NAKANISHI'S OKAY WITH ALL OF THAT...
...THAT JUST MEANS THAT ASAMI CAN GO OUT AND DO THAT STUFF, TOO.

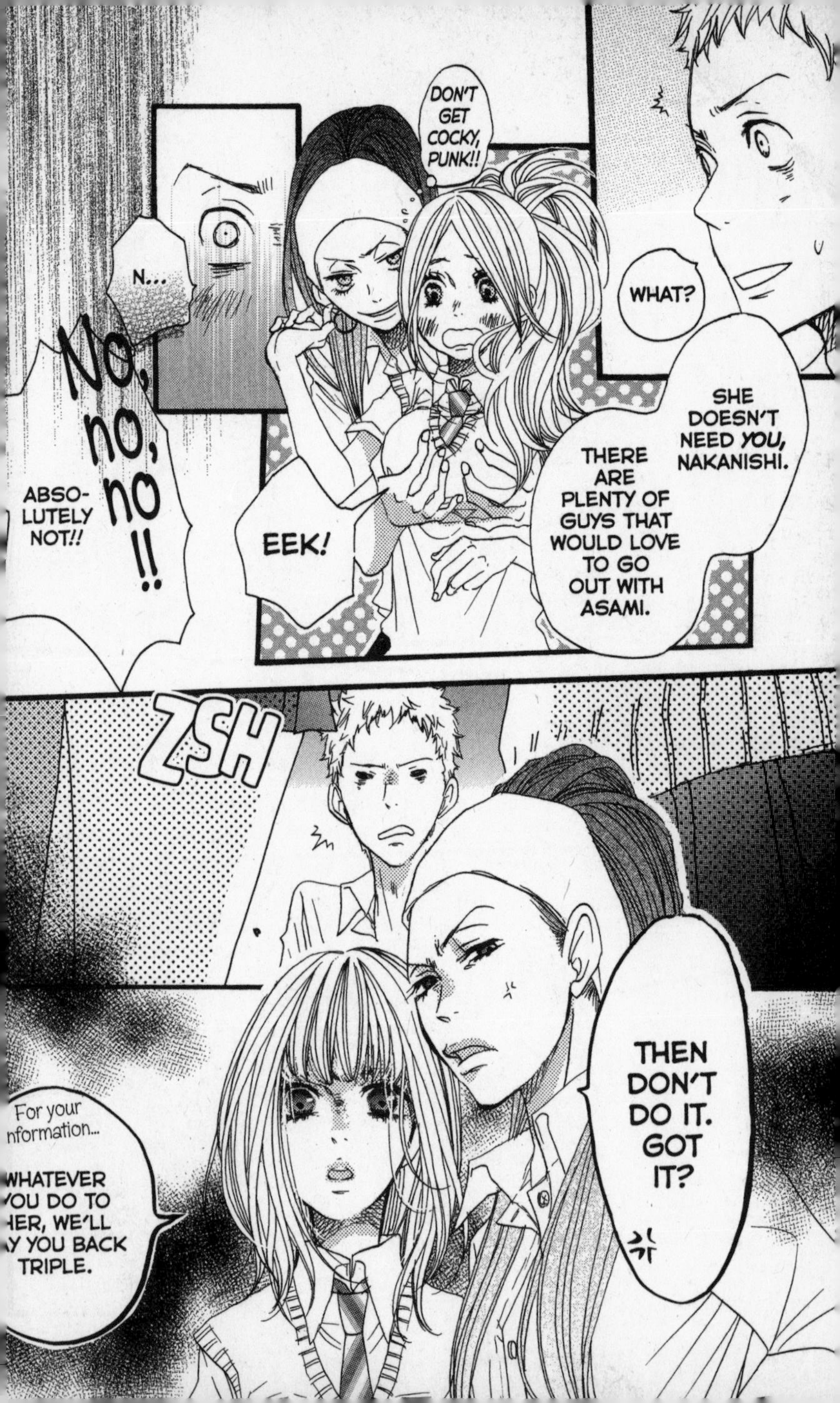
WHAT?
DON'T GET COCKY, PUNK!!
SHE DOESN'T NEED *YOU*, NAKANISHI.
THERE ARE PLENTY OF GUYS THAT WOULD LOVE TO GO OUT WITH ASAMI.
EEK!
N...
No, no, no!!
ABSOLUTELY NOT!!
ZSH
THEN DON'T DO IT. GOT IT?
For your nformation...
WHATEVER OU DO TO ER, WE'LL Y YOU BACK TRIPLE.

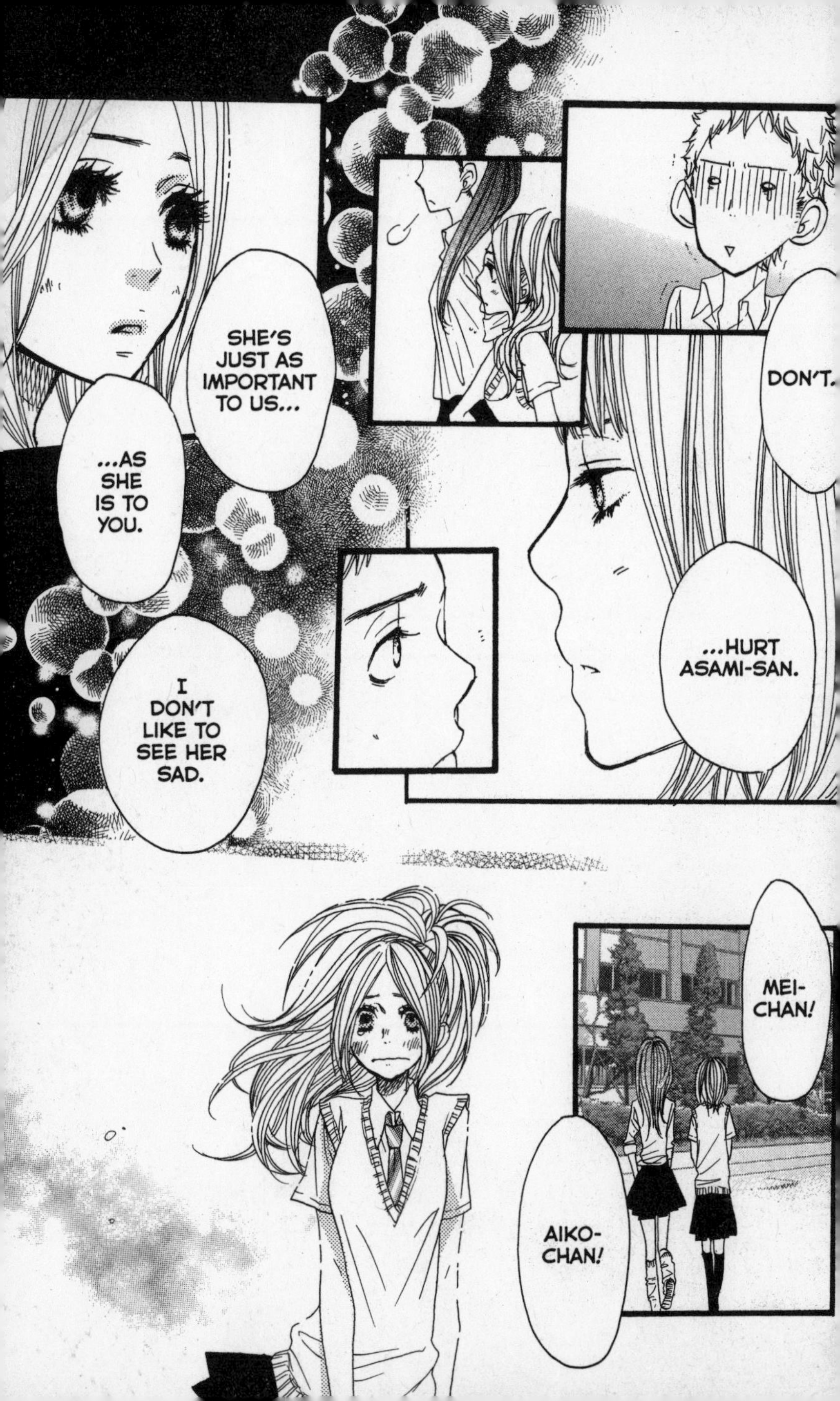
DON'T.
...HURT ASAMI-SAN.
SHE'S JUST AS IMPORTANT TO US...
...AS SHE IS TO YOU.
I DON'T LIKE TO SEE HER SAD.
MEI-CHAN!
AIKO-CHAN!

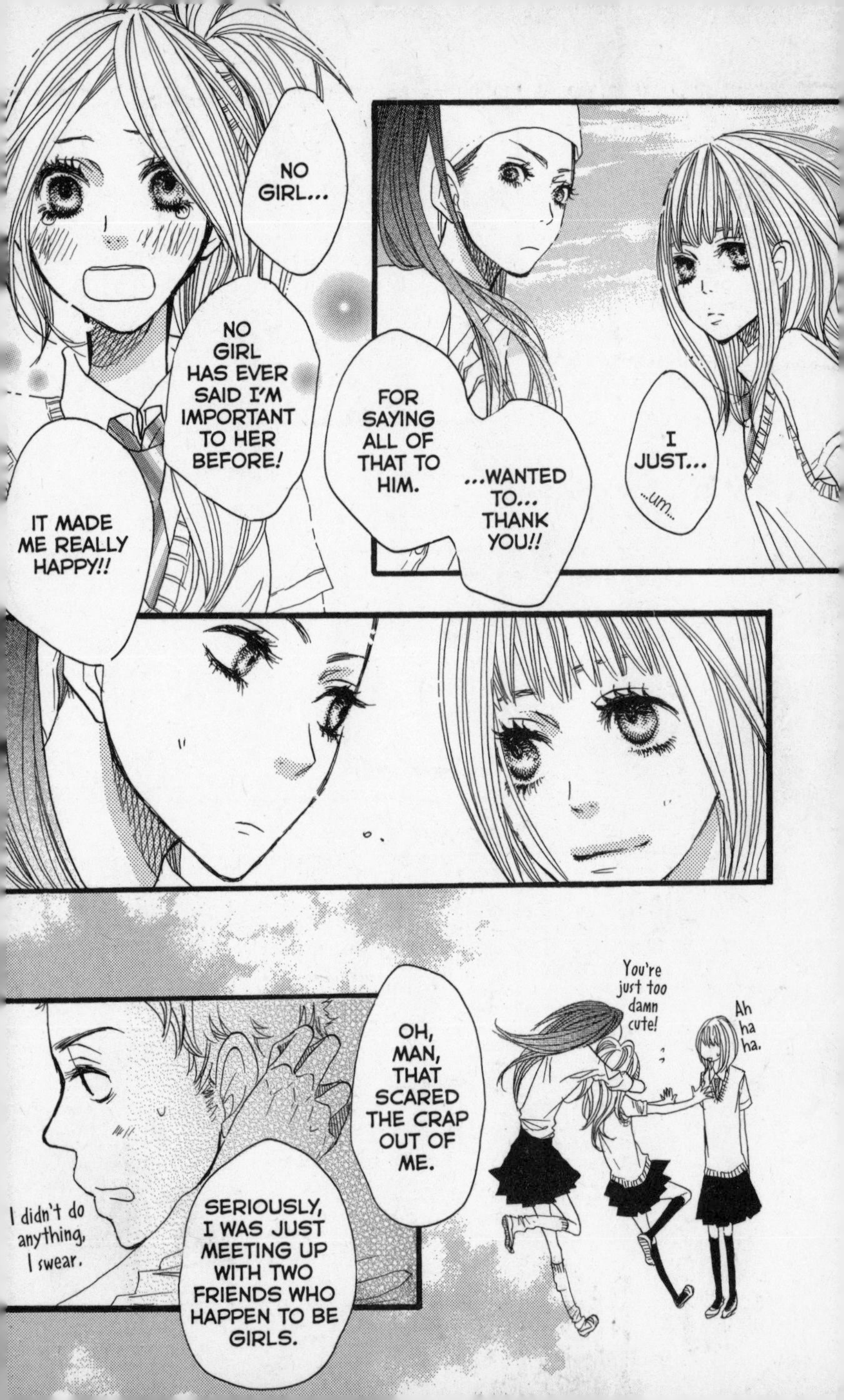
I JUST...
...um...
...WANTED TO... THANK YOU!!
FOR SAYING ALL OF THAT TO HIM.
NO GIRL...
NO GIRL HAS EVER SAID I'M IMPORTANT TO HER BEFORE!
IT MADE ME REALLY HAPPY!!
Ah ha ha.
You're just too damn cute!
OH, MAN, THAT SCARED THE CRAP OUT OF ME.
SERIOUSLY, I WAS JUST MEETING UP WITH TWO FRIENDS WHO HAPPEN TO BE GIRLS.
I didn't do anything, I swear.

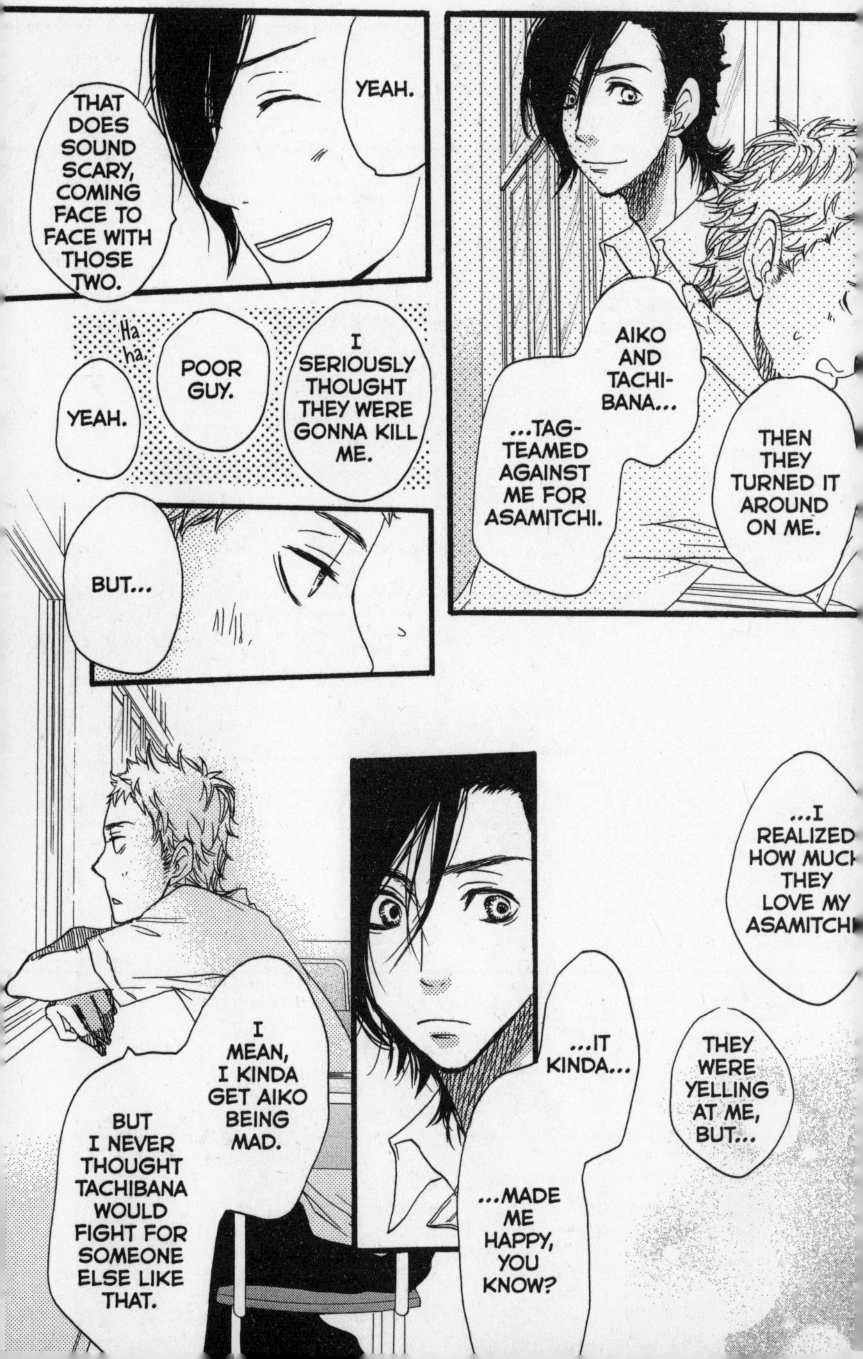
AIKO AND TACHI-BANA...
...TAG-TEAMED AGAINST ME FOR ASAMITCHI.
THEN THEY TURNED IT AROUND ON ME.
YEAH.
THAT DOES SOUND SCARY, COMING FACE TO FACE WITH THOSE TWO.
I SERIOUSLY THOUGHT THEY WERE GONNA KILL ME.
POOR GUY.
Ha ha.
YEAH.
BUT...
...I REALIZED HOW MUC THEY LOVE MY ASAMITCH
THEY WERE YELLING AT ME, BUT...
...IT KINDA...
...MADE ME HAPPY, YOU KNOW?
I MEAN, I KINDA GET AIKO BEING MAD.
BUT I NEVER THOUGHT TACHIBANA WOULD FIGHT FOR SOMEONE ELSE LIKE THAT.

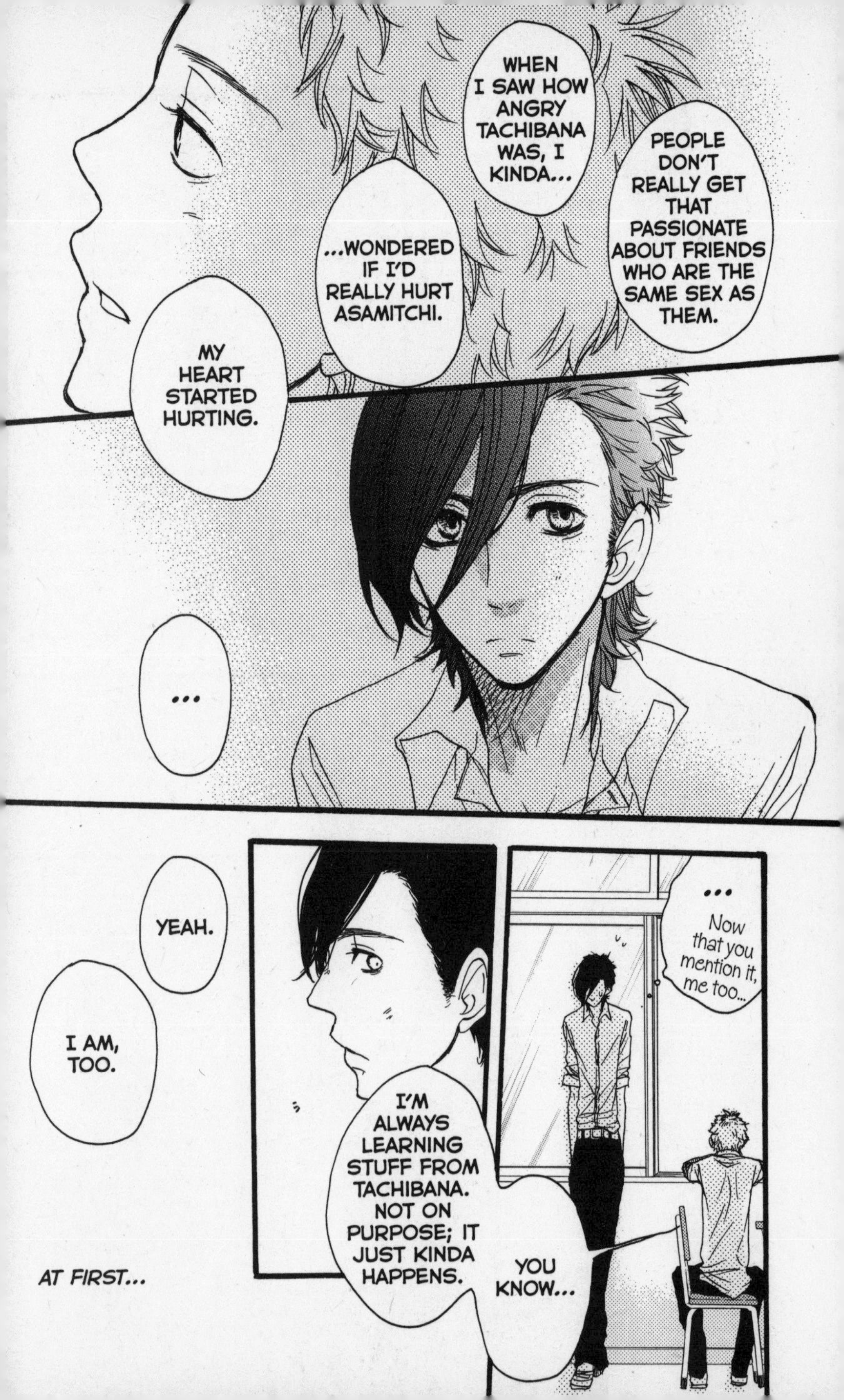
PEOPLE DON'T REALLY GET THAT PASSIONATE ABOUT FRIENDS WHO ARE THE SAME SEX AS THEM.
WHEN I SAW HOW ANGRY TACHIBANA WAS, I KINDA...
...WONDERED IF I'D REALLY HURT ASAMITCHI.
MY HEART STARTED HURTING.
...
...
Now that you mention it, me too...
YOU KNOW...
I'M ALWAYS LEARNING STUFF FROM TACHIBANA. NOT ON PURPOSE; IT JUST KINDA HAPPENS.
YEAH.
I AM, TOO.
AT FIRST...

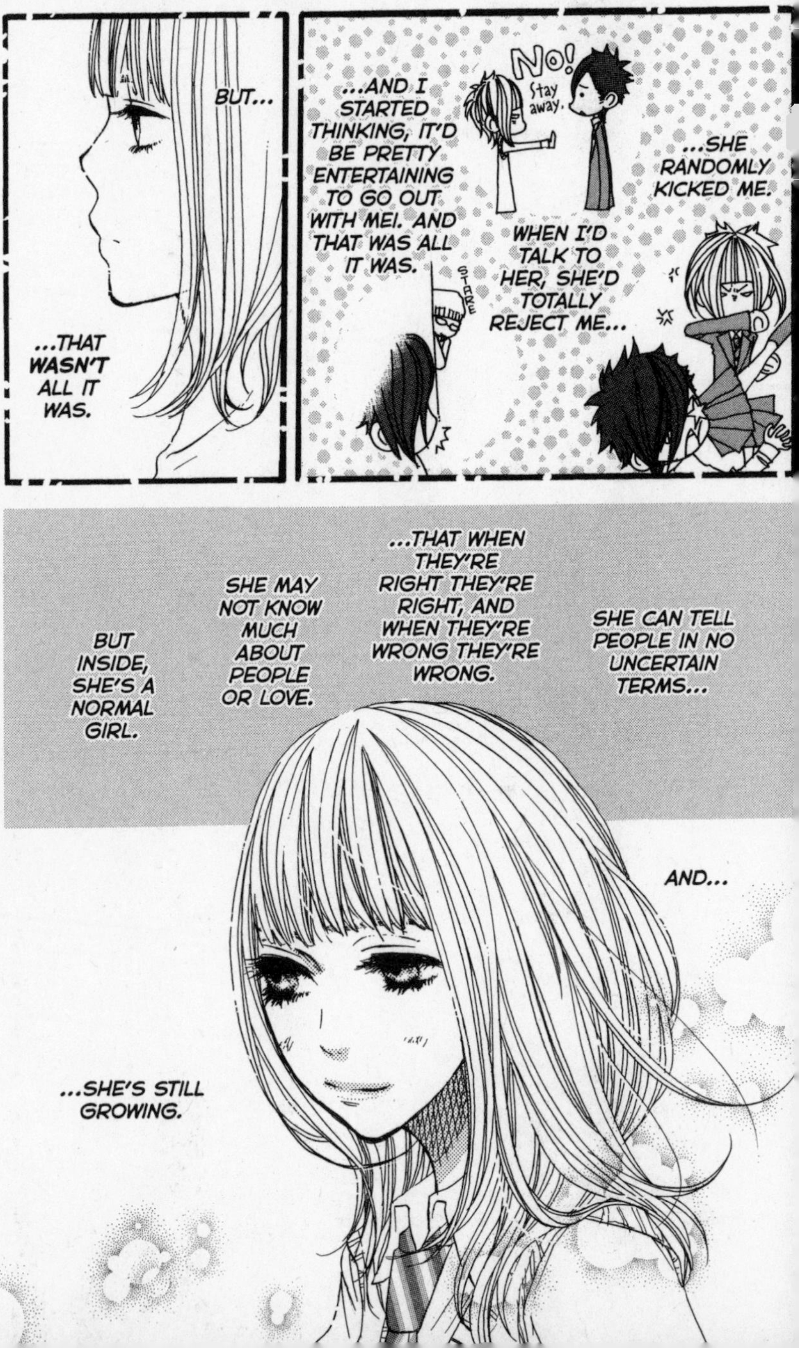

No!
Stay away.
...SHE RANDOMLY KICKED ME.
WHEN I'D TALK TO HER, SHE'D TOTALLY REJECT ME...
STARE
...AND I STARTED THINKING, IT'D BE PRETTY ENTERTAINING TO GO OUT WITH MEI. AND THAT WAS ALL IT WAS.
BUT...
...THAT WASN'T ALL IT WAS.
SHE CAN TELL PEOPLE IN NO UNCERTAIN TERMS...
...THAT WHEN THEY'RE RIGHT THEY'RE RIGHT, AND WHEN THEY'RE WRONG THEY'RE WRONG.
SHE MAY NOT KNOW MUCH ABOUT PEOPLE OR LOVE.
BUT INSIDE, SHE'S A NORMAL GIRL.
AND...
...SHE'S STILL GROWING.

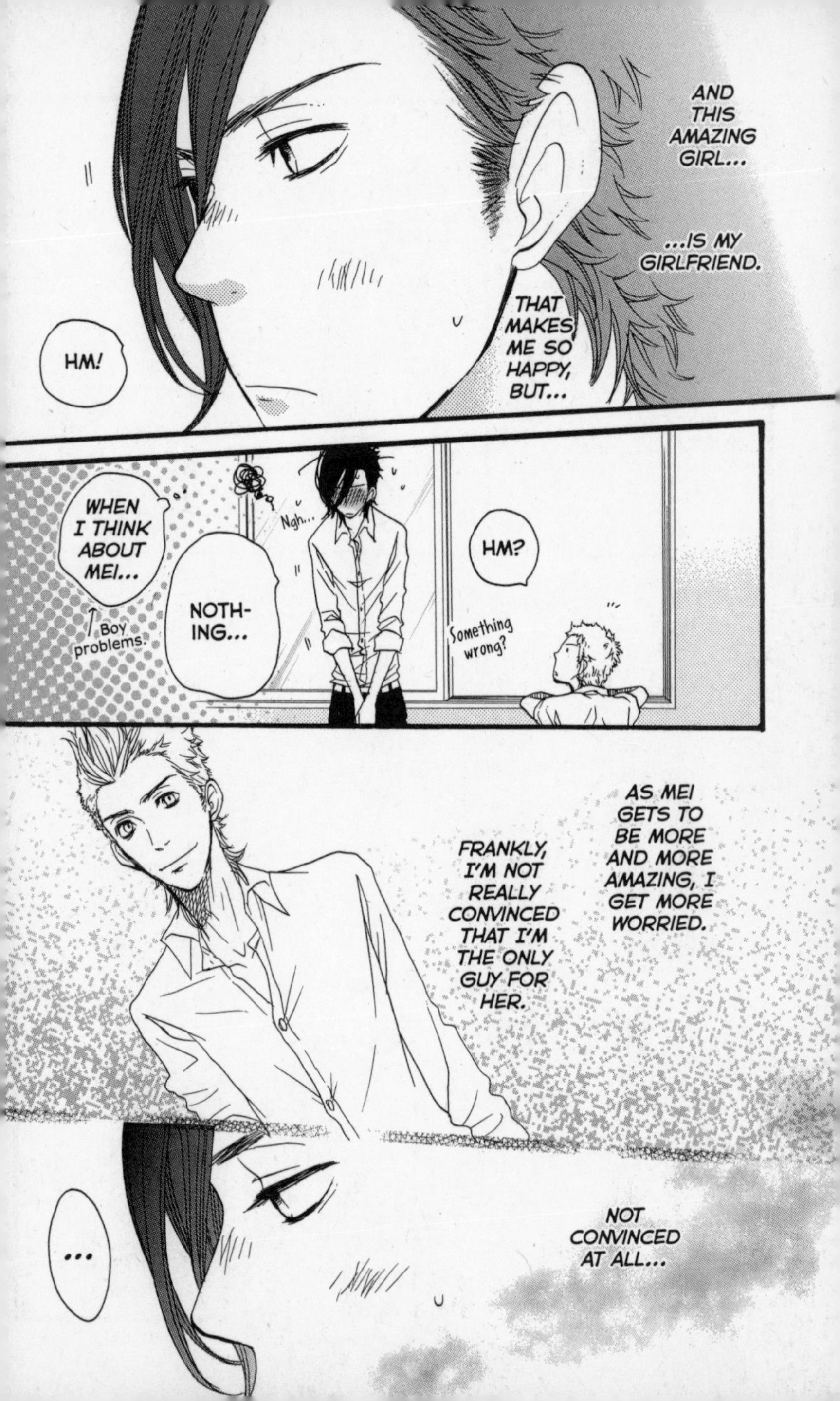
AND THIS AMAZING GIRL...
...IS MY GIRLFRIEND.
THAT MAKES ME SO HAPPY, BUT...
HM!
HM?
Something wrong?
Ngh...
NOTH-ING...
WHEN I THINK ABOUT MEI...
Boy problems.
AS MEI GETS TO BE MORE AND MORE AMAZING, I GET MORE WORRIED.
FRANKLY, I'M NOT REALLY CONVINCED THAT I'M THE ONLY GUY FOR HER.
NOT CONVINCED AT ALL...
...

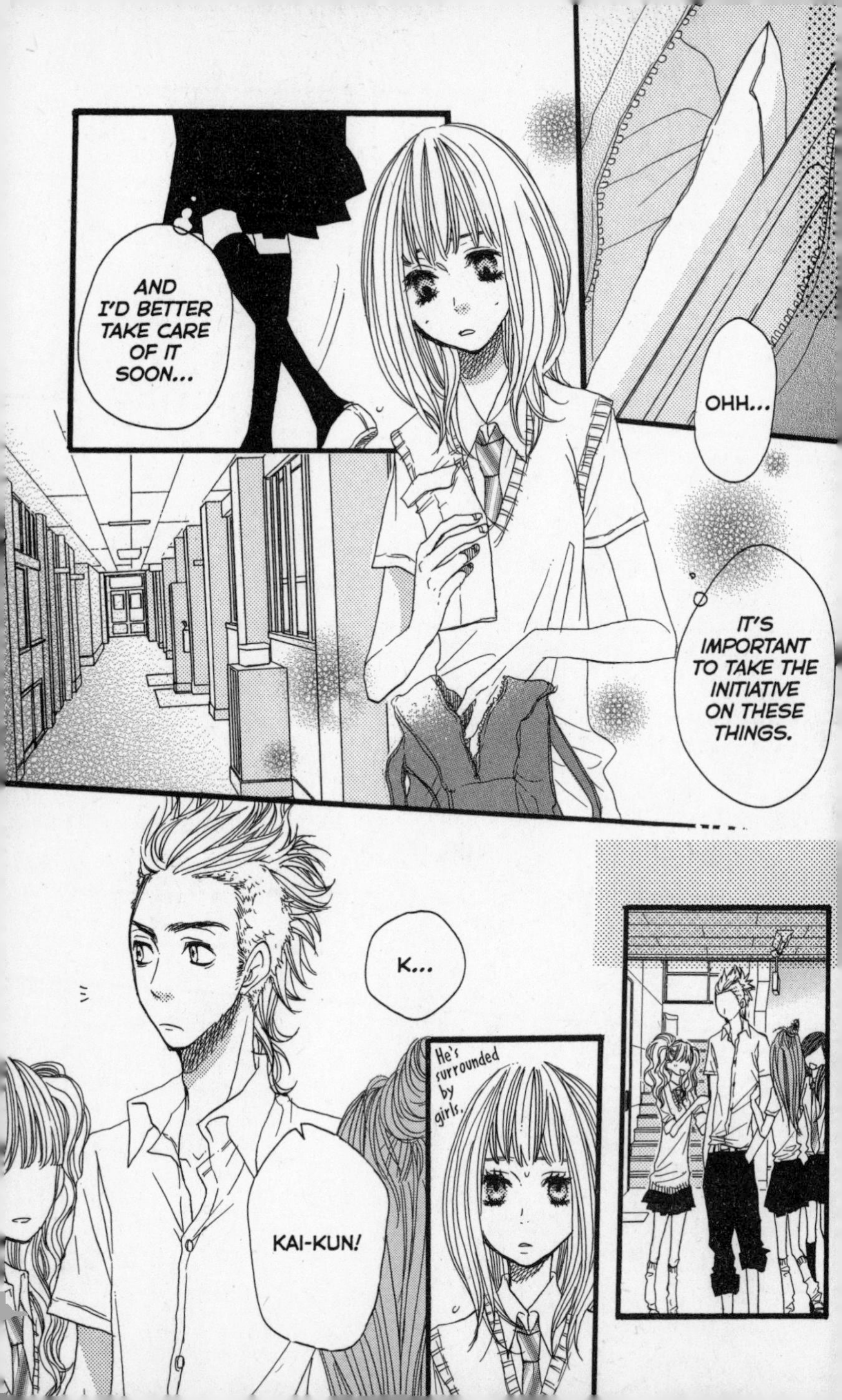
OHH...
AND I'D BETTER TAKE CARE OF IT SOON...
IT'S IMPORTANT TO TAKE THE INITIATIVE ON THESE THINGS.
K...
He's surrounded by girls.
KAI-KUN!

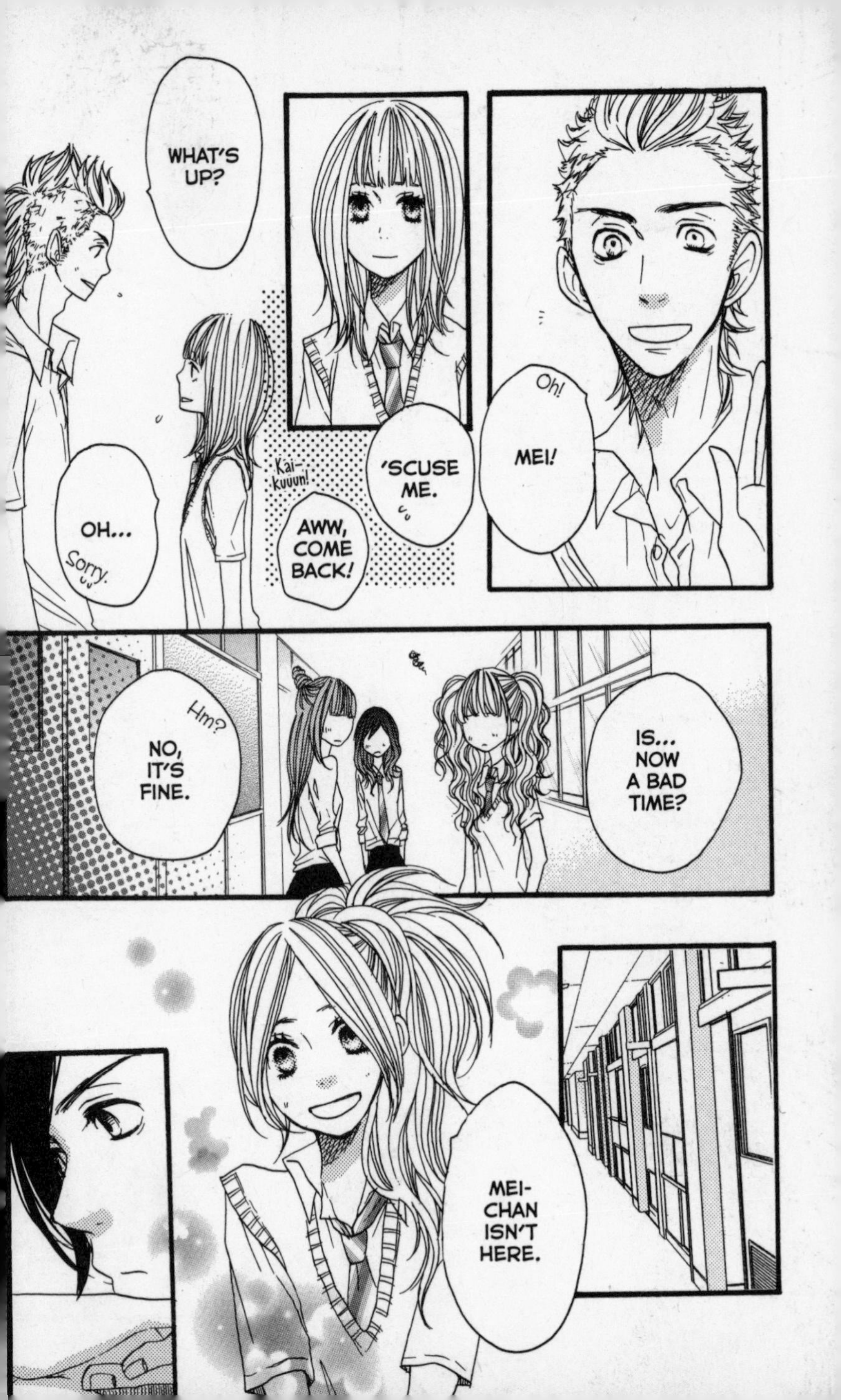
Oh!
MEI!
'SCUSE ME.
Kai-kuuun!
AWW, COME BACK!
WHAT'S UP?
OH...
Sorry.
IS... NOW A BAD TIME?
Hm?
NO, IT'S FINE.
MEI-CHAN ISN'T HERE.

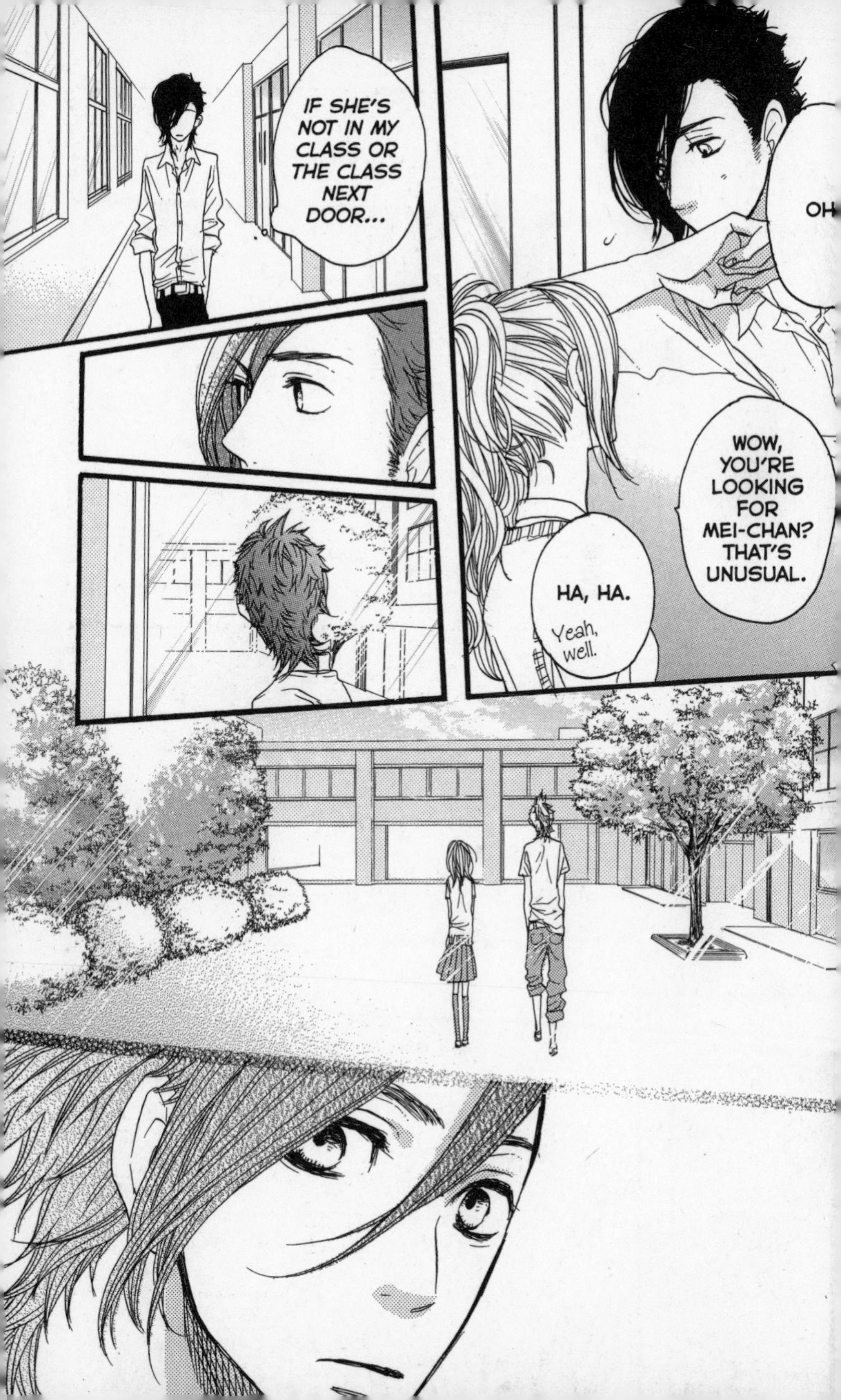
OH
WOW, YOU'RE LOOKING FOR MEI-CHAN? THAT'S UNUSUAL.
HA, HA.
Yeah, well.
IF SHE'S NOT IN MY CLASS OR THE CLASS NEXT DOOR...

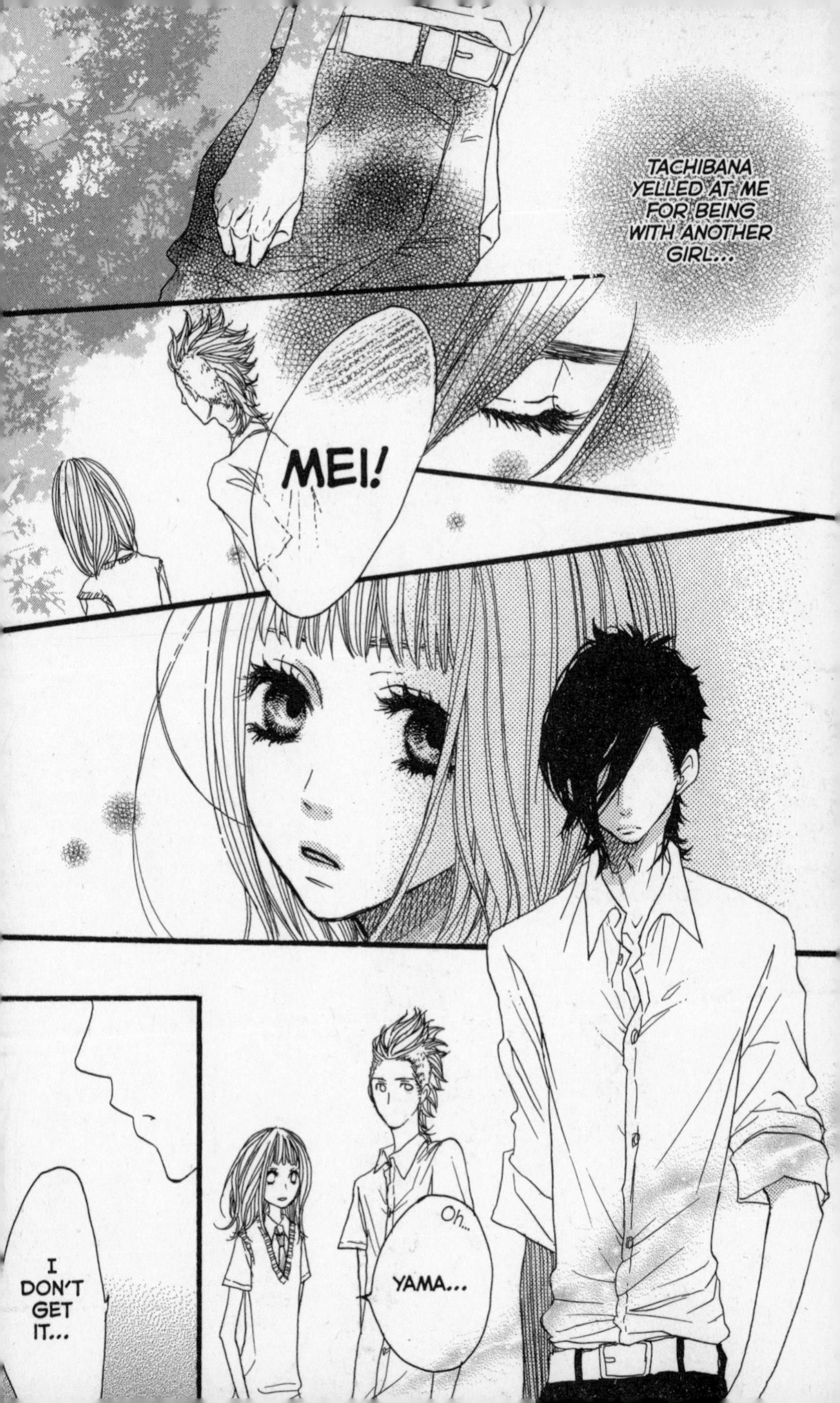
TACHIBANA YELLED AT ME FOR BEING WITH ANOTHER GIRL...
MEI!
Oh...
YAMA...
I DON'T GET IT...

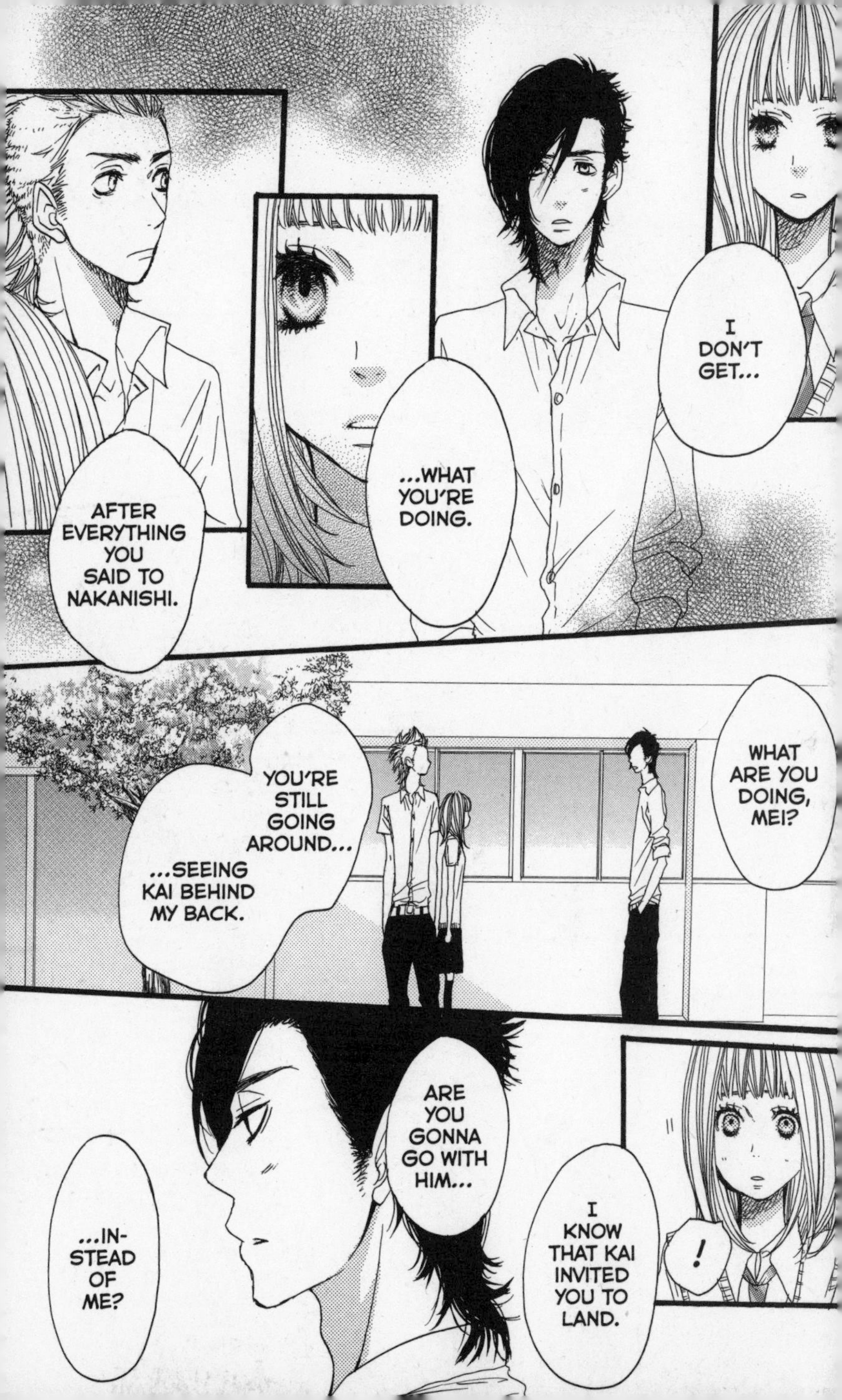
I DON'T GET...
...WHAT YOU'RE DOING.
AFTER EVERYTHING YOU SAID TO NAKANISHI.
WHAT ARE YOU DOING, MEI?
YOU'RE STILL GOING AROUND...
...SEEING KAI BEHIND MY BACK.
!
I KNOW THAT KAI INVITED YOU TO LAND.
ARE YOU GONNA GO WITH HIM...
...IN-STEAD OF ME?

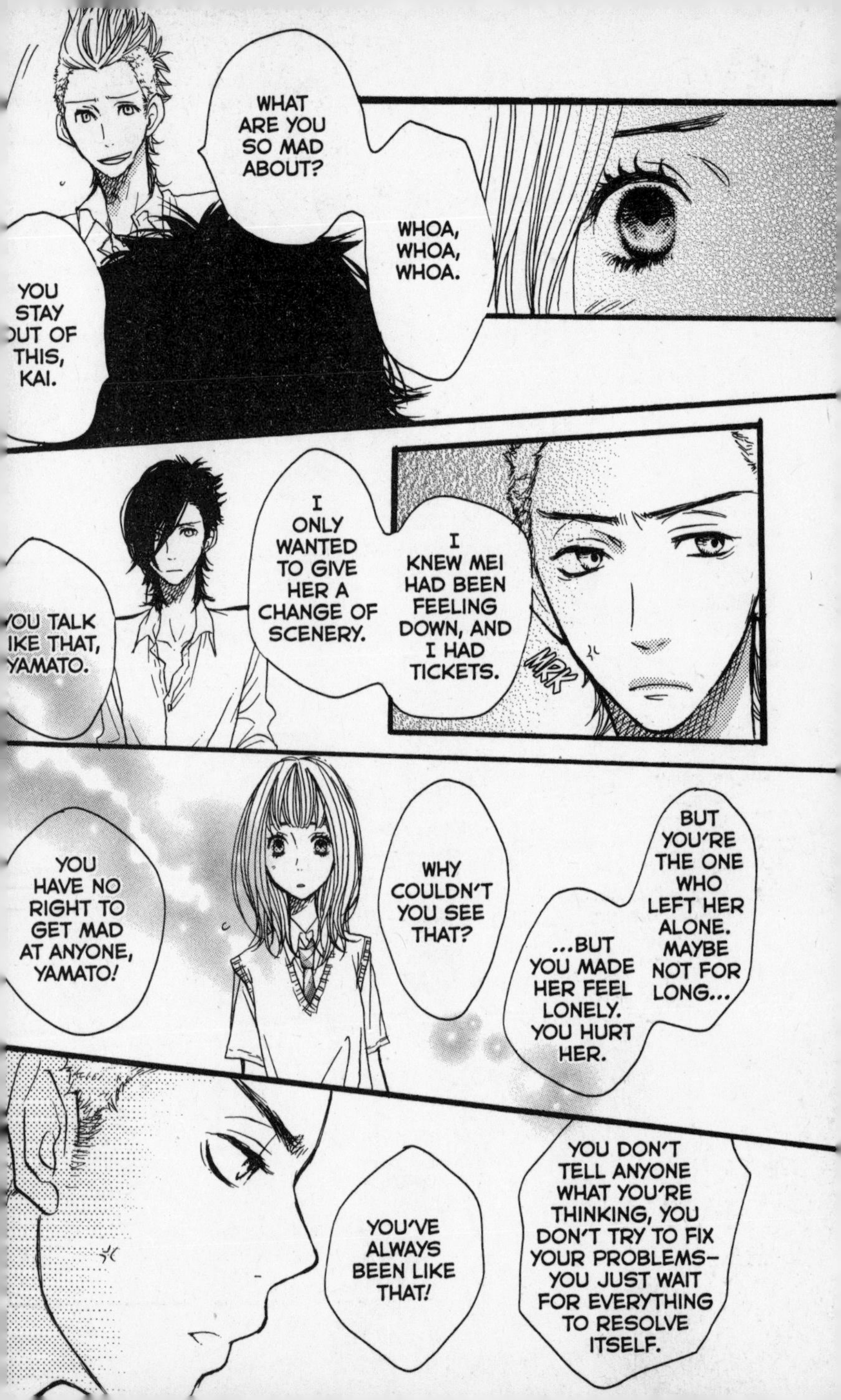

WHOA, WHOA, WHOA.
WHAT ARE YOU SO MAD ABOUT?
YOU STAY OUT OF THIS, KAI.
MRK
I KNEW MEI HAD BEEN FEELING DOWN, AND I HAD TICKETS.
I ONLY WANTED TO GIVE HER A CHANGE OF SCENERY.
OU TALK IKE THAT, YAMATO.
BUT YOU'RE THE ONE WHO LEFT HER ALONE. MAYBE NOT FOR LONG...
...BUT YOU MADE HER FEEL LONELY. YOU HURT HER.
WHY COULDN'T YOU SEE THAT?
YOU HAVE NO RIGHT TO GET MAD AT ANYONE, YAMATO!
YOU DON'T TELL ANYONE WHAT YOU'RE THINKING, YOU DON'T TRY TO FIX YOUR PROBLEMS—YOU JUST WAIT FOR EVERYTHING TO RESOLVE ITSELF.
YOU'VE ALWAYS BEEN LIKE THAT!

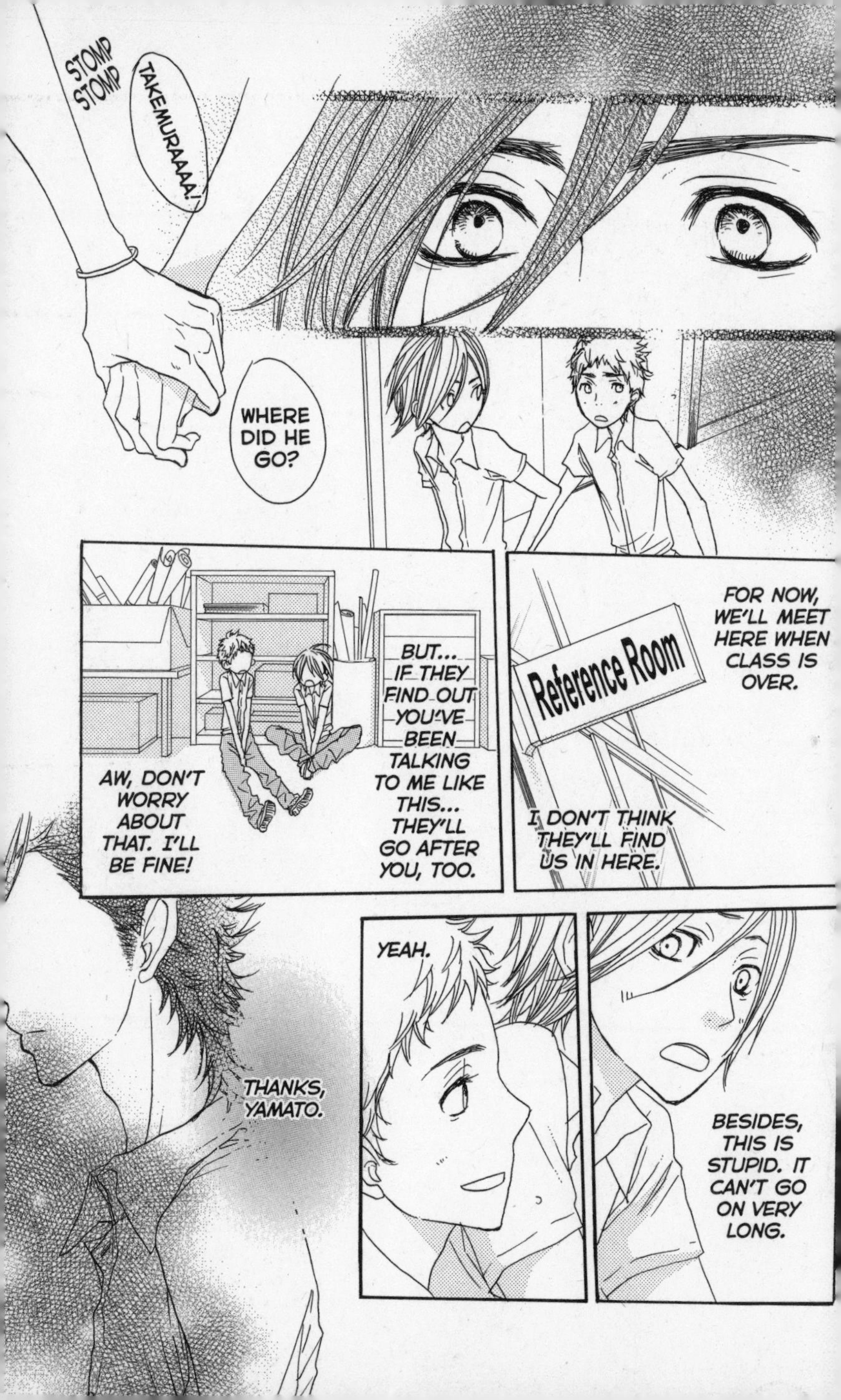
STOMP STOMP
TAKEMURAAAA!
WHERE DID HE GO?
FOR NOW, WE'LL MEET HERE WHEN CLASS IS OVER.
Reference Room
I DON'T THINK THEY'LL FIND US IN HERE.
BUT... IF THEY FIND OUT YOU'VE BEEN TALKING TO ME LIKE THIS... THEY'LL GO AFTER YOU, TOO.
AW, DON'T WORRY ABOUT THAT. I'LL BE FINE!
BESIDES, THIS IS STUPID. IT CAN'T GO ON VERY LONG.
YEAH.
THANKS, YAMATO.

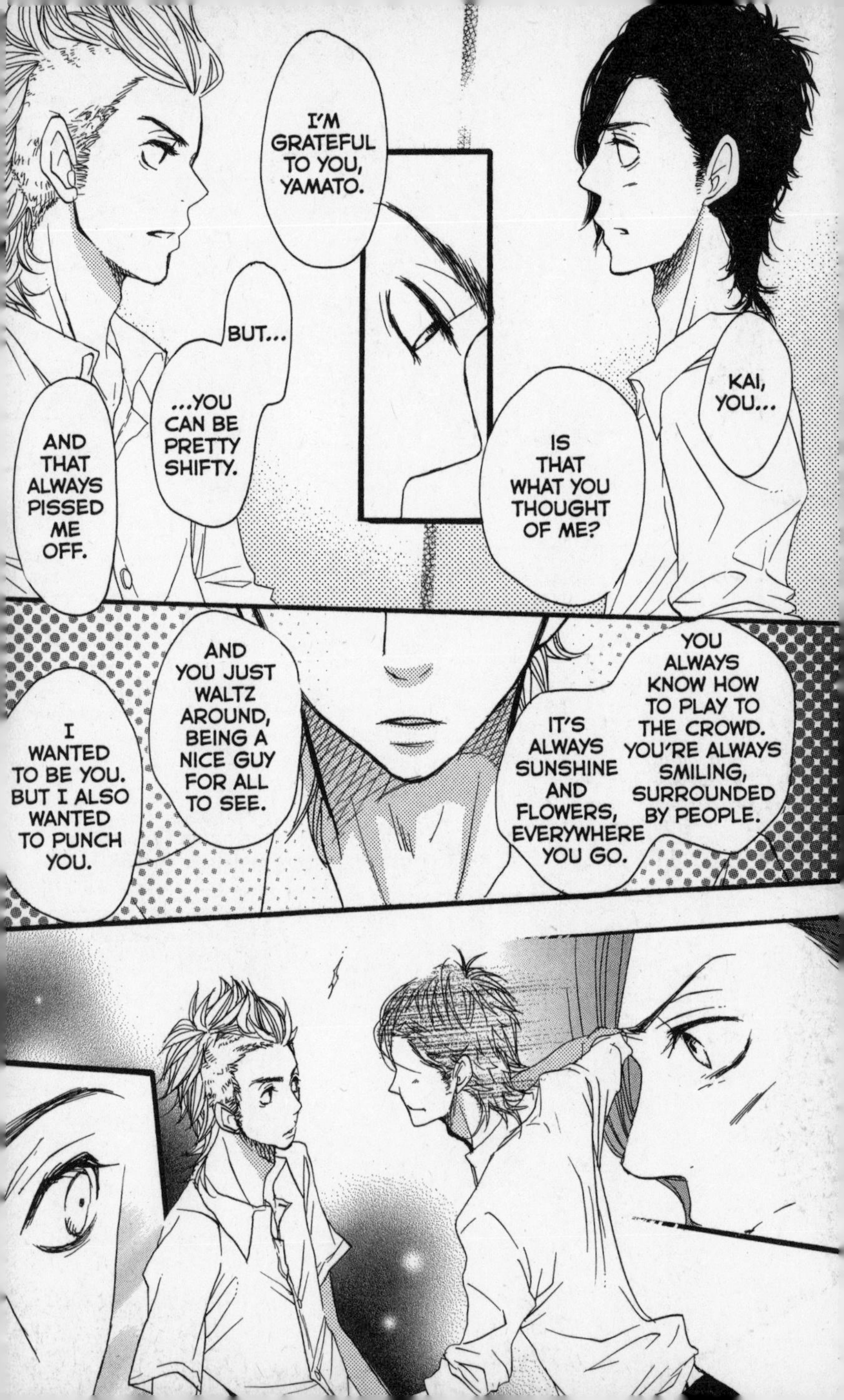
I'M GRATEFUL TO YOU, YAMATO.
BUT...
...YOU CAN BE PRETTY SHIFTY.
AND THAT ALWAYS PISSED ME OFF.
KAI, YOU...
IS THAT WHAT YOU THOUGHT OF ME?
YOU ALWAYS KNOW HOW TO PLAY TO THE CROWD. YOU'RE ALWAYS SMILING, SURROUNDED BY PEOPLE.
IT'S ALWAYS SUNSHINE AND FLOWERS, EVERYWHERE YOU GO.
AND YOU JUST WALTZ AROUND, BEING A NICE GUY FOR ALL TO SEE.
I WANTED TO BE YOU. BUT I ALSO WANTED TO PUNCH YOU.

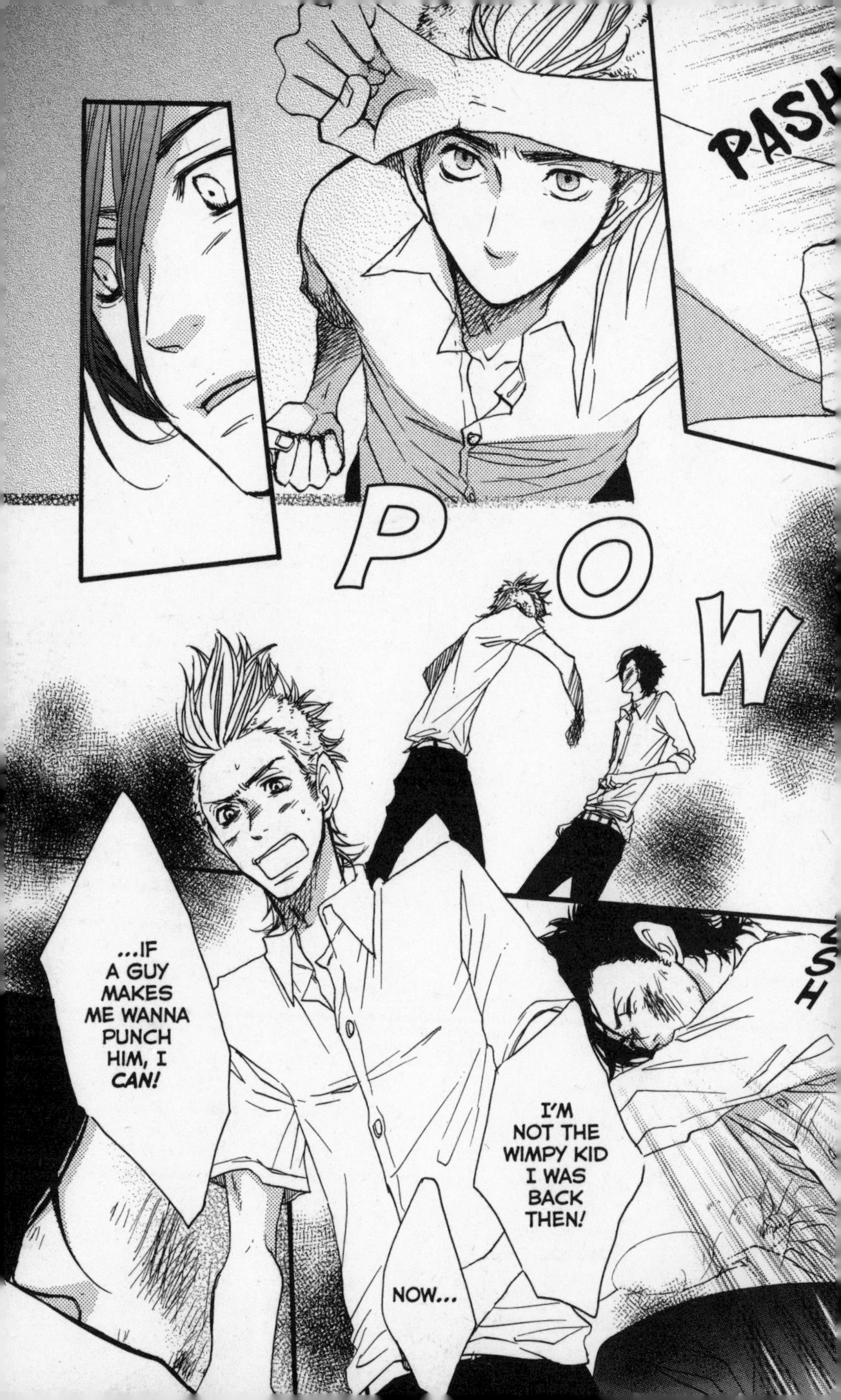
PASH
POW
SH
I'M NOT THE WIMPY KID I WAS BACK THEN!
...IF A GUY MAKES ME WANNA PUNCH HIM, I CAN!
NOW...

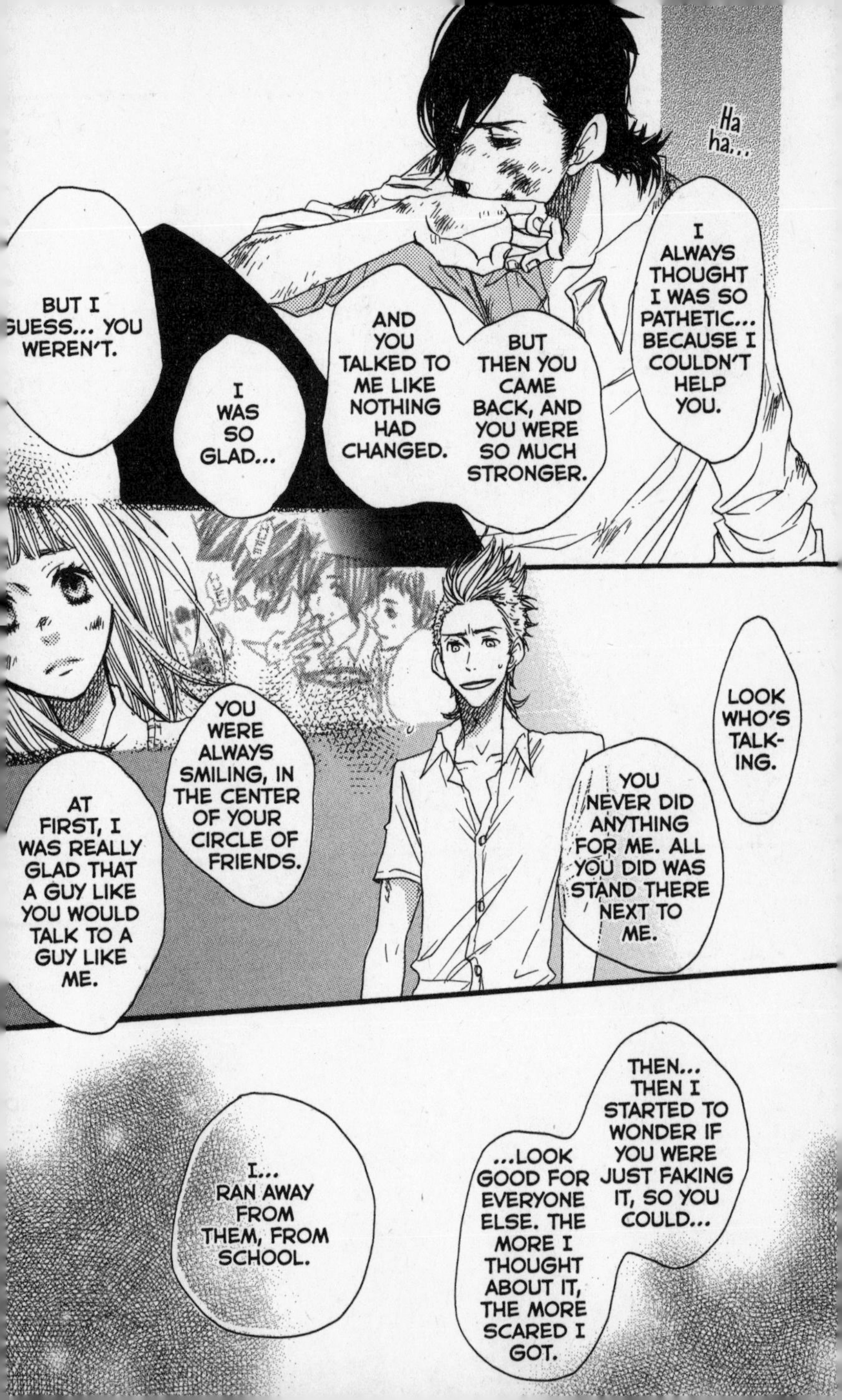
Ha ha...
I ALWAYS THOUGHT I WAS SO PATHETIC... BECAUSE I COULDN'T HELP YOU.
BUT THEN YOU CAME BACK, AND YOU WERE SO MUCH STRONGER.
AND YOU TALKED TO ME LIKE NOTHING HAD CHANGED.
I WAS SO GLAD...
BUT I GUESS... YOU WEREN'T.
LOOK WHO'S TALK-ING.
YOU NEVER DID ANYTHING FOR ME. ALL YOU DID WAS STAND THERE NEXT TO ME.
YOU WERE ALWAYS SMILING, IN THE CENTER OF YOUR CIRCLE OF FRIENDS.
AT FIRST, I WAS REALLY GLAD THAT A GUY LIKE YOU WOULD TALK TO A GUY LIKE ME.
THEN... THEN I STARTED TO WONDER IF YOU WERE JUST FAKING IT, SO YOU COULD...
...LOOK GOOD FOR EVERYONE ELSE. THE MORE I THOUGHT ABOUT IT, THE MORE SCARED I GOT.
I... RAN AWAY FROM THEM, FROM SCHOOL.

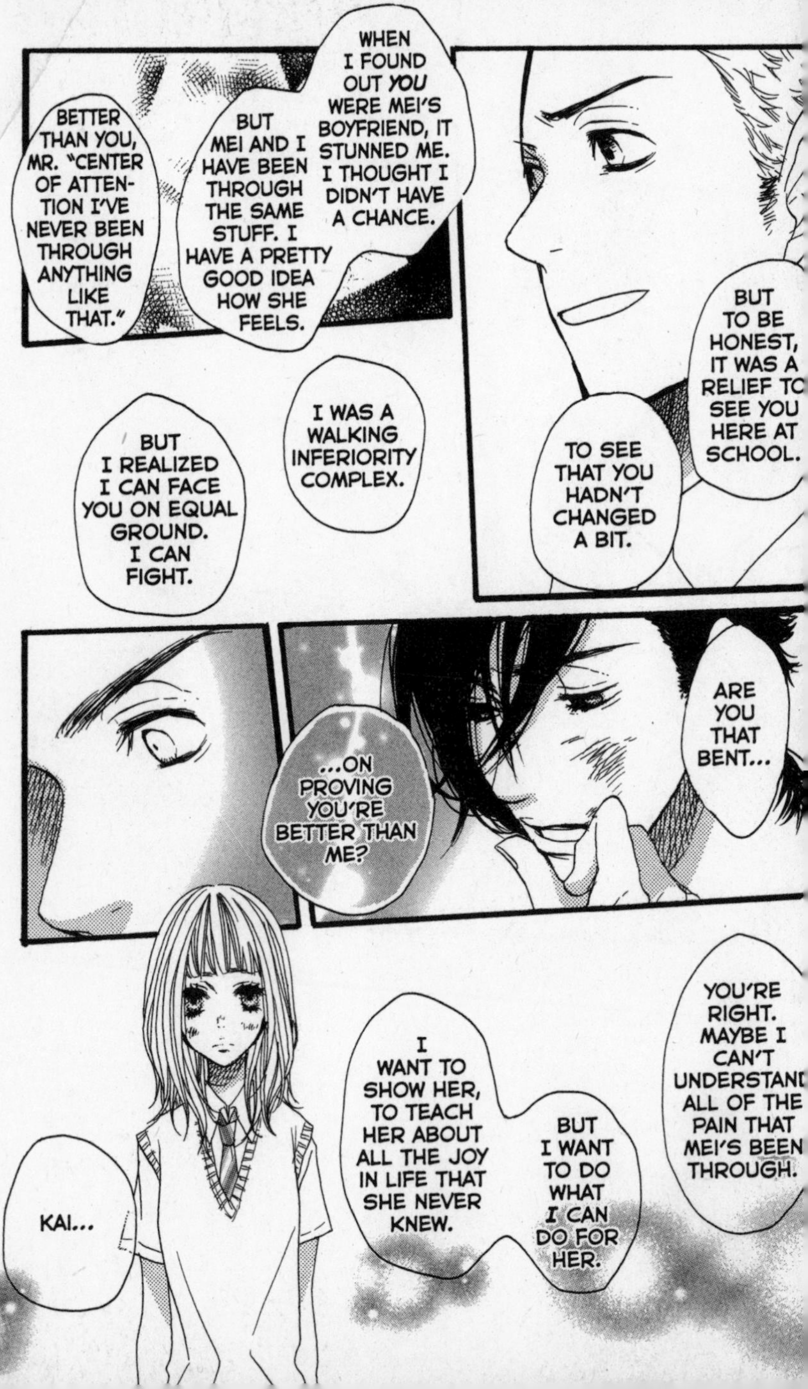
BUT TO BE HONEST, IT WAS A RELIEF TO SEE YOU HERE AT SCHOOL.
TO SEE THAT YOU HADN'T CHANGED A BIT.
WHEN I FOUND OUT *YOU* WERE MEI'S BOYFRIEND, IT STUNNED ME. I THOUGHT I DIDN'T HAVE A CHANCE.
BUT MEI AND I HAVE BEEN THROUGH THE SAME STUFF. I HAVE A PRETTY GOOD IDEA HOW SHE FEELS.
BETTER THAN YOU, MR. "CENTER OF ATTENTION I'VE NEVER BEEN THROUGH ANYTHING LIKE THAT."
I WAS A WALKING INFERIORITY COMPLEX.
BUT I REALIZED I CAN FACE YOU ON EQUAL GROUND. I CAN FIGHT.
ARE YOU THAT BENT...
...ON PROVING YOU'RE BETTER THAN ME?
YOU'RE RIGHT. MAYBE I CAN'T UNDERSTAND ALL OF THE PAIN THAT MEI'S BEEN THROUGH.
BUT I WANT TO DO WHAT *I* CAN DO FOR HER.
I WANT TO SHOW HER, TO TEACH HER ABOUT ALL THE JOY IN LIFE THAT SHE NEVER KNEW.
KAI...

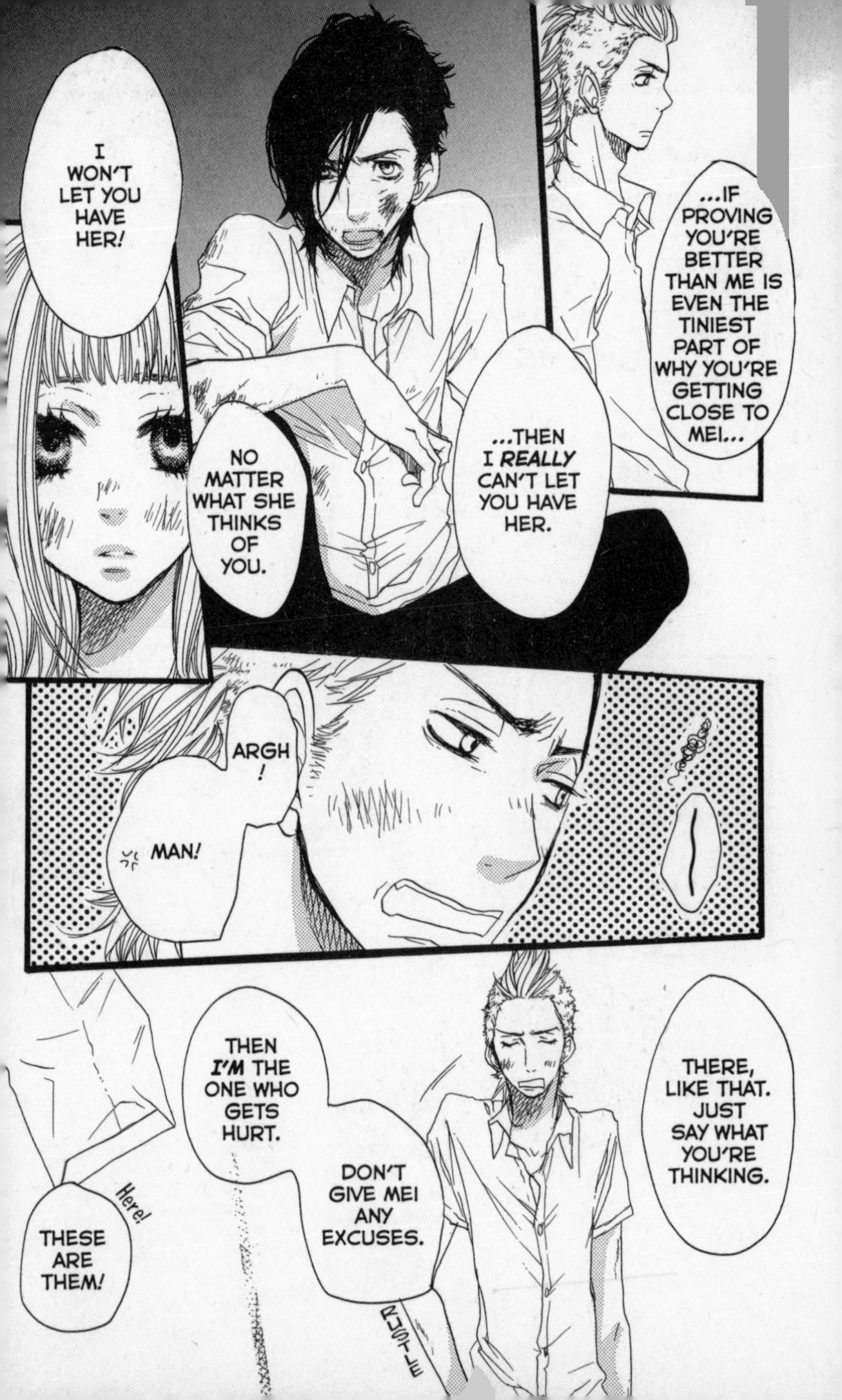
...IF PROVING YOU'RE BETTER THAN ME IS EVEN THE TINIEST PART OF WHY YOU'RE GETTING CLOSE TO MEI...
...THEN I *REALLY* CAN'T LET YOU HAVE HER.
NO MATTER WHAT SHE THINKS OF YOU.
I WON'T LET YOU HAVE HER!
ARGH!
MAN!
THERE, LIKE THAT. JUST SAY WHAT YOU'RE THINKING.
THEN *I'M* THE ONE WHO GETS HURT.
DON'T GIVE MEI ANY EXCUSES.
RUSTLE
Here!
THESE ARE THEM!

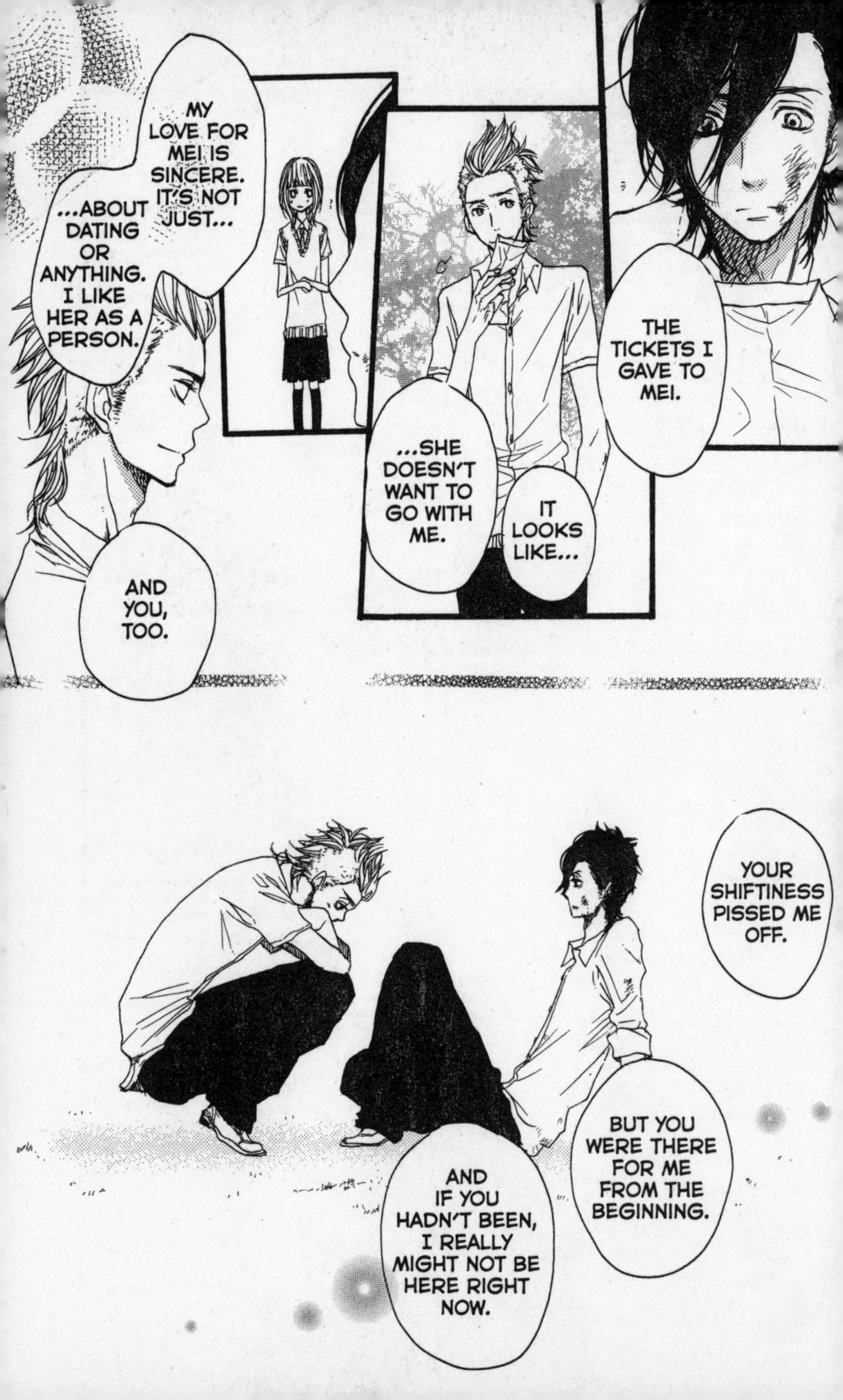
THE TICKETS I GAVE TO MEI.
IT LOOKS LIKE...
...SHE DOESN'T WANT TO GO WITH ME.
MY LOVE FOR MEI IS SINCERE. IT'S NOT JUST...
...ABOUT DATING OR ANYTHING. I LIKE HER AS A PERSON.
AND YOU, TOO.
YOUR SHIFTINESS PISSED ME OFF.
BUT YOU WERE THERE FOR ME FROM THE BEGINNING.
AND IF YOU HADN'T BEEN, I REALLY MIGHT NOT BE HERE RIGHT NOW.

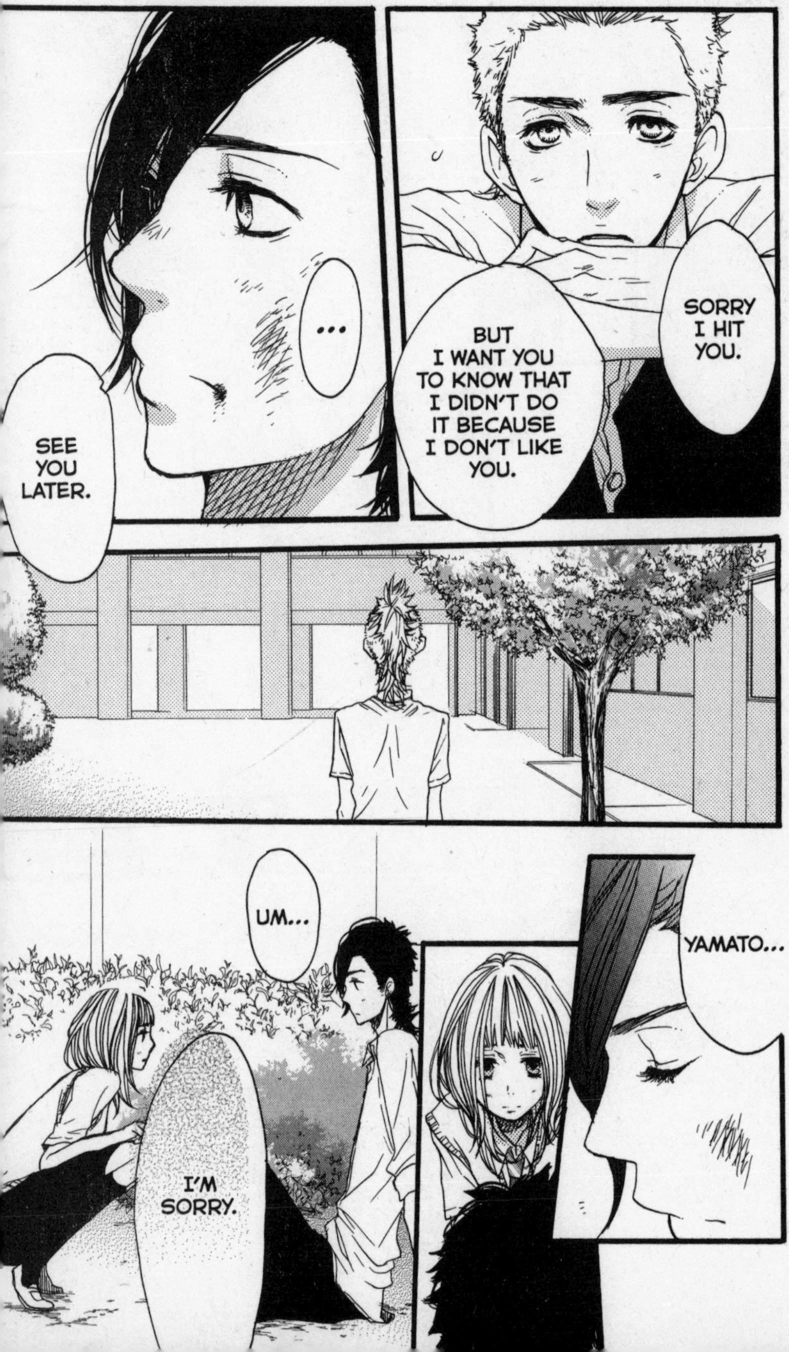
SORRY I HIT YOU.
BUT I WANT YOU TO KNOW THAT I DIDN'T DO IT BECAUSE I DON'T LIKE YOU.
...
SEE YOU LATER.
YAMATO...
UM...
I'M SORRY.

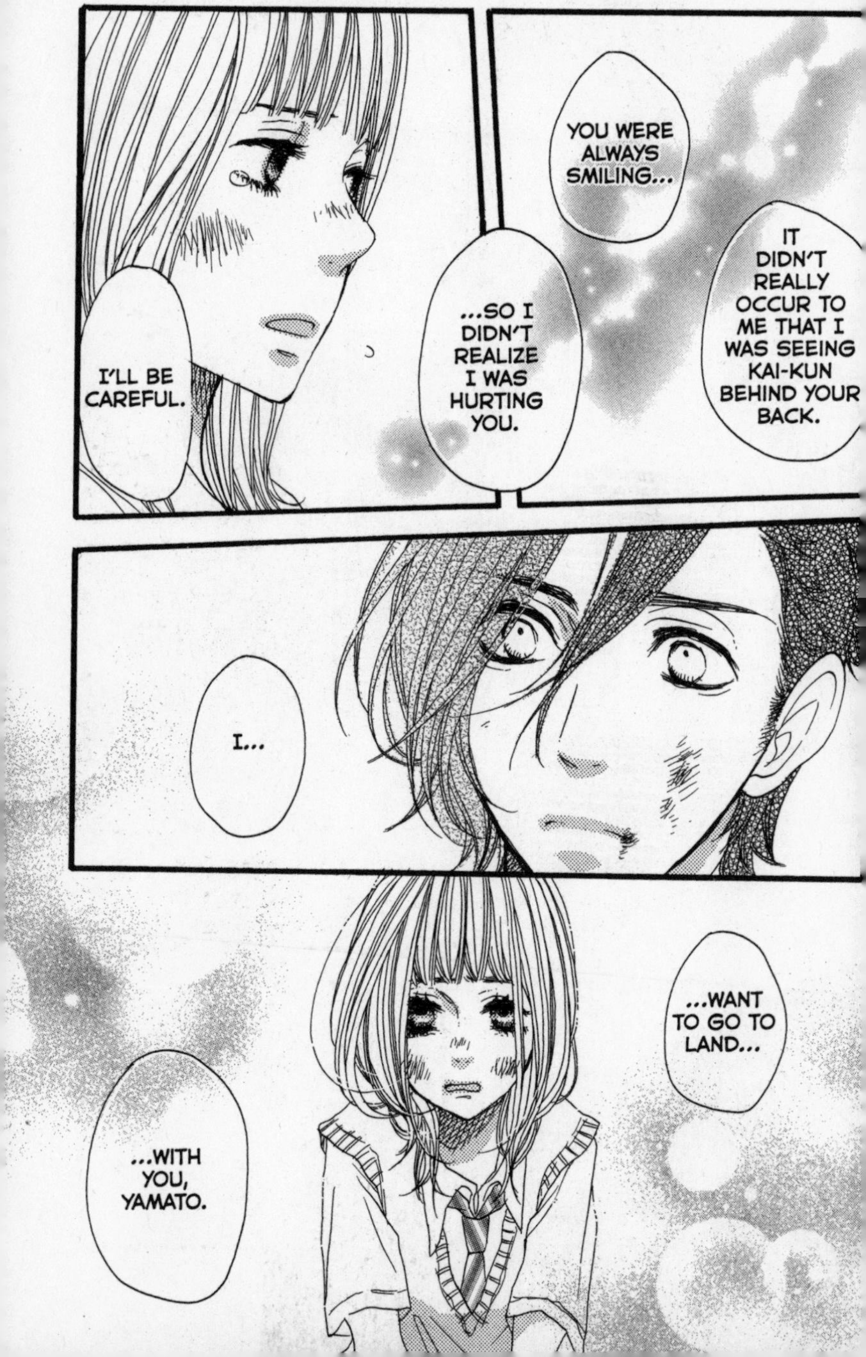
IT DIDN'T REALLY OCCUR TO ME THAT I WAS SEEING KAI-KUN BEHIND YOUR BACK.
YOU WERE ALWAYS SMILING...
...SO I DIDN'T REALIZE I WAS HURTING YOU.
I'LL BE CAREFUL.
I...
...WANT TO GO TO LAND...
...WITH YOU, YAMATO.

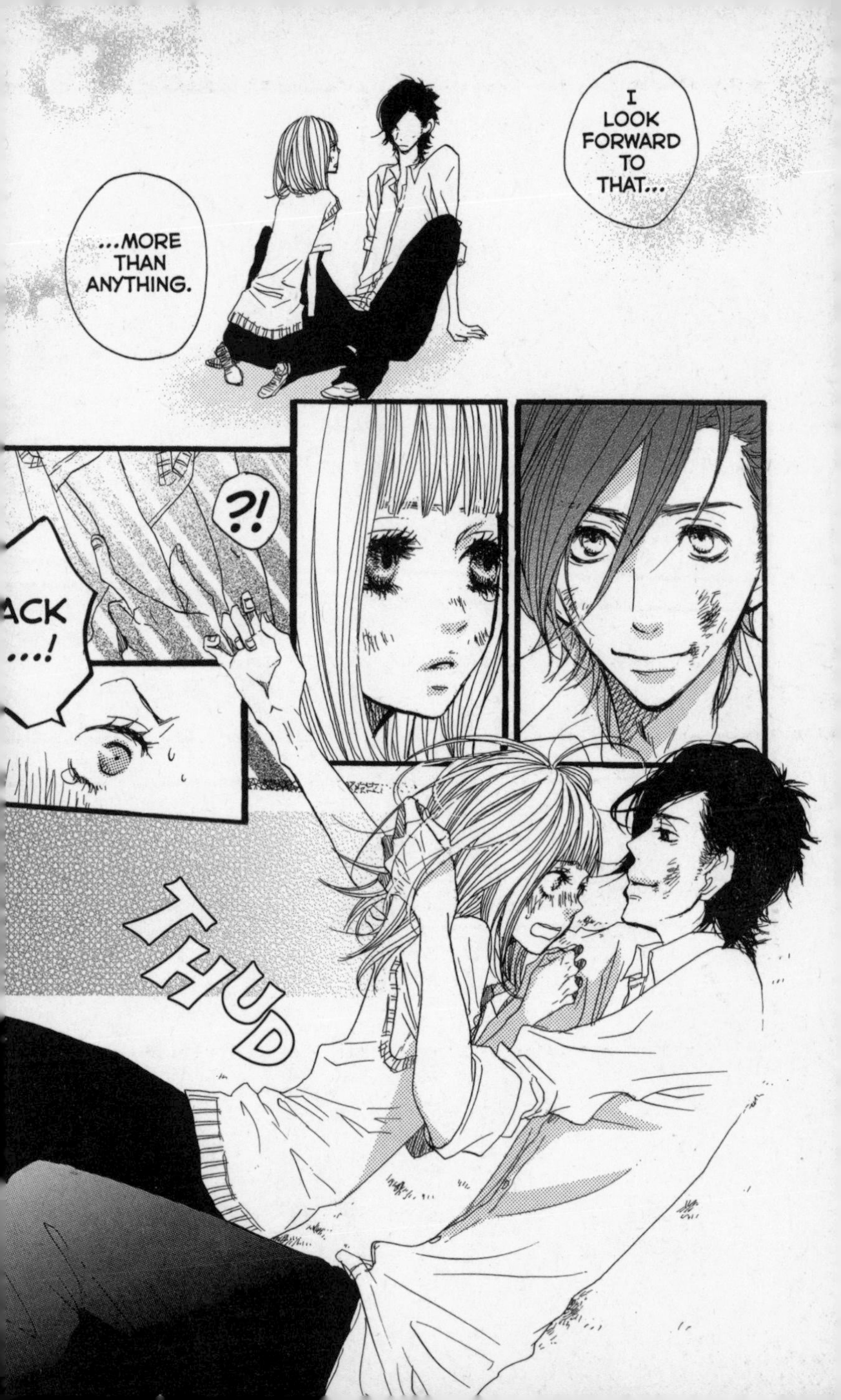
I LOOK FORWARD TO THAT...
...MORE THAN ANYTHING.
?!
ACK ...!
THUD

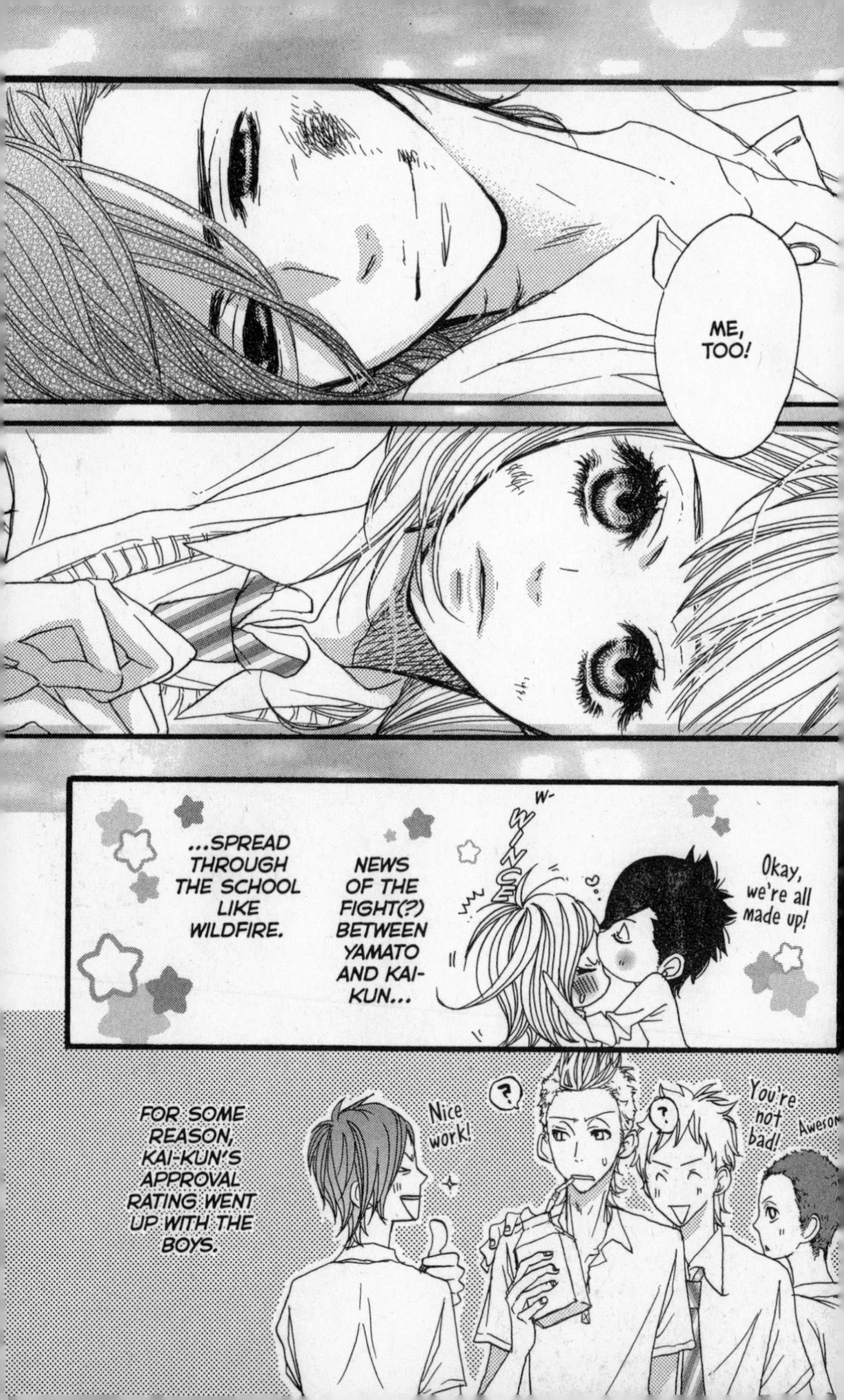
ME, TOO!
Okay, we're all made up!
W- WINCE
NEWS OF THE FIGHT(?) BETWEEN YAMATO AND KAI-KUN...
...SPREAD THROUGH THE SCHOOL LIKE WILDFIRE.
Awesom
You're not bad!
Nice work!
FOR SOME REASON, KAI-KUN'S APPROVAL RATING WENT UP WITH THE BOYS.

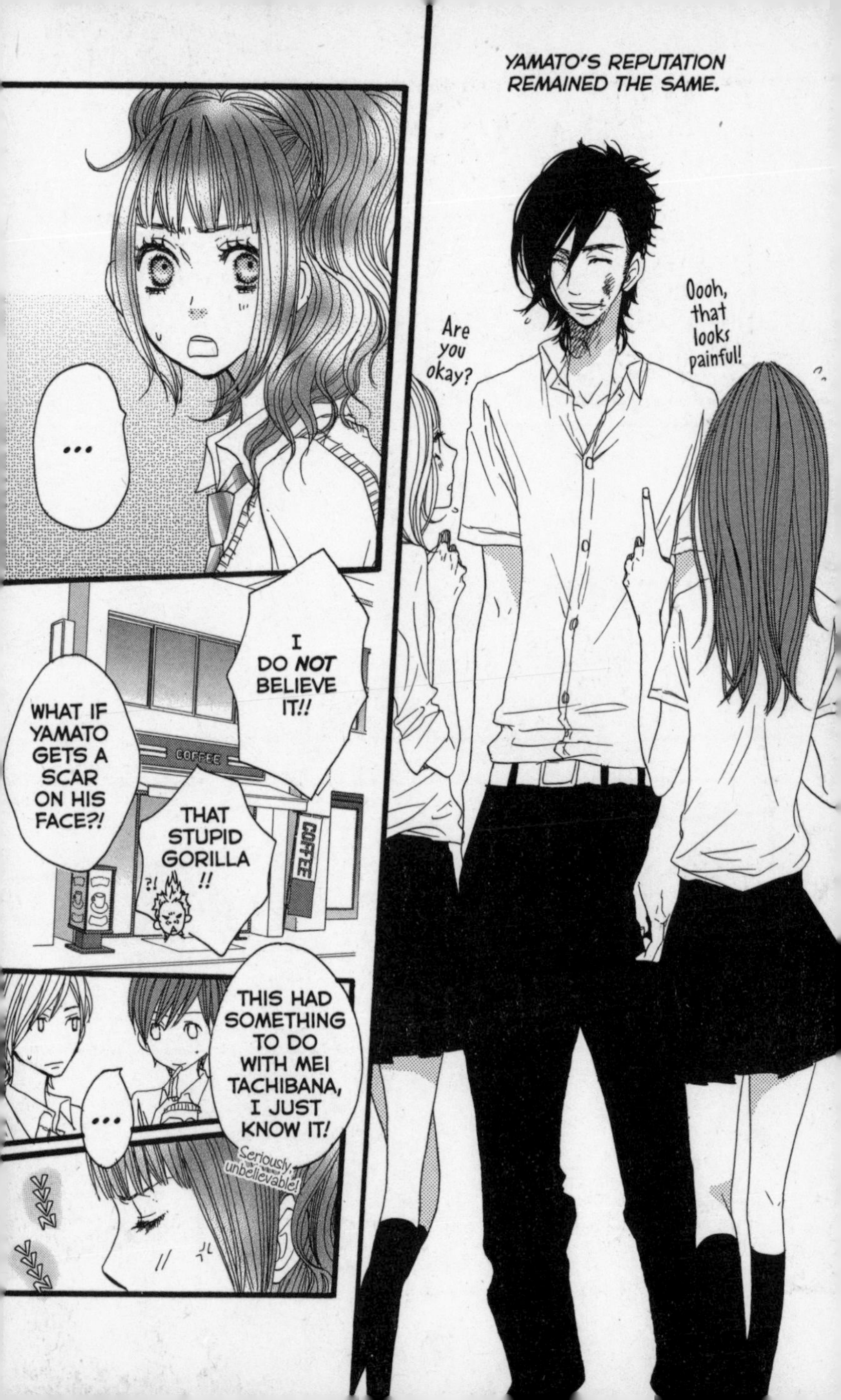
YAMATO'S REPUTATION REMAINED THE SAME.
Oooh, that looks painful!
Are you okay?
...
I DO *NOT* BELIEVE IT!!
WHAT IF YAMATO GETS A SCAR ON HIS FACE?!
THAT STUPID GORILLA!!
THIS HAD SOMETHING TO DO WITH MEI TACHIBANA, I JUST KNOW IT!
Seriously, unbelievable!
...

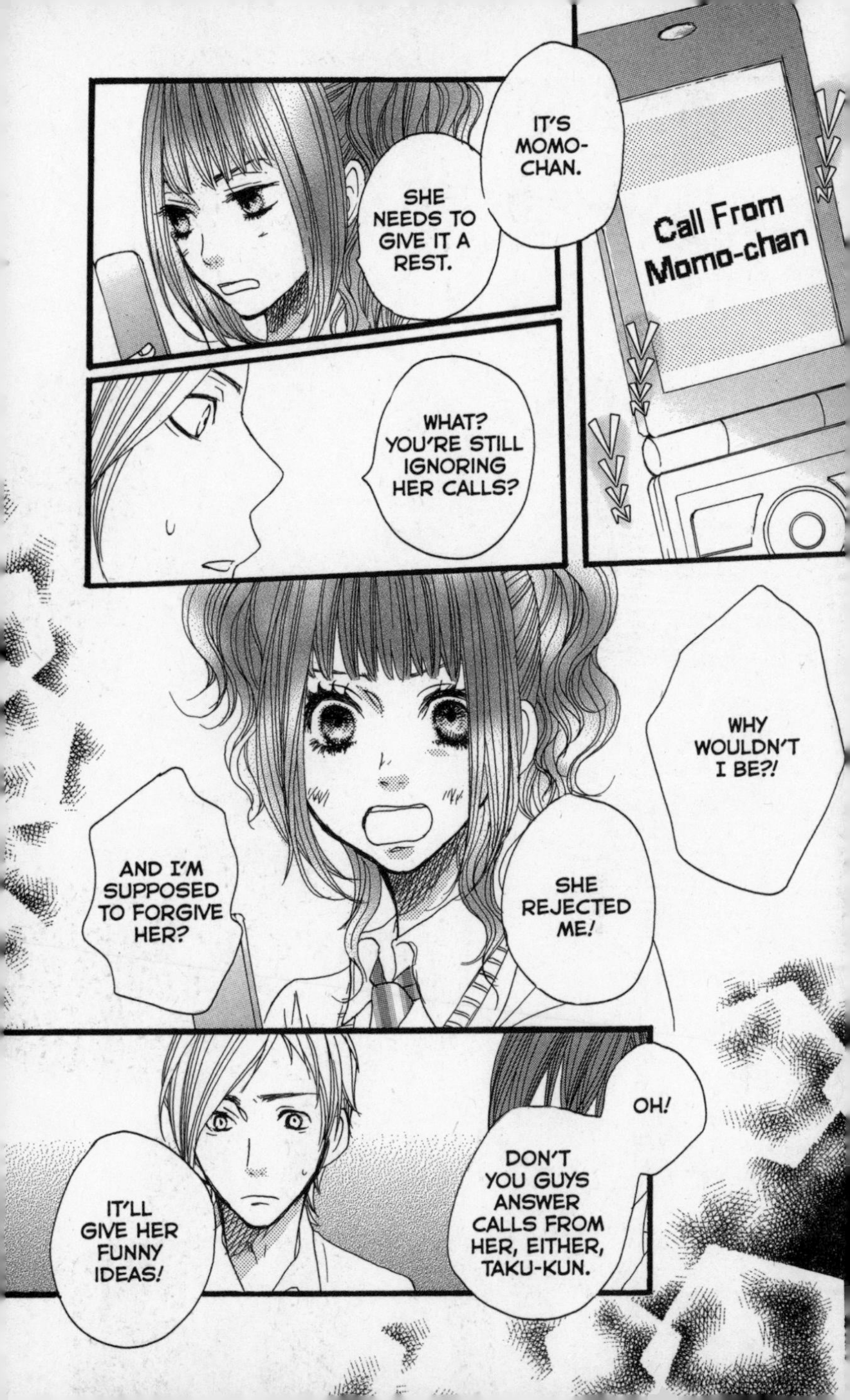
Call From Momo-chan
IT'S MOMO-CHAN.
SHE NEEDS TO GIVE IT A REST.
WHAT? YOU'RE STILL IGNORING HER CALLS?
WHY WOULDN'T I BE?!
SHE REJECTED ME!
AND I'M SUPPOSED TO FORGIVE HER?
OH!
DON'T YOU GUYS ANSWER CALLS FROM HER, EITHER, TAKU-KUN.
IT'LL GIVE HER FUNNY IDEAS!

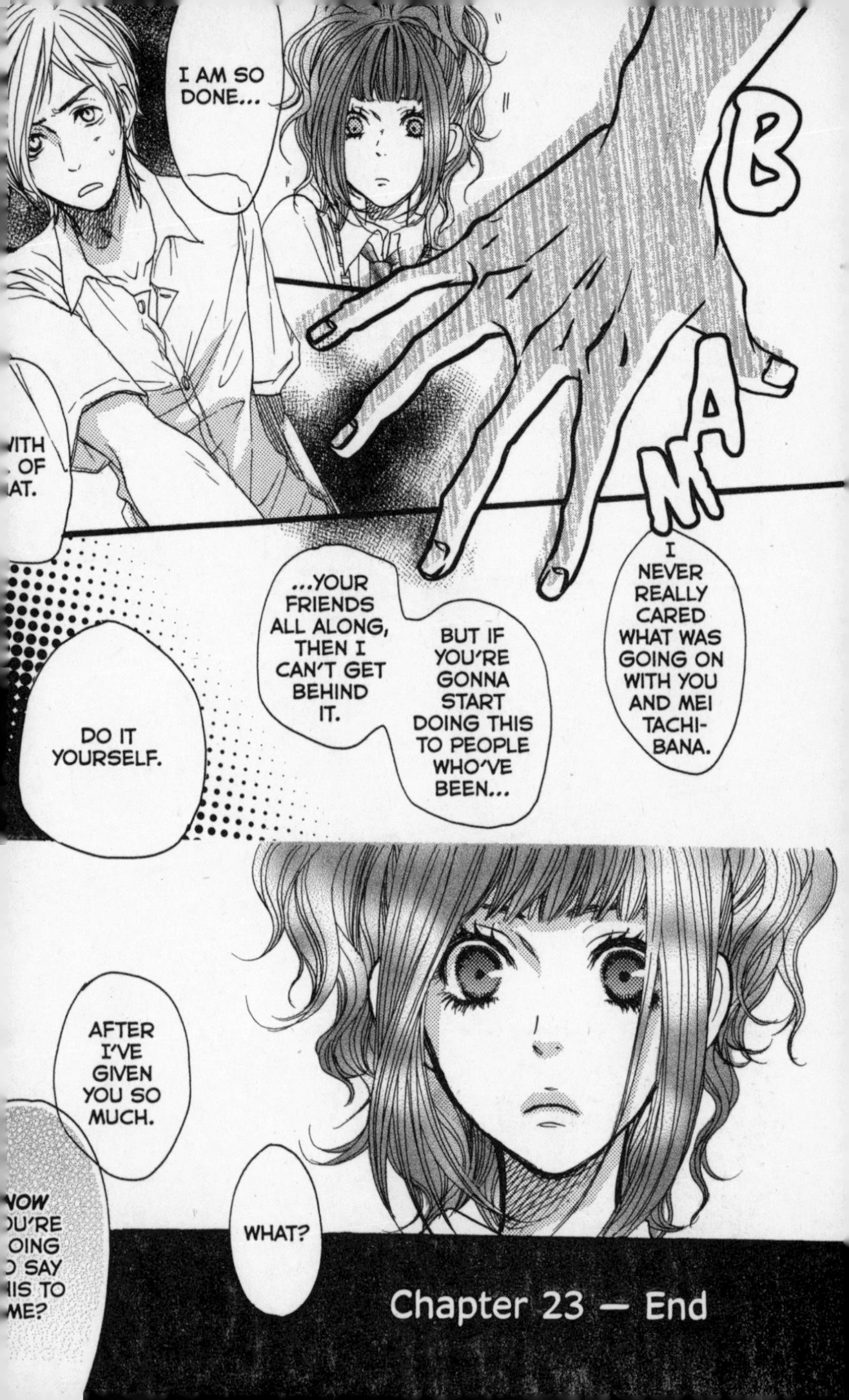
BAM
I AM SO DONE...
I NEVER REALLY CARED WHAT WAS GOING ON WITH YOU AND MEI TACHI-BANA.
BUT IF YOU'RE GONNA START DOING THIS TO PEOPLE WHO'VE BEEN...
...YOUR FRIENDS ALL ALONG, THEN I CAN'T GET BEHIND IT.
DO IT YOURSELF.
WHAT?
AFTER I'VE GIVEN YOU SO MUCH.

Chapter 23 — End

Say
"I love you".
Kanae Hazuki

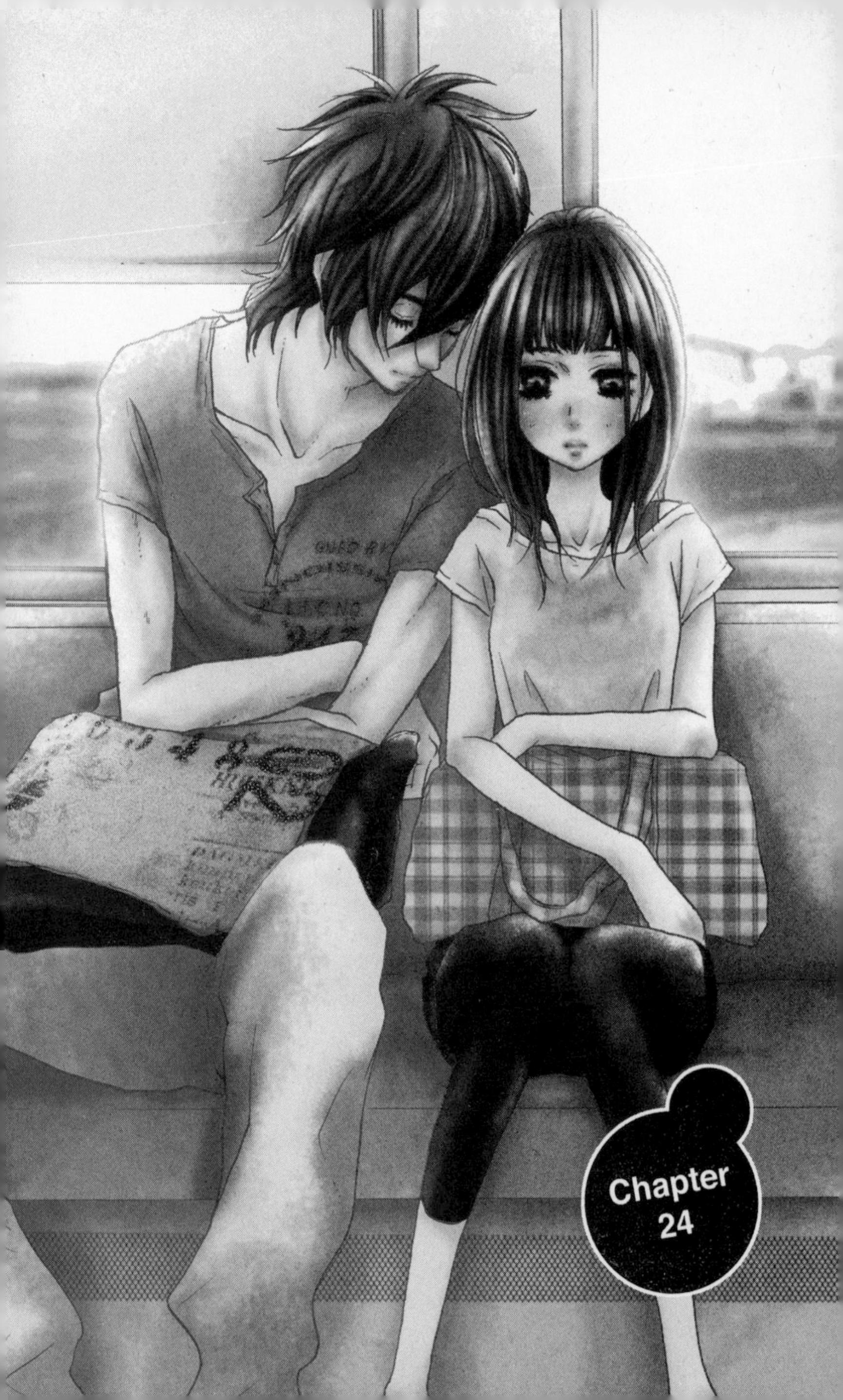
Chapter
24

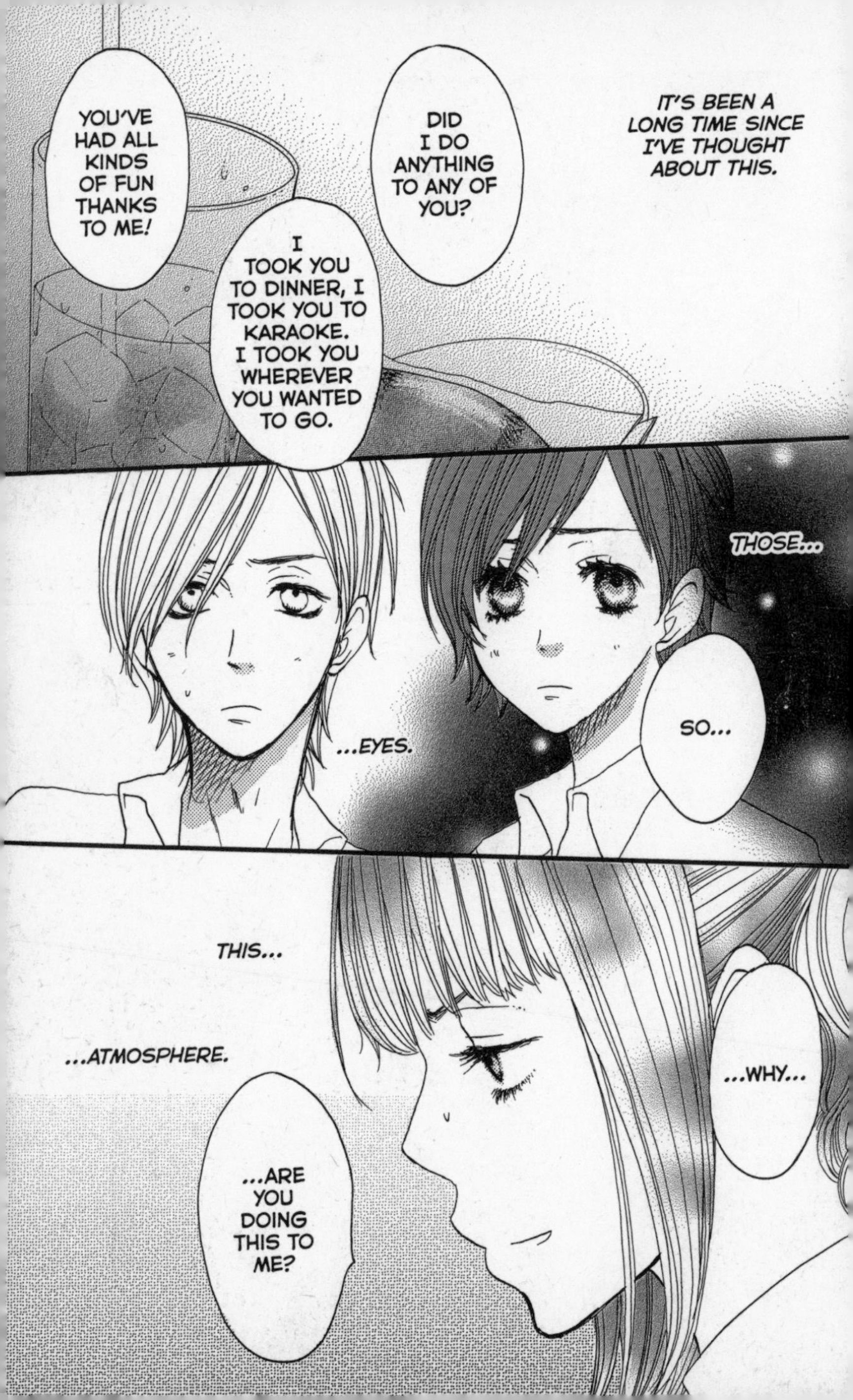
IT'S BEEN A LONG TIME SINCE I'VE THOUGHT ABOUT THIS.
DID I DO ANYTHING TO ANY OF YOU?
YOU'VE HAD ALL KINDS OF FUN THANKS TO ME!
I TOOK YOU TO DINNER, I TOOK YOU TO KARAOKE. I TOOK YOU WHEREVER YOU WANTED TO GO.
THOSE...
SO...
...EYES.
...WHY...
THIS...
...ATMOSPHERE.
...ARE YOU DOING THIS TO ME?

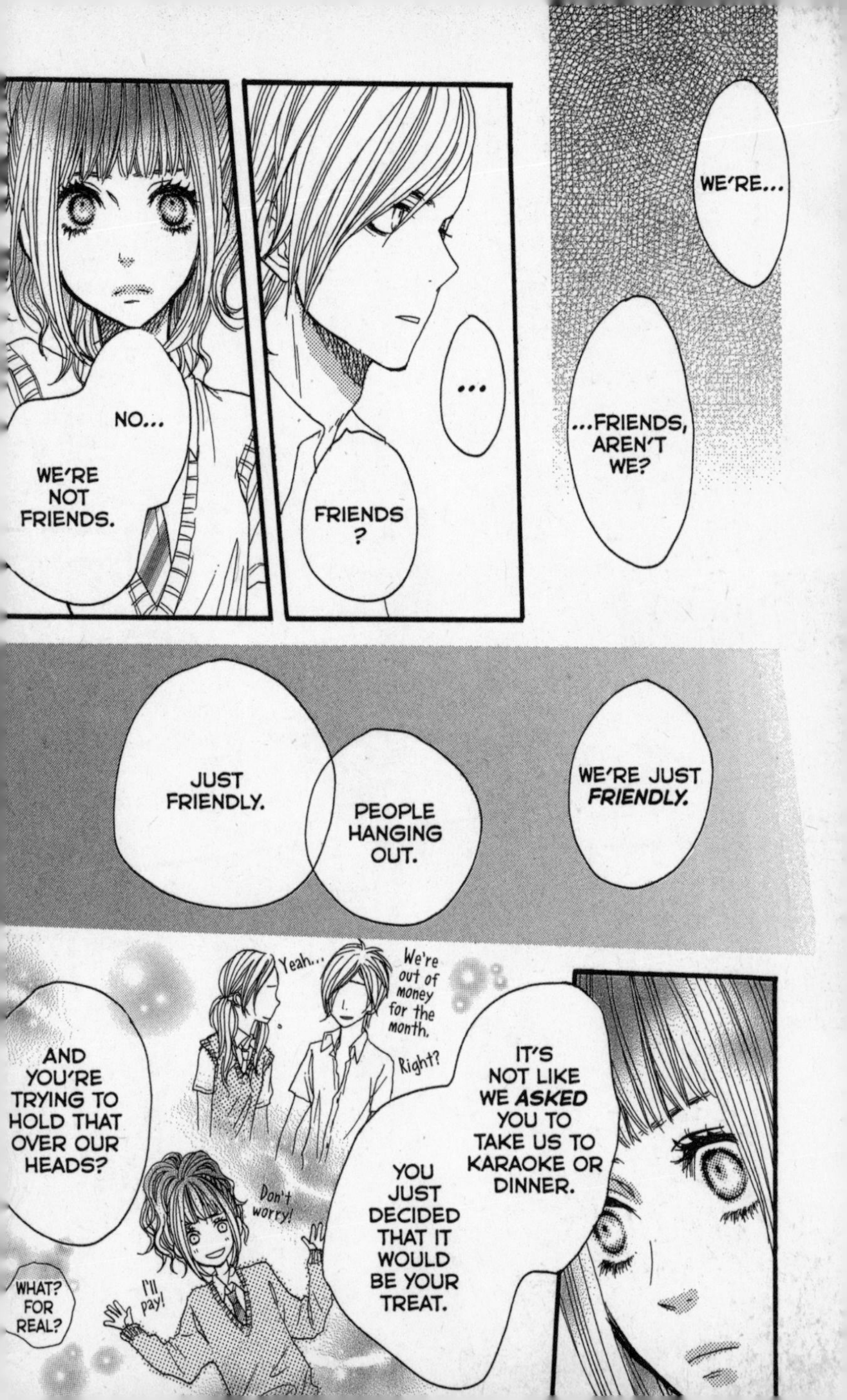
WE'RE...
...FRIENDS, AREN'T WE?
...
FRIENDS?
NO...
WE'RE NOT FRIENDS.
WE'RE JUST *FRIENDLY.*
PEOPLE HANGING OUT.
JUST FRIENDLY.
IT'S NOT LIKE WE *ASKED* YOU TO TAKE US TO KARAOKE OR DINNER.
YOU JUST DECIDED THAT IT WOULD BE YOUR TREAT.
We're out of money for the month.
Yeah...
Right?
Don't worry!
I'll pay!
AND YOU'RE TRYING TO HOLD THAT OVER OUR HEADS?
WHAT? FOR REAL?

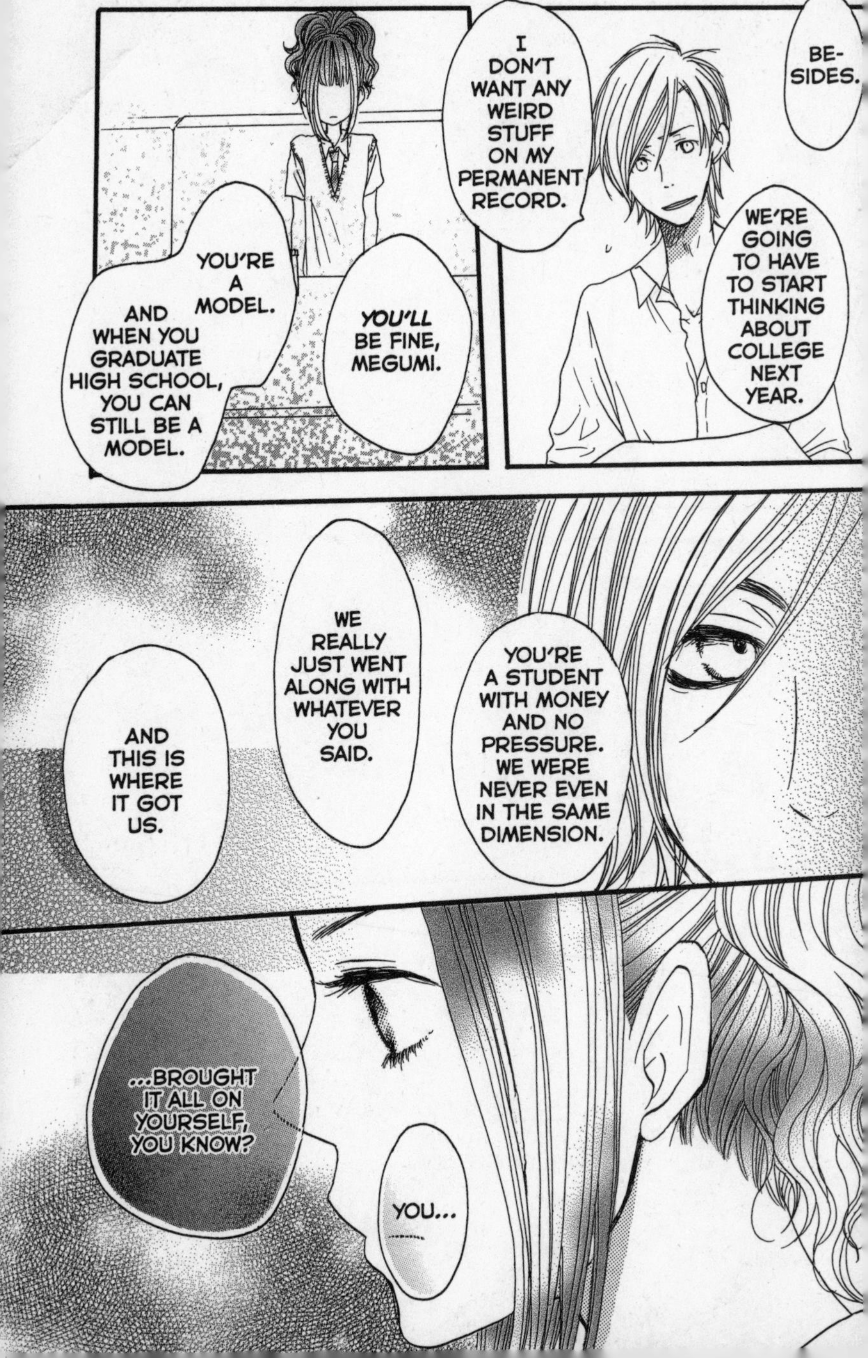
BE-SIDES.
I DON'T WANT ANY WEIRD STUFF ON MY PERMANENT RECORD.
WE'RE GOING TO HAVE TO START THINKING ABOUT COLLEGE NEXT YEAR.
YOU'LL BE FINE, MEGUMI.
YOU'RE A MODEL.
AND WHEN YOU GRADUATE HIGH SCHOOL, YOU CAN STILL BE A MODEL.
YOU'RE A STUDENT WITH MONEY AND NO PRESSURE. WE WERE NEVER EVEN IN THE SAME DIMENSION.
WE REALLY JUST WENT ALONG WITH WHATEVER YOU SAID.
AND THIS IS WHERE IT GOT US.
YOU...
...BROUGHT IT ALL ON YOURSELF, YOU KNOW?

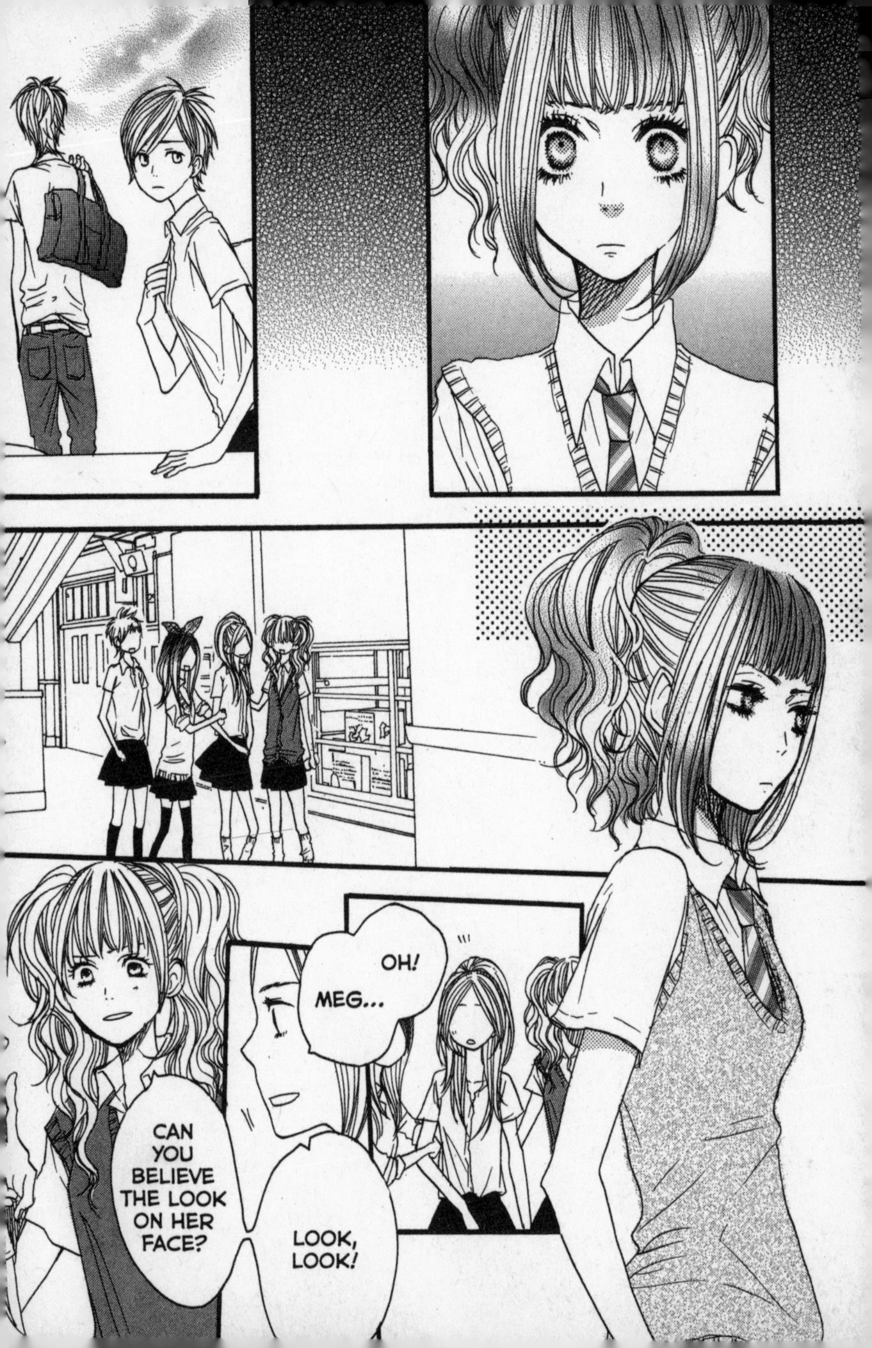
OH! MEG...
LOOK, LOOK!
CAN YOU BELIEVE THE LOOK ON HER FACE?

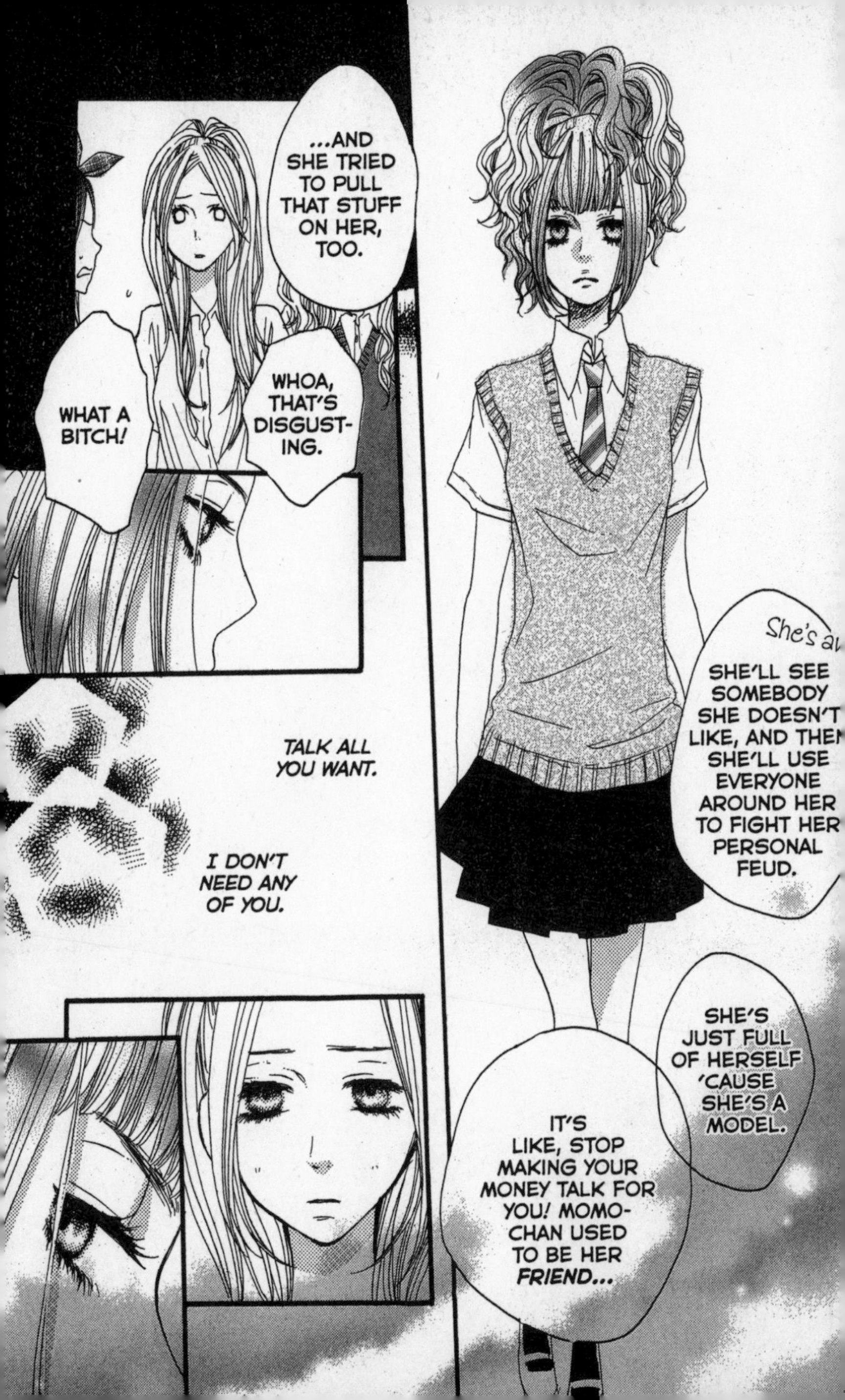
She's
SHE'LL SEE SOMEBODY SHE DOESN'T LIKE, AND THEN SHE'LL USE EVERYONE AROUND HER TO FIGHT HER PERSONAL FEUD.
SHE'S JUST FULL OF HERSELF 'CAUSE SHE'S A MODEL.
IT'S LIKE, STOP MAKING YOUR MONEY TALK FOR YOU! MOMO-CHAN USED TO BE HER *FRIEND*...
...AND SHE TRIED TO PULL THAT STUFF ON HER, TOO.
WHOA, THAT'S DISGUST-ING.
WHAT A BITCH!
TALK ALL YOU WANT.
I DON'T NEED ANY OF YOU.

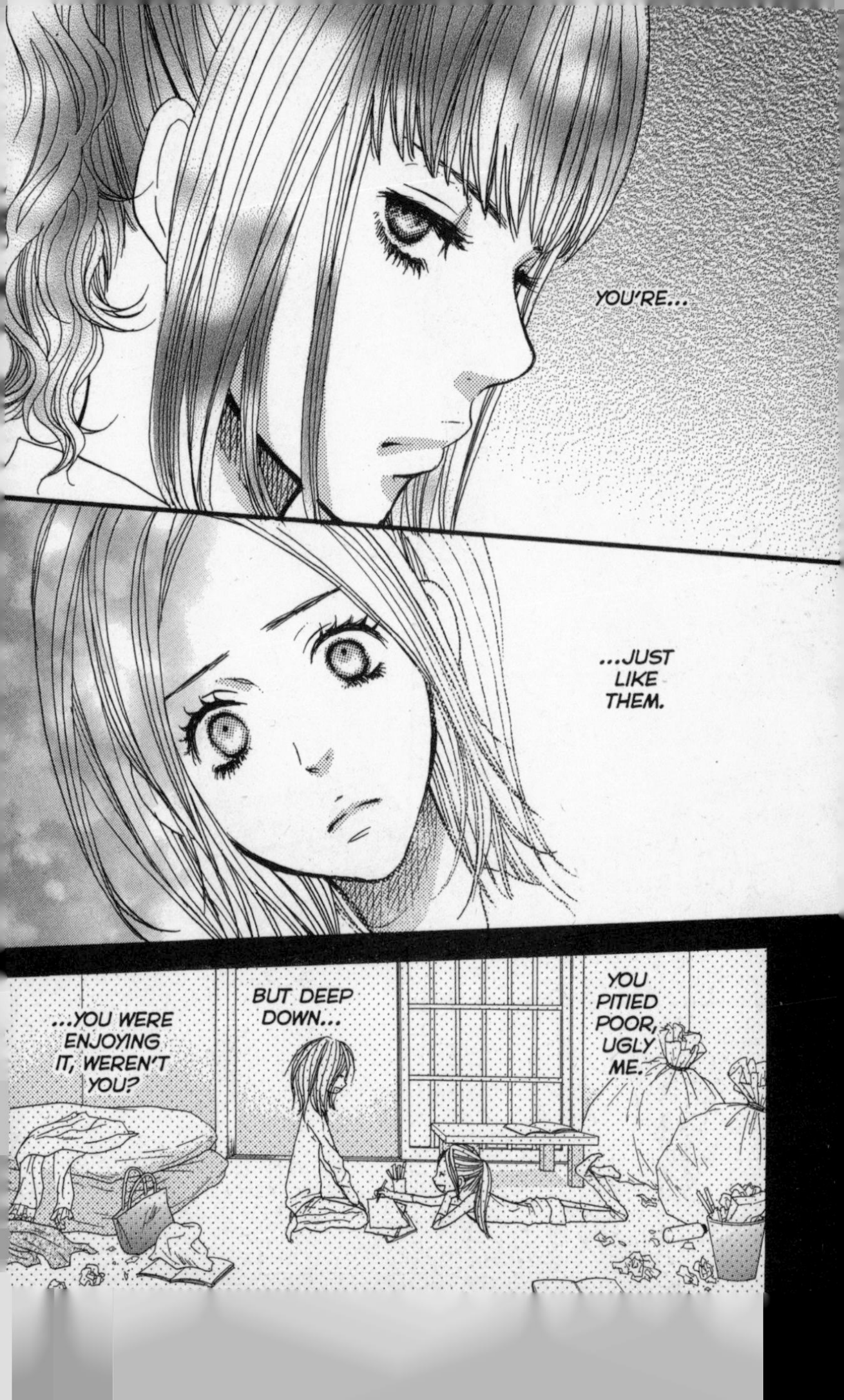
YOU'RE...
...JUST LIKE THEM.
YOU PITIED POOR, UGLY ME.
BUT DEEP DOWN...
...YOU WERE ENJOYING IT, WEREN'T YOU?

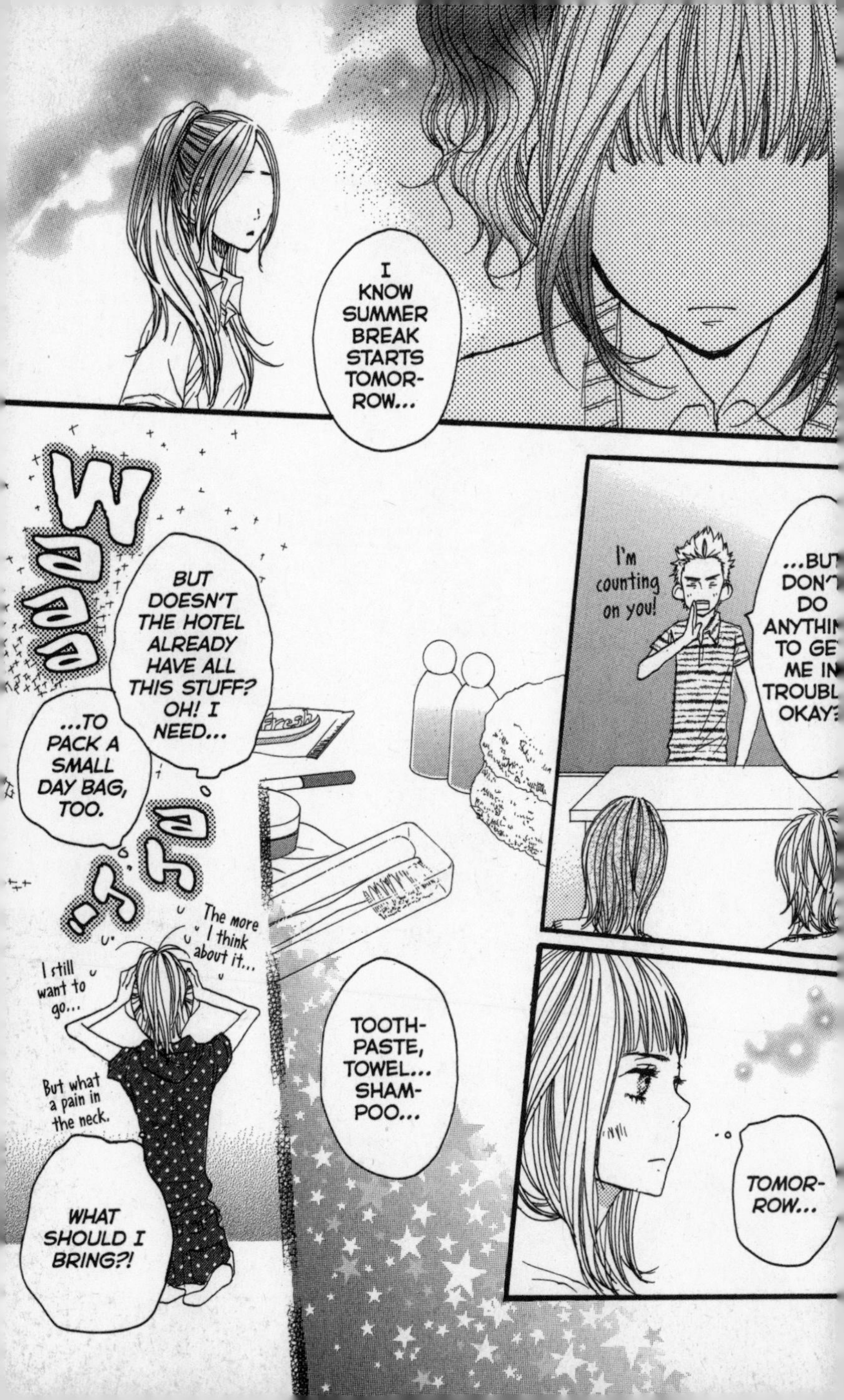
I KNOW SUMMER BREAK STARTS TOMORROW...
...BUT DON'T DO ANYTHIN TO GE ME IN TROUBL OKAY?
I'm counting on you!
TOMORROW...
TOOTHPASTE, TOWEL... SHAMPOO...
BUT DOESN'T THE HOTEL ALREADY HAVE ALL THIS STUFF? OH! I NEED...
...TO PACK A SMALL DAY BAG, TOO.
Waaa
The more I think about it...
I still want to go...
But what a pain in the neck.
WHAT SHOULD I BRING?!

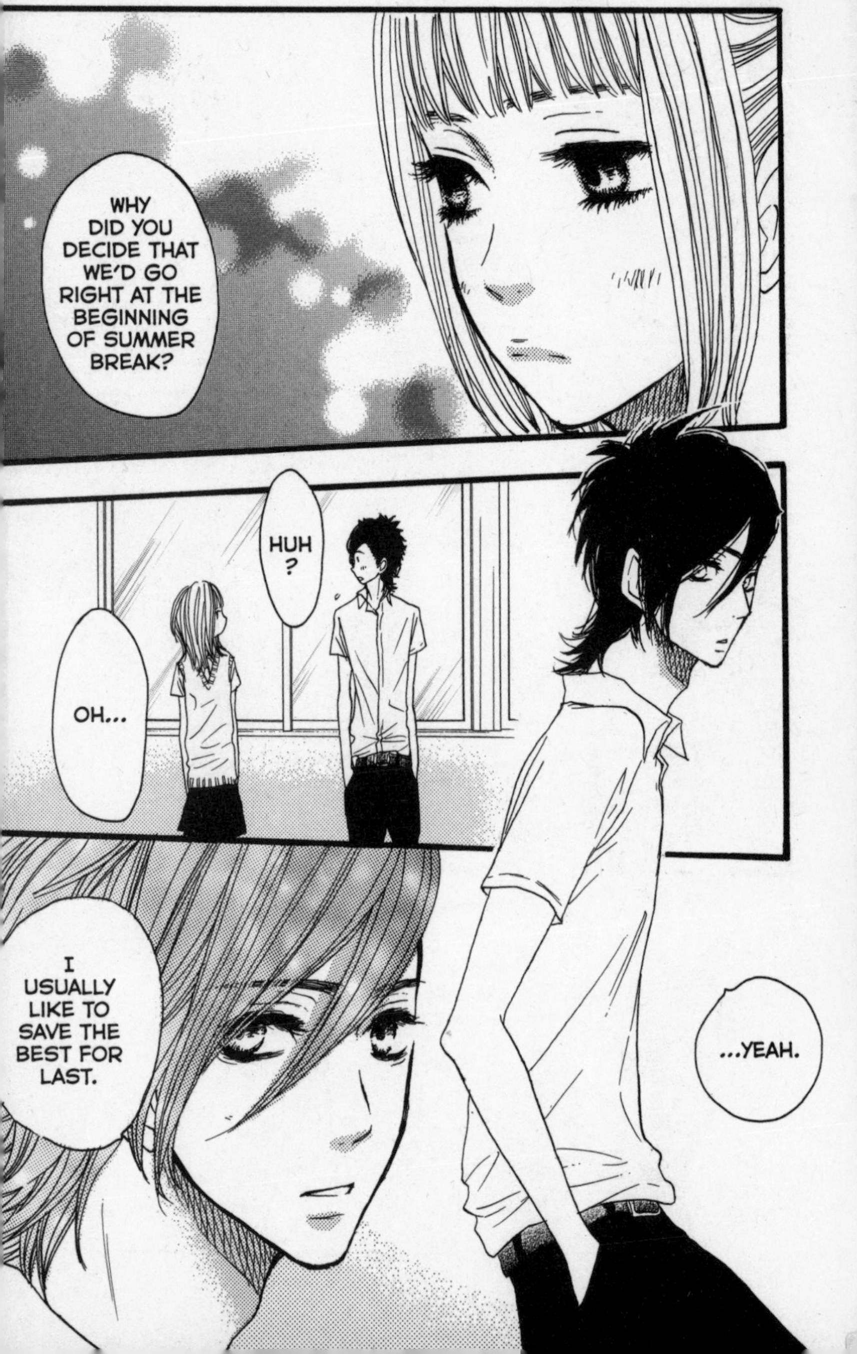
WHY DID YOU DECIDE THAT WE'D GO RIGHT AT THE BEGINNING OF SUMMER BREAK?
HUH?
OH...
I USUALLY LIKE TO SAVE THE BEST FOR LAST.
...YEAH.

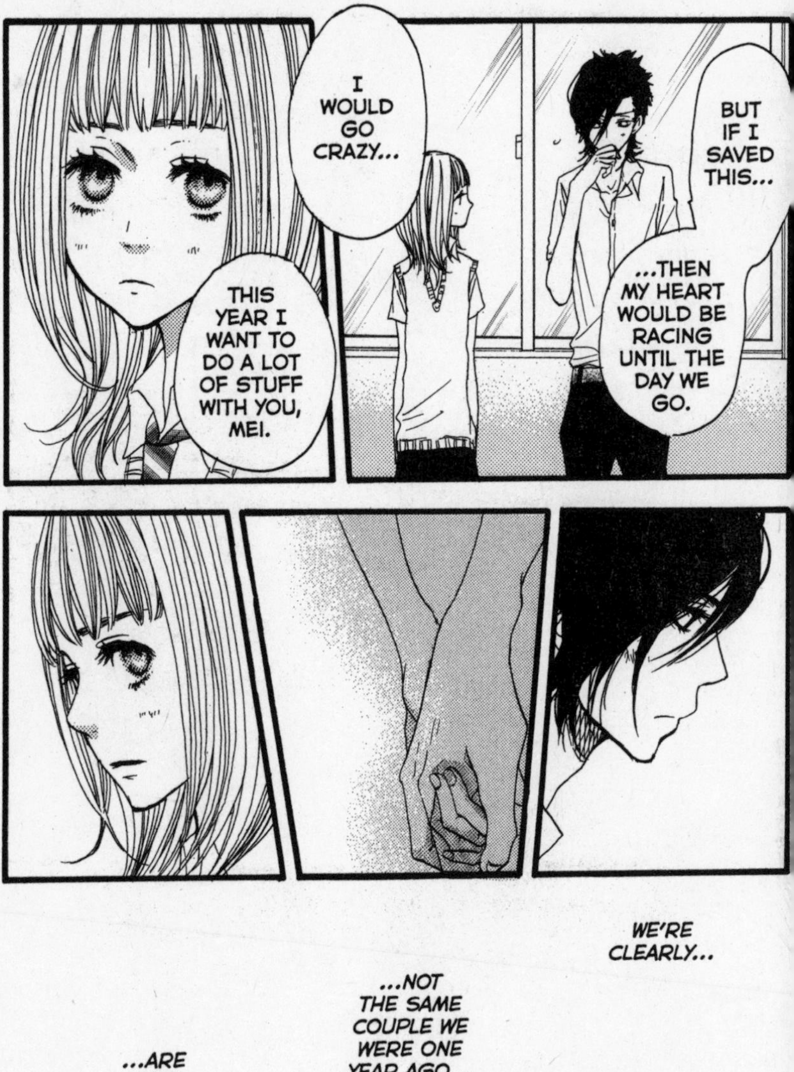
BUT IF I SAVED THIS...
...THEN MY HEART WOULD BE RACING UNTIL THE DAY WE GO.
I WOULD GO CRAZY...
THIS YEAR I WANT TO DO A LOT OF STUFF WITH YOU, MEI.
WE'RE CLEARLY...
...NOT THE SAME COUPLE WE WERE ONE YEAR AGO...
...ARE WE?

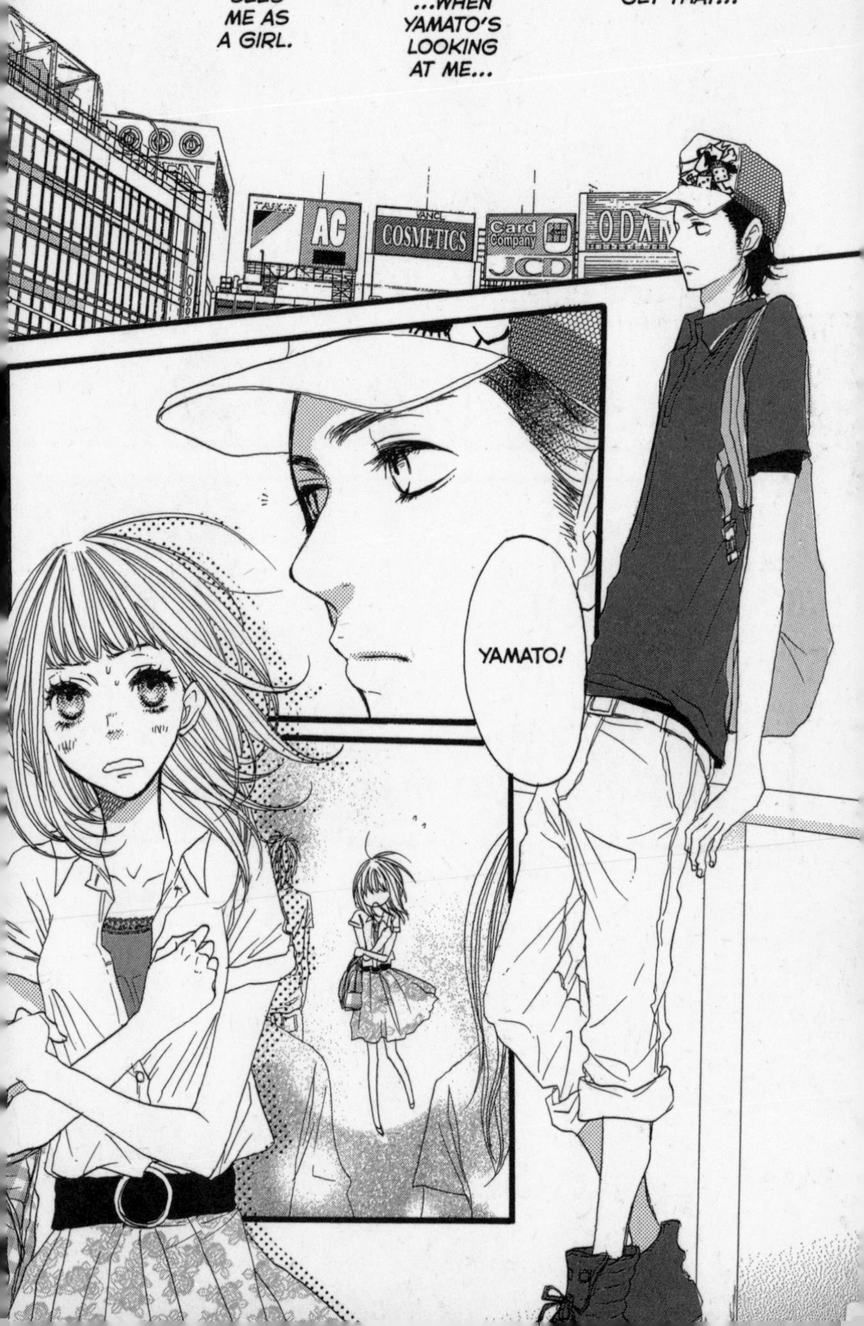
I FINALLY GET THAT...
...WHEN YAMATO'S LOOKING AT ME...
...HE SEES ME AS A GIRL.
COSMETICS
Card Company
JCD
AC
YAMATO!

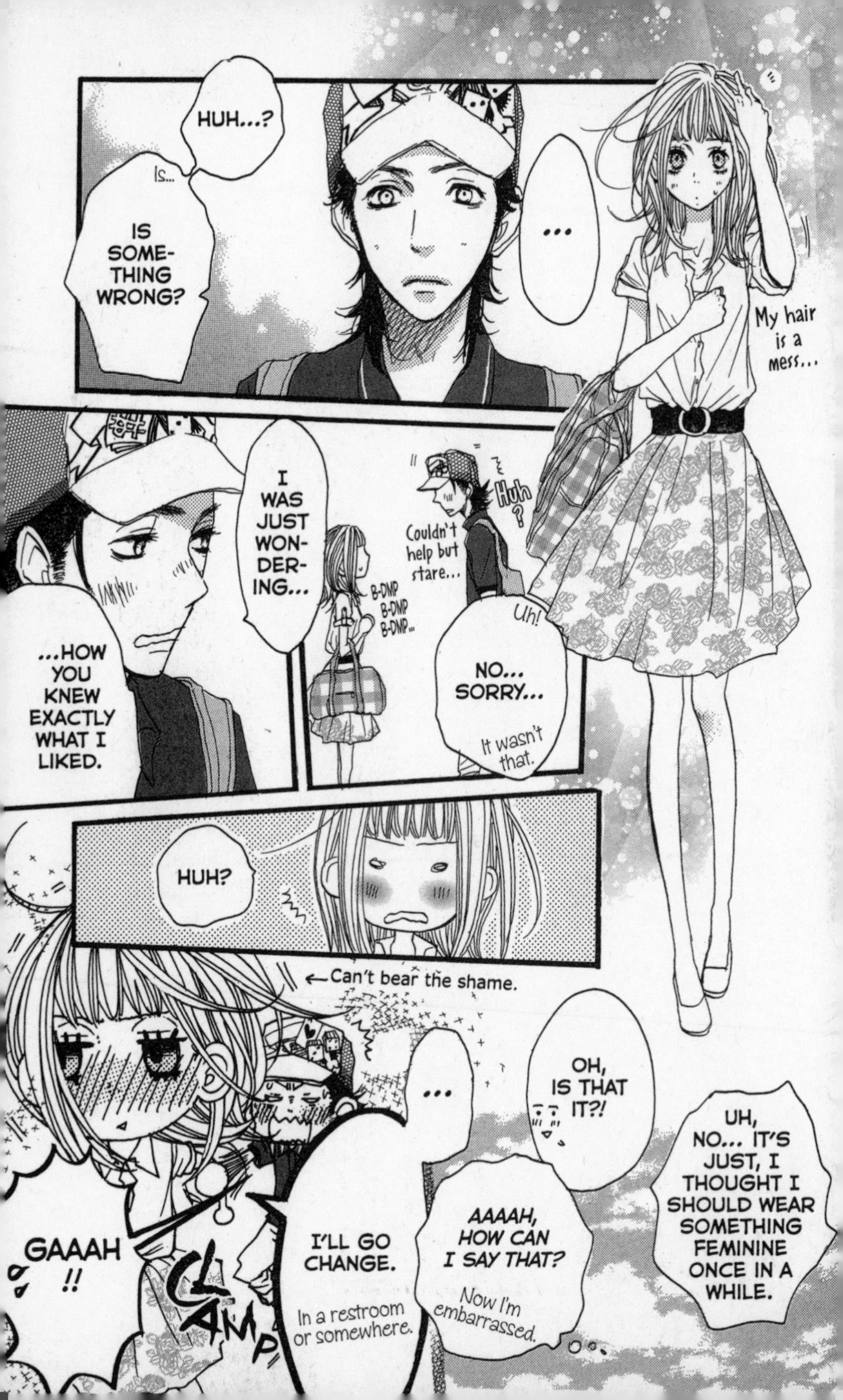
...
HUH...?
Is...
IS SOME-THING WRONG?
My hair is a mess...
Huh ?
Couldn't help but stare...
Uh!
NO... SORRY...
It wasn't that.
B-DMP B-DMP B-DMP...
I WAS JUST WON-DER-ING...
...HOW YOU KNEW EXACTLY WHAT I LIKED.
HUH?
UH, NO... IT'S JUST, I THOUGHT I SHOULD WEAR SOMETHING FEMININE ONCE IN A WHILE.
OH, IS THAT IT?!
...
AAAAH, HOW CAN I SAY THAT?
Now I'm embarrassed.
I'LL GO CHANGE.
In a restroom or somewhere.
← Can't bear the shame.
CLAMP
GAAAH !!

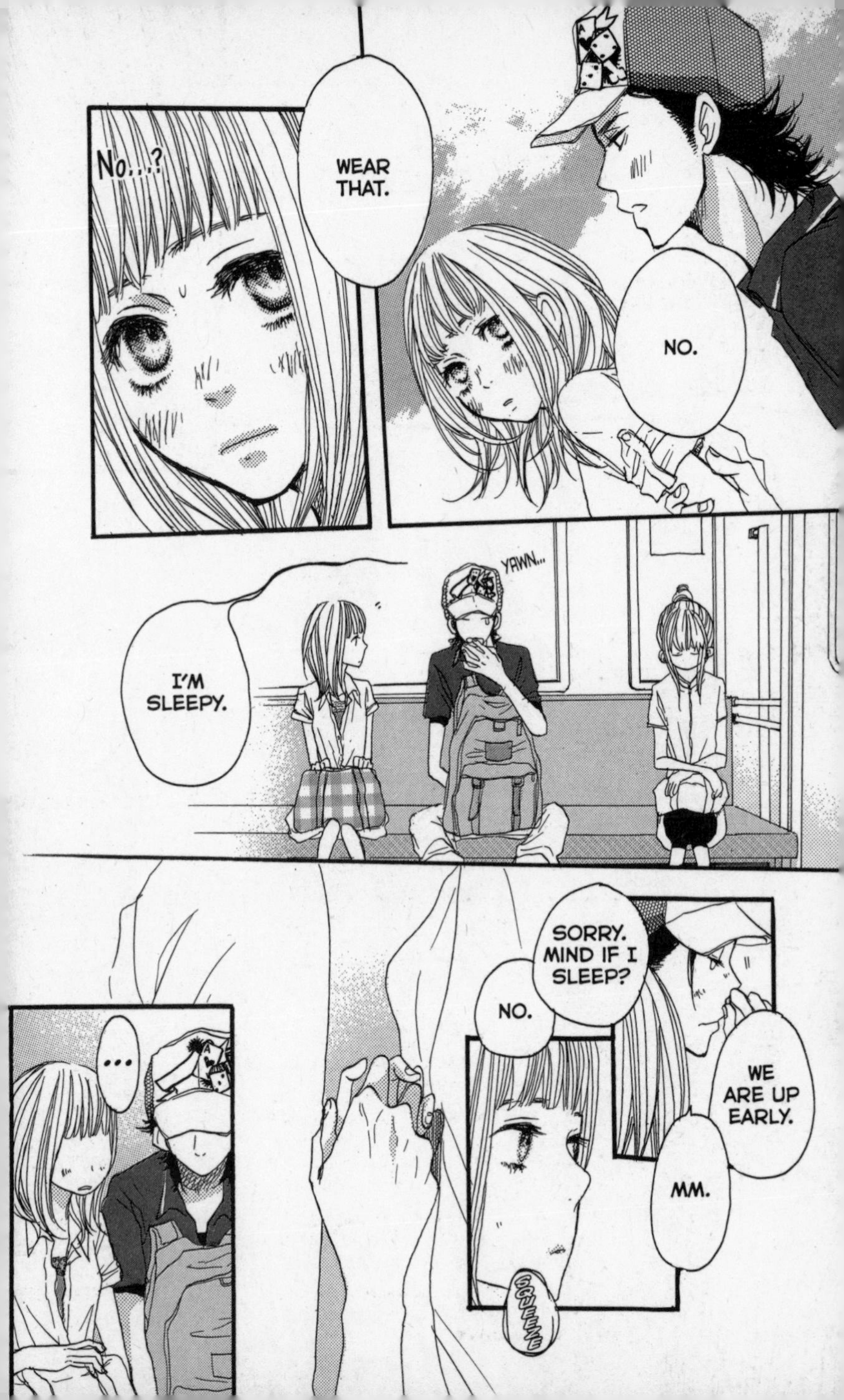
WEAR THAT.
NO.
No...?
YAWN...
I'M SLEEPY.
SORRY. MIND IF I SLEEP?
NO.
WE ARE UP EARLY.
MM.
SQUEEZE
...

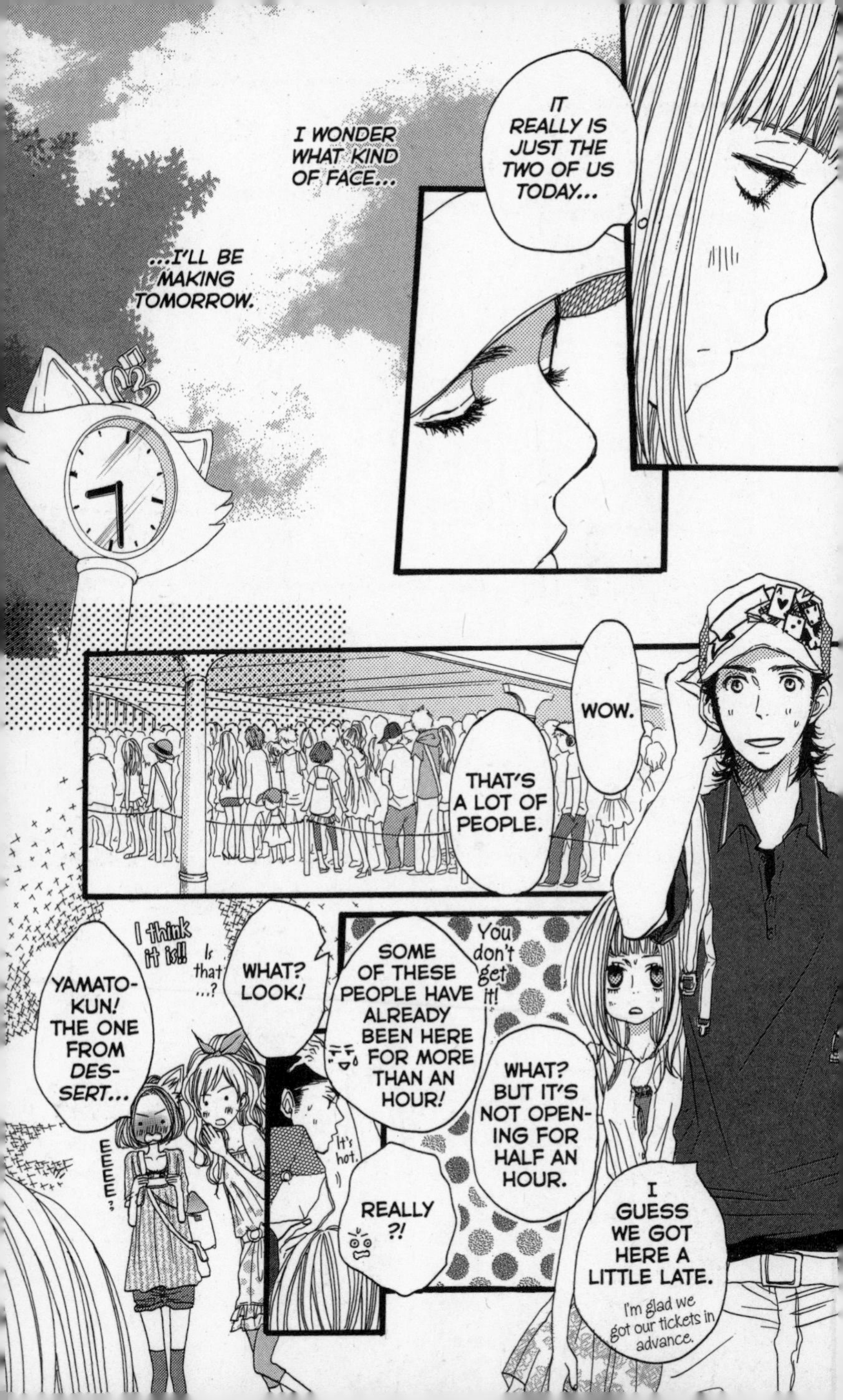
IT REALLY IS JUST THE TWO OF US TODAY...
I WONDER WHAT KIND OF FACE...
...I'LL BE MAKING TOMORROW.
WOW.
THAT'S A LOT OF PEOPLE.
I GUESS WE GOT HERE A LITTLE LATE.
I'm glad we got our tickets in advance.
WHAT? BUT IT'S NOT OPEN-ING FOR HALF AN HOUR.
You don't get it!
SOME OF THESE PEOPLE HAVE ALREADY BEEN HERE FOR MORE THAN AN HOUR!
It's hot.
REALLY?!
WHAT? LOOK!
Is that ...?
I think it is!!
YAMATO-KUN! THE ONE FROM DES-SERT...
EEEE?

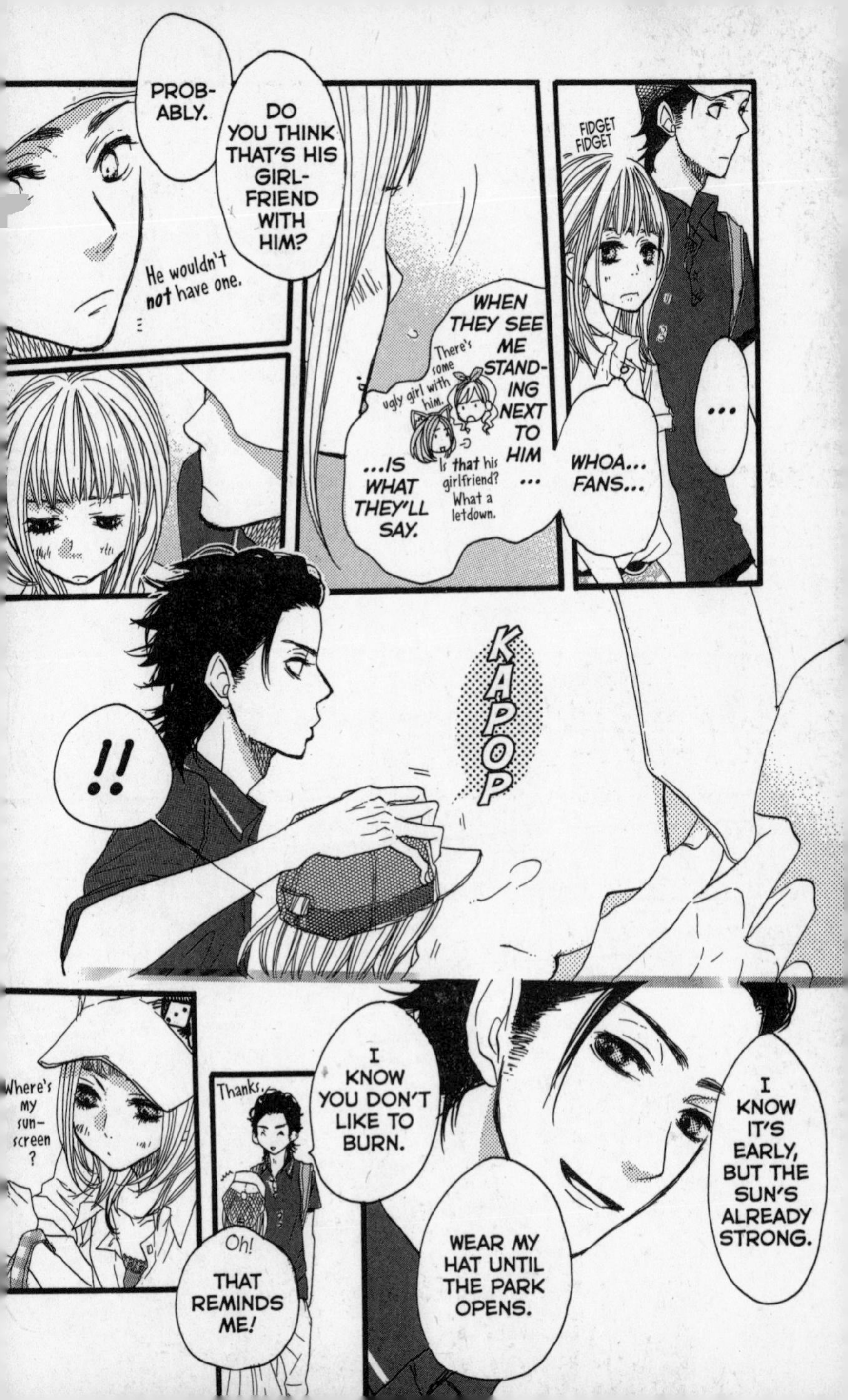
FIDGET FIDGET
WHOA... FANS...
...
WHEN THEY SEE ME STANDING NEXT TO HIM...
There's some ugly girl with him.
Is that his girlfriend? What a letdown.
...IS WHAT THEY'LL SAY.
DO YOU THINK THAT'S HIS GIRLFRIEND WITH HIM?
PROBABLY.
He wouldn't **not** have one.
KAPOP
!!
I KNOW IT'S EARLY, BUT THE SUN'S ALREADY STRONG.
WEAR MY HAT UNTIL THE PARK OPENS.
I KNOW YOU DON'T LIKE TO BURN.
Thanks.
Oh! THAT REMINDS ME!
Where's my sunscreen?

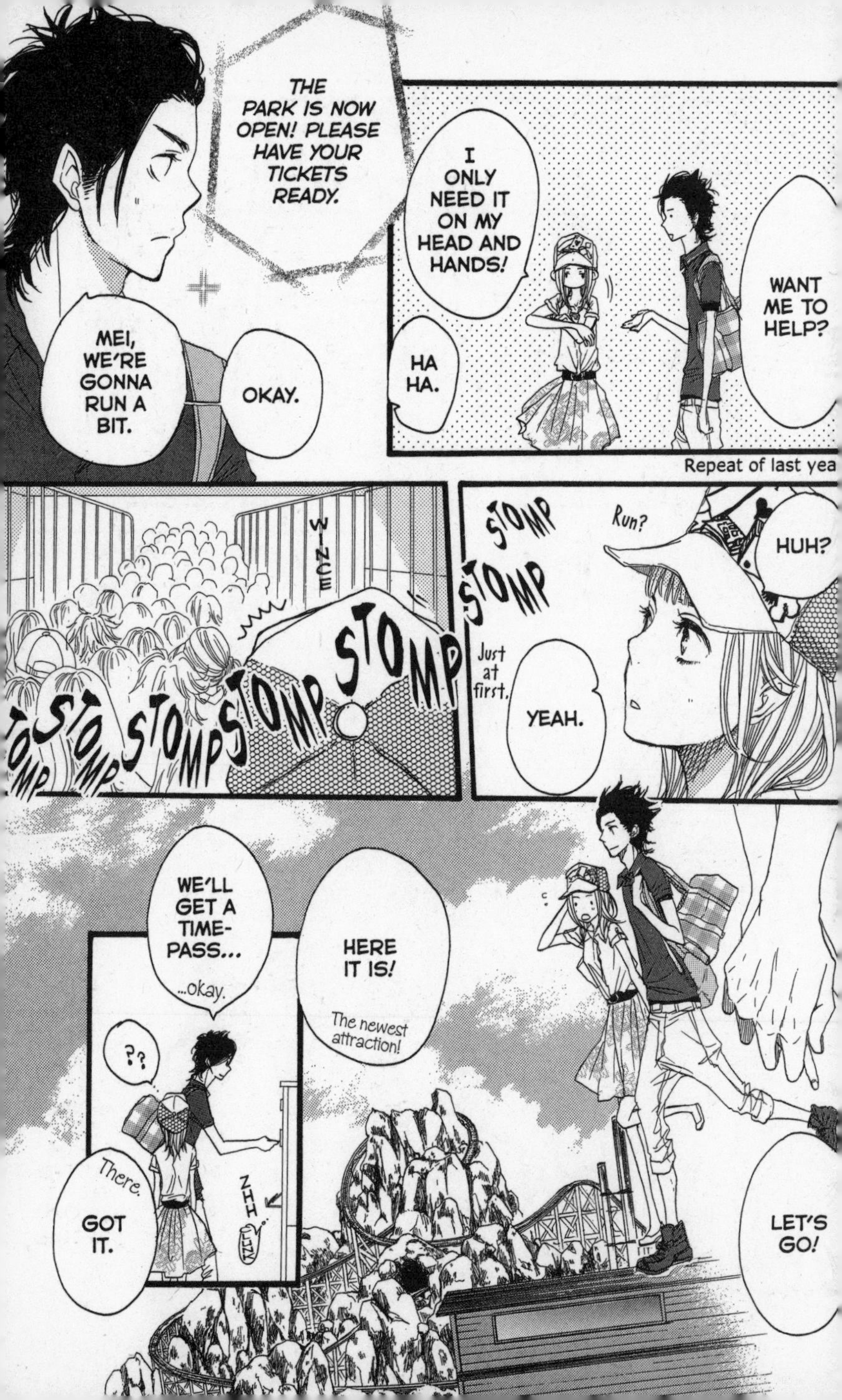
WANT ME TO HELP?
I ONLY NEED IT ON MY HEAD AND HANDS!
HA HA.
Repeat of last yea
THE PARK IS NOW OPEN! PLEASE HAVE YOUR TICKETS READY.
MEI, WE'RE GONNA RUN A BIT.
OKAY.
HUH?
Run?
STOMP
STOMP
Just at first.
YEAH.
WINCE
STOMP
STOMP
STOMP
STOMP
STOMP
LET'S GO!
HERE IT IS!
The newest attraction!
WE'LL GET A TIME-PASS...
...okay.
??
There.
GOT IT.
ZHH
CLUNK

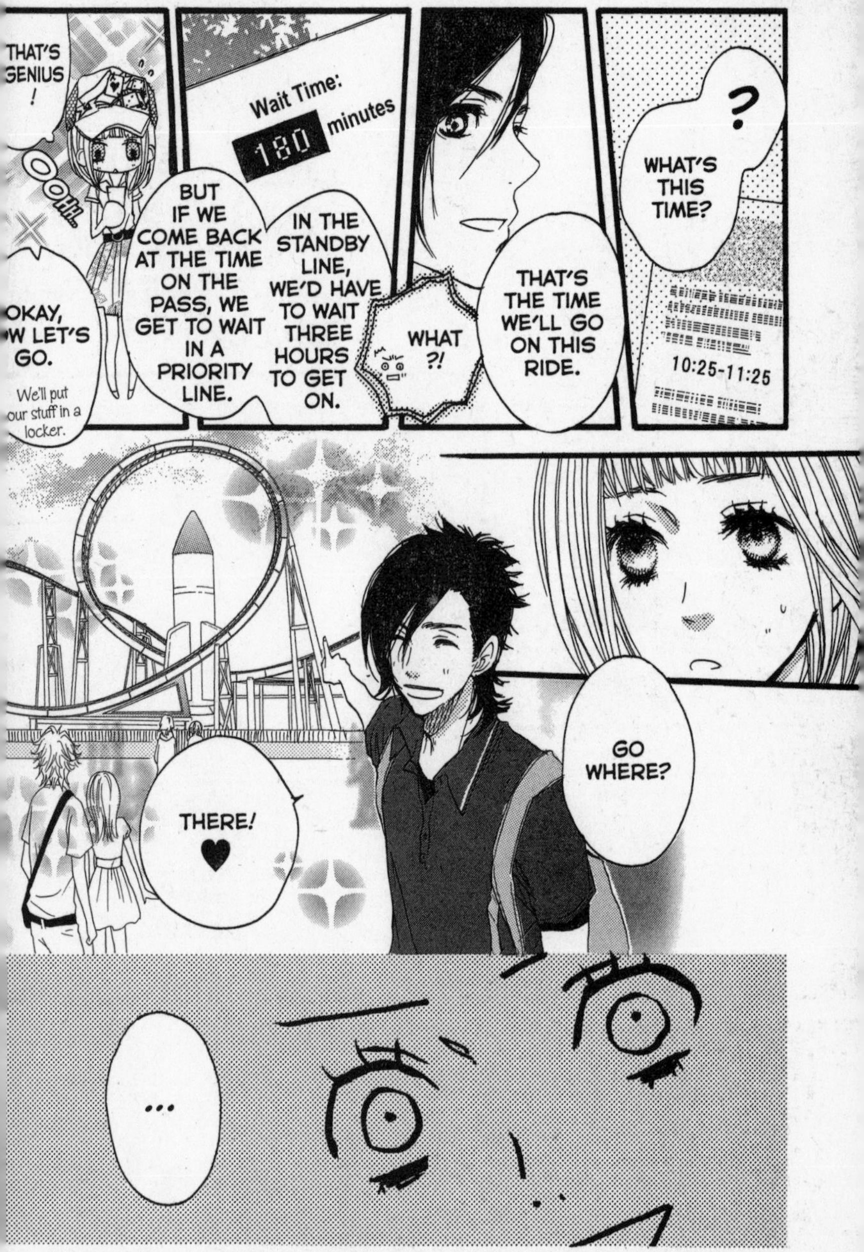
?
WHAT'S THIS TIME?
10:25-11:25
THAT'S THE TIME WE'LL GO ON THIS RIDE.
WHAT ?!
Wait Time: 180 minutes
IN THE STANDBY LINE, WE'D HAVE TO WAIT THREE HOURS TO GET ON.
BUT IF WE COME BACK AT THE TIME ON THE PASS, WE GET TO WAIT IN A PRIORITY LINE.
THAT'S GENIUS!
OOOH!
OKAY, W LET'S GO.
We'll put our stuff in a locker.
GO WHERE?
THERE! ♥
...

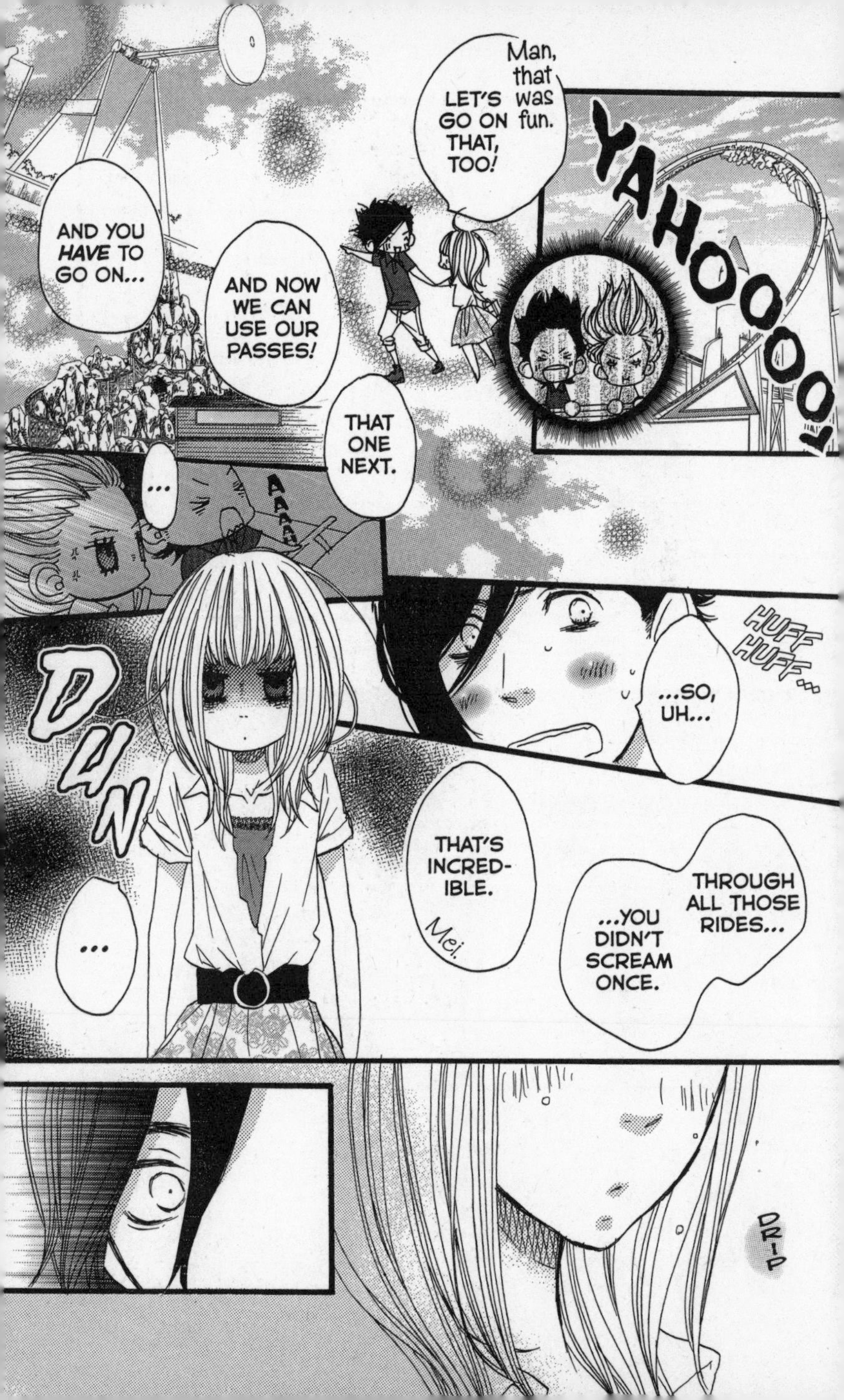
YAHOOOOO
Man, that was fun.
LET'S GO ON THAT, TOO!
AND NOW WE CAN USE OUR PASSES!
AND YOU *HAVE* TO GO ON...
THAT ONE NEXT.
AAAA
...
HUFF HUFF...
...SO, UH...
THROUGH ALL THOSE RIDES...
...YOU DIDN'T SCREAM ONCE.
THAT'S INCRED-IBLE.
Mei.
DUN
...
DRIP

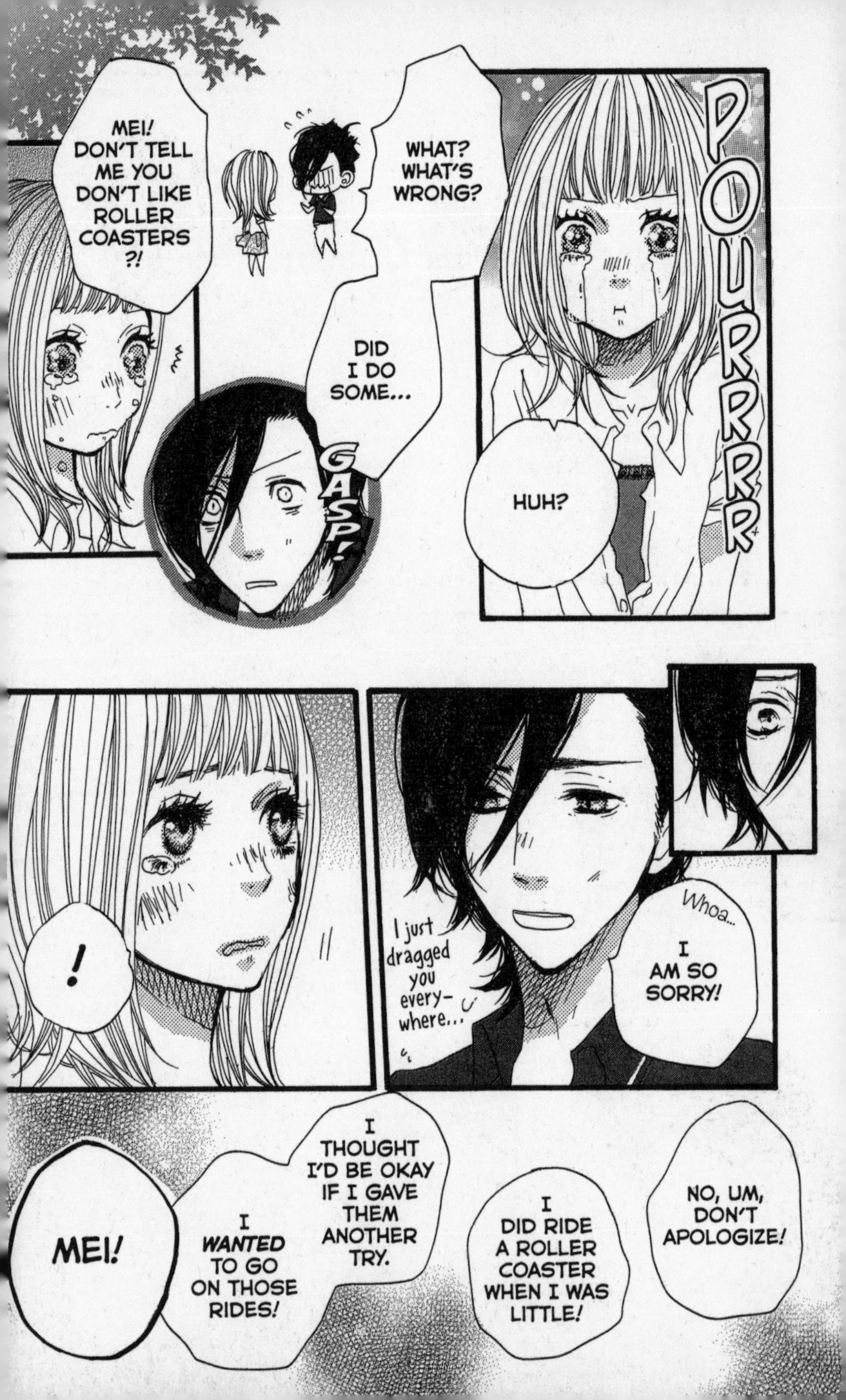
POURRRR
HUH?
WHAT? WHAT'S WRONG?
DID I DO SOME...
GASP!
MEI! DON'T TELL ME YOU DON'T LIKE ROLLER COASTERS ?!
Whoa...
I AM SO SORRY!
I just dragged you every-where...
!
NO, UM, DON'T APOLOGIZE!
I DID RIDE A ROLLER COASTER WHEN I WAS LITTLE!
I THOUGHT I'D BE OKAY IF I GAVE THEM ANOTHER TRY.
I *WANTED* TO GO ON THOSE RIDES!
MEI!

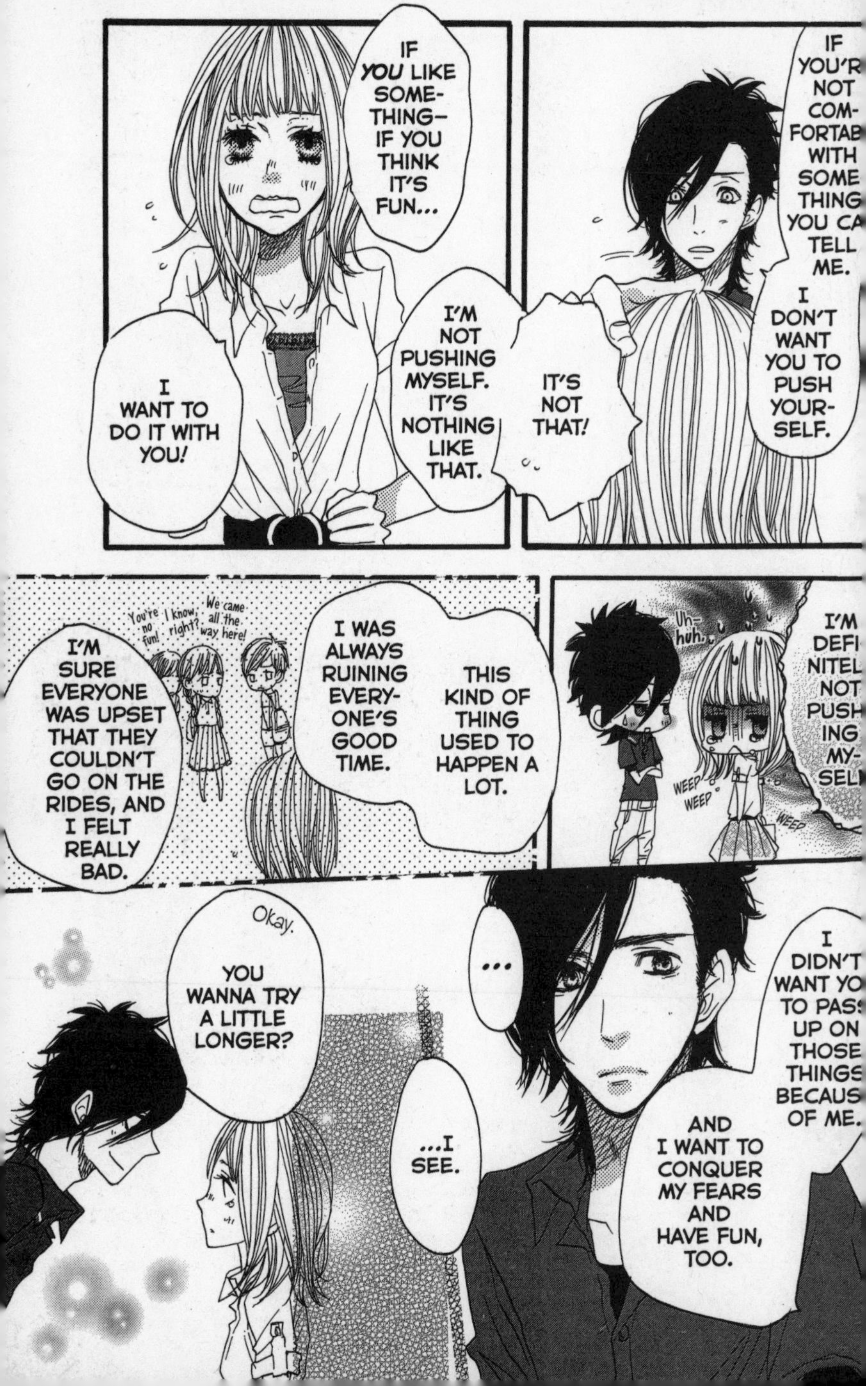

IF YOU'R NOT COM- FORTAB WITH SOME THING YOU CA TELL ME.
I DON'T WANT YOU TO PUSH YOUR- SELF.
IT'S NOT THAT!
IF *YOU* LIKE SOME- THING— IF YOU THINK IT'S FUN...
I'M NOT PUSHING MYSELF. IT'S NOTHING LIKE THAT.
I WANT TO DO IT WITH YOU!
I'M DEFI NITEL NOT PUSH ING MY- SEL
Uh-huh.
WEEP WEEP
WEEP
THIS KIND OF THING USED TO HAPPEN A LOT.
I WAS ALWAYS RUINING EVERY- ONE'S GOOD TIME.
We came all the way here!
I know, right?
You're no fun!
I'M SURE EVERYONE WAS UPSET THAT THEY COULDN'T GO ON THE RIDES, AND I FELT REALLY BAD.
I DIDN'T WANT YO TO PAS UP ON THOSE THINGS BECAUS OF ME.
AND I WANT TO CONQUER MY FEARS AND HAVE FUN, TOO.
...
...I SEE.
Okay.
YOU WANNA TRY A LITTLE LONGER?

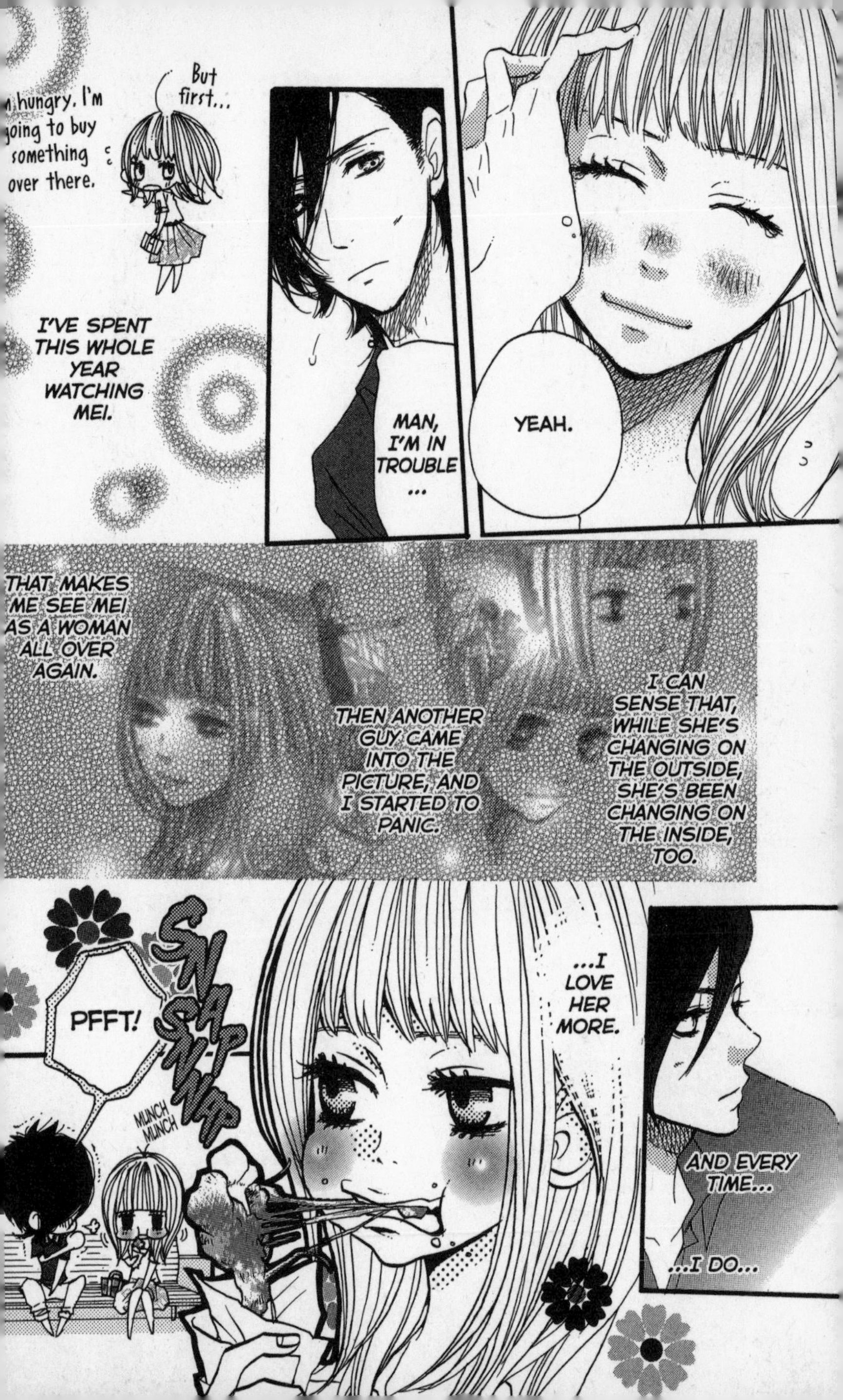

YEAH.
MAN, I'M IN TROUBLE...
But first...
hungry. I'm going to buy something over there.
I'VE SPENT THIS WHOLE YEAR WATCHING MEI.
I CAN SENSE THAT, WHILE SHE'S CHANGING ON THE OUTSIDE, SHE'S BEEN CHANGING ON THE INSIDE, TOO.
THEN ANOTHER GUY CAME INTO THE PICTURE, AND I STARTED TO PANIC.
THAT MAKES ME SEE MEI AS A WOMAN ALL OVER AGAIN.
AND EVERY TIME...
...I DO...
...I LOVE HER MORE.
SNAP SNAP
PFFT!
MUNCH MUNCH

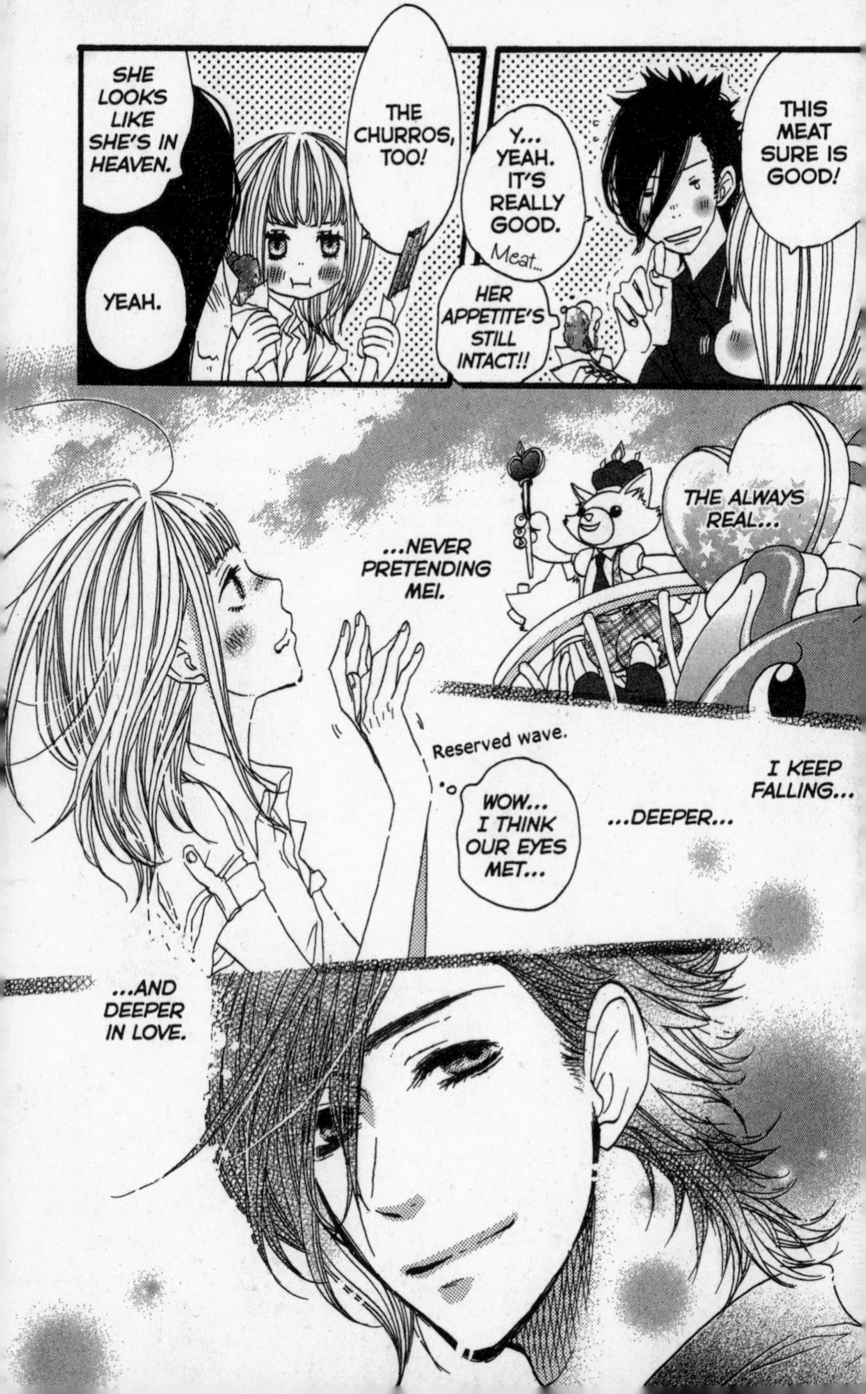
THIS MEAT SURE IS GOOD!
Y... YEAH. IT'S REALLY GOOD.
Meat...
HER APPETITE'S STILL INTACT!!
THE CHURROS, TOO!
SHE LOOKS LIKE SHE'S IN HEAVEN.
YEAH.
THE ALWAYS REAL...
...NEVER PRETENDING MEI.
I KEEP FALLING...
...DEEPER...
Reserved wave.
WOW... I THINK OUR EYES MET...
...AND DEEPER IN LOVE.

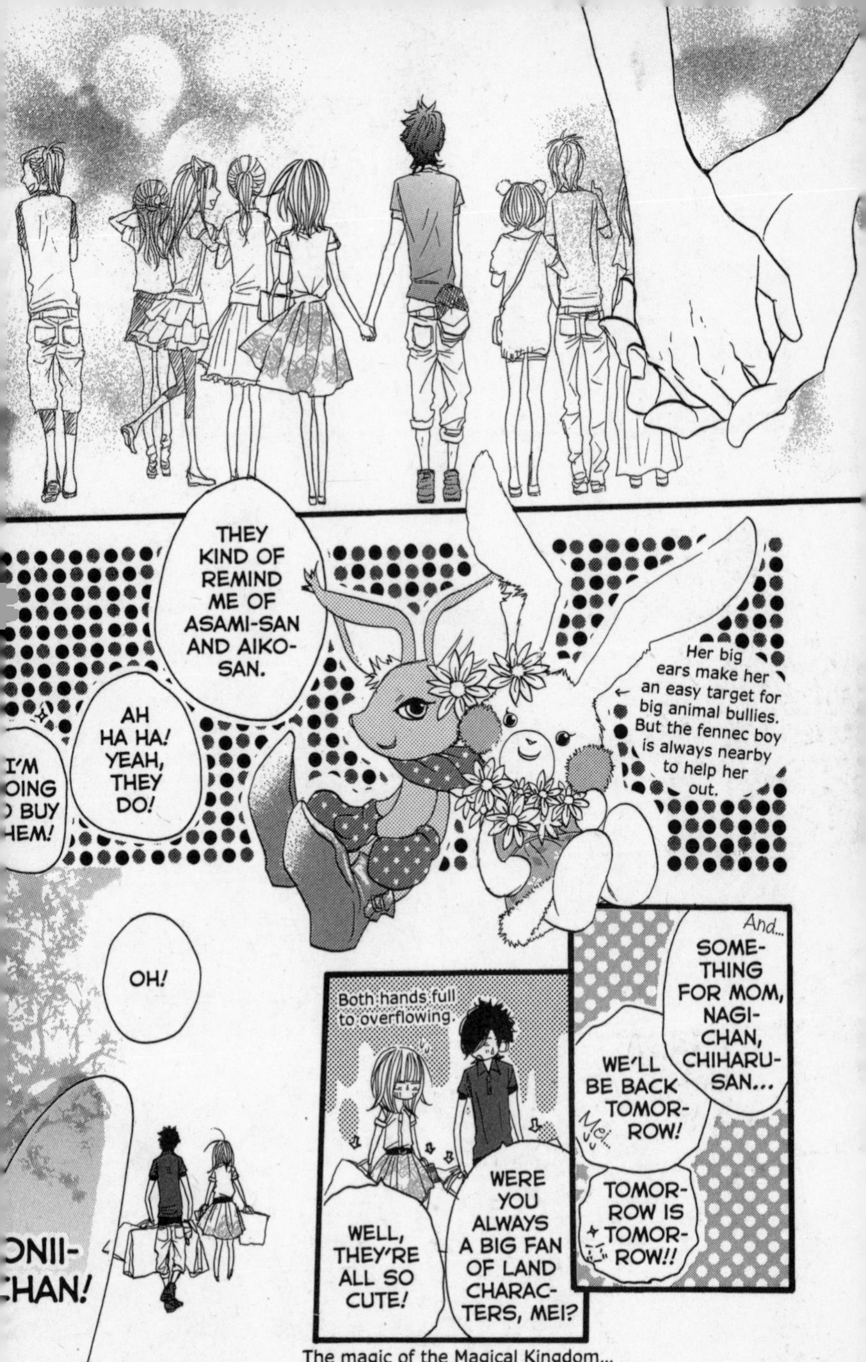
Her big ears make her an easy target for big animal bullies. But the fennec boy is always nearby to help her out.
THEY KIND OF REMIND ME OF ASAMI-SAN AND AIKO-SAN.
AH HA HA! YEAH, THEY DO!
I'M OING D BUY HEM!
And...
SOME-THING FOR MOM, NAGI-CHAN, CHIHARU-SAN...
WE'LL BE BACK TOMORROW!
Mei...
TOMORROW IS TOMORROW!!
Both hands full to overflowing.
WERE YOU ALWAYS A BIG FAN OF LAND CHARACTERS, MEI?
WELL, THEY'RE ALL SO CUTE!
OH!
ONII-CHAN!

The magic of the Magical Kingdom...

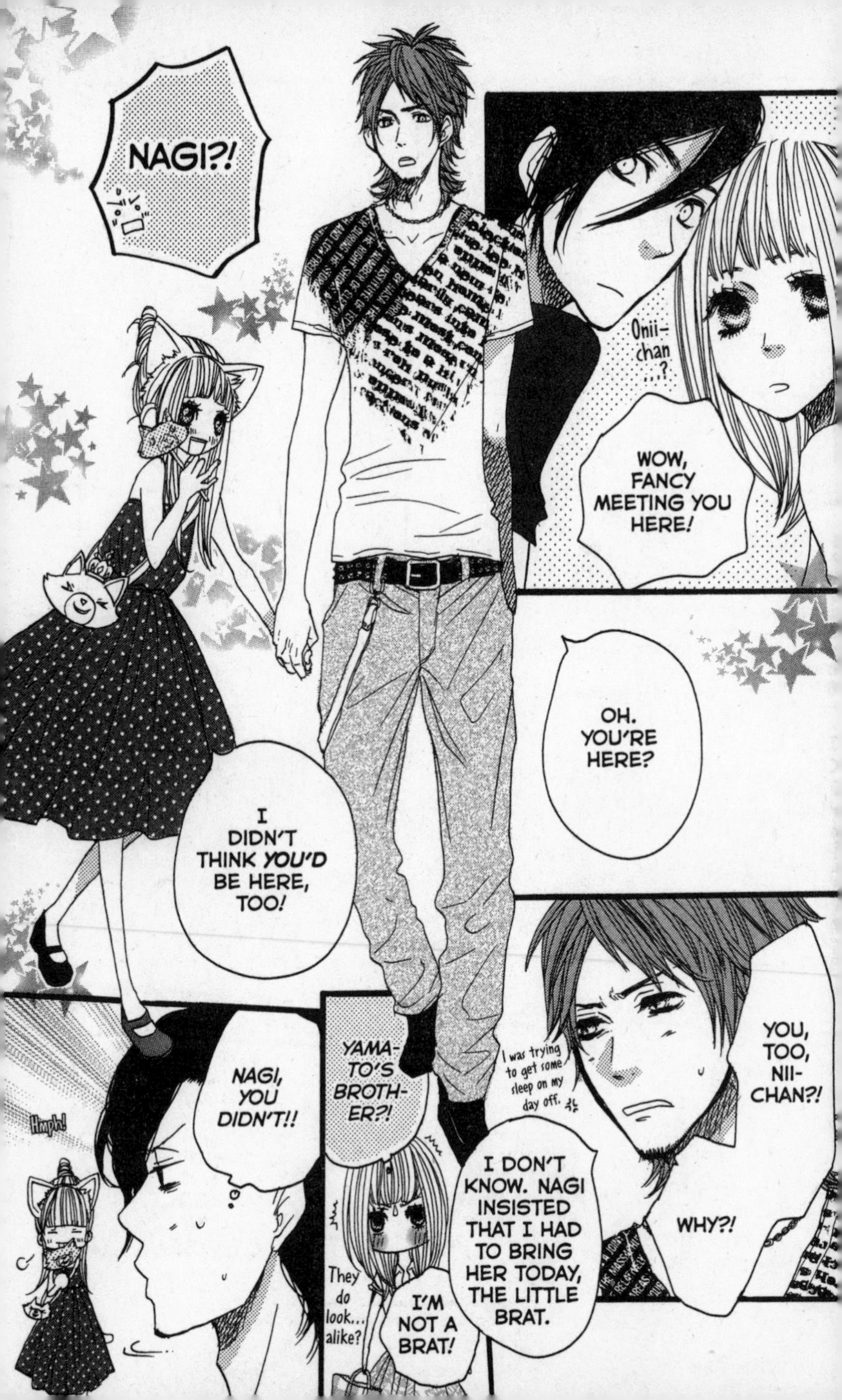
Onii-chan ...?
WOW, FANCY MEETING YOU HERE!
OH. YOU'RE HERE?
YOU, TOO, NII-CHAN?!
I was trying to get some sleep on my day off.
WHY?!
NAGI?!
I DIDN'T THINK YOU'D BE HERE, TOO!
YAMATO'S BROTHER?!
I DON'T KNOW. NAGI INSISTED THAT I HAD TO BRING HER TODAY, THE LITTLE BRAT.
I'M NOT A BRAT!
They do look... alike?
NAGI, YOU DIDN'T!!
Hmph!

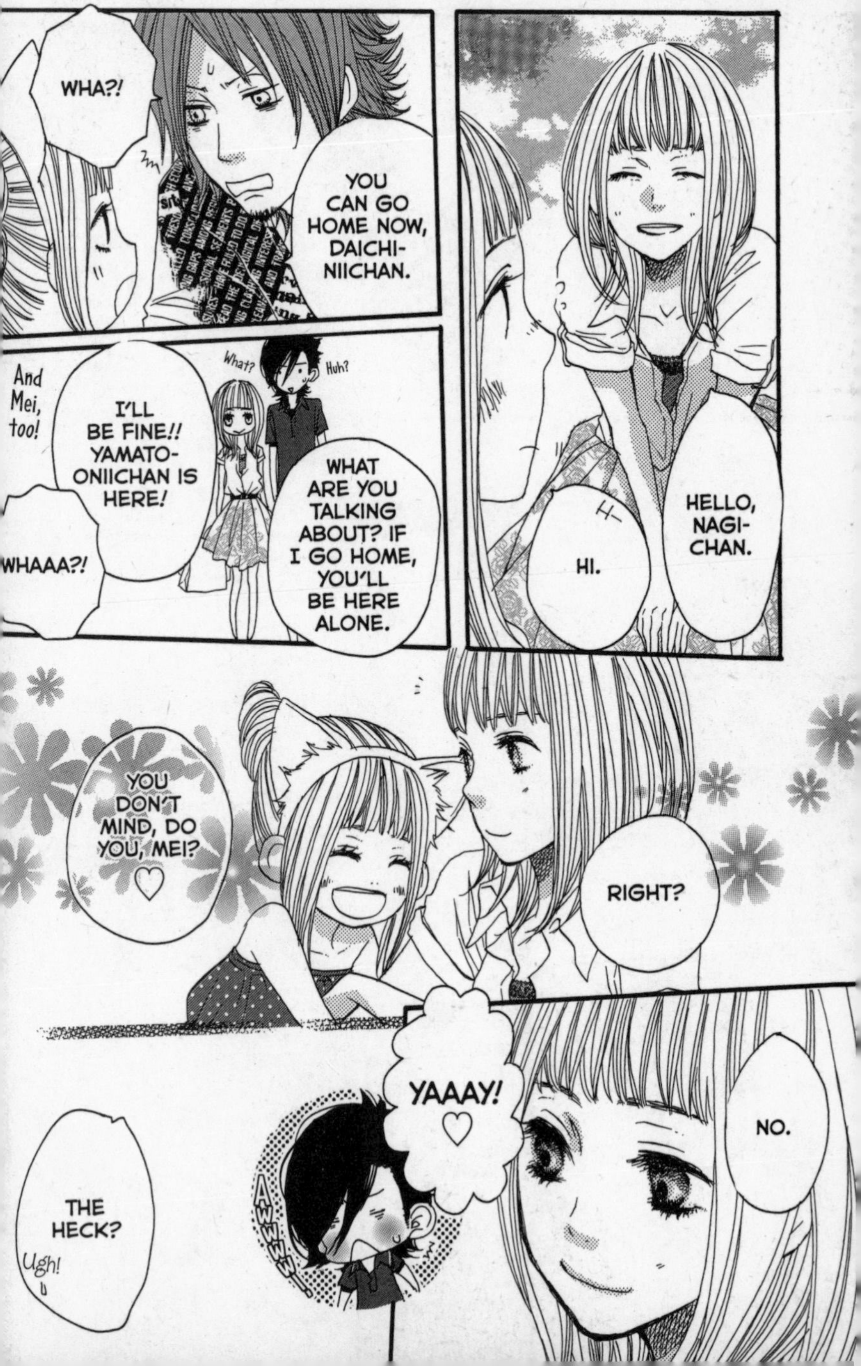
HELLO, NAGI-CHAN.
HI.
YOU CAN GO HOME NOW, DAICHI-NIICHAN.
WHA?!
Huh?
What?
WHAT ARE YOU TALKING ABOUT? IF I GO HOME, YOU'LL BE HERE ALONE.
I'LL BE FINE!! YAMATO-ONIICHAN IS HERE!
And Mei, too!
WHAAA?!
RIGHT?
YOU DON'T MIND, DO YOU, MEI? ♡
NO.
YAAAY! ♡
AWWWW
THE HECK?
Ugh!

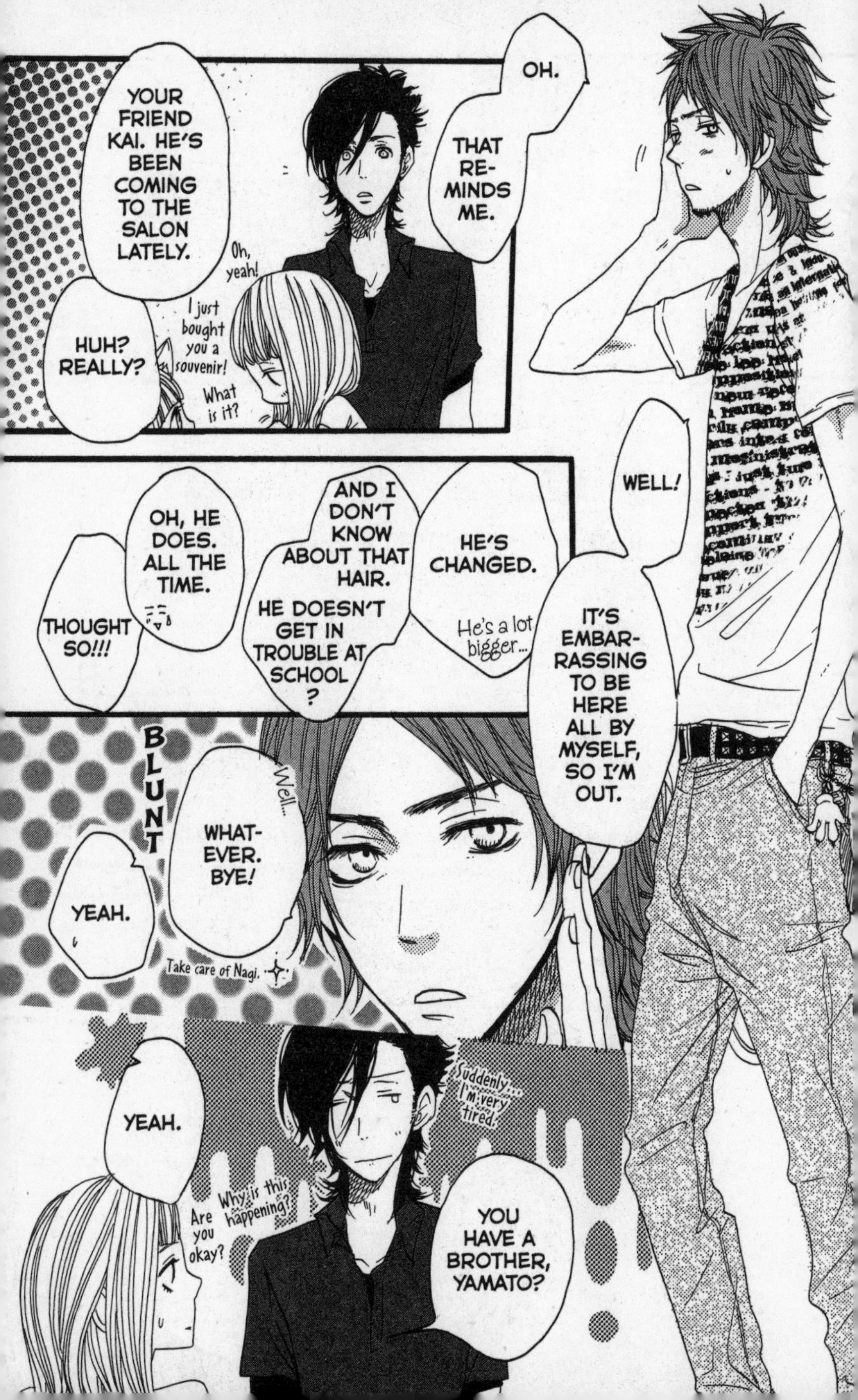
OH.
THAT RE-MINDS ME.
YOUR FRIEND KAI. HE'S BEEN COMING TO THE SALON LATELY.
Oh, yeah!
I just bought you a souvenir!
HUH? REALLY?
What is it?
HE'S CHANGED.
He's a lot bigger...
AND I DON'T KNOW ABOUT THAT HAIR.
HE DOESN'T GET IN TROUBLE AT SCHOOL?
OH, HE DOES. ALL THE TIME.
THOUGHT SO!!!
WELL!
IT'S EMBAR-RASSING TO BE HERE ALL BY MYSELF, SO I'M OUT.
Well...
WHAT-EVER. BYE!
BLUNT
YEAH.
Take care of Nagi.
Suddenly... I'm very tired.
YOU HAVE A BROTHER, YAMATO?
Why is this happening?
YEAH.
Are you okay?

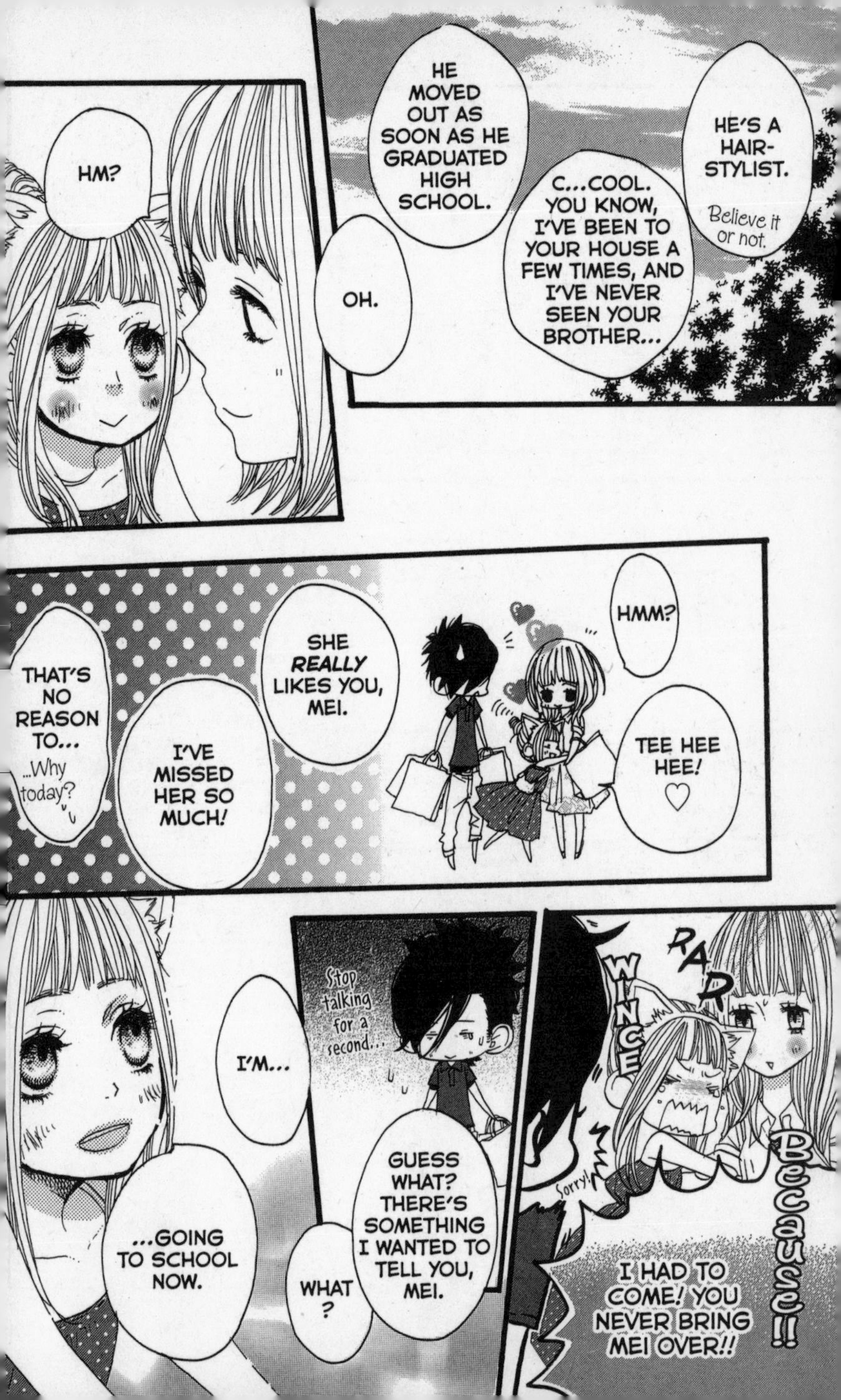
HE'S A HAIR-STYLIST.
Believe it or not.
C...COOL. YOU KNOW, I'VE BEEN TO YOUR HOUSE A FEW TIMES, AND I'VE NEVER SEEN YOUR BROTHER...
HE MOVED OUT AS SOON AS HE GRADUATED HIGH SCHOOL.
OH.
HM?
HMM?
TEE HEE HEE! ♡
SHE *REALLY* LIKES YOU, MEI.
I'VE MISSED HER SO MUCH!
THAT'S NO REASON TO...
...Why today?
RAR
WINCE
BECAUSE!!
I HAD TO COME! YOU NEVER BRING MEI OVER!!
Sorry!
Stop talking for a second...
GUESS WHAT? THERE'S SOMETHING I WANTED TO TELL YOU, MEI.
WHAT?
I'M...
...GOING TO SCHOOL NOW.

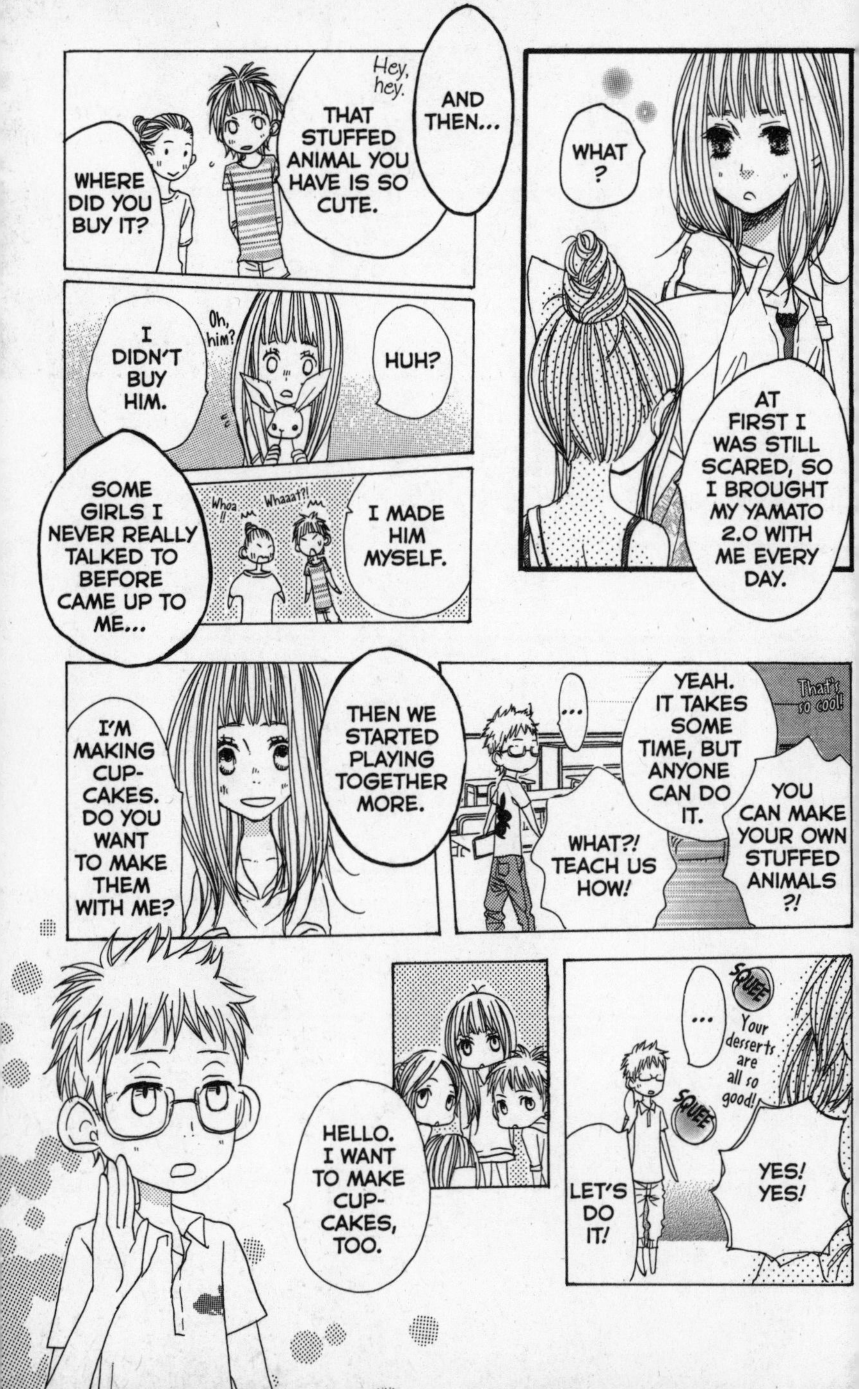
WHAT?
AT FIRST I WAS STILL SCARED, SO I BROUGHT MY YAMATO 2.0 WITH ME EVERY DAY.
AND THEN...
Hey, hey.
THAT STUFFED ANIMAL YOU HAVE IS SO CUTE.
WHERE DID YOU BUY IT?
HUH?
Oh, him?
I DIDN'T BUY HIM.
I MADE HIM MYSELF.
Whaaat?!
Whoa!!
SOME GIRLS I NEVER REALLY TALKED TO BEFORE CAME UP TO ME...
That's so cool!
YOU CAN MAKE YOUR OWN STUFFED ANIMALS?!
YEAH. IT TAKES SOME TIME, BUT ANYONE CAN DO IT.
WHAT?! TEACH US HOW!
...
THEN WE STARTED PLAYING TOGETHER MORE.
I'M MAKING CUP-CAKES. DO YOU WANT TO MAKE THEM WITH ME?
...
SQUEE
Your desserts are all so good!
SQUEE
YES! YES!
LET'S DO IT!
HELLO. I WANT TO MAKE CUP-CAKES, TOO.

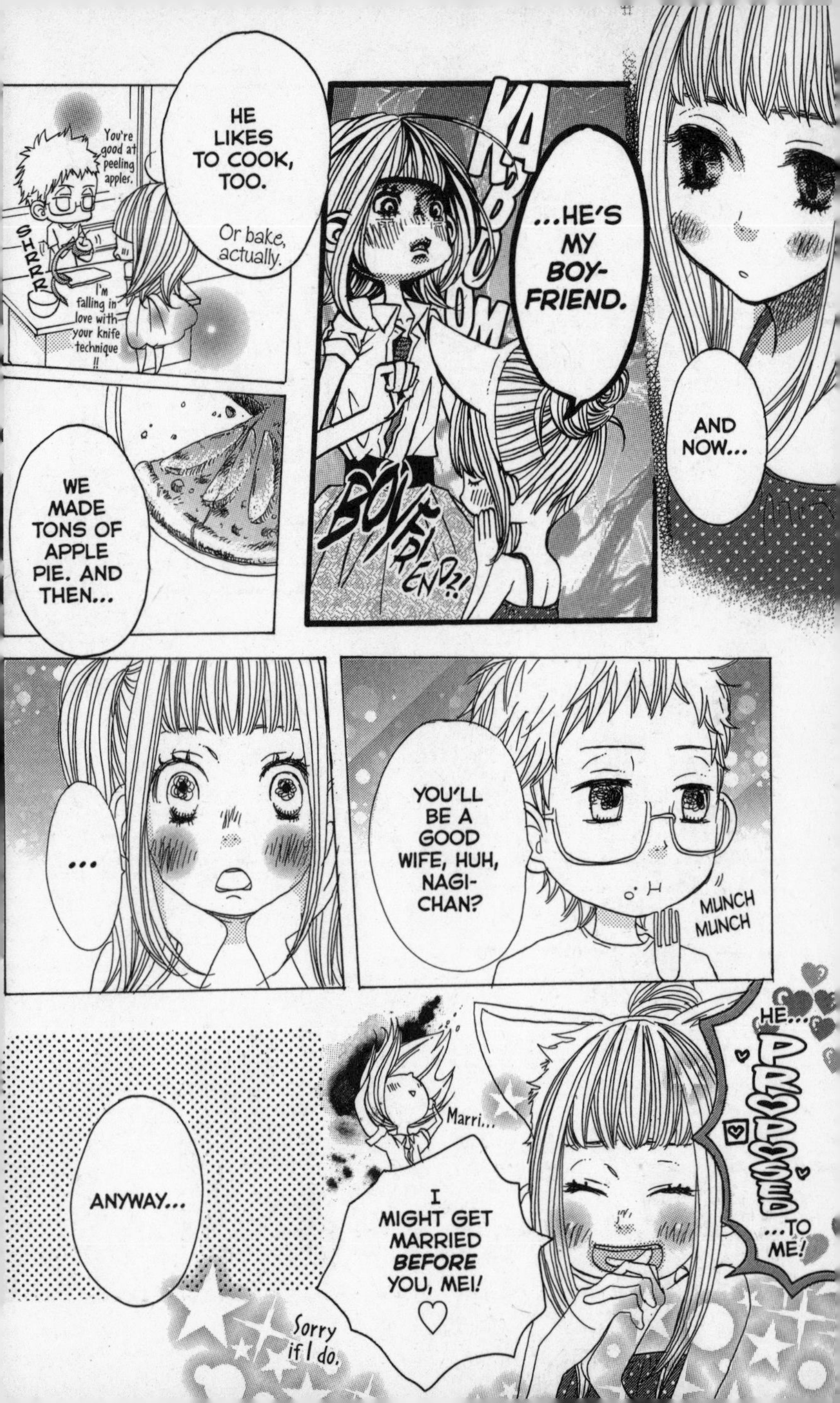
AND NOW...
KA
BOOM
...HE'S MY BOYFRIEND.
BOYFRIEND?!
HE LIKES TO COOK, TOO.
Or bake, actually.
You're good at peeling apples.
SHRRR
I'm falling in love with your knife technique!!
WE MADE TONS OF APPLE PIE. AND THEN...
YOU'LL BE A GOOD WIFE, HUH, NAGI-CHAN?
MUNCH MUNCH
...
HE... PROPOSED ...TO ME!
I MIGHT GET MARRIED BEFORE YOU, MEI!
Marri...
Sorry if I do.
ANYWAY...

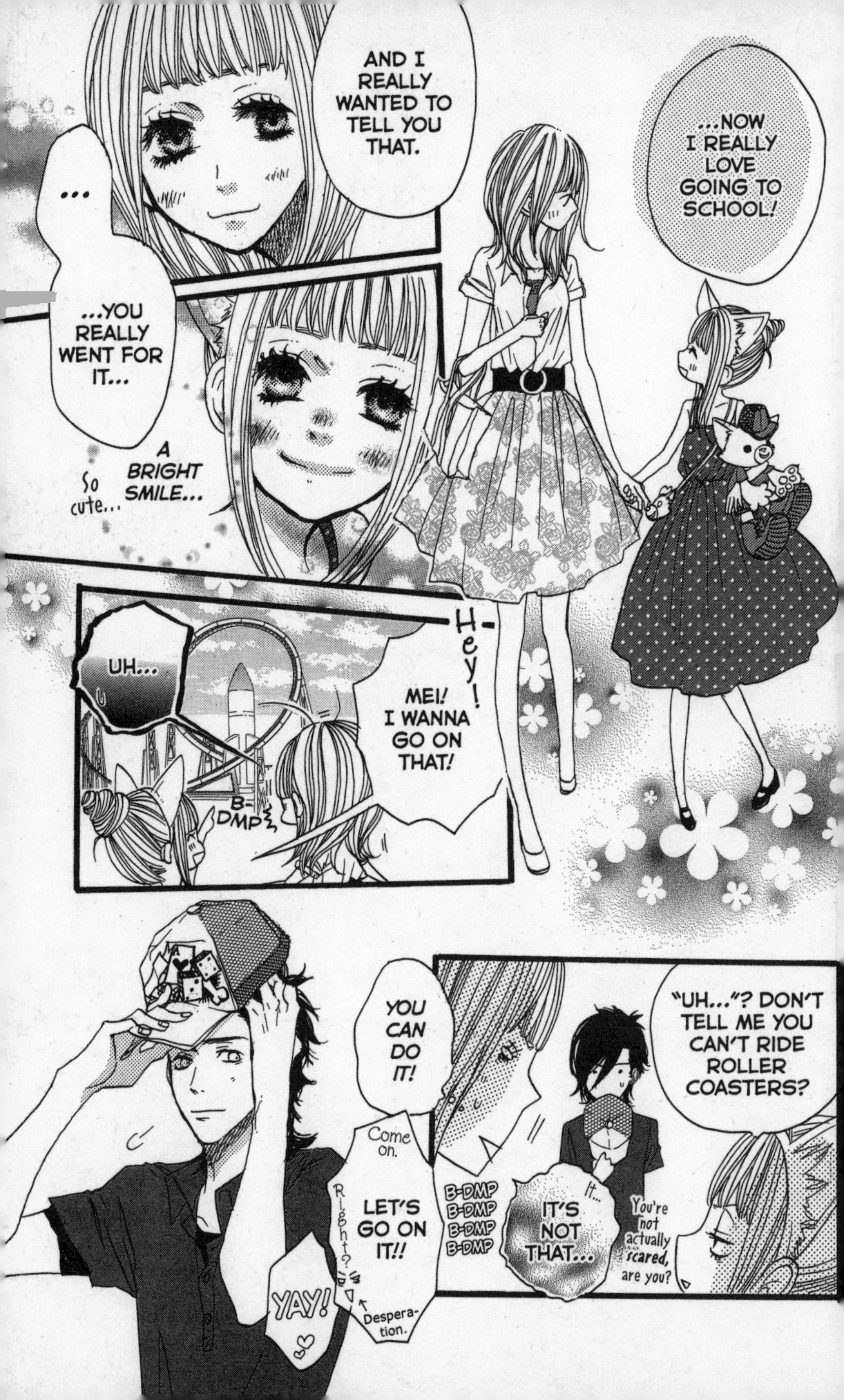

...NOW I REALLY LOVE GOING TO SCHOOL!
AND I REALLY WANTED TO TELL YOU THAT.
...
...YOU REALLY WENT FOR IT...
A BRIGHT SMILE...
So cute...
Hey!
MEI! I WANNA GO ON THAT!
UH...
B-DMP
"UH..."? DON'T TELL ME YOU CAN'T RIDE ROLLER COASTERS?
You're not actually scared, are you?
It...
IT'S NOT THAT...
B-DMP B-DMP B-DMP B-DMP
YOU CAN DO IT!
Come on.
LET'S GO ON IT!!
Right?
YAY!
Desperation.

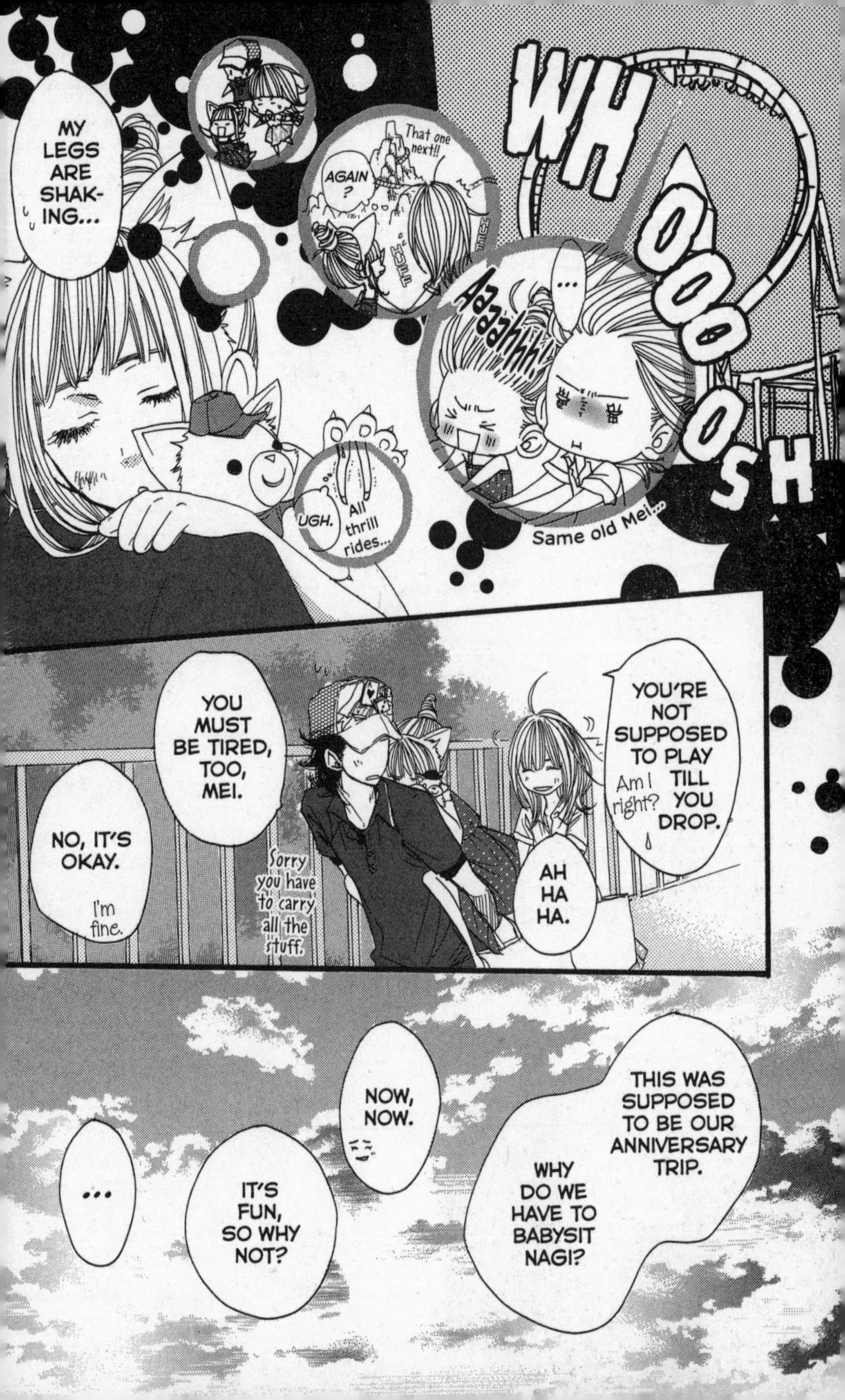
WHOOOOOSH
Aaaahhh!
...
Same old Mei...
That one next!!
AGAIN?
HUFF
All thrill rides...
UGH.
MY LEGS ARE SHAKING...
YOU'RE NOT SUPPOSED TO PLAY TILL YOU DROP.
Am I right?
AH HA HA.
YOU MUST BE TIRED, TOO, MEI.
Sorry you have to carry all the stuff.
NO, IT'S OKAY.
I'm fine.
THIS WAS SUPPOSED TO BE OUR ANNIVERSARY TRIP.
WHY DO WE HAVE TO BABYSIT NAGI?
NOW, NOW.
IT'S FUN, SO WHY NOT?
...

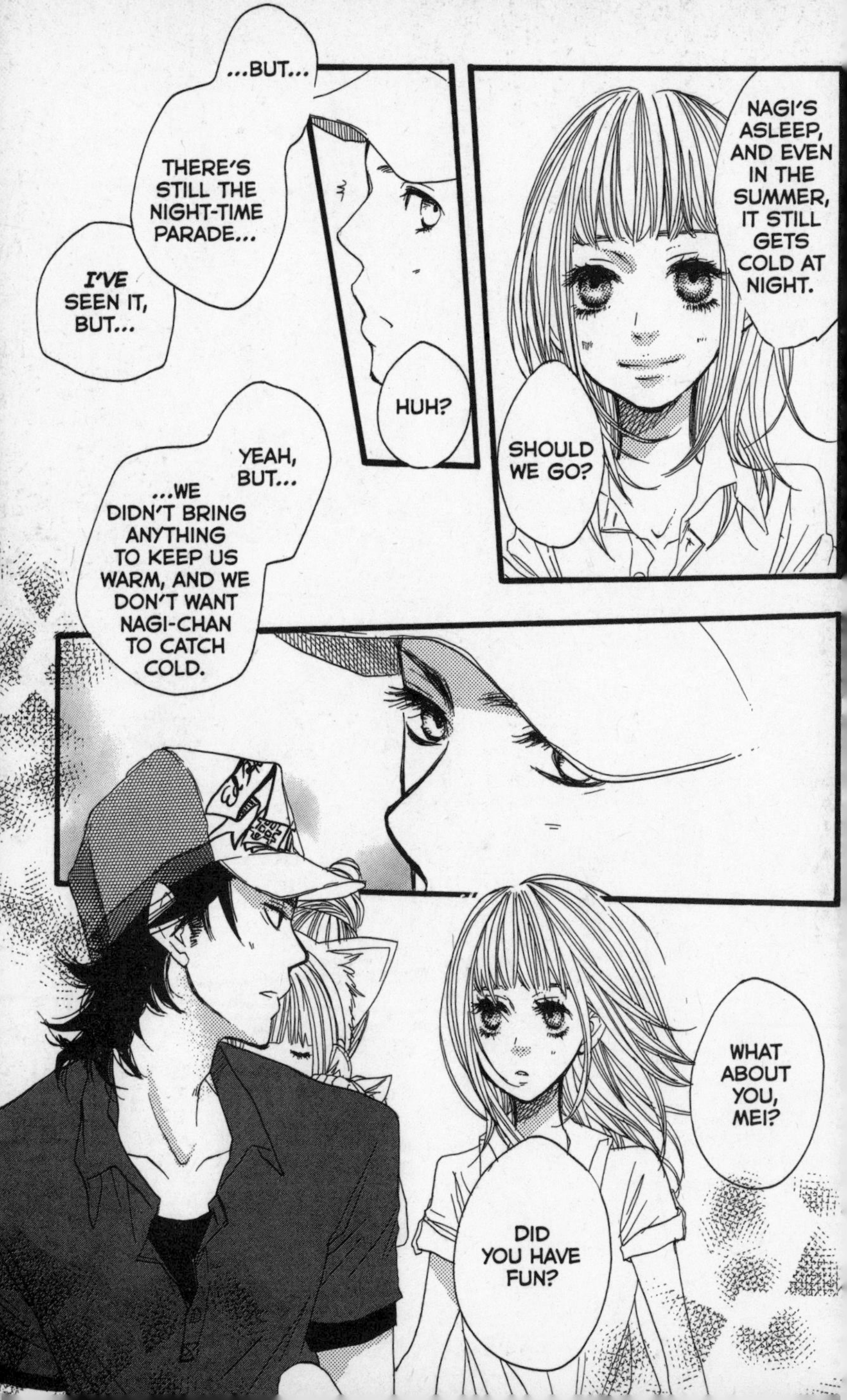
NAGI'S ASLEEP, AND EVEN IN THE SUMMER, IT STILL GETS COLD AT NIGHT.
SHOULD WE GO?
HUH?
...BUT...
THERE'S STILL THE NIGHT-TIME PARADE...
I'VE SEEN IT, BUT...
YEAH, BUT...
...WE DIDN'T BRING ANYTHING TO KEEP US WARM, AND WE DON'T WANT NAGI-CHAN TO CATCH COLD.
WHAT ABOUT YOU, MEI?
DID YOU HAVE FUN?

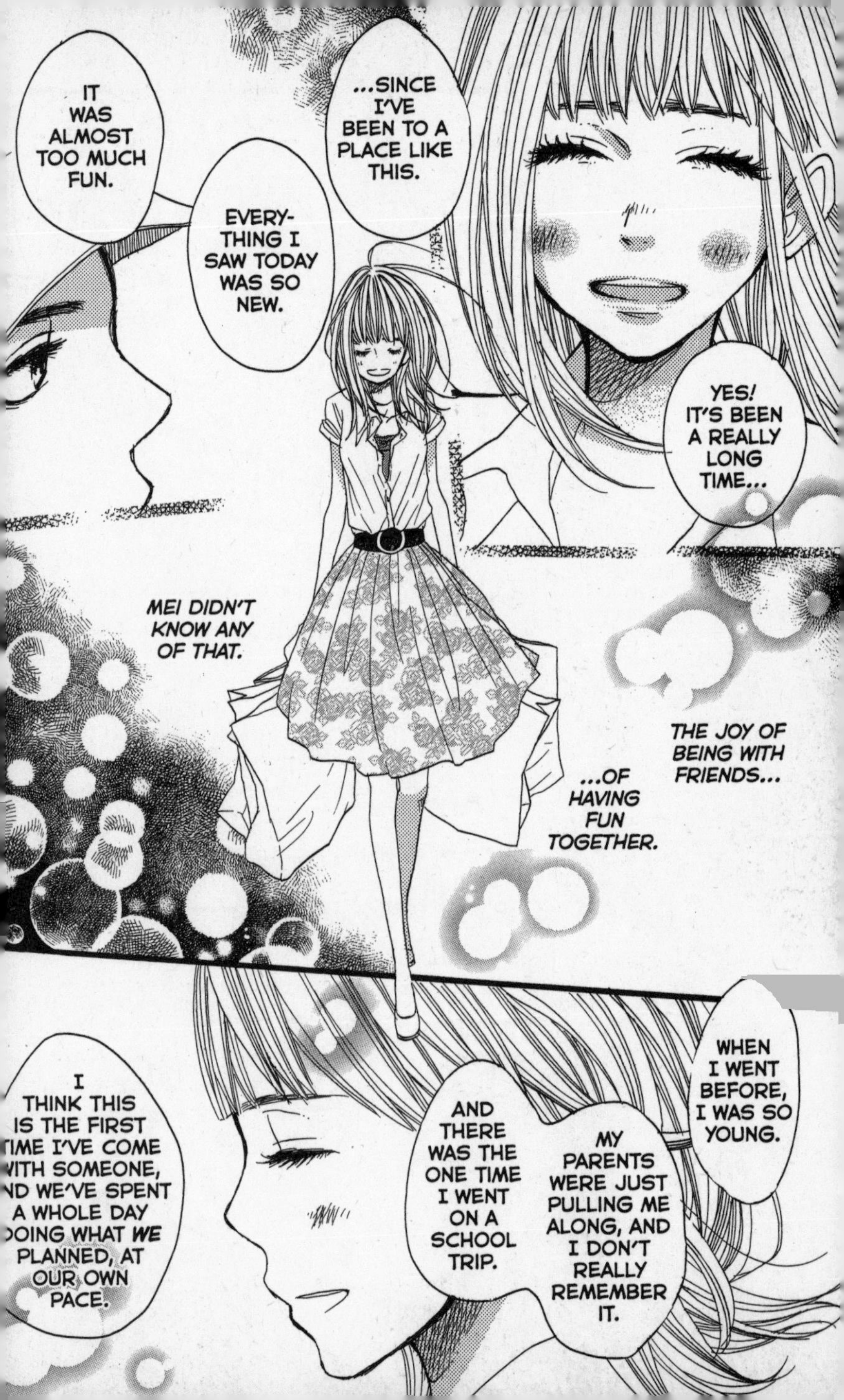

YES! IT'S BEEN A REALLY LONG TIME...
...SINCE I'VE BEEN TO A PLACE LIKE THIS.
EVERY-THING I SAW TODAY WAS SO NEW.
IT WAS ALMOST TOO MUCH FUN.
THE JOY OF BEING WITH FRIENDS...
...OF HAVING FUN TOGETHER.
MEI DIDN'T KNOW ANY OF THAT.
WHEN I WENT BEFORE, I WAS SO YOUNG.
MY PARENTS WERE JUST PULLING ME ALONG, AND I DON'T REALLY REMEMBER IT.
AND THERE WAS THE ONE TIME I WENT ON A SCHOOL TRIP.
I THINK THIS IS THE FIRST IME I'VE COME ITH SOMEONE, ND WE'VE SPENT A WHOLE DAY OING WHAT WE PLANNED, AT OUR OWN PACE.

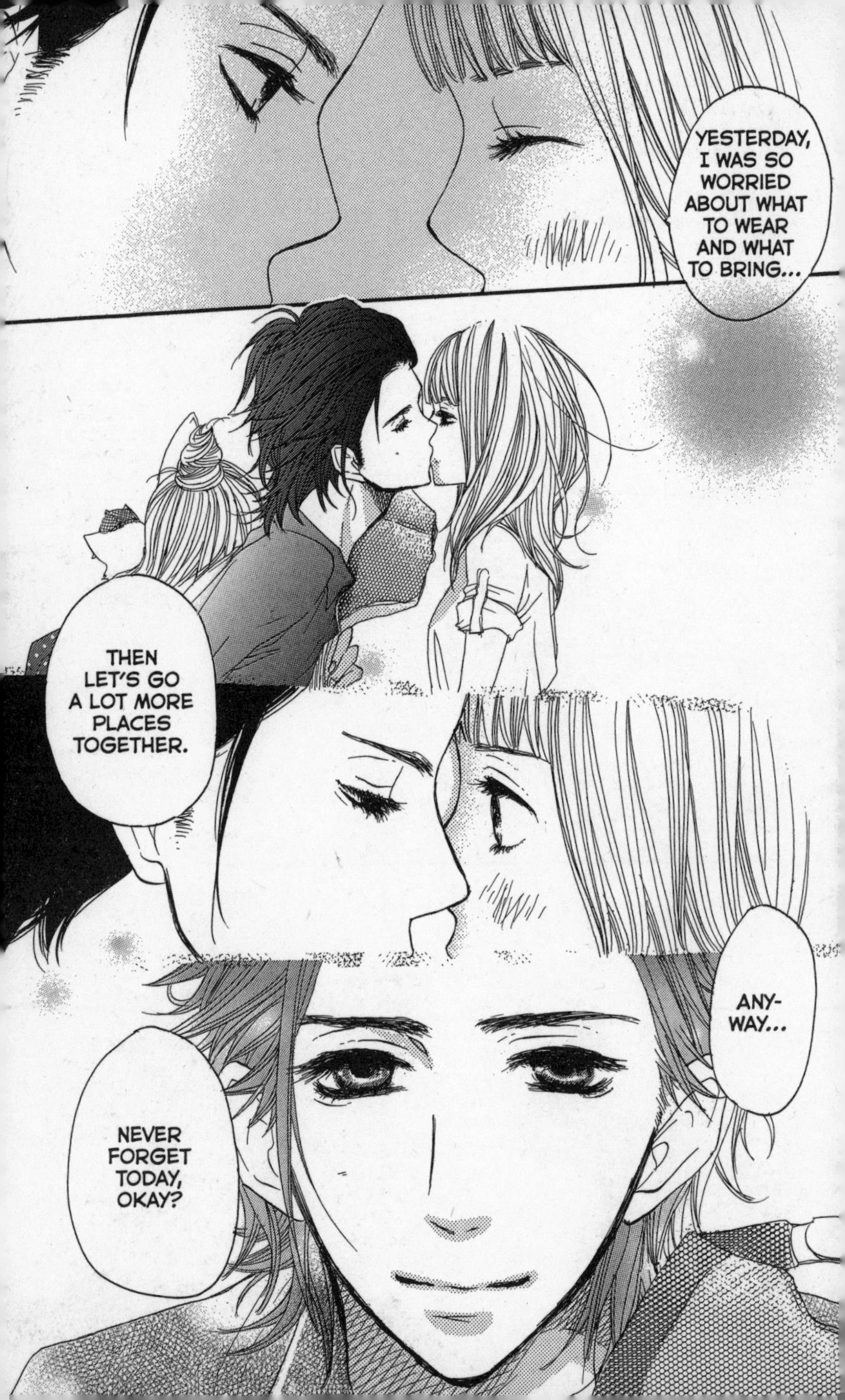
YESTERDAY, I WAS SO WORRIED ABOUT WHAT TO WEAR AND WHAT TO BRING...
THEN LET'S GO A LOT MORE PLACES TOGETHER.
ANY-WAY...
NEVER FORGET TODAY, OKAY?

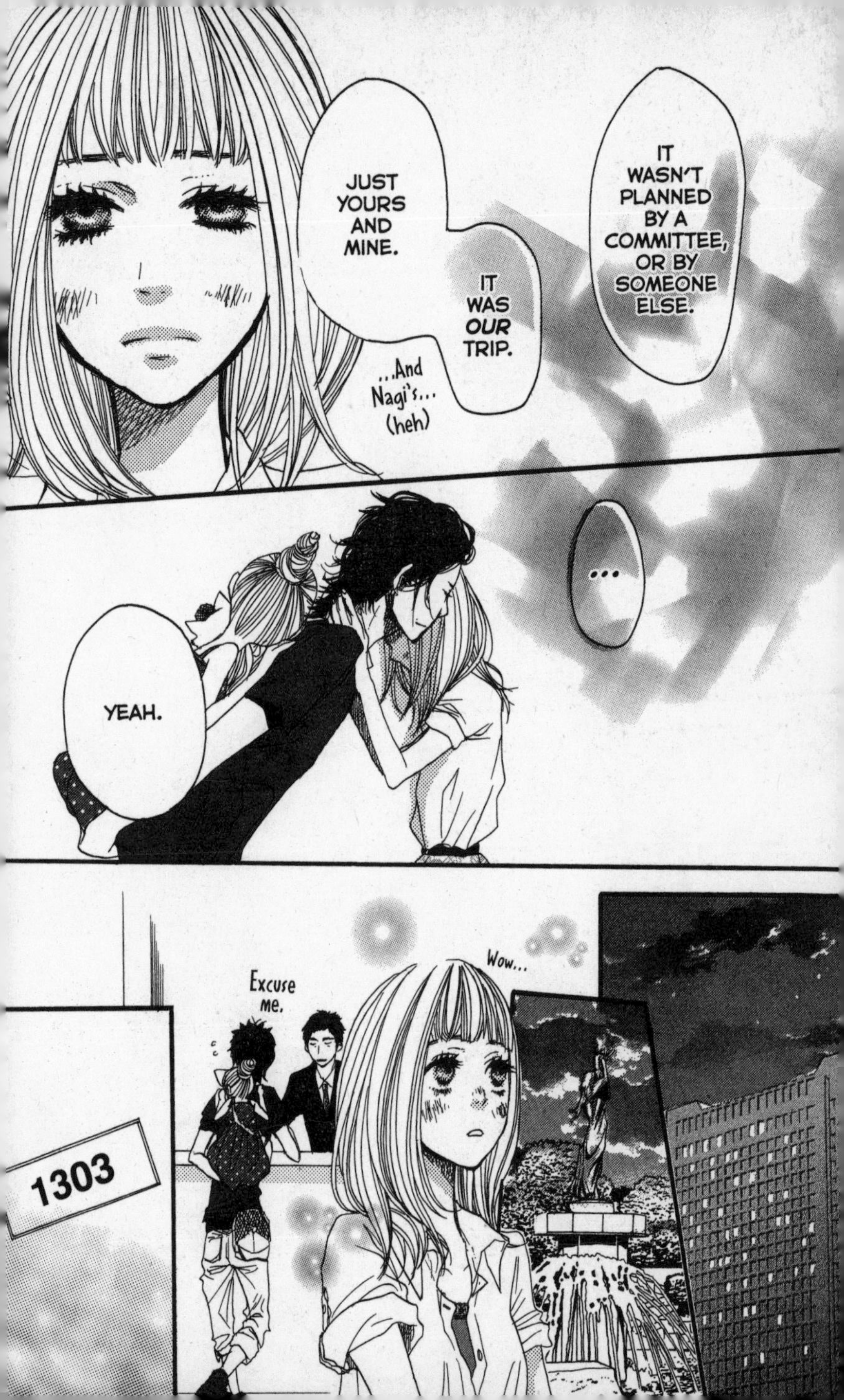
IT WASN'T PLANNED BY A COMMITTEE, OR BY SOMEONE ELSE.
IT WAS OUR TRIP.
JUST YOURS AND MINE.
...And Nagi's... (heh)
...
YEAH.
Wow...
Excuse me.
1303

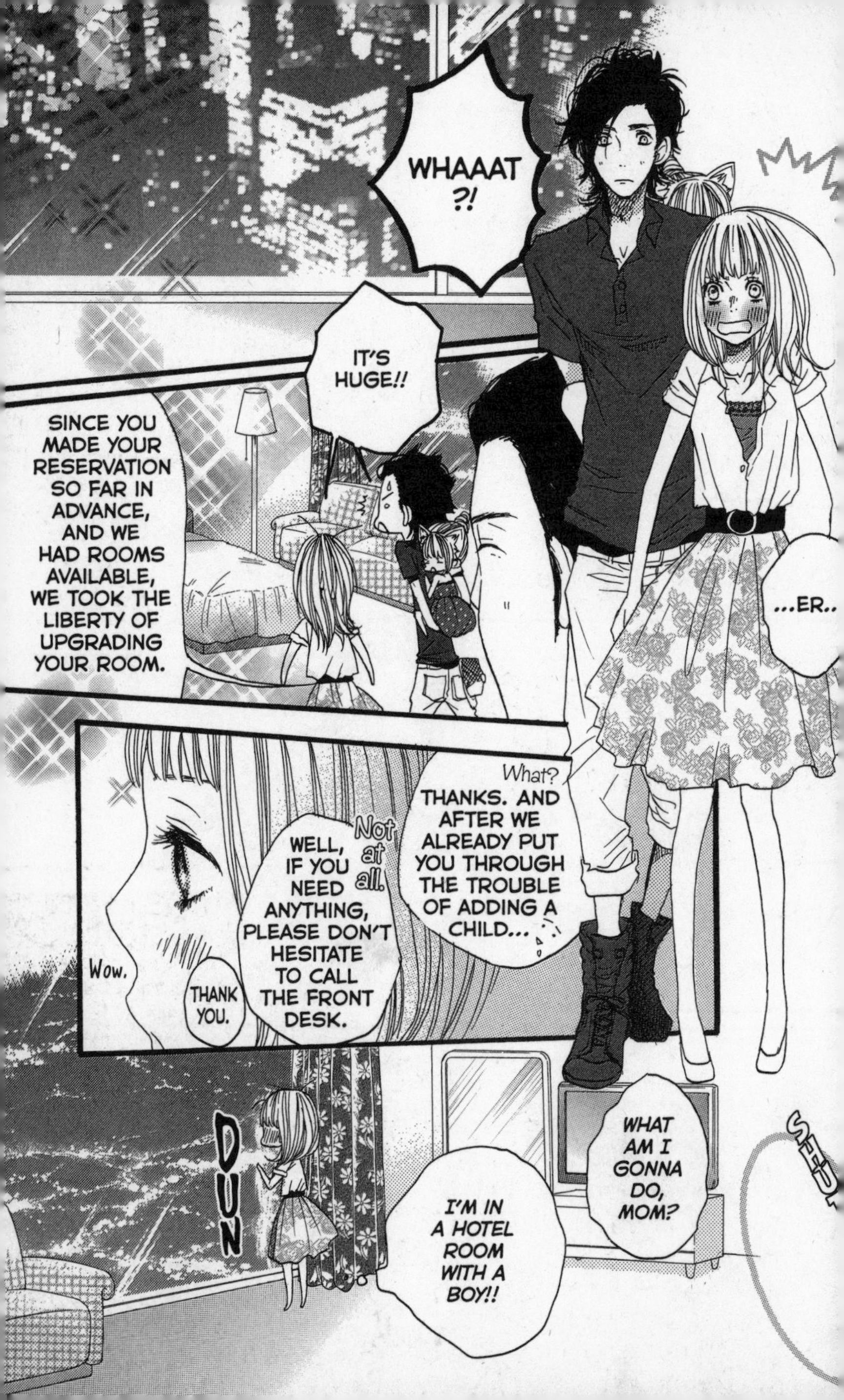
WHAAAT?!
...ER..
IT'S HUGE!!
SINCE YOU MADE YOUR RESERVATION SO FAR IN ADVANCE, AND WE HAD ROOMS AVAILABLE, WE TOOK THE LIBERTY OF UPGRADING YOUR ROOM.
What?
THANKS. AND AFTER WE ALREADY PUT YOU THROUGH THE TROUBLE OF ADDING A CHILD...
Not at all.
WELL, IF YOU NEED ANYTHING, PLEASE DON'T HESITATE TO CALL THE FRONT DESK.
THANK YOU.
Wow.
WHAT AM I GONNA DO, MOM?
I'M IN A HOTEL ROOM WITH A BOY!!
DUN
DUN

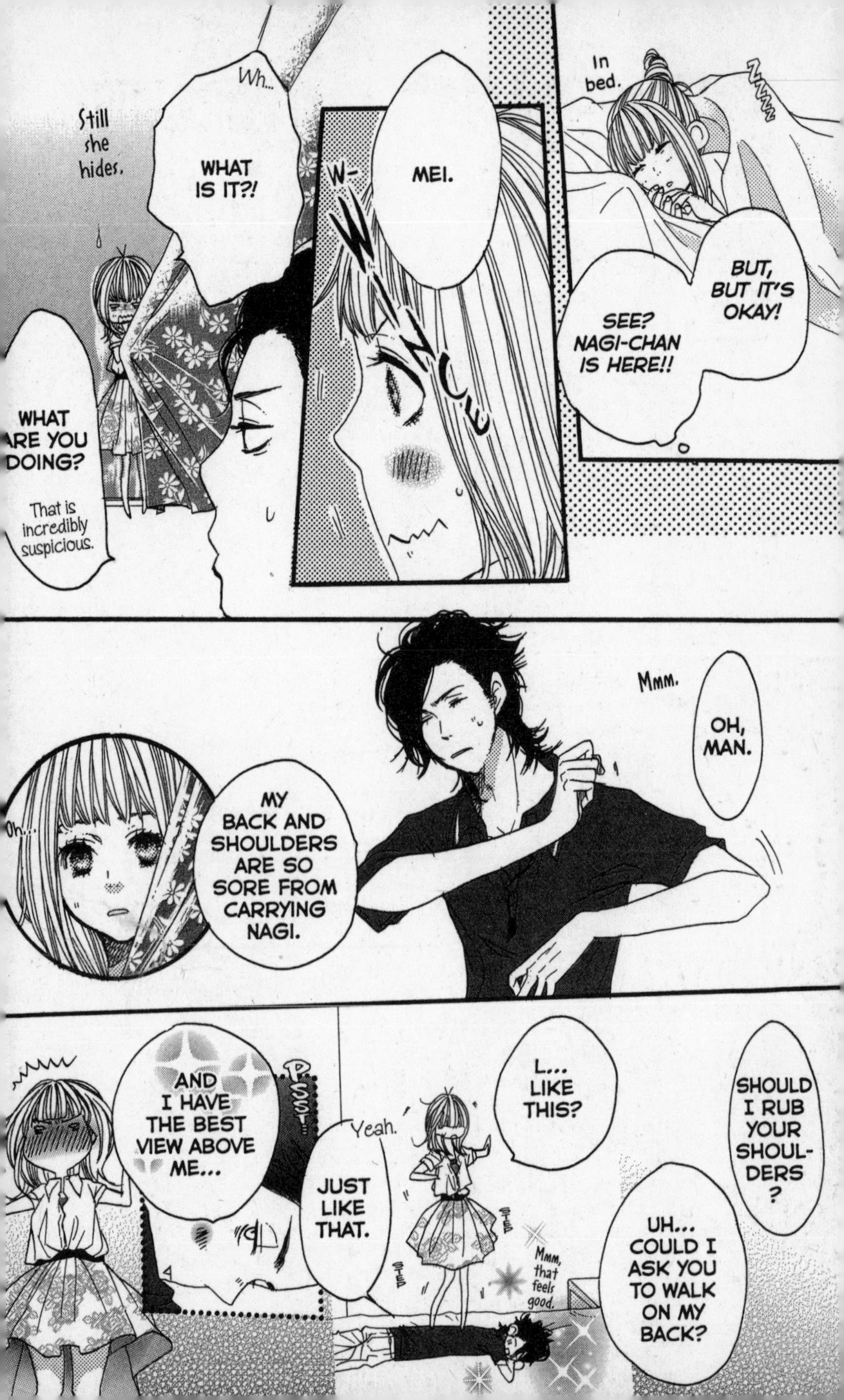
In bed.
BUT, BUT IT'S OKAY!
SEE? NAGI-CHAN IS HERE!!
MEI.
W-WINCE
WHAT IS IT?!
Wh...
Still she hides.
WHAT ARE YOU DOING?
That is incredibly suspicious.
OH, MAN.
Mmm.
MY BACK AND SHOULDERS ARE SO SORE FROM CARRYING NAGI.
Oh...
SHOULD I RUB YOUR SHOULDERS?
UH... COULD I ASK YOU TO WALK ON MY BACK?
L... LIKE THIS?
Yeah.
JUST LIKE THAT.
STEP
STEP
Mmm, that feels good.
PSST!!
AND I HAVE THE BEST VIEW ABOVE ME...

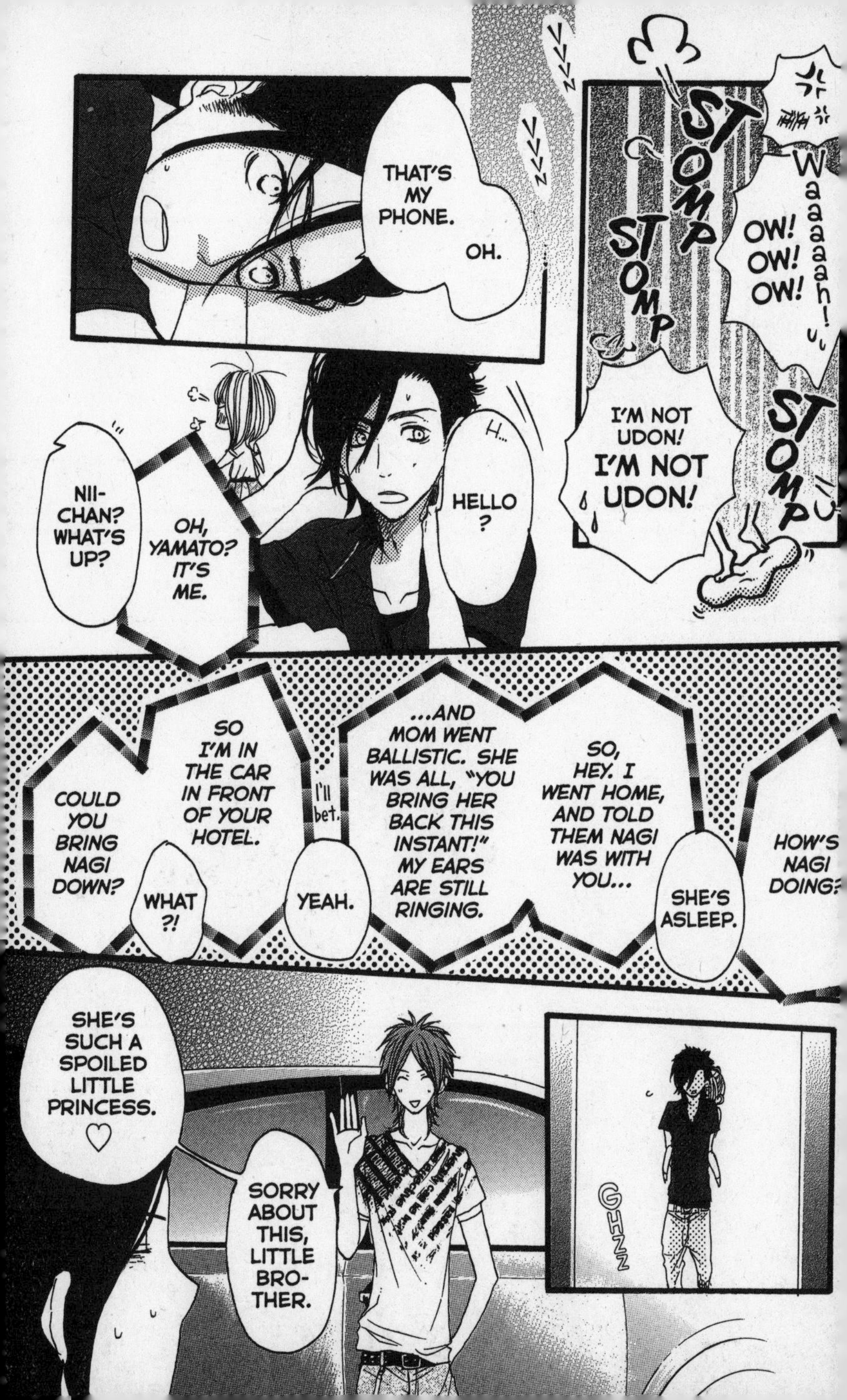
Waaaaah!
OW! OW! OW!
STOMP STOMP STOMP
I'M NOT UDON! I'M NOT UDON!
STOMP
THAT'S MY PHONE.
OH.
H...
HELLO?
OH, YAMATO? IT'S ME.
NII-CHAN? WHAT'S UP?
HOW'S NAGI DOING?
SHE'S ASLEEP.
SO, HEY. I WENT HOME, AND TOLD THEM NAGI WAS WITH YOU...
...AND MOM WENT BALLISTIC. SHE WAS ALL, "YOU BRING HER BACK THIS INSTANT!" MY EARS ARE STILL RINGING.
YEAH.
I'll bet.
SO I'M IN THE CAR IN FRONT OF YOUR HOTEL.
WHAT?!
COULD YOU BRING NAGI DOWN?
GHZZ
SORRY ABOUT THIS, LITTLE BROTHER.
SHE'S SUCH A SPOILED LITTLE PRINCESS. ♡

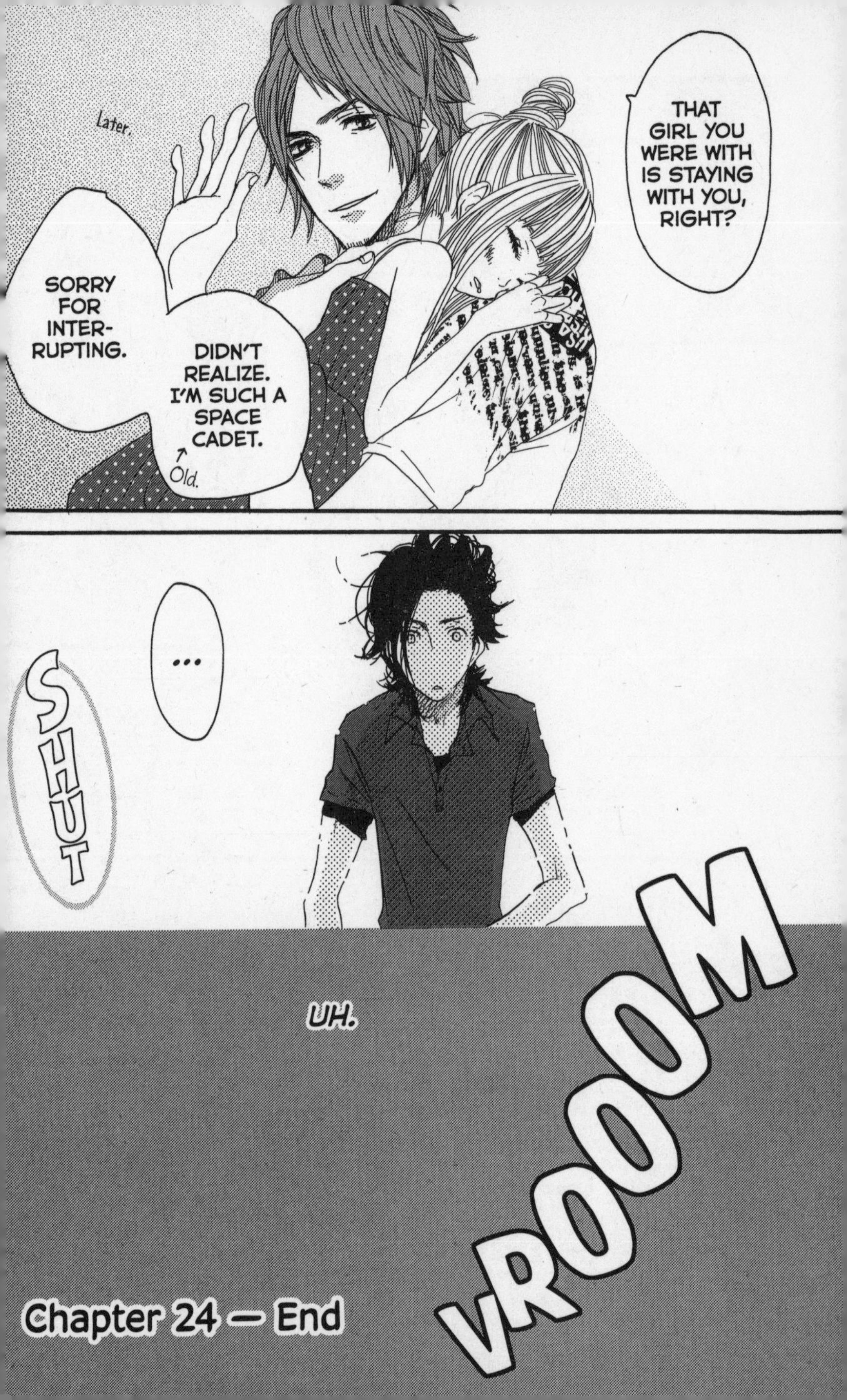
THAT GIRL YOU WERE WITH IS STAYING WITH YOU, RIGHT?
Later.
DIDN'T REALIZE. I'M SUCH A SPACE CADET.
Old.
SORRY FOR INTER-RUPTING.
...
SHUT
VROOOM
UH.
Chapter 24 — End

Hello, it's Kanae Hazuki. Thank you for reading this far. Every time I break my series length record, like with volume six, my heart starts to pound.

So this volume six was printed with a special edition that came with a CD drama*. Have you all listened to it? And since my manga was being turned into an audio play, this last November, I went to the recording session! As I listened to their voices, I was so grateful to all the voice actors who came together for this, and I was really impressed they created these scenes from the manga with just their voices! Their vocal expressions were amazing! Even when they had to redo something, they could get right into the scene and say their lines! I suppose this is what makes a real professional! I think a voice actor has to understand the story for everything they work on, and know their character twice as well as anyone else, or they can't do it. And not only the voice actors, but the entire recording staff. So when I think about that, and I think of all the people who came together that day for my manga, and the voice actors breathing life (voices) into my characters, it makes me so happy. I almost cried several times. And I was really happy that on the website, Sakurai-san, who voiced Yamato, wrote the comment, "Being strong is hard. I can really understand how encouraging it is to have someone there for you."

When it comes to physical strength and a strong image, you can get that any time you feel like it. But I don't think that's true strength. To get strength of the heart, you need to confront yourself, know yourself, and begin working on yourself from there. When I was a student, there was someone I thought must have a really strong heart, someone who didn't let everyone control her. Everyone liked her and she was surrounded by friends. When I told her, "You're so cool!" she said, "No, I'm not." But now that I've grown up and have started drawing manga, and seeing people other than myself, I'm starting to see that person's weakness, loneliness, and solitude through the people around her. When I think about myself as a student, telling this person, "You're so cool," I wonder how that must have sounded to her. But, however it might have sounded, she had learned to confront herself at a young age, and when I think about that, it's so endearing. I think she really was a strong, very cool person.

Megumi is in this volume a lot, and my friends' kids are always telling me she's really mean (lol), but I draw her because I think that, like Mei, there are a lot of normal modern girls like her. Everyone wants people to think well of them, and wants their friendships to go well. And everyone has their own past. The fact is, everyone is where they are because their pasts brought them there, and they can't change them. When you experience something once, and you don't like it, you don't want to go through it again. And sometimes that's why you draw a line between yourself and other people. When I think that that's all she can do to defend herself, I just can't hate her. I talk like I have it all figured out, but I'm still very weak, too. As proof, people always say I look scary, or like a bully, but then when I talk, they're surprised by the contrast between what I look like and how I talk (heh). I'm too scared to ever go into haunted houses, and the things I think about are so mundane...

*Available only in Japan.

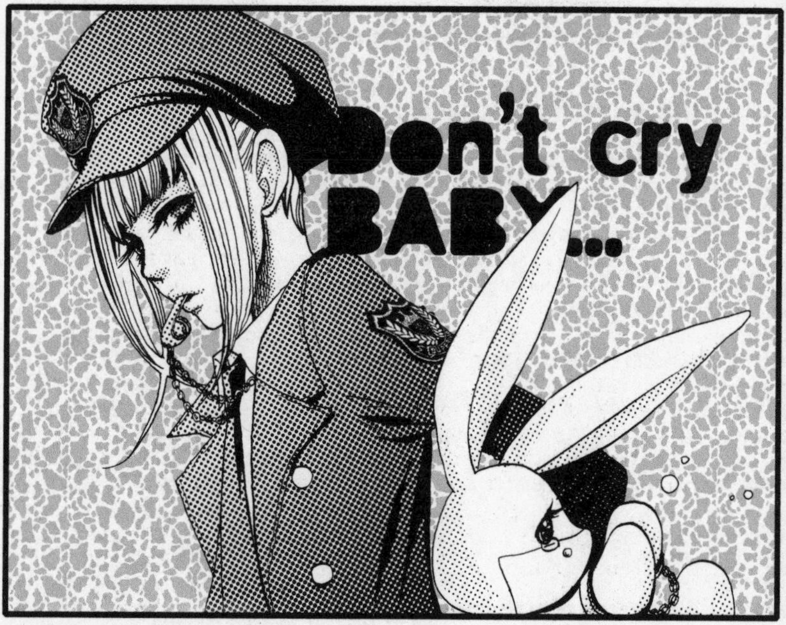
Don't cry
BABY...

Well, all that aside...

I'll finish with this question (opinion?) that I got on my blog. I thought I would address it here.

"I feel like Mei's hair is growing really slowly..."

Yeah. See, Mei's not used to growing her hair out, so when it got too long and started to bug her, she would trim it. So it took some time for her to get it to this length. ☺

That is all! (heh)

Thank you for all your blog comments, emails, and letters. ☺ When I read what you've written, I feel like I can picture you, working so hard to write them, and it makes me very happy. I'm writing responses to your letters, so please be patient.

Well then, I'll see you in the next volume.

—Kanae Hazuki

TRANSLATION NOTES

Page 57: A couple of posers

The word Megumi used in the Japanese is *miihaa*, which is a slang term for anyone who follows all the trends just because they're trends, and not necessarily because they actually care about whatever it is they're following.

Page 161: I'm not udon

Udon is a type of Japanese noodle. Part of the udon-making process involves putting dough in a plastic bag and stomping it to flatten it. Yamato is suggesting that perhaps Mei's stomping will flatten him if she doesn't ease up.

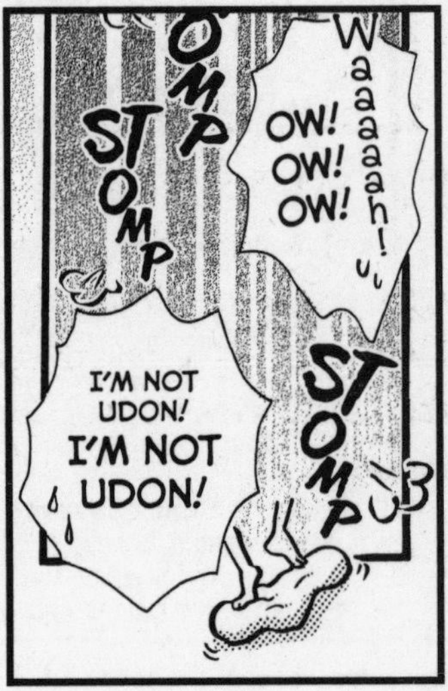
Waaaaah!
OW! OW! OW!
OMP
STOMP
STOMP
I'M NOT UDON! I'M NOT UDON!

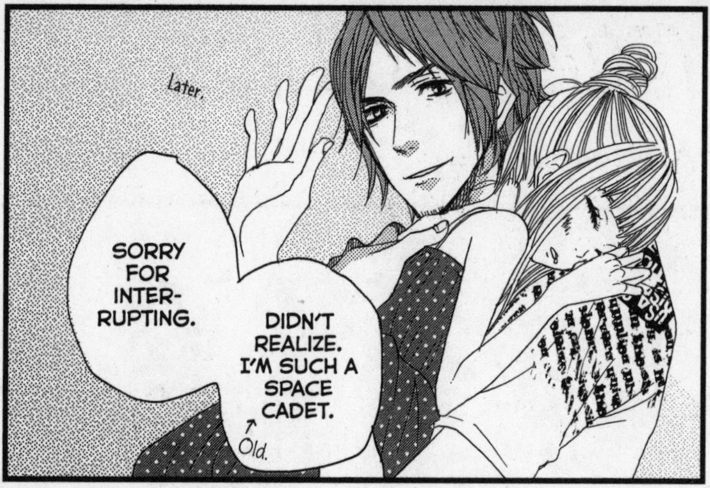
Later.
SORRY FOR INTER-RUPTING.
DIDN'T REALIZE. I'M SUCH A SPACE CADET.
Old.

Page 164: Space cadet

In the Japanese text, Daichi uses the slightly old Japanese slang, KY, which stands for *kûki o yomenai*, and literally means "can't read the air." It refers to someone who can't take a hint, like someone who leaves a small child with a couple who are very likely on a date.

Say I Love You. 7

Preview

KANAE HAZUKI

Say I Love You.

The following pages contain a preview of *Say I Love You.* Vol. 7, coming to print and digital formats from Kodansha Comics in March 2015. Check out our website for more details!

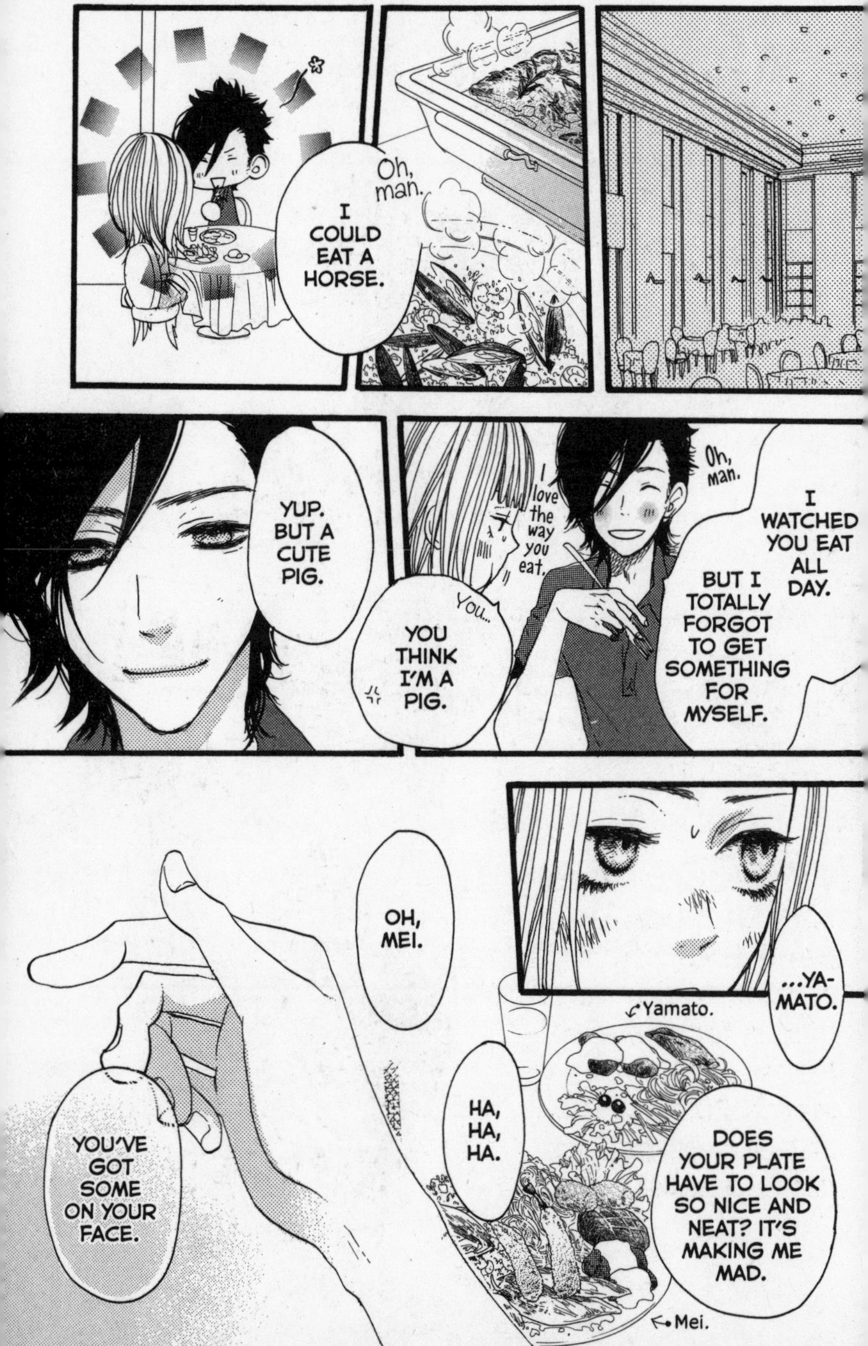
Oh, man.
I COULD EAT A HORSE.
Oh, man.
I WATCHED YOU EAT ALL DAY.
BUT I TOTALLY FORGOT TO GET SOMETHING FOR MYSELF.
I love the way you eat.
You...
YOU THINK I'M A PIG.
YUP. BUT A CUTE PIG.
...YA-MATO.
Yamato.
Mei.
DOES YOUR PLATE HAVE TO LOOK SO NICE AND NEAT? IT'S MAKING ME MAD.
HA, HA, HA.
OH, MEI.
YOU'VE GOT SOME ON YOUR FACE.

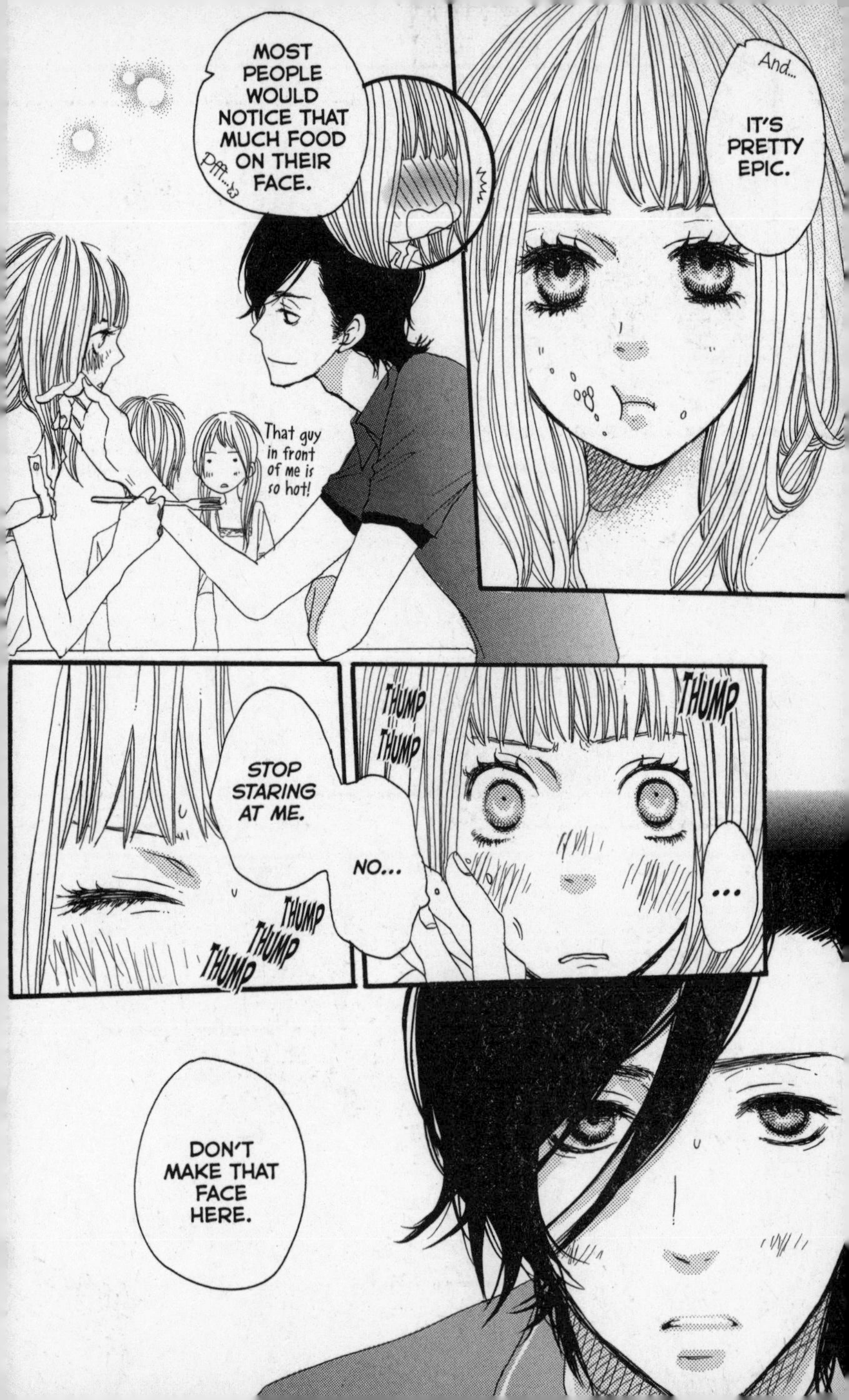

And...
IT'S PRETTY EPIC.
MOST PEOPLE WOULD NOTICE THAT MUCH FOOD ON THEIR FACE.
Pfft...
That guy in front of me is so hot!
THUMP
THUMP THUMP
...
NO...
STOP STARING AT ME.
THUMP THUMP THUMP
DON'T MAKE THAT FACE HERE.

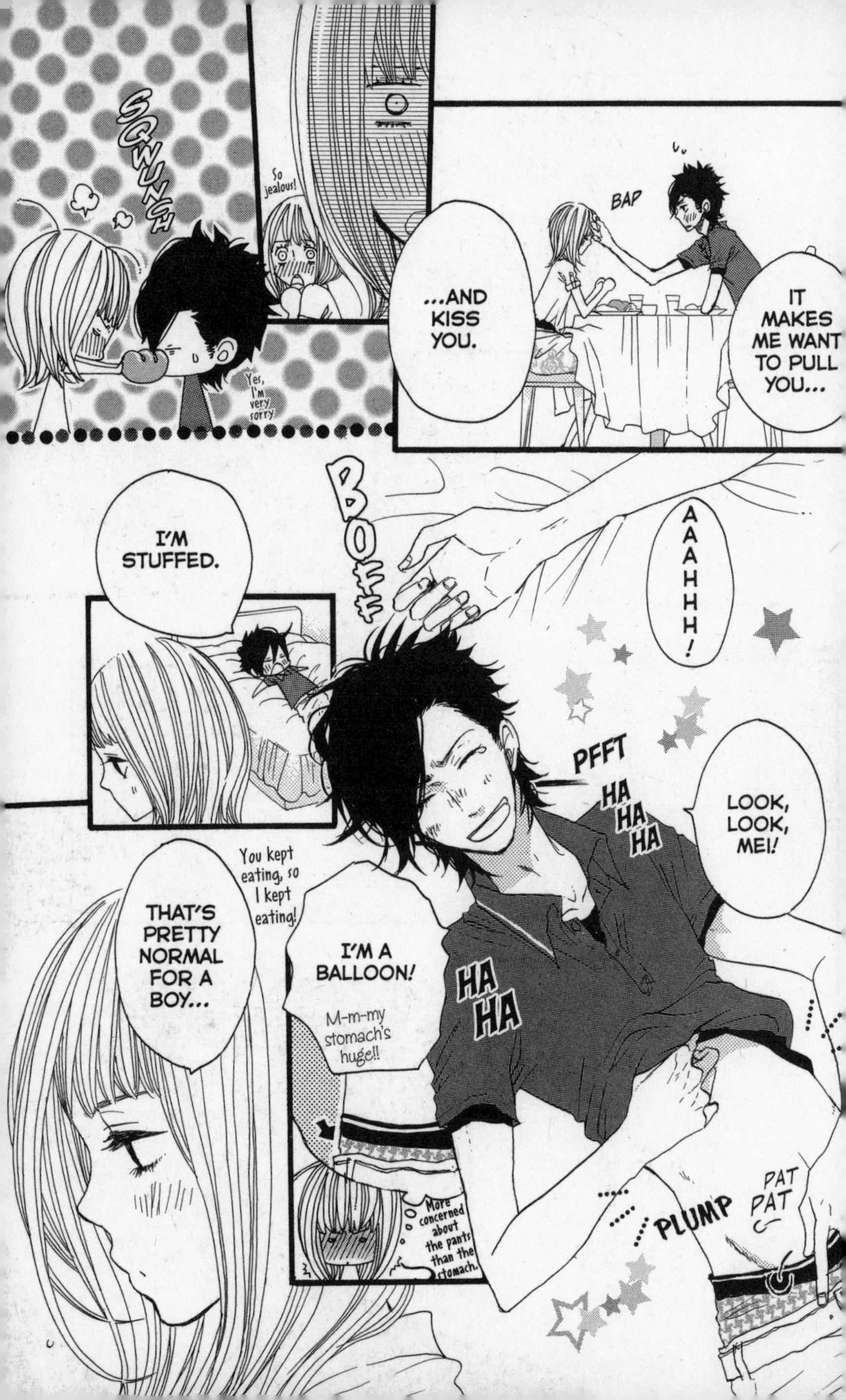
IT MAKES ME WANT TO PULL YOU...
BAP
...AND KISS YOU.
So jealous!
SQWUNCH
Yes, I'm very sorry
AAAHHH!
BOFF
LOOK, LOOK, MEI!
PFFT HA HA HA
I'M A BALLOON!
HA HA
M-m-my stomach's huge!!
PAT PAT
PLUMP
I'M STUFFED.
You kept eating, so I kept eating!
THAT'S PRETTY NORMAL FOR A BOY...
More concerned about the pants than the stomach.

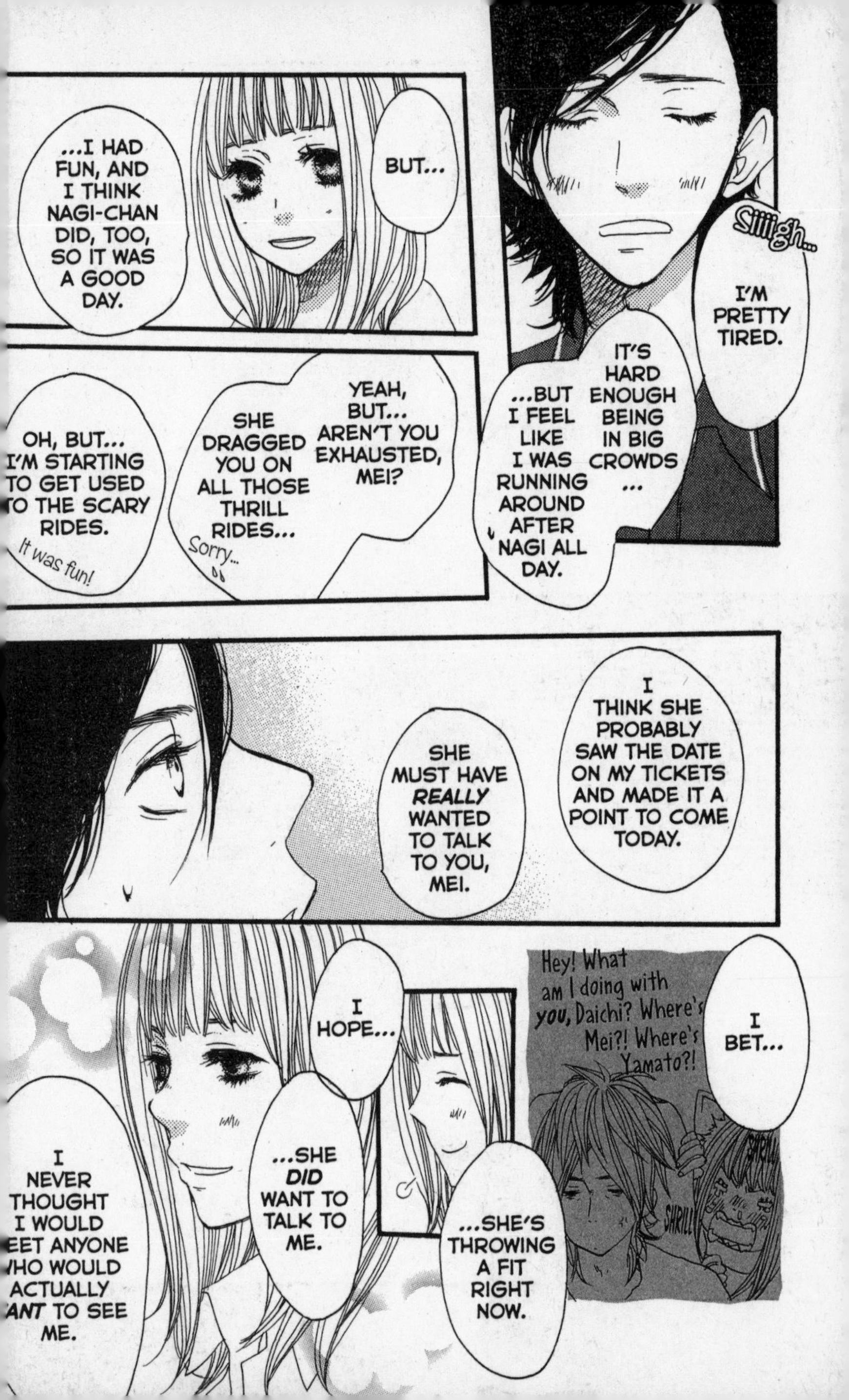
Siiiigh...
I'M PRETTY TIRED.
IT'S HARD ENOUGH BEING IN BIG CROWDS...
...BUT I FEEL LIKE I WAS RUNNING AROUND AFTER NAGI ALL DAY.
BUT...
...I HAD FUN, AND I THINK NAGI-CHAN DID, TOO, SO IT WAS A GOOD DAY.
YEAH, BUT... AREN'T YOU EXHAUSTED, MEI?
SHE DRAGGED YOU ON ALL THOSE THRILL RIDES...
Sorry...
OH, BUT... I'M STARTING TO GET USED TO THE SCARY RIDES.
It was fun!
I THINK SHE PROBABLY SAW THE DATE ON MY TICKETS AND MADE IT A POINT TO COME TODAY.
SHE MUST HAVE *REALLY* WANTED TO TALK TO YOU, MEI.
I BET...
Hey! What am I doing with *you*, Daichi? Where's Mei?! Where's Yamato?!
SHRILL
SHRILL
...SHE'S THROWING A FIT RIGHT NOW.
I HOPE...
...SHE *DID* WANT TO TALK TO ME.
I NEVER THOUGHT I WOULD EET ANYONE HO WOULD ACTUALLY ANT TO SEE ME.

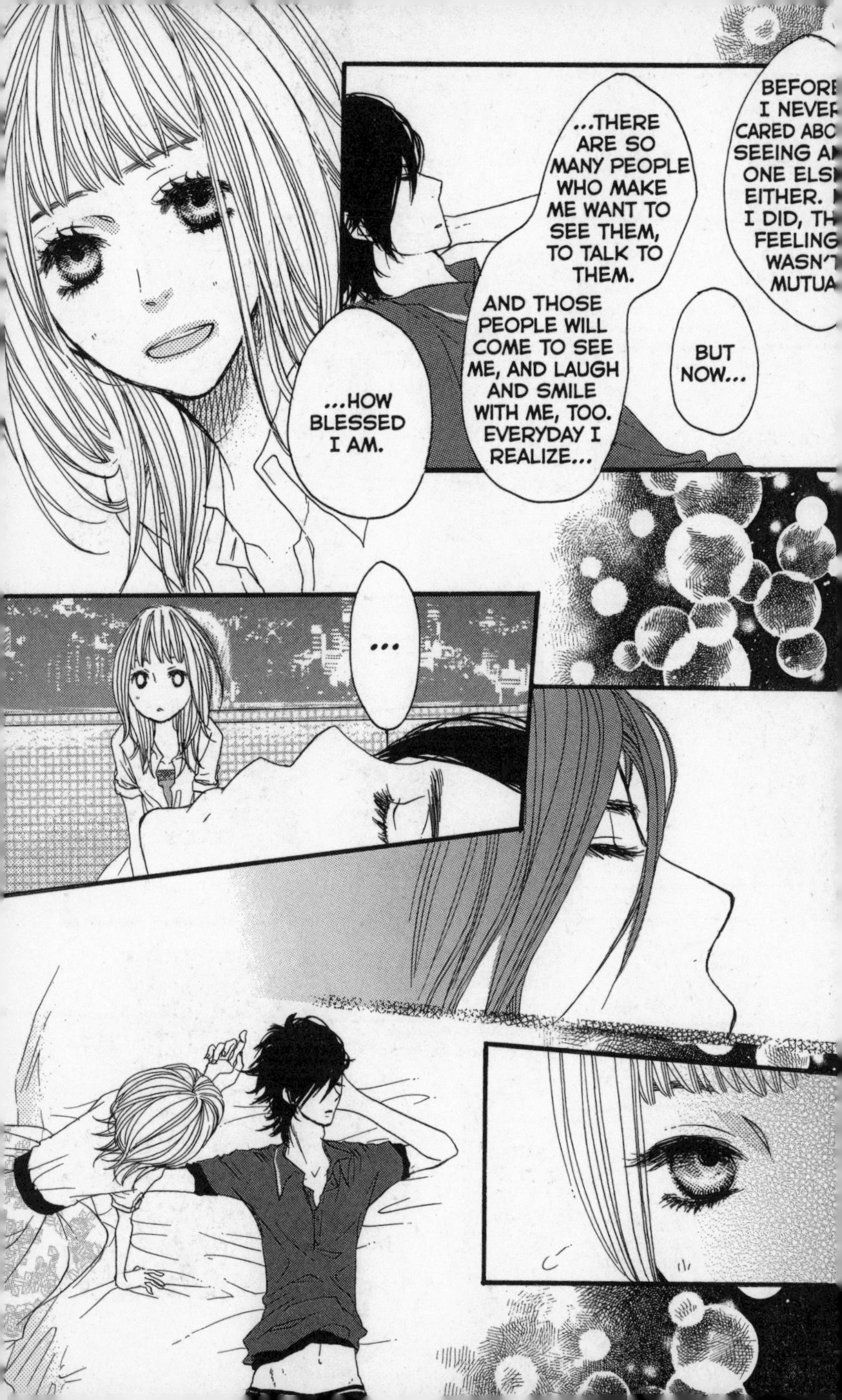
BEFORE I NEVER CARED ABO SEEING AN ONE ELSE EITHER. I DID, TH FEELING WASN'T MUTUA
BUT NOW...
...THERE ARE SO MANY PEOPLE WHO MAKE ME WANT TO SEE THEM, TO TALK TO THEM.
AND THOSE PEOPLE WILL COME TO SEE ME, AND LAUGH AND SMILE WITH ME, TOO. EVERYDAY I REALIZE...
...HOW BLESSED I AM.
...

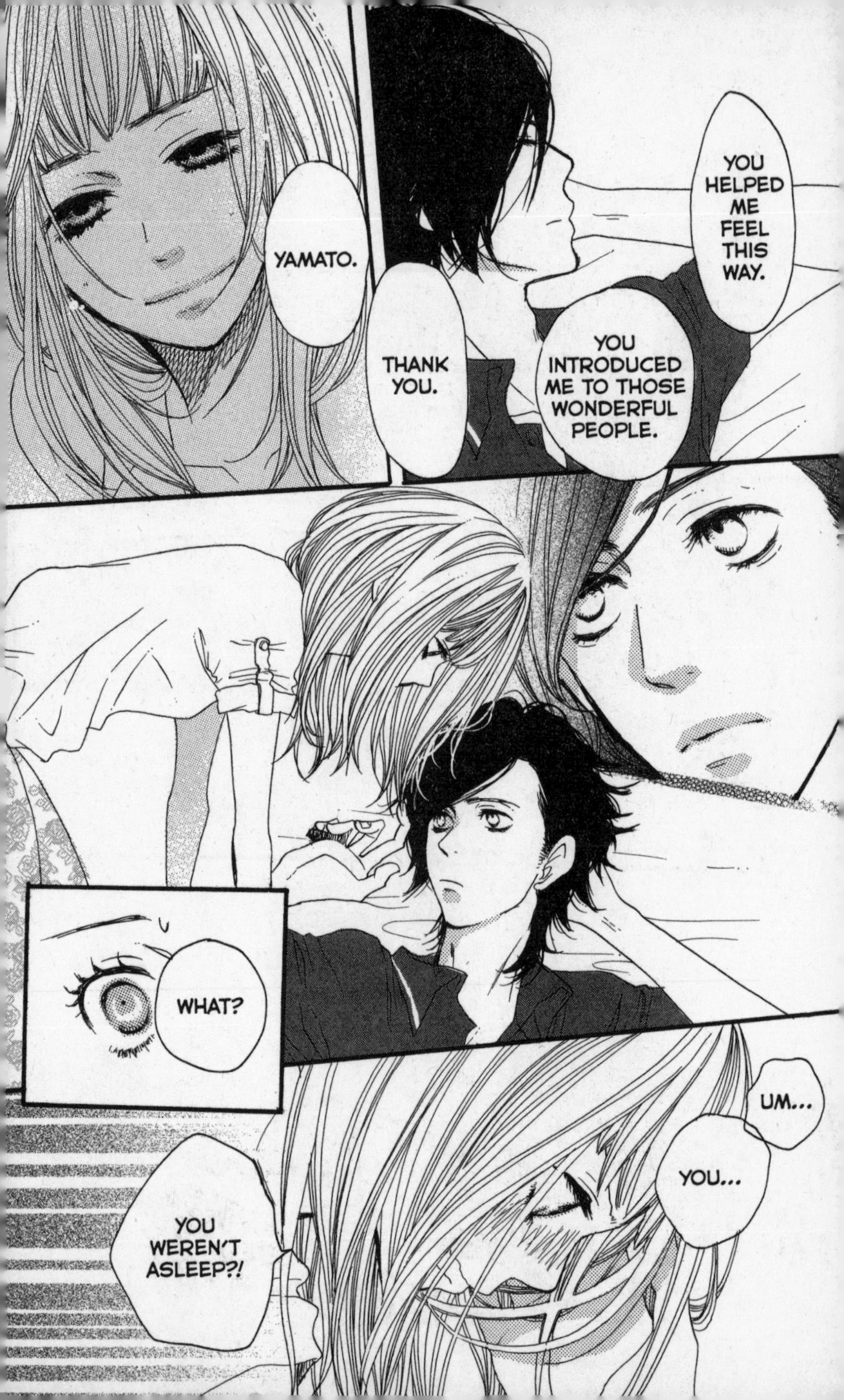
YOU HELPED ME FEEL THIS WAY.
YOU INTRODUCED ME TO THOSE WONDERFUL PEOPLE.
THANK YOU.
YAMATO.
WHAT?
UM...
YOU...
YOU WEREN'T ASLEEP?!

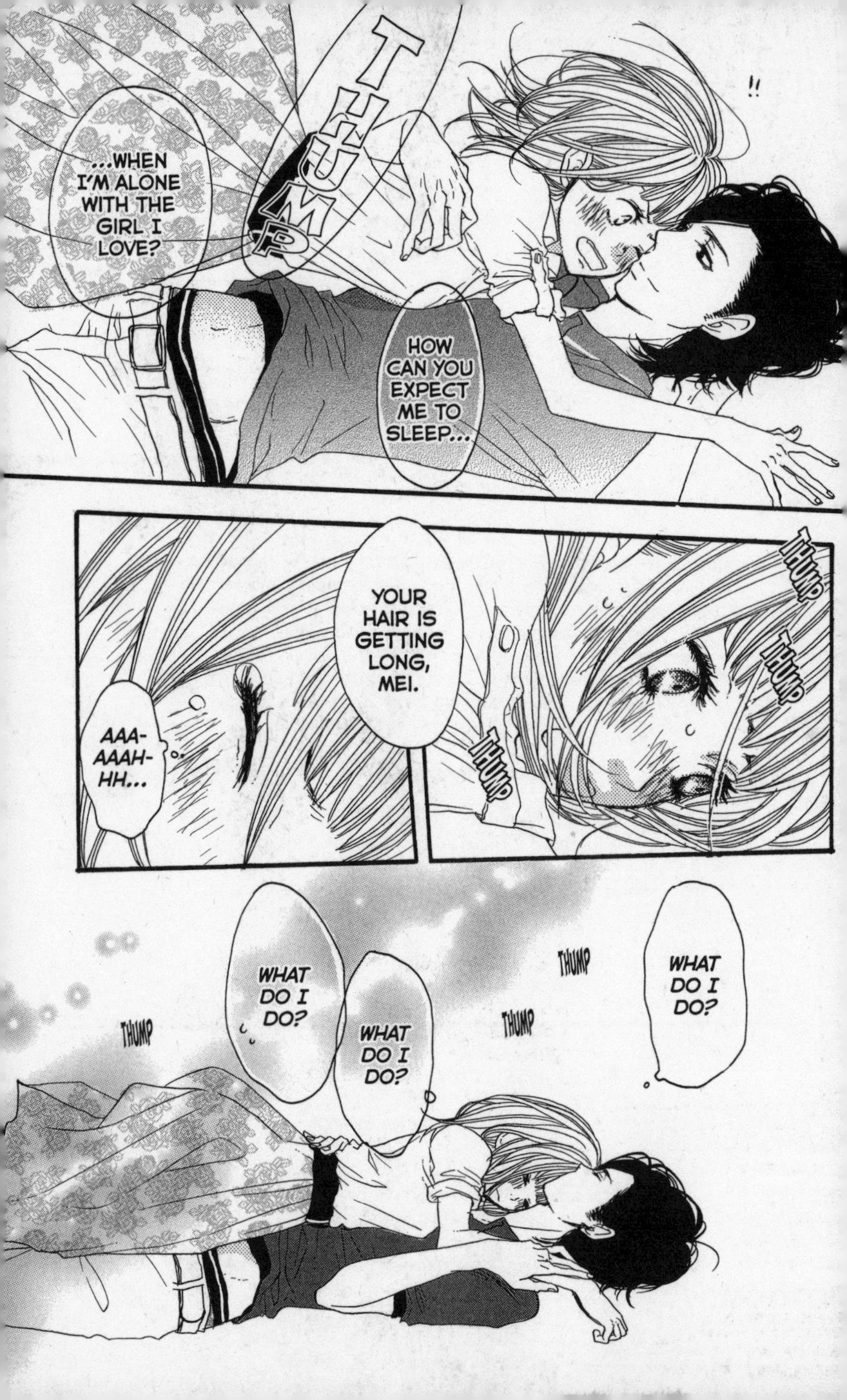
!!
THUMP
HOW CAN YOU EXPECT ME TO SLEEP...
...WHEN I'M ALONE WITH THE GIRL I LOVE?
THUMP
THUMP
THUMP
YOUR HAIR IS GETTING LONG, MEI.
AAA-AAAH-HH...
WHAT DO I DO?
THUMP
THUMP
WHAT DO I DO?
WHAT DO I DO?
THUMP

A Kodansha Comics Trade Paperback Original
Say I Love You. volume 6 copyright © 2011 Kanae Hazuki
English translation copyright © 2015 Kanae Hazuki

Published in the United States by Kodansha Comics, an imprint of Kodansha USA Publishing, LLC, New York.

Publication rights for this English edition arranged through Kodansha Ltd, Tokyo.

First published in Japan in 2011 by Kodansha Ltd., Tokyo as *Sukitte iinayo.* volume 6.

ISBN 978-1-61262-671-0

Printed in the United States of America.

www.kodanshacomics.com

9 8 7 6 5 4 3 2 1
Translation: Alethea and Athena Nibley
Lettering: John Clark
Editing: Ben Applegate
Kodansha Comics edition cover design by Phil Balsman